THE

ELDER SENECA

I

CONTROVERSIAE

1–6

463

THE
ELDER SENECA

DECLAMATIONS

IN TWO VOLUMES

TRANSLATED BY

M. WINTERBOTTOM

FELLOW OF WORCESTER COLLEGE, OXFORD

VOLUME I

CONTROVERSIAE

BOOKS 1–6

CAMBRIDGE, MASSACHUSETTS
HARVARD UNIVERSITY PRESS
LONDON
WILLIAM HEINEMANN LTD
MCMLXXIV

American ISBN 0–674–99510–4
British ISBN 0–434–99463–4

Printed in Great Britain

CONTENTS

FOREWORD

I am very grateful to Mrs. Miriam Griffin, who made helpful comments on my Introduction, to Dr. H. Vervliet, who advised me on the manuscript tradition and generously lent me a microfilm of the Vaticanus, and especially to Professor R. G. Austin, who gave my draft his scrupulous attention and saved me from many inaccuracies and inelegances.

Worcester College, Oxford   M.W.

INTRODUCTION

" The thing was born after me—that is why it is easy for me to have known it from its cradle." So Seneca the Elder (*C.* 1 pr. 12) on declamation. But he was thinking of the new emphases and recent popularity of something that went back well before his own time. Quintilian (2.4.41) knew that the treatment in schools of themes based on particular law-court cases and public debates had been practised as early as the time of Demetrius of Phaleron in the fourth century B.C.; while rhetorical exercises on generalised topics [1] had been employed in the schools of the sophists much earlier. The real flowering of Greek declamation, however, will have been in the Hellenistic centuries, when Hermagoras of Temnos elaborated rhetorical precept and the Greek cities began to stagnate, their independence lost. When the Romans took over Greek education along with the rest of Greek culture, declamation naturally came too. Themes for both legal and deliberative declamation are mentioned in Cicero's early work, the *De Inven-*

---

[1] *Theses* (cf. *C.* 1 pr. 12), distinguished by Hermagoras from the particular case (*hypothesis*). The general, of course, continued to lurk below the particular: see S. F. Bonner's interesting discussion in his *Roman Declamation*, 2–10, and especially *C.* 7.4.3: " Latro . . . made a sort of general topic (*tamquam thesim*) of the following: Should a son go to ransom a captive father or stay to support a blind mother? "

tione (dated to the 80s), and particularly in the related though anonymous *Rhetorica ad Herennium*. Cicero himself " declaimed in Greek up till his praetorship [66 B.C.], and in Latin even as an old man " (Suet. *Gr. Rhet.* 25.3). He perhaps preferred the older general and philosophical topics,[1] but Seneca (*C.* 1.4.7) seems to prove that Cicero on occasion spoke in a full-blown legal exercise of the kind so familiar later.

It is only during the second half of Cicero's century that the technical terms used by Seneca begin to crystallise. *Declamare*, earlier apparently used of loud and emphatic speech, begins to be restricted to school exercises.[2] *Controversia* comes to be used for the exercise based on legal cases, *suasoria* for that based on the giving of advice in a public meeting. The cant terms, *colores*, *sententiae* and the rest, proliferated as the exercise became more and more an end in itself. It was already that for many of the speakers [3] who appear in the pages of Seneca, men

---

[1] In the *Paradoxa Stoicorum* he gave oratorical treatment to matters discussed θετικῶς in the schools. Cf. too *ad Att.* 9.4 for a list of subjects for declamation suitable to Cicero's desperate position in 49 B.C.

[2] Perhaps not in Cicero before the 50s (Bonner, 28–9). *Controversia* and *suasoria* do not appear of the school exercise till Seneca.

[3] They are " declaimers " (*declamatores*) as a general term; " rhetors " (*rhetores*) ran schools where declamation was practised. "Schoolmen" (*scholastici*) is used by Seneca not of the young pupils but of men who spent most of their time in schools or in declamatory display. As a rule, *scholasticus* takes on a tinge of contempt, and Mr. D. A. Russell points out to me that in *C.* 7 pr. 4 it is beginning to have the connotations of folly found in Epictetus (1.11.39) and the Byzantine *Philogelos*.

(some of them) who died before Augustus died. The development is often ascribed to the loss of freedom of speech and the decay of oratory in real-life courts and assemblies after the fall of the Republic. But that can only be part of the reason. Many important cases were pleaded, even some important debates held after the battle of Actium. Training was still needed for those proposing to take their parts on these public stages, and declamation was supposed to provide that. If it forgot that role and was taken to an excess of unreality, that was rather the fault of the academics, who ran the schools, and the parents, who paid to send their sons there.[1] Neither academics nor parents had much time for philosophy,[2] the other possible source of advanced training. Rhetoric was what everybody wanted, and it was still of practical use; declamation was not *in principle* absurd even under the Principate.

As if to signal the new era, Cicero and the consuls of the next year, Hirtius and Pansa, practised declamation together after the murder of Caesar in 44 (*C.* 1 pr. 11); and had it not been for political circumstances, Lucius Annaeus Seneca, a Spaniard of equestrian family [3] from Cordoba, might have heard them (*ibid.*). That may imply [4] that he was then of an age to appreciate such entertainment—born, in that case, as early as 55 B.C. Though he is often

---

[1] This is the diagnosis of Quintilian later (see esp. 2.10).

[2] Seneca himself thought it unsuitable for his wife (see his son's *Helv.* 17.4). Cf. his remarks to his son Mela (*C.* 2 pr. 3–5); Sen. *Ep.* 108.22; Tac. *Agr.* 4.3.

[3] Tac. *Ann.* 14.53. For Cordoba, see Martial 1.61.7.

[4] It may not, as Mrs. Miriam Griffin argues in *J.R.S.* 62 (1972), 50.

called Seneca Rhetor, he was never a professional rhetorician, perhaps not even an advocate; but he was a friend of rhetoricians, and an assiduous frequenter of their public performances. Hence a knowledge of declaimers from his teacher Marullus in the thirties B.C. to Quinctilius Varus under Tiberius: declaimers not only in Rome but also in his native Spain, where he doubtless spent much time, looking after his estates. It was there that he married Helvia, there that at least one of his sons, the philosopher Seneca, was born at about the turn of the eras.

At one time, Seneca had had a prodigious memory (*C.* 1 pr. 2–3).[1] And it was the remnants of this memory that enabled him in his old age to gather together at the request of his sons the best sayings of declaimers of his time, particularly those they had never seen. They were keener on epigram and the flashy side of rhetoric than he;[2] and towards the end of his book he affects a disgust with the whole business (*C.* 10 pr. 1). But he kept his interest up long enough to give us what even in the truncated form now extant is our richest source of information on the rhetorical practices of the early Roman empire.

It is true that to supplement Seneca on the *educational* use of declamation we need to look at another

---

[1] Not so unusual then as now. Cf. the declaimer Latro (*C.* 1 pr. 18–19), Themistocles, Mithridates, Crassus and the orator Hortensius. For a striking modern instance, see A. R. Luria, *The Mind of a Mnemonist* (Cape, 1969). It may be that Seneca in fact relied more on notes than he tells us. And he certainly had *some* written sources (Bornecque, *Les Déclamations* . . ., 28–9).

[2] *C.* 1 pr. 22; 4 pr. 1. Cf. also *S.* 6.16 for their distaste for history.

source, the collection attributed to the great teacher Quintilian and known as the Minor Declamations. From this we learn that in a *controversia* the schoolteacher would propose a theme [1] (e.g. " A rapist hung himself. The girl he had raped chooses his property "), often related to a stated law (in this case " A girl who has been raped may choose her seducer's death or his property "). He would then give advice on the treatment (the sections entitled *sermo*), and a model speech (*declamatio*), put in the mouth either of one of the parties in the case or of an advocate.[2] The schoolboys (of what we should call secondary age) would give speeches of their own, on one side or the other.[3]

Declamation was intended to train for the lawcourt,[4] and it was natural that a school speech should be influenced in form by schemes dictated by the rhetoricians to real-life speeches. The *sermo* of the pseudo-Quintilian often alludes to the parts of a

[1] This had to be kept to very strictly. A declaimer could do what he liked in the way of imputing motive and inventing accessory information, but to " alter the facts of the case . . . would be to upset the theme (*thema evertere*) and defeat the object of the declamation " (Bonner, 51, citing, e.g., *C.* 9.5.10–11). It was, however, permissible to point out faults (*vitia*) in the theme: see Gell. 9.15–16.

[2] An advocate would be " granted " (e.g. *C.* 1.7.13) if a woman or slave were in question, or if the circumstances of the case made speech in person embarrassing (see *Decl.* 260 *sermo*). Declaimers, however, preferred to take the role of one of the parties, and prided themselves on their ability to speak in character (ἠθικῶς: e.g. *C.* 2.3.23).

[3] The early chapters of the second book of Quintilian are a prime source for the Roman school.

[4] Quintilian 2.10 has sensible words on the interplay of declamation and reality.

speech,[1] proem and epilogue (beginning and end), the narration of the facts and the arguments over their interpretation. It was of course these arguments that had particular relevance to legal training. " Quintilian " made his model speeches emphasise them. The poet Ovid preferred the *suasoria* because he found all argumentation boring (*C.* 2.2.12); but even in *controversiae* declaimers (according to the complaint of Votienus Montanus in *C.* 9 pr. 1) could leave aside argument and go for what appealed more to them and to their audience. Particularly and increasingly popular were epigrams, *sententiae,* short pointed sayings that carried a special punch when they neatly summarised an argument or concluded a section.[2] But audiences gave applause too to the brilliant descriptive digression,[3] and to apt (or inept [4]) historical instances (*exempla*).

The themes of declamations were later much derided; [5] and even those in Seneca's collection often

---

[1] e.g. *Decl.* 338 *sermo.* For parts of a speech in Seneca himself, see Bonner, 54: note esp. *C.* 1.1.25, 1.6.9, 1.7.15. Seneca sometimes introduces groups of epigrams with phrases like " Narration of Cestius Pius " (*C.* 1.3.2).

[2] Instances of various types in Bonner, 54–5.

[3] Fabianus made them easy to spot by starting them: " I wish to describe love " (or whatever): see *C.* 2.1.26. Descriptions (e.g. of storms, natural beauty) merged into " commonplaces," *loci communes,* which " have no intimate connection with the particular *controversia,* but can be quite aptly placed elsewhere too, such as those on fortune, cruelty, the age, riches " (*C.* 1 pr. 23). See my Index of Commonplaces.

[4] See the criticisms in *C.* 7.5.12–13, and the mockery in Lucian, *Rhet. Praec.* 20. The Index of Names will give an idea of the favourite historical personages.

[5] Most entertainingly by Petronius at the start of what

seem to stray far from reality. This is largely because many of them derive from Greek schools, which had manufactured them with the stock characters (rich man, poor man, good son, prodigal son) and implausible situations (pirates and poisons, coincidences and sudden discoveries) of New Comedy in mind. S. F. Bonner has argued in an important study [1] that genuine parallels in Roman law exist for many of the laws on which the themes are based. And of course every now and again the whirligig of time threw up a striking similarity to even the most outré imaginings.[2] The fact remains that declamation *could* have been far nearer to reality than it was. Boys were trained to argue about ancient lights and the government of the Roman empire by exercises on pirates and the battle of Thermopylae.

Roman schoolmasters kept their schools going because enough parents thought the education they offered worth while. At this bread and butter level, as we have seen, " Quintilian " may be a more reliable guide than Seneca. For " the Senecan declamations were mostly delivered at gatherings of quite mature people. . . . Most of (them) . . . appear to have been based upon debates where rival professors used the school-subjects to exhibit their powers and win the plaudits . . . of their contemporaries " (Bonner, 39). Latro is marked out as unusual (*C.* 9.2.23) because he " would never hear pupils

---

remains of the *Satyricon.* See also Tacitus *Dial.* 35, and in general Bonner, c. 4.

[1] *op. cit.,* cc. 5–6.

[2] Bonner, 36–7.

declaim—he merely declaimed himself,[1] saying he was a pattern, not a school-teacher." That implies that the normal *scholasticus* did run a school of his own, very much as did Quintilian later. But like the sophists of fifth-century Athens, he was able to combine with his teaching a practice of display speaking (*epideixis*) that brought him before the public and might make him known to great men and even emperors. Latro (*C.* 2.4.12) declaimed in the presence of Augustus, Maecenas and Agrippa, very much as Virgil used to recite portions of his poems before imperial personages. The great men themselves sometimes condescended to join in, for example (behind closed doors) the consular historian Asinius Pollio (*C.* 4 pr. 2). We cannot be very sure how the system worked. Probably there was a whole range of possibilities, ranging from ordinary teaching behind closed doors through open lessons [2] to the professorial debate envisaged by Bonner.

As we shall see, both the content and the style of declamation had a large effect upon the literature of the Silver age; and the extravagances recounted by Seneca were certainly not restricted to occasions when professors were trying to impress each other outside school. Ancient criticism makes it certain that the faults of declamation pervaded the whole set up. But certainly the rhetoricians were not at their most sober on the public stage, and Seneca has many

---

[1] Latro's preliminary remarks, made while he was still seated, are the epideictic equivalent of the ordinary school *sermo* (*C.* 1 pr. 21: cf. *C.* 3 pr. 11 on Pompeius Silo).

[2] Observe the behaviour of Albucius, who only spoke five or six times a year in public (*C.* 7 pr. 1).

criticisms to make. As to content, his sympathies lay with the down-to-earth Cassius Severus against the unworldly schoolman Cestius (*C. 3 pr.*) He often remarks on foolish *colores* (see below), where the facts were absurdly represented.[1] And as to style, he is severe on the more ridiculous epigrams. The luckless Saenianus " said a very stupid thing " (*C. 5.2*), " produced an epigram with the hallmark of stupidity " (*C. 7.5.10*), made a remark " with its own kind of insanity " (*C. 9.2.28*). Declaimers are said to display " bad taste " (*cacozelia*), their style is branded as "corrupt," they are unduly Asianic. These were to be the watchwords for critics of extremes of style as the century went on.[2]

It is now time to see how Seneca put his collection of *controversiae* together. Originally there were ten books, each treating between six and nine themes, and each (it seems) with a preface. Each preface gave details of the style and personalities of one or more individual declaimers; Seneca compares himself to a giver of gladiatorial shows: " I am not bringing all my declaimers on at once: let a book always have something new, to keep you on your toes by means of the novelty of the speakers as well as of the

---

[1] The dream-monger Junius Otho is a particular figure of fun.

[2] For *cacozelia*, see *C. 9.1.15*, with Russell's note on " Longinus " 3.4. Quintilian later wrote a lost book on the causes of the corruption of eloquence. Asianism was at first purely geographical in connotation; but the bombastic style frequent in the Greek cities of Asia Minor made this a useful term with which to smear Cicero (see Quintilian 12.10.12, with Austin's notes). Many of Seneca's Greek declaimers really were Asians; but he seems to use *Asianus* as a term of stylistic abuse at *C. 1.2.23*.

epigrams " (*C.* 4 pr. 1). Each book gave epigrams to illustrate the particular declaimers described in its preface.[1] This simple schema often breaks down: Votienus Montanus is introduced in the preface to the ninth book, though an epigram of his had appeared in *C.* 7.5.12; and once a declaimer has been introduced —like Latro in *C.* 1 pr.—his epigrams may appear in any succeeding book.

Each declamation is treated in much the same manner. Seneca first gives the law (if any) on which the theme depends (so, e.g., *C.* 1.1), then the theme itself. Then come epigrams from the declamations of a number of speakers, first on one side of the case, then on the other.[2] Sometimes only one epigram is given for a particular person (so, e.g., for Albucius in *C.* 1.1.10); but often a series is given.[3] Only very rarely do we have a continuous extract from a speech. Latro's remarks in *C.* 2.7.1–9, unfortunately cut short by a defect in the manuscripts, seem to be the only attempt to give a full declamation. Sometimes a continuous section is given (e.g. Fabianus in *C.* 2.1.10–13). But normally the epigrams are extracted like cherries from a cake, and we are left to infer a context for them. Hence the main difficulty in

[1] See especially *C.* 2 pr. 5.

[2] Declaimers did sometimes speak on both sides; see Müller's note on *C.* 9.4.12. It is unclear whether this happened on the same occasion.

[3] My impression is that Seneca groups the epigrams in the order in which they came in the declamation. It may be remarked here that Seneca's concentration on epigrams gives a perhaps false view of the overall style of a declamation. The epigrams will have been used to give a pungent ending to a paragraph more rotundly expressed (a point not quite made by Bonner, 65).

INTRODUCTION

understanding the book, in Latin and in English. The reader must get on the declamatory wavelength, and realise the cleverness of the declaimers (and its limits) before he can really see what is going on. I have provided notes wherever the context seemed more than usually elusive. But I have sometimes had to guess, and the reader will have to guess too. Nor is it always easy to see where one epigram ends and the next begins. To help the English reader while not wholly prejudicing the issues, I have divided the epigrams by dashes *in the translation only*, where I judged best.

On the epigrams follow the " division." In the schoolroom the practice was for the master to lay down the main lines along which his pupils were to argue;[1] these lines " Quintilian " calls the " bare bones of the *controversia*," to be clothed in flesh in his own model declamation and the speeches of his pupils.[2] Similarly, before declaiming Latro used to announce the " questions " he proposed to raise.[3] And when Seneca (as he very often does, e.g. *C.* 1.1.13) gives Latro's division of a declamation, he may have drawn on these preliminary remarks. All the same he often, in giving Latro's division, backs up the questions by extracts in direct speech, apparently taken from the actual declamation (so, e.g., *C.* 1.5.4). Now when Seneca describes Latro's practice (*C.* 1 pr. 21), he makes it sound unusual. And it would

[1] Quintilian 2.6.1.
[2] *Decl.* 270 *sermo*.
[3] This was not at all the same thing as giving a summary of the speech as a whole, for that had far more in it than merely arguments.

seem that the divisions which Seneca attributes to other declaimers may be the result of his own analysis of their arguments. Occasionally a declaimer would give a division in the course of the speech itself, formally. But this happened only rarely even in the law-court; it was surely infrequent in the epideictic declamation.

The divisions are usually of a standard plan, exploiting the contrast of law and equity, *ius* and *aequitas*. Thus in *C.* 1.1.13, Latro distinguishes between the questions, *Can* he be disinherited? i.e. is the law such that this can happen? and *Should* he be, i.e. is there any moral justification? Seneca's terminology is not altogether consistent, but he often distinguishes between " questions," matters of law, and " treatment " (*tractatio*), applied to matters of morality and justification.[1] The contrast of *ius* and *aequitas* is traditional; it is exploited by Cicero, e.g. in the speech for Caecina (51 *seq.*). Here at least is a solid link between declamation and reality. Seneca, however, is critical of further divisions and subdivisions displaying more ingenuity than sense.

The *colores* follow the division. A " colour " (as it seems easiest to translate) was a line of approach to the case, a method of interpreting the facts that was to the advantage of the speaker. Seneca gives a selection of possible approaches, often commenting on their usefulness or good sense, citing freely from the declamations, and getting diverted into engaging anecdotes. Colours could often be summarised in epigrams, and this section often ends with something

[1] See, e.g., *C.* 1.1.14, 2.2.5. Bonner, 57, and esp. H. Bornecque, *Les Déclamations* . . ., 51–2.

of a rag-bag:[1] and here (for some reason) Seneca places the Greek epigrams, which our defective texts often omit or gravely corrupt.

The whole book indeed has been seriously damaged in the course of its transmission. Two quite separate manuscript traditions are available. The first alone gives the *full* text of the *Controversiae* so far as we possess it—that is, Books 1, 2, 7, 9 and 10. It also gives Seneca's prefaces to Books 7, 9 and 10. The second tradition covers all ten books, and is the only source of the titles of the separate *Controversiae*; but it gives only excerpts under each declamation theme. Comparison between the full and excerpted texts, where we possess both, show how savage the excerpting was. Normally only epigrams are reproduced, and by no means all of those: nor are they attributed to individual declaimers. Divisions and colours largely go overboard; a few spicy anecdotes survive from the wreck. Worse still, the excerpts *adapt* the full text even where they do not suppress it. A fascinating study has shown how the excerptor re-handled the epigrams to improve their rhythm.[2] He also tampered with the epigrams to make them clearer, adding subjects and objects not present in the original. Occasionally he mistook the meaning, and produced a new epigram out of the flotsam of the old.

---

[1] Thus in *C.* 1.3 Seneca is still thinking of colours at the start of §12; but the remarks of Hispanus, Triarius and Marullus are noted apropos of nothing.

[2] H. Hagendahl in *Apophoreta Gotoburgensia Vilelmo Lundström oblata* (Göteborg, 1936), 299 *seq*. The original text is sporadically clausulated; Seneca probably kept faithfully to the differing practice of the declaimers.

INTRODUCTION

The excerpts do, however, preserve in full the prefaces to Books 1–4, 7 and 10.[1]

The effect is that we possess the following:

> Books 1–2 (with prefaces), in full and in excerpt
> 3–4 (with prefaces), in excerpt
> 5–6 (without prefaces), in excerpt
> 7 (with preface), in full and in excerpt
> 8 (without preface), in excerpt
> 9–10 (with prefaces), in full and in excerpt

Critical editions print the whole of the excerpts separately. I have only given the excerpts where the full text is not available; but I have indicated in the full text which words also appear, *in one form or another*, in the excerpts.

Seneca can hardly have started writing his book of *controversiae* much before A.D. 37;[2] we do not know whether he lived to publish it, or whether his son, the philosopher, published it for him. But the old man certainly went on[3] to write a second partially preserved work, a collection of *suasoriae*. In these declamations, the theme is of the type: " X, in circumstances Y, deliberates." The declaimer has to advise X what to do. This type was employed in the schools for younger pupils;[4] and though it was presumably designed as a training for deliberative oratory, the connection with reality had been much weakened by the time the Romans inherited it from the Greeks.

---

[1] And they can be used, with due caution, to emend the text offered by the full version of the declamations.

[2] Bornecque, *op. cit.*, 24.

[3] *C.* 2.4.8 proves the priority of the *Controversiae*.

[4] Tac. *Dial*. 35.4.

In *S.* 6 and 7 the themes are related to Roman history; the others are from Greek history and even mythology (*S.* 3).

Just as in his other book, Seneca shows us the professors at play. No introduction survives.[1] Epigrams from individual declaimers follow the statement of the theme. Then comes the division. Colours are out of place here, and Seneca usually ends with a wealth of anecdote, the Greek epigrams again being placed last of all. The modern reader may well find the *Suasoriae* more congenial than the *Controversiae*.

Three fragments traditionally assigned to Seneca's collections of declamations are printed at the end of my second volume. None is certain, for all (and in particular the second) might refer to the philosopher. In the first, Quintilian may mean loosely by Seneca one of the declaimers reported by him; the third, from Donatus, refers to Julius Montanus, who appears once in the extant books of the *Controversiae*.

The fragments of the Histories, which I have added for the sake of completeness, are a more difficult case. That Seneca wrote a history of Rome " from the beginning of the civil wars right down almost to the day of his death " is stated by a fragment of his son's life of him.[2] When that life was written, the history had

---

[1] But the one book we have is otherwise fairly complete. *S.* 6.27 shows that there were never more than seven declamations. The beginning of the first is missing.

[2] See Haase's edition of the younger Seneca, 3.436–7. For the elder Seneca as a historian see most recently I. Hahn, *Acta Antiqua Academiae Scientiarum Hungaricae* 12 (1964), 169–206 and F. Klingner, *Mus. Helv.* 15 (1958), 199: together with Schanz-Hosius, *Gesch. d. röm. Lit.* 2.341.

not been published, and it is not certain that it ever was. There has been, and still is, much controversy [1] about one alleged fragment, that on the " Ages of Rome " from Lactantius, and its relation to a similar passage in Florus. But there is a good chance that both this and the second fragment (from Suetonius) are to be attributed to the son. Certainly Quintilian does not mention any historical work in his summary of the younger Seneca's oeuvre (10.1.129); but history can be discussed outside history books, and there are many lost works of the philosopher into which these fragments could be fitted. More properly to be related to the old man's book are the details on Cicero's death in *S.* 6; Seneca clearly had collated the authorities for this episode. And we should note too the remarks to his declamation-hungry sons on the more solid fare of history (*S.* 6.16).

Whether the history was eventually to see the light of day or not, the old man was clearly busy with it and with his rhetorical writings at the very end of his life. For he was dead by 41. That was the year when Seneca the younger was exiled to Corsica by the emperor Gaius; and in consoling his mother Helvia (*Helv.* 2.4) for that further loss, he wrote: " Within thirty days [of an uncle's death], you buried your very dear husband, by whom you were the mother of three children."

*   *   *

[1] The bibliography is given by M. Lausberg, *Untersuchungen zu Senecas Fragmenten* (Berlin, 1970), 3 n. 10; see also Mrs. Griffin's article (p. ix, n. 4, above), which I have followed in the matter of the Histories.

INTRODUCTION

The modern will find a good deal of the elder Seneca's material unreal, unfamiliar and even tedious. He will skip many of the epigrams, and concentrate on the lively prefaces and the incidental anecdote. But anyone, lay or scholar, who wishes to understand the essence of Silver Latin will have to take the rough with the smooth and nerve himself to read at least a fair sample of the whole. All writers of Latin prose and verse from the Augustan age to the end of antiquity had their secondary education in schools that taught declamation; and even the greatest of them could not keep—did not wish to keep—their style unmarked by the experience.[1] We can read in Seneca himself of the relation between the declamation and the poetry of Ovid [2] (*C.* 2.2.8–12, perhaps the most illuminating section of the whole work). Even Virgil, when he resoundingly concludes a speech " Timeo Danaos et dona ferentis," is producing a *sen-*

---

[1] It is a matter both of content (exaggerated horrors of storm, poison and torture) and, more especially, of style: epigram, clever lines of argument, allusiveness and the extravert declamatory tone. Bonner, c. 8 summarises helpfully.

[2] Worked out, e.g., by C. Brück, *De Ovidio scholasticarum declamationum imitatore* (Giessen, 1909). For Lucan, see Bonner, *A.J.P.* 87 (1966), 257–89, and M. P. O. Morford, *The Poet Lucan* (Blackwell, 1967). For the younger Seneca, E. Rolland, *De l'influence de Sénèque le père . . . sur Sénèque le philosophe* (Gand, 1906), with C. Preisendanz, *Philologus* 67 (1908), 68–112. For Juvenal, J. de Decker, *Juvenalis declamans* (Ghent, 1913). I have drawn on these and other works and on my own reading to give an indication in the notes of parallels for the epigrams listed by Seneca, keeping the number down by weighting the selection in favour of authors with full commentaries (e.g. Juvenal) which can easily be consulted for further material.

tentia. Later, Lucan in verse, the younger Seneca in prose, were soaked in the declamatory manner. And at the end of the century Juvenal and Tacitus (with more reservations) can be seen as a similar pair. The criticism levelled at declamation had no effect on its increasing unreality.[1] The Major Declamations attributed to Quintilian take the story down to the fourth century. And even the medievals had their share of wizards and pirates from this source, for the ever popular *Gesta Romanorum* sometimes draw on declamation themes. When we call Latin after the fall of the Republic rhetorical, we mean that it was declamatory. And to track declamation to its lair, we must go to the elder Seneca.

---

[1] The establishment of public " chairs " for teachers of rhetoric under the Flavians marks the respectability of the declaimers, but does not seem to have kept their fantasies in check. Meanwhile in Greece the rhetoricians of the second sophistic, of whom Philostratus gives a vivid picture, were no less prone to see declamation as an end in itself.

BIBLIOGRAPHY

The basic facts about the elder Seneca are collected by the handbooks, e.g. *Prosopographia Imperii Romani* [2] no. 616; Pauly-Wissowa, *Real-Encyclopädie* 1.2237–40 (O. Rossbach); and especially Schanz-Hosius, *Geschichte d. römischen Literatur*, 2.338–42. The pioneer work on Seneca and declamation was H. Bornecque, *Les Déclamations et les Déclamateurs d'après Sénèque le père* (Lille, 1902), but readers will find S. F. Bonner, *Roman Declamation* (Liverpool, 1949) both more reliable and wider in its perspectives. I cannot stress too strongly what I owe to this fine book.

Bonner and Bornecque between them will provide further bibliography. Here I need mention only, on education, M. L. Clarke, *Rhetoric at Rome* (Routledge, 1953) and *Higher Education at Rome* (Routledge, 1971); on literary terminology, H. Bardon, *Le vocabulaire de la critique littéraire chez Sénèque le Rhéteur* (Paris, 1940); and on Silver Latin generally, W. C. Summers, *Select Letters of Seneca* (Macmillan, 1910), Introduction.

For a useful summary of past work, see J. E. G. Whitehorn, *Prudentia* 1 (1969), 14–27.

A NOTE ON THE TEXT AND TRANSLATION

The elder Seneca has only once been translated in
full before, by H. Bornecque (ed. 2, Garnier, Paris,
1932): though passages have been put into English
(the prefaces by L. A. Sussman, *Speech Monographs* 37
[1970], 135–51. If I have at all improved on Bornecque, that would only be because it is easier to
stand on the shoulders of others than to carry others
oneself. Where I differ from him, I do so with trepi-
dation; I owe much to his acute feel for the declamatory nuance.

There has been no commentary on the *Controversiae* since the eighteenth century; for the *Suasoriae* we have W. A. Edward, *The Suasoriae of Seneca
the Elder* (Cambridge, 1928), with translation.

The major critical edition is that of H. J. Müller
(Vienna, 1887; Hildesheim, 1963), the culmination of
nineteenth-century work on the author.[1] What went
before—C. Bursian (Leipzig, 1857) and A. Kiessling
(Leipzig, 1872)—is now of less value, though often
more acute in judgement. Müller gives a very complete apparatus, with full and extremely accurate
collations of the manuscripts that matter (and some

---

[1] The elder Seneca is so often referred to by Müller's pages
that I have given his pagination in the right-hand margin of
the Latin text in the form 16M, etc.

that do not). Since then, little has been done on the
text, except for scattered conjectures. The many
articles by R. Novák in *Wiener Studien* between 1895
and 1915 amass much information on Seneca's lin-
guistic practices, but show little critical judgement.
I have learnt much more from E. Thomas, *Philologus*
Suppl.-Bd. 8 (1899), 159–298, and D. R. Shackleton
Bailey, *C.Q.* 19 (1969), 320–29. Much work has been
done on the manuscripts of the " full " tradition by
Dr. H. Vervliet of Antwerp; some of his results
appear in *Scriptorium* 13 (1959), 80–81 and *L'Antiquité
classique* 33 (1964), 431–41.

The text I present here is in effect a corrected
Müller. Müller printed far too many conjectures;
where I return to the reading of the manuscripts, I
usually do so without a note: my translation should
make it clear in each case what my interpretation is.
As to the many places where I do diverge from the
manuscript tradition, the limitations of a Loeb edition naturally make it impossible to give all the
details;[1] but I have tried to indicate all important
conjectures, with particular attention paid to passages where the text is gravely in doubt. Where I
print a conjecture unknown to Müller or not accepted
by him, I *always* attribute it. In my critical notes,
unattributed readings are those of the primary manuscripts (for which see below); I have normally relied
on Müller's reports, but have occasionally checked
dubious points on a microfilm of *V* most kindly lent
to me by Dr. Vervliet.

---

[1] In particular, I hardly ever note variations between the
" full " text and that of the excerpta.

Müller rightly regarded *A*, *B* and *V* as the primary manuscripts of the full text. The three descend from one archetype: and it is normally supposed that *A* and *B* are further linked by a hyparchetype. *V*, however, is highly " corrected " and interpolated, and the prudent editor will always weigh its readings with suspicion. *AB*, even when wrong, are often nearer the truth.

I almost never cite later manuscripts of the full text: Dr. Vervliet's unpublished thesis shows that all descend ultimately from *V*; or, for that matter, of the excerpta, where Müller's reliance on the oldest manuscript, *M*, though merely intuitive, would doubtless be justified if the matter were to be properly investigated. Except under extreme provocation, I follow Müller's orthography.

In the Latin text of Books 1, 2, 7, 9 and 10 of the *Controversiae* italics indicate sentences or parts of sentences excerpted from the full version in one branch of the tradition (see Introduction, p. xx). The excerptor sometimes adapted the material to his own purposes, and it should not be assumed that the italicised words necessarily give the actual form of the excerpts; these are readily available in the major printed editions.

Attention may be drawn to two idiosyncrasies of my translation. I often employ inverted commas without attribution of speaker to represent the frequent Latin use of *inquit*. And I often phrase in the positive questions raised in the *divisio* where the Latin uses the negative (so at 7.4.4 " an lex de alendis parentibus *non* pertineret ad matres vivis patribus "). I hope that my licence in these cases will not mislead.

Finally as to the notes: they are to be used in conjunction with the Index of Names, where the information given about historical and legendary persons should elucidate allusions in the text.

SIGLA OF THE MANUSCRIPTS

" Full " text of the Controversiae, plus the Suasoriae

A   Antwerp, Bibliothèque Publique, MS. 411 (tenth century)

B   Brussels, Bibliothèque Royale, MS. 9594 (ninth century)

V   Vaticanus lat. 3872 (tenth century)

D   Brussels, Bibliothèque Royale, MS. 9144 (fifteenth century)

Excerpta (=E) from the Controversiae

M   Montpellier University Library (Section de Médecine), MS. 126 (tenth century)

ABBREVIATIONS

I hope that all abbreviations used in the notes are self-explanatory, or can easily be elucidated by reference, e.g., to the list in the *Oxford Classical Dictionary* (ed. 2), ix *seq.* The following, however, may puzzle:

RLM = *Rhetores Latini Minores*, ed. K. Halm (Leipzig, 1863, reprinted 1964).

References to the collections of Minor and Major Declamations attributed to Quintilian are given *either* as *Decl.* with a page reference to Ritter (for the Minor) or Lehnert (for the Major) *or* as *Decl.* with a declamation number; in the latter case single or double figure numbers will be from the Major collection, three figure from the Minor.

CONTROVERSIARUM

LIBER PRIMUS

SENECA NOVATO, SENECAE, MELAE FILIIS SALUTEM.

1 Exigitis rem magis iucundam mihi quam facilem: iubetis enim quid de his declamatoribus sentiam qui in aetatem meam inciderunt indicare, et si qua memoriae meae nondum elapsa sunt ab illis dicta colligere, ut, quamvis notitiae vestrae subducti sint, tamen non credatis tantum de illis sed et iudicetis. Est, fateor, iucundum mihi redire in antiqua studia melioresque ad annos respicere, et vobis querentibus quod tantae opinionis viros audire 2 non potueritis detrahere temporum iniuriam. Sed cum multa iam mihi ex meis desideranda senectus 2M fecerit, oculorum aciem retuderit, aurium sensum hebetaverit, nervorum firmitatem fatigaverit, inter ea quae rettuli memoria est, res ex omnibus animi partibus maxime delicata et fragilis, in quam primam senectus incurrit. Hanc aliquando ⟨adeo⟩[1] in me

---

[1] *Supplied by C. F. W. Müller.*

2

THE CONTROVERSIAE

BOOK 1

PREFACE

SENECA TO HIS SONS NOVATUS, SENECA AND MELA
GREETINGS

What you ask is something I find agreeable rather 1 than easy. You tell me to give you my opinion of the declaimers who have been my contemporaries, and to put together such of their sayings as I haven't yet forgotten, so that, even though you were not acquainted with them, you may still form your own judgement on them without trusting merely to hearsay. Yes, it *is* agreeable for me to return to my old studies, to look back on better years, and simultaneously to remove the sting of your complaint against Time—that you were unable to listen to men of such reputation. But 2 by now old age has made me regret the loss of many of my faculties. It has dimmed my eyesight, dulled my hearing, made my strong muscles tired: but among these things I mention it is memory, of all parts of the mind the most vulnerable and fragile, that old age first assaults. I do not deny that my own memory [1] was at one time so powerful as to be

[1] For Seneca's memory, see Introduction, p. x.

floruisse ut non tantum ad usum sufficeret sed in miraculum usque procederet non nego; nam et duo milia nominum recitata quo erant ordine dicta reddebam, et ab his qui ad audiendum praeceptorem mecum convenerant singulos versus a singulis datos, cum plures quam ducenti efficerentur, ab ultimo inci-
3 piens usque ad primum recitabam. Nec ad complectenda tantum quae vellem velox mihi erat memoria, sed etiam ad continenda quae acceperat solebat bonae fidei esse: [1] nunc et aetate quassata et longa desidia, quae iuvenilem quoque animum dissolvit, eo perducta est ut, etiamsi potest aliquid praestare, non possit promittere. Diu ab illa nihil repetivi: nunc quia iubetis quid possit experiar et illam omni cura scrutabor.

Ex parte enim bene spero: nam quaecumque apud illam aut puer aut iuvenis deposui, quasi recentia aut 3M modo audita sine cunctatione profert; at si qua illi intra proximos annos commisi, sic perdidit et amisit ut, etiamsi saepius ingerantur, totiens tamen tam-
4 quam nova audiam. Ita ex memoria mea quantum vobis satis sit superest; neque enim de his me interrogatis quos ipsi audistis, sed de his qui ad vos usque non pervenerunt.

Fiat quod vultis: mittatur senex in scholas. Illud necesse est inpetrem, ne me quasi certum aliquem ordinem velitis sequi in contrahendis quae mihi occurrent; necesse est enim per omnia studia mea errem et passim quidquid obvenerit adprehendam.
5 Controversiarum sententias fortasse pluribus locis ponam in una declamatione dictas; non enim ⟨sem-

---

[1] solebat—esse *is given by the MSS after* repetivi *below.*

positively prodigious, quite apart from its efficiency in ordinary use. When two thousand names had been reeled off I would repeat them in the same order; and when my assembled school-fellows each supplied a line of poetry, up to the number of more than two hundred, I would recite them in reverse. My memory used to be swift to pick up what I wanted 3 it to; but it was also reliable in retaining what it had taken in. Now it has been undermined by age, and by a long period of idleness—which can play havoc with young minds too: to such an extent that though it may be able to come up with something, it cannot make any promises. It is a long time since I asked anything of it. But now, since you require it, I will see what it can do, and pry into its recesses with every care.

To some extent I am quite hopeful: whatever I entrusted to it as a boy or young man it brings out again without hesitation as though new and just heard. But things I have deposited with it these last years it has lost so entirely that even if they are repeatedly dinned into me, I hear them each time as new. Hence enough of my memory is left for your 4 purposes—for you aren't asking me about speakers you have heard yourselves, but about those who came before your time.

Be it as you wish, then: let an old man be sent to school. But I must ask you not to insist on any strict order in the assembling of my memories; I must stray at large through all my studies, and grab at random whatever comes my way. I shall, perhaps, dis- 5 tribute over a number of passages epigrams which were actually spoken in one *controversia*: I don't

per⟩ [1] dum quaero aliquid invenio, sed saepe quod
quaerenti non comparuit aliud agenti praesto est;
quaedam vero, quae obversantia mihi et ex aliqua
parte se ostendentia non possum occupare, eadem
securo et reposito animo subito emergunt; aliquando
etiam seriam rem agenti et occupato sententia diu
frustra quaesita intempestive molesta est. Necesse
est ergo me ad delicias conponam memoriae meae
quae mihi iam olim precario paret.

6   Facitis autem, iuvenes mei, rem necessariam et
utilem quod non contenti exemplis saeculi vestri
prioris quoque vultis cognoscere. Primum quia,
quo plura exempla inspecta sunt, plus in eloquentiam
proficitur. Non est unus, quamvis praecipuus sit,
imitandus, quia numquam par fit imitator auctori.
Haec rei natura est: semper citra veritatem est 4M
similitudo. Deinde ut possitis aestimare in quantum
cotidie ingenia decrescant et nescio qua iniquitate
naturae eloquentia se retro tulerit: quidquid Romana
facundia habet quod insolenti Graeciae aut opponat
7 aut praeferat circa Ciceronem effloruit; omnia ingenia quae lucem studiis nostris attulerunt tunc nata
sunt. In deterius deinde cotidie data res est, sive
luxu temporum—nihil enim tam mortiferum ingeniis

---

[1] semper *supplied here by Gertz.*

---

[1] For the concept of imitation, see Quintilian 10.2 (esp. 24–6,
on the desirability of having more than one model, and 11 for
the inferiority of copy to original).
[2] The first statement of a theme often sounded in the
first century A.D. The principal text is Tacitus' *Dialogus.*

always find what I want when I'm looking for it—but often what escaped me when I was searching for it comes to me when I am on some other tack. Some things, that I cannot quite catch as they hover before me only partly visible, suddenly come up clearly when I am relaxed and at leisure. Sometimes, even, an epigram that I have long hunted in vain comes at the wrong moment and is a nuisance when I'm occupied with some serious business. I have got, therefore, to adapt myself to the whims of my memory, which for some time has obeyed me only on sufferance.

Well, my dear young men, you are doing some- 6 thing necessary and useful in refusing to be satisfied with the models provided by your own day and wanting to get to know those of the preceding generation too. For one thing, the more patterns one examines, the greater advantage to one's eloquence. You should not imitate one man, however distinguished: [1] for an imitator never comes up to the level of his model. This is the way it is; the copy always falls short of the reality. Moreover, you can by this means judge how sharply intellectual standards are falling every day, how far some grudge on nature's part has sent eloquence into a decline.[2] Everything that Roman oratory has to set alongside or even above the haughty Greeks reached its peak in Cicero's day: all the geniuses who have brought brilliance to our 7 subject were born then. Since, things have got daily worse. Perhaps this is due to the luxury of the age

Others are conveniently collected by H. Caplan in *Studies in Speech and Drama in honor of Alexander M. Drummond* (Ithaca, N.Y., 1944), 295 *seq.* = *Of Eloquence* (Cornell, 1970), 160 *seq.*

quam luxuria est—sive, cum pretium pulcherrimae
rei cecidisset, translatum est omne certamen ad
turpia multo honore quaestuque vigentia, sive fato
quodam, cuius maligna perpetuaque in rebus omnibus lex est ut ad summum perducta rursus ad in-
fimum, velocius quidem quam ascenderant, relaban-
tur.

8   Torpent ecce ingenia desidiosae iuventutis nec in
unius honestae rei labore vigilatur; somnus lan-
guorque ac somno et languore turpior malarum rerum
industria invasit animos: cantandi saltandique obscena
studia effeminatos tenent, [et] capillum frangere et
ad muliebres blanditias extenuare vocem, mollitia 5M
corporis certare cum feminis et inmundissimis se
excolere munditiis nostrorum adulescentium speci-
9 men est. Quis aequalium vestrorum quid dicam
satis ingeniosus, satis studiosus, immo quis satis vir
est? Emolliti enervesque quod nati sunt in vita[1]
manent, expugnatores alienae pudicitiae, neglegentes
suae. In hos ne dii tantum mali ut cadat eloquentia:
quam non mirarer nisi animos in quos se conferret
eligeret. Erratis, optimi iuvenes, nisi illam vocem
non M. Catonis sed oraculi creditis. Quid enim est
oraculum? nempe voluntas divina hominis ore enun-
tiata; et quem tandem antistitem sanctiorem sibi invenire divinitas potuit quam M. Catonem per quem
humano generi non praeciperet sed convicium
faceret? Ille ergo vir quid ait? "Orator est,

---

[1] in vita *Kiessling:* inuiti *or* muti.

(nothing is so fatal to talent as luxury); perhaps, as this glorious art became less prized, competitiveness transferred itself wholly to sordid businesses that bring great prestige and profit; perhaps it is just Fate, whose grim law is universal and everlasting— things that get to the top sink back to the bottom, faster than they rose.

Look at our young men: they are lazy, their intel- 8 lects asleep; no-one can stay awake to take pains over a single honest pursuit. Sleep, torpor and a perseverance in evil that is more shameful than either have seized hold of their minds. Libidinous delight in song and dance transfixes these effeminates. Braiding the hair, refining the voice till it is as caress-ing as a woman's, competing in bodily softness with women, beautifying themselves with filthy fineries— this is the pattern our youths set themselves.[1] Which 9 of your contemporaries—quite apart from his talent and diligence—is sufficiently a man? Born feeble and spineless, they stay like that throughout their lives: taking others' chastity by storm, careless of their own. God forbid *them* to be blessed with elo-quence—something for which I should have scant respect if it exercised no choice in those on whom it bestowed itself. That well-known saying of Cato was really an oracle—and you are wrong, my excellent young men, if you fail to appreciate the fact: for surely an oracle is the divine will given human expression; and what high priest could the gods have found more holy than Marcus Cato, not so much to teach mankind as to scold it? What then was it that the great man said? "An orator, son Marcus, is a

[1] A declamatory topic taken up by Sen. *N.Q.* 7.31.2.

10 Marce fili, vir bonus dicendi peritus." Ite nunc et
in istis vulsis atque expolitis et nusquam nisi in libidine viris quaerite oratores. Merito talia habent
exempla qualia ingenia. Quis est qui memoriae
studeat? quis est qui non dico magnis virtutibus sed 6M
suis placeat? Sententias a disertissimis viris iactas
facile in tanta hominum desidia pro suis dicunt, et
sic sacerrimam eloquentiam, quam praestare non
possunt, violare non desinunt. Eo libentius quod
exigitis faciam, et quaecumque a celeberrimis viris
facunde dicta teneo, ne ad quemquam privatim pertineant, populo dedicabo.

11 Ipsis quoque multum praestaturus videor, quibus
oblivio inminet nisi aliquid quo memoria eorum
producatur posteris tradetur.[1] Fere enim aut
nulli commentarii maximorum declamatorum extant aut, quod peius est, falsi. Itaque ne aut ignoti
sint aut aliter quam debent noti, summa cum fide
suum cuique reddam. Omnes autem magni in eloquentia nominis excepto Cicerone videor audisse;
ne Ciceronem quidem aetas mihi eripuerat, sed
bellorum civilium furor, qui tunc orbem totum perva-
gabatur, intra coloniam meam me continuit: alioqui
in illo atriolo in quo duos grandes praetextatos ait
secum declamasse potui adesse, illudque ingenium

---

[1] tradetur *Gertz:* tradatur.

good man skilled in speaking."[1] Well, go and look 10
for orators among the smooth and hairless of today,
men only in their lusts. Quite properly, they have
models as depraved as their intellects. Who cares for
his future renown? Who is made popular—I won't
say by great qualities—but even by his own? Un-
detected by so casual a public, they can easily pass off
for their own epigrams thrown off by the really able,
thus constantly violating the holiness of an eloquence
they cannot attain. So much the more gladly will I
comply with your request, making a present to the
public of all the eloquent sayings of famous men that
I can remember, so that they aren't mere private
possessions of someone.

Indeed, I think I shall be doing a great service to 11
the declaimers themselves, who face being forgotten
unless something to prolong their memory is handed
on to posterity; for in general there are no extant
drafts from the pens of the greatest declaimers, or,
what is worse, there are forged ones. So to prevent
them being unknown, or known in the wrong light, I
shall be scrupulous in giving each his due. I think I
heard everyone of great repute in oratory, with the
exception of Cicero; and even Cicero I was deprived
of not by my age, but by the raging civil wars, which
at that time were traversing the entire world, and
which kept me behind the walls of my colony;[2]
otherwise I might have been present in that little hall
where he says two grown-up boys declaimed with

---

[1] A definition adopted with enthusiasm by Quintilian
(12.1.1). For Cato as an oracle, cf. Sen. *Ep.* 94.28.

[2] See Introduction, p. ix.

quod solum populus Romanus par imperio suo habuit 7M
cognoscere, et, quod vulgo aliquando dici solet, sed in
illo proprie debet, potui vivam vocem audire.

12   Declamabat autem Cicero non quales nunc controversias dicimus, ne tales quidem quales ante
Ciceronem dicebantur, quas thesis vocabant. Hoc
enim genus materiae quo nos exercemur adeo novum
est ut nomen quoque eius novum sit: controversias
nos dicimus; Cicero causas vocabat. Hoc vero alterum nomen Graecum quidem, sed in Latinum ita
translatum ut pro Latino sit, scholastica, controversia multo recentius est, sicut ipsa " declamatio "
apud nullum antiquum auctorem ante Ciceronem
et Calvum inveniri potest, qui declamationem
⟨a dictione⟩ [1] distinguit; ait enim declamare iam se
non mediocriter, dicere bene; alterum putat domes-
ticae exercitationis esse, alterum verae actionis.
Modo nomen hoc prodiit; nam et studium ipsum
nuper celebrari coepit: ideo facile est mihi ab
incunabulis nosse rem post me natam.

13   In aliis autem an beneficium vobis daturus sim
nescio, in uno accipio: Latronis enim Porcii, 8M
carissimi mihi sodalis, memoriam saepius cogar retrac-
tare, et a prima pueritia usque ad ultimum eius diem
perductam familiarem amicitiam cum voluptate

---

[1] *Supplied by Gertz.*

---

[1] Cicero according to Suet. *Gr. Rhet.* 25.3 declaimed in
Greek up to his praetorship, in Latin as an older man with
Hirtius and Pansa (consuls in 43 B.C.), " quos discipulos (*ad*

him,[1] and got to know that genius, the only possession of Rome to rival her empire: and, to use a common saying that is particularly appropriate of him, I could have heard the " living voice." [2]

Now Cicero [3] used to declaim, but not the *contro-* 12 *versiae* we speak nowadays, or even the kind called *theses* which were spoken before Cicero. The type of theme we now use for our exercises is so new that its name too is new. We speak of *controversiae*. Cicero called them " causes." A second name, *scholastica*, a Greek word to be sure, but taken over to serve as a Latin one, is much more recent than *controversia*: just as *declamatio* itself can be found in no old author before Cicero and Calvus. Calvus distinguishes *declamatio* from *dictio*, saying that he is by now not bad at " declaiming " but good at " speaking." The former he regards as to be used of exercises at home, the other of a real speech. The name has emerged recently, the practice itself having become popular not long ago: the thing was born after me—that is why it is easy for me to have known it from its cradle.

In general, I may—or may not—be doing you a 13 service; in one respect I am receiving one. For I shall frequently have to revive memories of my dearest friend, Porcius Latro, and recall with the highest pleasure an intimate friendship that lasted from our early childhood to his last day. **The man**

Fam. 9.16.7, dated 46 B.C.) et grandis praetextatos vocabat."
The *praetexta* was discarded at sixteen; Hirtius and Pansa were, like Seneca, " sent to school " again.

[2] Otto, *Sprichwörter*, 378.

[3] For the difficulties of the following account, see Introduction, p. viii.

maxima repetam. Nihil illo viro gravius, nihil suavius, nihil eloquentia [sua] [1] dignius; nemo plus ingenio suo imperavit, nemo plus indulsit.

In utramque partem vehementi viro modus deerat: nec intermittere studium sciebat nec repetere. 14 Cum se ad scribendum concitaverat, iungebantur noctibus dies, et sine intervallo gravius sibi instabat, nec desinebat nisi defecerat; rursus cum se remiserat, in omnes lusus, in omnes iocos se resolvebat; cum vero se silvis montibusque tradiderat, in silvis ac montibus natos, homines illos agrestis, laboris patientia et venandi sollertia provocabat, et in tantam perveniebat sic vivendi cupiditatem ut vix posset ad priorem consuetudinem retrahi. At cum sibi iniecerat manum et se blandienti otio abduxerat, tantis viribus incumbebat in studium ut non tantum nihil perdidisse sed multum adquisisse de- 15 sidia videretur. Omnibus quidem prodest subinde 9M animum relaxare; excitatur enim otio vigor, et omnis tristitia, quae continuatione pertinacis studii adducitur, feriarum hilaritate discutitur: nulli tamen intermissio manifestius proderat. Quotiens ex intervallo dicebat, multo acrius violentiusque dicebat; exultabat enim ⟨animo⟩ [2] novato atque integro robore, et tantum a se exprimebat quantum concupierat. Nesciebat dispensare vires suas, sed inmoderati adversus se imperii fuit, ideoque studium eius prohiberi debebat quia regi non poterat. Itaque sole-

---

[1] *Deleted by Kiessling.*
[2] *Supplied here by Gertz.*

was uniquely serious and charming, uniquely worthy of being eloquent. No-one was more in control of his genius—yet no-one more indulged it.

This passionate man lacked moderation in two respects: he could not stop work—and could not start it again. When he had roused himself to write, day 14 and night merged—he over-pressed himself ceaselessly, and stopped only when he was exhausted. But when he relaxed, he let himself go on all kinds of amusement and frivolity; yet when he had yielded himself up to the woods and mountains, he rivalled for endurance of hardship and skill in the hunt the country folk who had been born in those woods and mountains, and used to be so entranced with the idea of living like that that he could scarcely be brought back to his former pursuits. Yet when he had taken a grip on himself, and torn himself away from the allurements of leisure, he would throw himself into his work so energetically that he seemed to have lost nothing, even gained much, by his sloth. Of course, 15 everyone is benefited by occasional mental relaxation; leisure rouses one's energy, and all the melancholy induced by extended hard work is dispelled by the gaiety of a vacation; but no-one was more obviously so helped than Latro. When he spoke after a gap, it was much more keenly and vehemently; he would exult in the renewal of his mind and the perfection of his powers; and he would get out of himself as much as he wished. He had no idea how to husband his strength, but ruled himself ruthlessly—his zest had to be stopped altogether just because it could not be regulated. And so he himself, broken by constant and unremitting effort, used to feel a las-

bat et ipse, cum se assidua et numquam intermissa
contentione fregerat, sentire ingenii lassitudinem,
quae non minor est quam corporis, sed occultior.

16   Corpus illi erat et natura solidum et multa exercitatione duratum, ideoque numquam impetus
ardentis animi deseruit. Vox robusta, sed surda,
lucubrationibus et neglegentia, non natura infuscata;
beneficio tamen laterum extollebatur, et, quamvis
inter initia parum attulisse virium videretur, ipsa
actione adcrescebat. Nulla umquam illi cura vocis
exercendae fuit; illum fortem et agrestem et Hispa-
nae consuetudinis morem non poterat dediscere:
utcumque res tulerat, ita vivere, nihil vocis causa fac-   10M
ere, non illam per gradus paulatim ab imo ad summum
perducere, non rursus a summa contentione paribus
intervallis descendere, non sudorem unctione dis-
17 cutere, non latus ambulatione reparare. Saepe
cum per totam lucubraverat noctem, ab ipso cibo statim ad declamandum veniebat. Iam vero quin rem
inimicissimam corpori faceret vetari nullo modo
poterat: post cenam fere lucubrabat, nec patiebatur
alimenta per somnum quietemque aequaliter digeri,
sed perturbata ac dissipata in caput agebat; itaque
et oculorum aciem contuderat et colorem mutaverat.

    Memoria ei natura quidem felix, plurimum tamen
arte adiuta. Numquam ille quae dicturus erat
ediscendi causa relegebat: edidicerat illa cum scrip-
serat. Id eo magis in illo mirabile videri potest quod
non lente et anxie sed eodem paene quo dicebat
18 impetu scribebat. Illi qui scripta sua torquent, qui

situde of mind that is as debilitating as bodily tired-
ness, though less obvious.

He had a body that nature had made strong and 16
exercise hard, so that it never failed the impulses of
his passionate spirit. His voice was strong but dull,
thickened not by nature but by over-work and lack of
care. But it was capable of being raised, thanks to
the strength of his lungs, and though at the start of a
speech it might be thought to have too little power in
reserve it grew with the impetus of the speech itself.
He never took any trouble to exercise his voice; he
could not put off his steadfast, rustic, Spanish character: his motto was to live as circumstances suggested,
without doing anything for the sake of his voice (such
as gradually taking it up from low to high, and then
going down again from the highest pitch by equal in-
tervals), and without inhibiting sweat by means of oil
or renewing his lungs by walking. Often, having 17
stayed up all night, he would come to declaim straight
from a meal. Again, he could just not be put off
doing something very harmful to the body: he
generally worked into the night after dinner,[1] so that
his food, instead of being smoothly digested in a rest-
ful sleep, was driven to his head, disturbed and scattered—hence his weak eyesight and bad complexion.

His memory was naturally good, and much improved by technique. He would never read over
again what he was going to say in order to learn it off
—he had learnt it off as he wrote: which is the more
remarkable because he used to write not slowly and
painstakingly but with almost the same impetuosity
as marked his speech. Those who put their writings 18

[1] Compare the remarks of Celsus 1.2.5; Sen. *Ep.* 94.20.

de singulis verbis in consilium eunt, necesse est quae totiens animo suo admovent novissime adfigant; at quorumcumque stilus velox est, tardior 11M memoria est. In illo non tantum naturalis memoriae felicitas erat, sed ars summa et ad conprehendenda quae tenere debebat et ad custodienda, adeo ut omnes declamationes suas quascumque dixerat teneret etiam. Itaque supervacuos sibi fecerat codices; aiebat se in animo scribere. Cogitata dicebat ita ut in nullo umquam verbo eum memoria deceperit. Historiarum omnium summa notitia: iubebat aliquem nominari ducem et statim eius acta cursu reddebat: adeo quaecumque semel in animum eius descenderant in promptu erant.

19   Video vos, iuvenes mei, plus iusto ad hanc eius virtutem obstupescere; alia vos mirari in illo volo: hoc, quod tantum vobis videtur, non operosa arte tradi potest. Intra exiguum paucissimorum dierum tempus poterit quilibet facere illud quod Cineas fecit, qui missus a Pyrrho legatus ad Romanos postero die novus homo et senatum et omnem urbanam circumfusam senatui plebem nominibus suis persalutavit; aut quod ille fecit qui recitatum a poeta novum carmen dixit suum esse et protinus ⟨ex⟩ memoria recitavit, cum hoc ille cuius carmen erat facere non posset; aut quod fecit Hortensius, qui a Sisenna 12M provocatus in auctione persedit per diem totum et omnes res et pretia et emptores ordine suo argentariis recognoscentibus ita ut in nulla re falleretur

---

[1] For techniques of memorising, see Quintilian 11.2, where (§24) the story of Hortensius recurs (cf. Cic. *Brut.* 301). For Cineas' memory, see Cic. *Tusc.* 1.59; Plin. *N.H.* 7.88.

on the rack, holding debates over every word, inevitably end up by fixing in the mind what has so often engaged it; but those who write quickly are slower to remember. Not only had nature blessed Latro with a fine memory, but he had supreme technique for grasping and for retaining what he had to remember, so that he could recall all the declamations he had ever spoken. He had thus made books superfluous—he used to say he wrote in his mind. What he had mentally rehearsed he used to speak without his memory ever failing in a single word. He had vast knowledge of the whole range of history; he would ask someone to name a general to him, and then immediately detail his feats with fluency—so true was it that he had at his finger-tips whatever had once come his way.

I can see, my dear young men, that you are more 19 astonished by this talent of Latro than you should be; I want you to admire other qualities in him—this one, which you make so much of, can be acquired by a technique that requires little trouble.[1] Within the small space of a very few days, anyone can do what Cineas did: this man, sent as ambassador to Rome by Pyrrhus, next day, as a newcomer, greeted by their correct names the senate and the whole crowd of townspeople around the senate. Or he can emulate the man who, hearing a new poem recited by its author, said it was his own, and proceeded to recite it from memory, even though its *author* could not do the same; or Hortensius, who, challenged by Sisenna, sat all day at an auction, and then listed without a mistake and in the right order all the articles, their prices and purchasers, with the bankers authenticating the

recensuit. Cupitis statim discere? Suspendam cupiditatem vestram et faciam alteri beneficio locum;
interim hoc vobis in quo iam obligatus sum persol-
vam.

20 Plura fortasse de Latrone meo videor vobis quam
audire desiderastis exposuisse; ipse quoque hoc futurum provideram, ut memoriae eius quotiens occasio fuisset difficulter avellerer. Nec his tamen
ero contentus; sed quotiens me invitaverit memoria,
libentissime faciam ut illum totum et vos cognoscatis
et ego recognoscam. Illud unum non differam, fals-
am opinionem de illo in animis hominum convaluisse:
putant enim fortiter quidem sed parum subtiliter eum
dixisse, cum in illo, si qua alia virtus fuit, et subtilitas fuerit.

21 Id, quod nunc a nullo fieri animadverto, semper
fecit: antequam dicere inciperet, sedens quaestiones
eius quam dicturus erat controversiae proponebat.
Quod summae fiduciae est: ipsa enim actio multas
latebras habet, nec facile potest, si quo loco subtilitas
defuit, apparere, cum orationis cursus audientis
iudicium impediat, dicentis abscondat; at ubi nuda 13M
proponuntur membra, si quid aut numero aut
ordine excidit manifestum est. Quid ergo? unde
haec de illo fama? Nihil est iniquius his qui nusquam putant esse subtilitatem nisi ubi nihil est
praeter subtilitatem; et in illo cum omnes oratoriae

---

[1] It is difficult to translate *subtilitas* in such a way as to
cover the range of meaning Seneca illustrates in §21; he is

details. You want to learn straight away? I will keep your eagerness in suspense, and leave myself room to do you a second service; meanwhile I shall discharge my present debt to you.

You may think that I have given you more details 20 about my friend Latro than you wanted to hear. I had myself expected that I should find it hard to tear myself away, whenever I had a chance to recall him. Nor shall I be content with what I have already said, but whenever my memory lures me on, I shall be very glad to make sure you get to know him—and I get to know him again—in the round. And one thing I shall say at once: a false idea has gained ground— men think that he spoke strongly but not acutely enough. In fact, if he had any quality, it was acuteness.[1]

I don't notice anyone nowadays doing what he 21 always did: before beginning a speech he used, while still seated, to set out the points at issue in the *controversia* he was to declaim—a mark of supreme confidence. An actual speech gives much scope for concealment; if acuteness is anywhere lacking, the lack is not obvious, for the impetus of the speech prevents the audience judging—and hides the judgement of the speaker. But when the bones of the speech are set out in advance unadorned, it is obvious if anything is left out or misplaced. Well then, how did the story get around? Nothing is more unfair than to think that acuteness is only present when there is nothing present but acuteness. Latro possessed every oratorical quality, so that this

thinking particularly of intellectual precision as shown in the organisation of a declamation.

virtutes essent, hoc fundamentum superstructis tot
et tantis molibus obruebatur, nec deerat in illo sed
non eminebat. Et nescio an maximum vitium sub-
tilitatis sit nimis se ostendere. Magis nocent in-
sidiae quae latent: utilissima est dissimulata subtilitas, quae effectu apparet, habitu latet.

22   Interponam itaque quibusdam locis quaestiones
controversiarum, sicut ab illo propositae sunt, nec
his argumenta subtexam, ne et modum excedam et
propositum, cum vos sententias audire velitis et
quidquid ab illis abduxero molestum futurum sit.
Hoc quoque Latro meus faciebat, ut sententias
amaret. Cum condiscipuli essemus apud Marullum
rhetorem, hominem satis aridum, paucissima belle,
sed non vulgato genere dicentem, cum ille exilitatem
orationis suae imputaret controversiae et diceret:
" necesse me est per spinosum locum ambulantem
suspensos pedes ponere," aiebat Latro: " non
mehercules tui pedes spinas calcant, sed habent ";
et statim ipse dicebat sententias quae interponi   14M
argumentis cummaxime declamantis Marulli possent.

23   Solebat autem et hoc genere exercitationis uti,
ut aliquo die nihil praeter epiphonemata scriberet,
aliquo die nihil praeter enthymemata, aliquo die
nihil praeter has translaticias quas proprie sententias
dicimus, quae nihil habent cum ipsa controversia

---

[1] The first example is at 1.1.13.
[2] *Epiphonemata* were exclamatory epigrams bringing a

foundation was obscured by the vast superstructure, and so, though present, was not obvious: indeed, perhaps the greatest fault of acuteness is to flaunt itself unduly. Plots that are hidden are more dangerous; the most useful sort of acuteness is the sort you hide—its effect is plain to see, its presence obscure.

So I shall put in [1] at various places the points at 22 issue in the *controversiae* just as he set them out: but I won't add the arguments that went with them— that would be excessive and irrelevant, for it is the epigrams you want to hear, and any space I deprive them of will annoy you. My friend Latro, of course, was keen on epigrams too. Once we were studying together under the rhetor Marullus, a rather dry man, who said very little prettily, though his style was unusual. Marullus put the blame for the meagreness of a speech of his on to the theme of the *controversia*, saying: " I am walking through a thorny place, and have to tread carefully." " To be sure, it's not that your feet are treading thorns," said Latro. " The thorns are in *them*." And he proceeded himself to point out the epigrams which could have been interspersed in the arguments of Marullus, still in mid-declamation.

He practised another sort of exercise: one day he 23 would write only " exclamations," [2] one day only enthymemes, one day nothing but the traditional passages we properly call *sententiae*, that have no intimate connection with the particular *controversia*,

passage to a climax (Quintilian 8.5.11). Enthymemes were " rhetorical syllogisms," arguments in quasi-syllogistic form based on probabilities.

inplicitum, sed satis apte et alio transferuntur,
tamquam quae de fortuna, de crudelitate, de saeculo,
de divitiis dicuntur; hoc genus sententiarum supellec-
tilem vocabat. Solebat schemata quoque per se,
quaecumque controversia reciperet, scribere. Et
putant illum homines hac virtute caruisse, cum ingenium quidem eius et hac dote abundaverit?
Iudicium autem fuit strictius; non placebat illi orationem inflectere nec umquam recta via decedere
nisi cum hoc aut necessitas coegisset aut magna suas-
24 isset utilitas. Schema negabat decoris causa
inventum, sed subsidii, ut quod [palam][1] aures
offensurum esset si palam diceretur, id oblique et
furtim subreperet. Summam quidem esse dement- 15M
iam detorquere orationem cui esse rectam liceret.

Sed iam non sustineo diutius vos morari: scio
quam odiosa res mihi sit Circensibus pompa. Ab
ea controversia incipiam quam primam Latronem
meum declamasse memini admodum iuvenem in
Marulli schola, cum iam coepisset ordinem ducere.

---

[1] *Deleted by Gronovius.*

but can be quite aptly placed elsewhere too, such as those on fortune, cruelty, the age, riches.[1] This type of *sententia* he called his " stock." He also used to write out figures [2] on their own, such as would go into a *controversia*. And yet people think he lacked this quality. In fact he had abundant natural talent here also; but his taste was pretty restrained—he didn't like to twist language, to leave the straight and narrow path, unless he had to, or unless there was some great advantage to sway him. He said figures 24 were not discovered to beautify but to aid, enabling something that, said openly, would offend the ear, to creep in from the flank, furtively. But he thought it the height of madness to distort language if it *could* be straightforward.

But I won't delay you any longer; I know how tedious I find the procession at the circus.[3] I shall begin with the *controversia* which was the first I heard my friend Latro declaim when he was quite a young man in Marullus' school, but had already begun to lead the class.[4]

---

[1] Seneca means commonplaces, *loci communes*.

[2] Variations from the ordinary straightforward means of expression, elaborately classified by the rhetoricians.

[3] For the elaborate procession before the Ludi Circenses, see Tert. *Spect.* 7.

[4] For competition in Roman schools, see Quintilian 1.2.24.

I

Patruus Abdicans

Liberi parentes alant aut vinciantur.

Duo fratres inter se dissidebant; alteri filius erat. Patruus in egestatem incidit; patre vetante adulescens illum aluit; ob hoc abdicatus tacuit. Adoptatus a patruo est. Patruus accepta hereditate locuples factus est. Egere coepit pater: vetante patruo alit illum. Abdicatur.

1 ⟨Porci Latronis.⟩ Quid mihi obicis? puto luxuriam: quidquid umquam inmodesta largitione effudimus, id omne †consumatur† in alimentum duorum senum. Cum vetaret me pater, aiebat: "ipse mihi, ⟨si⟩ egerem, alimenta non daret." 16M *Eo iam perductus erat ut omnem spem ultimorum alimentorum in ea domo poneret in qua habebat* ⟨et⟩ [1]

¹ *Supplied by Kiessling.*

---

¹ Literally "feed." I have translated "support," "give alms to," "feed," according to convenience.
² This law is Greek, and has no known Roman counterpart before the second century A.D. (Bonner, 95–6).
³ That is, he did not (as on the present occasion) bring a court case objecting to the *abdicatio*. *Abdicatio*, translated conveniently but misleadingly "disinheritance" throughout this book, was not a legal act at Rome (as was ἀποκήρυξις in Greece) and could not give rise to a court case for reinstate-

1

THE MAN WHO DISINHERITED HIS NEPHEW

Children must support[1] their parents, or be imprisoned.[2]

Two brothers were at loggerheads. One had a son. The uncle fell into need; though his father told him not to, the youth supported him: as a result he was disinherited, without protest.[3] He was adopted by his uncle. The uncle received a bequest and became rich. The father has fallen into need, and the youth is supporting him against his uncle's wishes. Now he is being disinherited.

For the son

PORCIUS LATRO. What is your reproach against 1 me? Extravagance, I suppose. All my excessive expenditure has been lavished on supporting two old men.—When my father told me not to, he said: "*He* wouldn't support me if *I* were in need." Now he was in such a plight that his last hope of support lay in the house where there lived the son he disinherited and the brother who hated him.—Suppose

ment. Bonner (p. 102), however, points out that declamations based on *abdicatio* would be good practice for cases where sons challenged the wills of their dead fathers. Nor was there anything unusual in the *practice* of *abdicatio*. Valerius Maximus gives one formula: "I judge him unworthy of the state and of my house, and I order him to leave my sight forthwith" (5.8.3).

27

abdicatum et inimicum. Ecce oppresserit mors egentem: quid facturus es? pluris tibi frater efferendus quam alendus est. Quisquis rogatus est, ait: " quid porro? tam locuples frater alere non potest?"[1] Miserrimus senex divitiis tuis etiam blandimentum

2 in stipem perdidit. *" Ipse " inquit " me ali vetuit." Imitationem alienae culpae innocentiam vocas?* Ne eo quidem aestimas quanta ista crudelitas sit, quod, si quis fratrem non alit, ne a filio quidem alendus est? Quid adoptionem iactas? tunc ad te veni cum haberem divitem patrem. Parcius, quaeso, patres: praesentes habemus deos. Scis tuto te facere: etiamsi abdicaveris, alam. Fatendum est crimen meum: tardius miseritus sum; itaque do poenas:

3 egeo. Parentibus meis, cum in cetera odium sit, tantum in meam notam convenit. O felix spectaculum si vos in gratiam possum reducere: faciamque hoc, vultus quoque vestri hortantur. Surgite patres, adeste iudices: alter mihi ex parentibus servatus, alter servandus est. Porrigite mutuas 17M in gratiam manus; me foederi medium pignus addite: inter contendentes duos medius elidor. Ergo fame morientem videbo per cuius cineres iuraturus sum? *Omnis instabilis et incerta felicitas est: quis crederet iacentem supra crepidinem Marium aut fuisse consulem*

---

[1] i.e. he cannot say: " Even my brother is poor."

he dies in poverty? What will you do? It will cost you more to bury your brother than to feed him.— Everyone he begs says: "What? Is so rich a brother unable to keep you?" The wretched old man, thanks to your riches, has lost even cajoleries for getting alms.[1]—"*He* gave orders I wasn't to be sup- 2 ported." You call imitating another's guilt inno- cence?—Don't you even measure the extent of your cruelty from the fact that someone who refuses to support his brother does not deserve support even from his son?—Why do you boast of your adoption of me? I came to you when I had a rich father.—Please restrain your attacks on me, fathers both. I have the gods on my side.—You know you're on firm ground; even if you disinherit me, I shall support you.—I must confess my crime: I was slow to pity [2]—hence I pay the penalty: I am poor.—My parents, who quarrel on 3 every other topic, agree only in censuring me. Happy sight, if I can reconcile the two of you! And I shall do it—even your expressions encourage me. Rise, fathers, attend, judges: one of my parents has been saved—the other needs to be saved. Put out your hands alike in token of reconciliation; make me the pledge, the middle-man in your treaty. I am getting crushed in the middle of the two contestants. —Shall I then see dying of hunger the man by whose ashes I shall swear?—All happiness is unstable and uncertain.[3] Who would believe that Marius, as he lay in the gutter, had been consul—and would be

[2] Because he had to be *asked* for help (§§16, 19). The son intends the uncle to take the moral to heart.

[3] The *locus de fortuna*, for which see Index of Common-places.

aut futurum? Quid porro tam longe exempla repeto, tamquam domi [1] desit? [2] qui illum vidit *quid non timendum felicibus putat, quid desperandum infelicibus?*

4 IUNI GALLIONIS. Ego indicabo cur me abdices: tu indica cur adoptaveris. Quae iam [3] accedunt nova? Equidem [nova] [4] illud non miror, quod misericordia obicitur: illud miror, quod hic obicit; sic enim me gessi ut hoc crimine duos patres obligarem. Uterque me amat, uterque ali miser desiderat, uterque prohibet. Nec secum nec cum fortuna bene convenit. Conponite aliquando bonos quidem sed contumaces viros. Uter discordiae causam praebuerit nolite a me exigere: uterque patruus est, uterque pater est. Transit ad istum fratris sui et fortuna et animus. Misericors sum: non mutassem [5] patrem si naturam mutare potuissem!

5 P. ASPRENATIS. Fortunae lex est praestare quae exegeris. Miserere: mutabilis est casus; dederunt 18M victis terga victores et quos provexerat fortuna destituit. Quid referam Marium sexto consulatu Carthagini mendicantem, septimo Romae imperantem?

---

[1] domi *Bursian:* modo.
[2] desit *Müller:* sit *AB:* non sit *V*.
[3] quae iam *Summers:* quaedam.
[4] *Deleted by Bursian.*
[5] mutassem *Schott:* muto.

---

[1] Cf. §5: *C.* 7.2.6. For details of Marius' career (as for other proper names), see Index of Names. This phase of his adventures is a well-known *exemplum*: see Mayor on Juv.

again?[1]   But why do I look for instances so far afield, as if there were a shortage at home?   Anyone who has seen *him* realises that the fortunate should always fear, the unfortunate never despair.

JUNIUS GALLIO.   *I* shall reveal why you are dis- 4 inheriting me; *you* must reveal why you adopted me.[2] What new factors have entered the situation since then?—I am not surprised that I am reproached with pity, but that it is this man who reproaches me: for such has been my behaviour that I have put both fathers under an obligation by means of this fault. Both love me, both, falling into distress, require supporting, both forbid it.—They don't get on well with each other, or with fortune.   Bring together at long last two men who are good but stubborn.   Don't ask me which of them started the quarrel; both are my uncle, both my father.—This one has had passed on to him his brother's fate—and his mentality.—I am prone to pity: I shouldn't have changed fathers if I could have changed nature![3]

PUBLIUS ASPRENAS.   It is the law of Fortune to do 5 what you demand of others.   Show pity!   Chance is fickle.   Victors flee before the vanquished, fortune deserts those whom it advanced.   No need to bring up Marius, in his sixth consulship a beggar in Carthage, in his seventh ruler of Rome.   I don't need

10.276–82, and esp. Manil. 4.46–8: " quod, consul totiens, exul, quod de exule consul / adiacuit Libycis compar iactura ruinis / eque crepidinibus cepit Carthaginis urbem." The *crepido* was really a footpath, stand for beggars (cf. Petr. 9.1).

[2] In each case for the son's acts of charity.

[3] Purposely ambiguous: my nature—or his? Cf. §10 Romanius Hispo.

*Ne circa plura instabilis fortunae exempla te mittam,
vide quis alimenta rogetur et quis roget.*

Iuni Othonis patris. Time mutationem: et
ille nihil prius ex bonis quam filium perdidit.

6 Arelli Fusci patris. Ecquid aperis mihi penates
tuos? *Non sum hospes gravis, unum senem adduco:
hoc tibi vitio, pater, placui.* Venit ignotus senex;
volo transire tacentem; per patrem rogat. Ergo
aliquis peribit fame qui filium suum optat superstitem? Quid hoc esse dicam quod me tam pericu-
lose abdicant? quod totiens ist fortunam mutant
quotiens ego patrem? Redite in gratiam: inter
funestas acies armatae manus in foedus porriguntur.
Perierat totus orbis nisi iram finiret misericordia. Aut
si tam pertinacia placent odia, parcite: *iactatus
inter duos patres, utriusque filius, semper tamen felicioris
abdicatus,* positus inter duo pericula, quid faciam?
Qui alunt abdicantur, mendicant qui non alunt.
Illud tamen, pater, deos testor: divitem te relinquo.

7 Cesti Pii. Tali me operi praeparaveram: volebam fratres in gratiam reducere. Hoc tu obicis?
At nisi impetravero ut boni fratres sint, impetrabo ne
mali patres sint? Uterque me amavit, uterque pro

---

[1] The natural father.

[2] A periphrasis for father, like §3 "the man by whose
ashes I shall swear." For fathers wishing their sons to survive
them, see Plaut. *Asin.* 16–17 and Quintilian 9.2.98 (both parts
of an oath).

to remind you of further instances of the mutability of fortune: look who is asked for support, and who is asking!

JUNIUS OTHO SENIOR. Fear change! He [1] too lost none of his possessions before he lost his son.

ARELLIUS FUSCUS SENIOR. Will you not open your 6 home to me? I am no troublesome guest: I bring with me only one old man. This was the fault, father, with which I pleased *you*.—There approaches an old man I do not know. I want to pass him by without him saying anything. But he begs me invoking the name of father. Shall then someone who prays for his own son to survive him [2] perish of hunger?—What of the fact that it is so dangerous for them to disinherit me?—that they change their fortunes as often as I my father?—Be reconciled: on a fatal battlefield armed hands stretch out to seal a treaty. The whole world would have been destroyed if pity did not put an end to anger. Or, if you like such unrelenting hatreds, spare *me*. What am I to do, bandied about between two fathers, the son of both, but always disinherited by the more fortunate, placed between two perils? Those who support their fathers get disinherited: those who do not have to beg.[3]—One thing, father, I call the gods to witness: I leave you a rich man.[4]

CESTIUS PIUS. This was what I had prepared for: 7 I wanted to bring back the brothers to friendship. Is this your reproach? Yet, if I cannot get them to be good brothers, shall I be able to get them to stop being bad fathers?—Both loved me, both prayed for

---

[3] Because of the law.
[4] But beware of the future!

me vota fecit; quantum est si dixero: "uterque me 19M
aluit"? Quae causa fuerit discordiae, nescio;
timeo ne iste prior ⟨iniuriam fecerit qui prior⟩ [1]
egere coepit. Quid obicis, pater? ⟨misericordiam?⟩ [2]
Scio quendam in hac civitate propter istud crimen
adoptatum. "Fratrem" inquit "alere noluit."
†Invenisti quod possem defendere.† Possum liberos tollere ut primum hoc illis narrem, avum
illorum fame perisse? Non fefelli te qualis essem:
scivisti cum adoptares. Bis abdicatus sum: volo
utramque causam meam agere, neutram per me volo;
adsit mihi altus: semper causa mea habebit ad-
vocatum patrem. Alter alterum amet: uterque me
amavit. Vis illum veras poenas dare? sentiat
quam bono fratri iniuriam fecerit.

8 POMPEI SILONIS. De patre ⟨vestro merui⟩ [3] bene,
quamquam eum per aetatem nosse non possum;
sed habet et ille beneficium meum: duos eius filios
alui. Surge, infelix senex. Quid? putatis illum
flere quod eget? immo quod abdicavit, quod ⟨non⟩ [4]
aluit.

ARGENTARI. Vides enim, liberalis in domo tua
esse coepi! Ille propter me duxit uxorem, cum
fortasse iuvenem adoptare posset. Haec abdicantis

---

[1] *Supplied by Schott and Bursian.*
[2] *Supplied by Müller.*
[3] *Supplied by Schultingh and Haase.*
[4] *Supplied by Faber.*

me: is it worth adding: Both supported me?[1]—I don't know what caused their quarrel: but I fear that the first offender was the one who first became poor. —What do you reproach me with, father? Pity? I know someone in this city who was adopted for that crime.—"He wouldn't support his own brother." You have found something I could defend.[2]—Can I rear children and make this my first story to tell them —how their grandfather died of hunger?—I didn't deceive you about my character; you knew when you adopted me.—I have twice been disinherited. I wish to plead both my causes—without taking part in either in person: let my advocate be the man I supported; my case will always have a father to plead it.—Let one love the other—they both loved me.— Do you want him to pay a real penalty? Let him realise what a good brother he injured.[3]

POMPEIUS SILO. I deserved well of the man who was father of you both, even though my age prevented me from knowing him; he too has had a service from me—I supported two of his sons.—Get up, poor old man. Do you think he weeps because he is poor? No, it is because he disinherited me, and did not support his brother.

ARGENTARIUS. You see, it was in your house [4] that I first became generous!—He married because of me,[5] though he could, perhaps, have adopted a young man. —These were his words as he disinherited me: "Go

---

[1] "Support" being, for the uncle, a dirty word.

[2] Text and sense uncertain.

[3] i.e. you should shame him by helping him in his distress.

[4] That of the natural father.

[5] i.e. to have a natural child. The son is explaining his kindness to his father.

fuere verba: "i ad illum quem magis amas quam patrem." Non omnibus imperiis patris parendum est. Nihil in te novi facio: scis me et priori patri non paruisse. Venit immissa barba capilloque deformi, non senectute sed fame membris trementibus, summissa et tenui atque elisa ieiunio voce, ut vix exaudiri posset, introrsus conditos oculos vix allevans: alui. Quomodo, quaeritis? quomodo istum.

9   CORNELI HISPANI. Puta me hodie non abdicari, sed adoptari. Volo quaedam futuro praedicere patri: Hic quem vis adoptare inimicum patris sui invito patre aluit. Reliquit aequo animo beatam domum, ut cum mendico viveret. Noveris oportet hoc eius vitium: ad praestandam calamitosis misericordiam contumax est. Nec tamen habeo quod de hoc vitio meo queri possim: hoc inveni patrem, hoc perdidi. Quam multi patres optant similem filium! bis abdicor. Homo est: non vis alam hominem? Civis est: non vis alam civem? Amicus est: non vis alam amicum? Propinquus est: non vis alam propinquum? Sic pervenitur ad patrem. Homo est, civis est, amicus est, propinquus est; ⟨ista⟩[1] condicione ergo non erit vitium porrexisse stipem nisi dixero: "pater est."

10   VIBI GALLI. *Circumibo tecum, pater, aliena limina; ostendam omnibus et me, qui alimenta dedi, et te, qui negasti.*

[1] *Supplied by Gertz.*

---

[1] "An old and exhausted question" (*C.* 2.1.20), discussed

to the man you love more than your father."—One should not obey all one's father's orders.[1] I am doing nothing new in your case: you know I disobeyed my former father, too.—He approached, his beard untrimmed, his hair dishevelled, his limbs trembling not with age but with hunger, his voice low, thin, stifled by hunger so as to be barely audible, scarcely raising his sunken eyes. I fed him. How, you [2] ask. The way I fed *this* man.

CORNELIUS HISPANUS. Suppose I am being adopted, 9 not disinherited today. I want to give a warning to my future father: " This man you wish to adopt supported his father's enemy against his father's will. He cheerfully left a rich home to live with a beggar. You should know of this vice of his: he is obstinate in his pity for the distressed." Yet I have no complaints about my vice: this was what enabled me to find a father—and lose one. How many fathers pray for a son like this! *I* get disinherited—twice.—He is a man. Don't you want me to help a man? He is a citizen. Don't you want me to help a citizen? He is a friend. Don't you want me to help a friend? He is a relation. Don't you want me to help a relation? So we come to a father. He is a man, a citizen, a friend, a relation. On this showing, then, it will only be a vice to give alms if I say: " He is my father."

VIBIUS GALLUS. Father, I will go round strangers' 10 doors with you. I will let everyone see me, who gave support, and you, who refused it.

at length by Gell. 2.7 and often alluded to in the declaimers (e.g. p. 109.19 *seq*. Ritter).
  [2] The judges.

ROMANI HISPONIS. Scio, pater, melius esse quod tu dicis: istud ego si possem, numquam abdicatus essem. Fateor, vitium est: hoc quoque in me prior 21M emendare voluit pater nec potuit. Impulisti me in fraudem: qui me abdicabat aiebat: "non oportebat fieri," tu dicebas oportere, tibi credidi. "Non dedit" inquit "mihi alimenta": defuerunt tibi? Quisquis alimenta a mendico rogatus est, nihil amplius quam monstrat: "i ad fratrem, i ad filium." Iam quidam nobis eandem fortunam precantur. Crede mihi, sacra populi lingua est.

ALBUCI SILI. Tollite vestras divitias, quas huc atque illuc incertae fortunae fluctus appellet; redite in gratiam: innocens sum.

11 Pars altera. VALLI SYRIACI. *Crescere ex mea proposuit invidia:* sequemur senes quo vocat ambitio iuvenilis et contionem illi praebebimus? *Melius se potest iactare quam defendere.* Ecquid *iustus metus meus est, ne heredem ingratum scribam, inimicum relinquam?* Inter cetera quae mihi cum inimico fateor esse communia et hoc est: infelicissimam ambo et tristissimam egimus vitam, excepto uno quod alter alterum egentem vidimus. Proici me adiectis verborum contumeliis iussit: ad caelum manus sustulit, fassus huius se spectaculi debitorem, et tunc primum fratri vitam precatus est. Laetitiam parati patri-

ROMANIUS HISPO. Father, I know that what you say is better. If I were capable of it, I should never have been disinherited. It is a fault, I agree. This was what my first father wanted to correct in me—and he failed.—It was you who drove me to deceit. My disinheritor said: "It was wrong." You said it was right—and I believed you.—"He did not support *me*." Did you *need* support?[1]—Whoever is dunned for alms by this beggar merely gestures: "Go to your brother, to your son."—Now there are some who are wishing us the same luck:[2] believe me, the people's tongue is divine.

ALBUCIUS SILUS. Destroy your riches, which the waves of inscrutable fortune will drive hither and thither.—Return to friendship—then I am innocent.

The other side

VALLIUS SYRIACUS. His intention was to advance 11 himself by stirring up hatred against me. Shall we old men follow the summons of a youth's ambition, and give him a platform? He is better able to vaunt himself than to defend himself.—Am I not justified in fearing to write an ungrateful youth into my will, to leave an enemy my heir?—There are many things that I agree I have in common with my enemy: one is that we have both lived most sad and unfortunate lives, with a single exception—we have each of us seen the other in need.—He ordered me to be flung out, heaping insults on me. He raised his hands to heaven, confessing his indebtedness for this spectacle: that was the first time he prayed his brother

[1] No—because *I* helped you.
[2] As my natural father's.

monii ut ex tanto calamitatium stupore nullam percepi, nisi quod isti daturus omnia eram, illi negaturus. Liquet nobis deos esse: qui non aluit eget, qui in domum suam fratrem non recepit in publico manet. Aequavit iam potentiam meam cum illius potentia 22M fortuna, nisi quod haec prior facere non possum. Adoptavi te cum abdicatus es: cum adoptas abdico.

12 VIBI RUFI. Cum egerem, aiebam: " satis se vindicavit, quod a dispensatore locupletis inimici consors modo omnis fortunae diurnum petam."

MARULLI. Ille vitam audebit rogare, qui mori malet quam sua verba sibi dici? Multis debeo misericordiam, multis tuli. Quisquis est qui me ulla calamitate similem effingit, perinde habeo ac si gradu cognationis attingat. Scio quam acerbum sit supplicare exteris; scio quam grave sit repelli a domesticis; scio quam crudele sit cotidie et mortem optare et vitam rogare. *Etiamsi tu non odisti eum qui mihi fecit iniuriam, ego odi eum qui fecit tibi.*

13 DIVISIO. Divisio controversiarum antiqua simplex fuit; recens utrum subtilior an tantum operosior ⟨sit⟩ [1] ipsi aestimabitis: ego exponam quae aut veteres invenerunt aut sequentes adstruxerunt.

---

[1] *Supplied by Gertz.*

---

[1] In order to suffer.
[2] To the son and not to the brother.
[3] i.e. be cruel to my brother.
[4] i.e. as it were adopting your father.
[5] Seneca contrasts the preceding generation (Latro) with the recent declaimers of §14.

should live.[1]—In the state of shock arising from all my troubles, I got no joy of the money I had acquired, except that I was going to leave everything to *him*, and deny it to *him*.[2]—It is obvious to us that the gods exist: the man who did not support is now in need; the man who did not take his brother into his house lives in the open air.—Now Fortune has put my power on a level with his—except that I cannot be the first to do these things.[3]—I adopted you when you had been disinherited; now that *you* are adopting,[4] I disinherit you.

Vibius Rufus. When I was in need, I used to say 12 to myself: " He has had full revenge; I shall have to ask for my daily bread from the steward of my rich enemy—though just now I too enjoyed every fortune."

Marullus. Will he dare to beg for his life?—he will prefer to die rather than hear said to him what he said to me.—I owe a debt of pity to many: I have given it to many. Whoever makes me his image by suffering any disaster, I regard as my relation. I know how bitter it is to beg from strangers, how hard to be rejected by one's kin, how cruel every day to wish for death—and have to beg a living.—Even if *you* do not hate the man who injured me, *I* hate the man who injured *you*.

Division

The old division of *controversiae* was straight- 13 forward; you shall judge for yourselves if the new one is more accurate—or just more trouble. *I* shall describe what the ancients [5] discovered, and what additions their successors have made.

Latro illas quaestiones fecit: divisit in ius et aequitatem, an abdicari possit, an debeat. ⟨An
possit⟩ [1] abdicari, sic quaesit: an necesse fuerit
illum patrem alere, et *ob id abdicari non possit quod
fecit lege cogente.* Hoc in has quaestiones divisit:
an abdicatus non *desinat filius esse;* an is desinat *qui
non tantum abdicatus sed etiam ab alio adoptatus est.*
Etiamsi filius erat, an quisquis patrem non aluit
puniatur, tamquam aeger, vinctus, captus; an aliquam filii lex excusationem accipiat; an ⟨in⟩ [2] hoc
accipere potuerit. An abdicari debeat, per haec 23M
quaesit: an, etiamsi ille indignus fuit qui aleretur,
hic tamen recte fecerit qui aluit; deinde an dignus
fuerit qui aleretur.

14   Novi declamatores Graecis auctoribus adiecerunt
primam illam quaestionem: an adoptatus abdicari
possit. Hac Cestius usus est. Adiecit quaestionem [Gallio] [3] alteram: an, si abdicari possit etiam
adoptatus, ⟨possit⟩ [4] ob id vitium quod antequam
adoptaretur notum fuit adoptanti. Haec autem
ex aequitatis parte pendet et tractatio magis est
quam quaestio.

   Gallio quaestionem primam Latronis duplicavit sic:

[1] *Supplied by Gronovius.*   [2] *Supplied by Bursian.*
[3] *Deleted by Gruppe.*   [4] *Supplied by Müller.*

Latro's points were these. He made a distinction between law and equity.[1] Can he be disinherited? Should he be? On the question, Can he be disinherited, he raised the following points: Was it necessary for him to support his father, and can he be disinherited for something he did because the law compelled him to? This he subdivided as follows: Does a disinherited son cease to be a son? Does someone who, besides being disinherited, has been adopted by another, cease to be a son? Even if he was still a son, should everyone who has failed to support his father be punished? Suppose he were sick, in prison, a captive?[2] Can the law accept an excuse on the part of a son? Could it accept it in this case? On the question, Should he be disinherited, he subdivided thus: Even if that man did not deserve to be supported, was this man nevertheless right to support him? Next, Was he worthy of support?

Recent declaimers, following a Greek lead, have 14 added a question before these two: Can an adopted son be disinherited? Cestius used this point. He added another: If even an adopted child can be disinherited, can he be disinherited for a fault that was known to the adopter before the adoption? But this is rather relevant to the heading of equity, and a piece of *treatment*[3] rather than a question.

Gallio doubled Latro's first point thus: It was per-

---

[1] For this distinction between the letter of the law and the claims of equity, frequently made in the declamations, see Bonner, 46–7.

[2] For this argument, see Quintilian 5.10.97, 7.6.5; *RLM* p. 107.22 *seq.*

[3] See Introduction, p. xviii.

licuit mihi alere etiam te vetante; deinde non licuit non alere. In priore parte hoc vindicavit, non posse filium ob id abdicari quod esset suae potestatis; nulli autem interdici misericordia: *Quid si flere me vetes cum vidi hominem calamitosum?* quid si vetes propter aliquod honestum factum periclitanti favere? *Adfectus nostri in nostra potestate non sunt. Quaedam iura non scripta, sed omnibus scriptis certiora sunt:* quamvis filius familiae sim, licet mihi et stipem porrigere mendico et humum cadaveri ⟨inicere⟩.[1] Iniquum est conlapsis manum non porrigere: commune hoc ius generis humani est. Nemo invidiosum ius postulat quo alteri profuturus est.

15 Latro illud vehementer pressit: Non feci ratione, adfectu victus sum. Cum vidissem patrem egentem, mens non constitit mihi; quid vetueris nescio. Hoc aiebat non esse tractandum tamquam quaestionem; 24M esse tamen potentius quam ullam quaestionem.

Fuscus Arellius pater hoc movit in ultimo tamquam quaestionem: putavi te, quamvis vetares, nihilominus velle ali fratrem: eo vultu vetabas aut mihi ita videbaris.

Cestius audacius; non fuit contentus dicere: " putavi velle te," adiecit: " voluisti et hodie quoque

───────────────

[1] *Supplied by Gertz.*

───────────────

[1] Sen. *Helv.* 17.1: " No emotion is our slave, least of all that arising from sorrow "; cf. *Decl.* p. 417.4 Ritter.

missible for me to support him even though you forbade it. Next, it was not permissible for me to fail to support him. In the first part, he claimed that a son could not be disinherited for something which he was free to do; no-one could be banned from pity. "What if you were to forbid me to weep when I saw a man in distress? What if you were to forbid me to take the side of one in danger of condemnation because of some good deed? We have no control over our emotions.[1] Some laws are unwritten—but more immutable than all written ones. I may be a son, dependent on my father; yet I can hand alms to a beggar, throw dust on a corpse.[2] It is wrong not to stretch out a hand to the prostrate: this is the common right of humanity. No-one becomes unpopular by claiming a right that enables him to help another."

Latro pressed this point vigorously: "I did not act 15 from reason, but overcome by emotion. When I saw my father in need, I could not control myself: what you forbade me, I forget." He said this should not be developed as a question, though it was more effective than any question.

Arellius Fuscus senior brought in at the end this point, out of which he made an issue: "I thought you wanted your brother supported, even though you forbade it. You had that sort of look when you forbade me—or at least so I thought."

Cestius was bolder; he was not content to say: "I thought you wanted . . ." He went on: "You did

---

[2] Gallio is clearly thinking of Antigone's symbolic burial of her brother (cf. too the "unwritten laws" above: Soph. *Ant.* 454).

vis," et sua figura dixit omnia propter quae velle
deberet. "Quare ergo abdicas? puto, indignaris
praereptum tibi officium."

16 Latro colorem simplicem pro adulescente ⟨intro-
duxit⟩:[1] habere non quo excuset, sed quo glorietur.
Non potui, inquit, sustinere illud durum spectaculum.
Offensam mihi putas tantum excidisse? mens excidit, non animus mihi constitit, non in ministerium
sustinendi corporis suffecerunt pedes, oculi subita
caligine obtorpuerunt: alioqui ego, si tunc meae
mentis fuissem, expectassem dum rogarer?

Fuscus illum colorem introduxit, quo frequenter uti
solebat, religionis: movit, inquit, me natura, movit
pietas, movit humanorum casuum tam manifesto
approbata exemplo varietas. Stare ante oculos
Fortuna videbatur et dicere talia: esuriunt[2] qui suos
non alunt.

17 Albucius hoc colore: accessit, inquit, ad me pater,   25M
nec summissis verbis locutus est; non rogavit, sciit[3]
quomodo agendum esset cum filio: alere me iussit;
recitavit legem, quam ego semper scriptam etiam
patruo putavi. Et deinde dixit: praestiti non
quantum patri praestare debui, sed quantum vetanti
subripere potui.

---

[1] *Supplied by Gertz (before* pro).
[2] esuriunt *Müller:* hae (hi *V*) sunt.
[3] sciit *Bursian:* siet *AB:* sed *V*.

want it, and you want it today, too." And by means of this figure [1] of his, he said everything that should lead him to want it. "Why then are you disinheriting me? I suppose because you are angry that your duty [2] has been snatched away from you."

Latro brought up a straightforward *colour* for the 16 youth. He had something to boast of, not to apologise for. "I could not tolerate that cruel sight. Do you think that I just forgot your wrong to me? I forgot everything; my consciousness dimmed, my feet were unable to support my body as they should, my eyes dulled in sudden darkness. Otherwise, if I had been in my right mind at that moment, should I have waited to be asked?"

Fuscus introduced, as he often did, the *colour* of religion: "Nature moved me, piety moved me, and the mutability of human fortune, so clearly exemplified. Fortune seemed to stand before my eyes and say: 'Those who do not support their own go hungry.'"

Albucius used this *colour*: "My father came to me, 17 and spoke to me in words that were not humble. He did not beg: he knew how one ought to behave towards a son—he gave me orders to feed him. He recited the law to me—a law that I have always supposed covers an uncle too." Then he said: "I gave less than I ought to have given to a father—but as much as I could slip past him who forbade me."

---

[1] Cf. *C.* 1 pr. 23 n. Seneca here (as often) uses *figure* in a slightly wider sense of a device for giving a whole declamation or part of one a "shape" other than the normal straightforward one.

[2] i.e. to help your brother.

Blandus colore diverso: Venit subito deformis
squalore, lacrimis. O graves, Fortuna, vices tuas!
Ille dives modo superbus rogavit alimenta, rogavit
filium suum, rogavit abdicatum suum. Interrogas
quam diu rogaverit? Ne di istud nefas patiantur,
ut diu rogaverit; diutius tamen quam tu. Quaeritis
quid fecerim? quod solebam.

18   Silo Pompeius hoc colore: Movit, inquit, me
quod nihil suo iure, nihil pro potestate, quod tamquam patruus accessit. Ego vero non expectavi
verba, non preces: complexus sum et osculatus sum
patrem, dedi alimenta. Hoc unum crudeliter feci,
quod dixi fratrem dedisse: non alere sed exprobrare
visus sum.

Triarius hoc colore: timui, inquit, si non aluissem,
ne abdicarer a patre; sciebam quomodo illi placuis-
sem.

Argentarius hoc colore: Accessit, inquit, ad me
pater obrutus sordibus, tremens deficientibus membris; rogavit alimenta. Interrogo vos, iudices,
quid me, haec si ⟨fiant⟩,[1] facere oporteat. Nam
istum non interrogo: scit quid facturus sim. Num
patiemini[2] ut alteri patri faciam iniuriam, alteri invidiam? Cum vetuisset me alimenta praestare, si   26M
qua est fides, non putavi illum ex animo vetare;
lenocinatur, inquam, gloriae meae, ut videar patrem
etiam prohibitus aluisse.

19   Marullus novo colore egit: Cecidit in pedes meos
senex squalidus barba capilloque. Novit, inquam,

---

[1] quid me, haec si fiant *Madvig:* quidem hec (haec quidem
V) si.

[2] num patiemini *Haase:* nam patrem.

Blandus had a different *colour*. " He appeared suddenly, made ugly by dirt and tears. Fortune, how bitter are your reversals! That once proud and rich man begged food, begged his son, begged the son he had disinherited. Do you ask how long he begged? God forbid he begged for long: but it was longer than you. Do you ask what I did? What I was accustomed to."

Pompeius Silo had this *colour*: " I was moved be- 18 cause he came asking nothing as of right, nothing as in his power—he came as though he were an uncle. *I* did not wait for words or for prayers. I embraced and kissed my—father; I gave him food. I did one cruel thing: I said his brother had provided it. It was as if I were reproaching him, not feeding him."

Triarius' *colour*: " I was afraid that if I didn't feed him I should be disinherited by my father: I knew how I had pleased *him*."

Argentarius' *colour*: " My father came to me filthy, his wasted limbs trembling, and asked for food. I ask you, judges, what I should do in such a situation. I do not ask *him*: he knows how I am likely to behave. Will you tolerate it if I do a wrong to one father and make the other unpopular? [1] Though he forbade me to give food (you must believe me) I did not think his ban was sincere. He is trying, I said to myself, to help my glory along, so that it will look as though I fed my father in spite of being forbidden."

Marullus employed a new *colour*: " There fell at 19 my feet an old man, beard and hair matted. This man, I said to myself, knows somehow that I feel pity.

---

[1] Because the people would see the brother starving.

49

nescio qui iste misericordiam meam. Adlevavi, cum ignorarem quis esset: vultis repellam quod pater est?

Cestius hoc colore: Haec mecum cogitavi: pater meus ⟨eget⟩;[1] egentem videt frater: non miseretur, non praestat alimenta; hoc est, inquam, non vult eripere filio officium, scit in hac fortuna meorum has iam meas esse partes. Hoc peccavi, quod non ultro ad patrem accessi; sed aiebam: nolo huic quicquam amplius praestare quam illi praestiti: non expectavi donec patruus ad me veniret? et nunc expectabo. Venit ad me pater: quid habui facere? perducere illum ad patruum? Non feci. Merito irascitur; potuit enim, si aluisset, levare quidem fortunam fratris, sed causam adgravare.

20. Buteonis colorem non probabat Latro: praestitisse se dixit exiguum, tantum quo spiritum posset producere; et cum descripsisset pallorem eius ac maciem, adiecit: apparet illum ab inimicis ali. Hunc colorem cum improbaret Latro hac sententia usus est: non est, inquit, abdicato quicquam ex gloria criminis sui detrahendum.

Hispanus hunc colorem venustius; nam et miserationi eius qui non benignissime alitur adiecit aliquid et pietati suae nihil detraxit: Quomodo autem, inquit, illum alo? exiguos furtive cibos mitto, et si 27M

---

[1] *Supplied by Gertz.*

I helped him up, not knowing who he was. Do you want me to reject him just because he is my father?"

This was Cestius' *colour*: "I thought to myself: My father is in need. His brother sees he is in need. He does not pity him, he gives him no support. That is, I said to myself, he does not want to deprive a son of the chance of doing his duty: he knows that when my relations are in such a plight, this is now *my* role. My fault was that I did not go to my father, unasked. But I said to myself: I don't want to give him any more than I gave the other. Didn't I wait for my uncle to come to me? I will wait now, too. My father came to me. What could I do? Take him to my uncle? I did not do it. He is angry, and he has reason to be: for if he had given him food, he could have relieved his brother's plight, while making his case worse." [1]

Latro disapproved of Buteo's *colour*. Buteo said he 20 had given a little food, just to keep life going. And, after describing his pallor and thinness, he added: "It is obvious that it is enemies who feed him." Latro, attacking this *colour*, employed the epigram: "The disinherited son should not make any detraction from the splendour of his crime."

Hispanus used this *colour* more prettily: he made the man so meanly fed more pitiable without detracting from the son's affection. "How do I feed him? I send him a few provisions secretly; what I proffer to the starving old man is anything I could

---

[1] He is angry with me for depriving him of the chance of feeding his brother because if he had done so he could, while relieving his distress, have put him in the wrong (cf. §7 n.).

quid de mensa mea detrahere potui, famelico seni porrigo. Non credis, qui scis quomodo te aluerim?

21   Colorem ex altera parte, quae durior est, Latro aiebat hunc sequendum, ut gravissimarum iniuriarum inexorabilia et ardentia induceremus odia Thyesteo more; aiebat patrem non irasci tantum debere sed furere. Ipse ⟨in⟩ declamatione usus est summis clamoribus illo versu tragico: "cur fugis fratrem? scit ipse."

Hunc colorem secutus Syriacus Vallius durum sensum videbatur non dure posuisse in narratione sic: infelicissimam ambo et tristissimam egimus vitam, excepto ⟨uno⟩ [1] quod alter alterum egentem vidimus. Aeque efficaciter odium videbatur expressisse fraternum hac sententia: vos, iudices, *audite quam valde eguerim: fratrem rogavi.*

22   Hanc partem memini *apud Cestium declamari ab Alfio Flavo*, ad quem audiendum me fama perduxerat; qui cum *praetextatus* esset, tantae opinionis fuit ut populo Romano puer eloquentia notus esset. Semper de illius ingenio Cestius et praedicavit et timuit: aiebat tam inmature magnum ingenium non esse vitale; sed tanto concursu hominum audiebatur ut raro auderet post illum Cestius dicere. Ipse omnia mala faciebat ingenio suo; naturalis tamen illa vis eminebat, quae post multos annos, iam et desidia obruta et carminibus enervata, vigorem

Supplied by Kiessling: cf. §11.

remove from my own table. Don't you believe me?
—you know how I fed *you*."

Latro said that on the other side, which is more 21
difficult, we should follow the *colour* of representing
unremitting and passionate hatred, arising from the
gravest injuries, Thyestes-wise. He said the father
should not merely be angry: he should rave. He
himself, in his declamation, employed the tragic
verse: "Why do you flee your brother? *He*
knows,"[1] which received great applause.

Vallius Syriacus, pursuing this *colour*, was thought
to have brought a harsh idea into his narrative very
smoothly, thus: "We have both lived most sad and
unfortunate lives, with a single exception—we have
each of us seen the other in need."[2] He was thought
to have represented the hatred between the brothers
equally effectively with the epigram: "Judges, hear
how badly I was in need. I had to beg my brother!"

I remember this side being declaimed at Cestius' 22
by Alfius Flavus. His reputation attracted me to go
and hear him. While still wearing the *toga praetexta*[3] he was so famous that here was a child known
country-wide for his eloquence. Cestius was always
remarking on his genius—and fearing for it. He said
a talent that was so great so early in life could not last.
Still, he used to be listened to by such a crowd of
people that Cestius rarely ventured to speak after
him. He harmed his talent himself, in all possible
ways: yet his natural force shone out. After many
years, overwhelmed by idleness and weakened by

[1] *Frg. Trag. Inc.* 115 Ribbeck².
[2] Cf. §11.
[3] That is, before the age of sixteen.

tamen suum tenuit. *Semper autem commendabat
eloquentiam eius aliqua res extra eloquentiam: in puero
lenocinium erat ingenii aetas,* in iuvene desidia.   28M

23   Hic cum declamaret partem abdicantis, hanc
summis clamoribus dixit sententiam: *Quis es tu qui
de facto patrum sententiam feras?* ille tunc peccavit,
tu nunc peccas. *Ad te arbitrum odia nostra non mit-
timus: iudices habemus deos.* Et illam sententiam:
Audimus fratrum fabulosa certamina et incredibilia
nisi nos fuissemus: impias epulas, detestabili parricidio fugatum[1] diem: hoc uno modo iste frater a
fratre ali meruit. Quam innocenter me contra
parricidium vindico! filium illi suum reddo.

24   Cestius hunc colorem tam strictum non probavit,
sed dixit temperandum esse, et ipse hoc colore usus
est, quem statim a principio induxit: Miratur aliquis quod, cum duo gravissimam [fratrum][2] acceperimus iniuriam, ego et filius, ego solus irascor?
Non est quod miretur: iam filio satisfactum est.

---

[1] fugatum *ed.:* futurum.
[2] *Deleted by Novák.*

---

[1] The uncle contrasts his mild behaviour in avenging himself
for his brother's neglect (which he calls parricide) with the
savagery of Atreus, who served up to his brother Thyestes his

indulgence in poetry, it still retained its vigour. But there was always something apart from his eloquence to set his eloquence off. As a boy, it was his age which played the pander to his talent; as a youth, his negligence.

Now when Alfius declaimed the role of the dis- 23 inheritor, he spoke amid great applause the epigram: "Who are you to pass judgement on your fathers' action? Then it was he who was in the wrong: now it is you. We do not send our quarrels for you to settle them. Our judges are the gods." And again: "We hear of mythical quarrels between brothers, quarrels that would be incredible if *we* had not existed. We hear of impious banquets, of the daylight banished by a shocking parricide. This was the only way this brother deserved to be fed by his brother! How harmlessly do I avenge myself for parricide: I give him back his son!"[1]

Cestius did not like this savage *colour*, and said it 24 should be toned down. He himself employed a *colour* which he brought[2] in right from the start. "Is anyone surprised that, though two have received the gravest injury, I and my son, I am the only one who is angry? There is no need for surprise. My son has already had his due.[3] You ought to have asked me

own children: "hoc est deos quod puduit, hoc egit diem / aversum in ortus" (Sen. *Thy.* 1035-6).

[2] Here and later Seneca possibly uses *inducere colorem* with allusion to the painters' technical sense "to lay on," "overspread a colour" (e.g. Pliny *N.H.* 35.102). But he also uses the verb simply as meaning "to bring in," "introduce."— *E.H.W.*

[3] That is, he had seen his father humiliated. Cestius proceeds to address the son.

Debuisti, inquit, me rogare ut ipse praestarem,
debuisti illum ad me perducere, debuisti recon-
ciliationem temptare, non famam pietatis ex nostra
captare discordia. Fortasse ego cum egerem fratrem rogassem si tu non fuisses; fortasse ille me
rogasset si tu non fuisses; poterit nobis convenire si
non fuerit in medio quem potius miseri contumaces
rogent.

25 Hermagoras in hac controversia transit a prooemio
in narrationem eleganter, rarissimo quidem genere,
ut ⟨in⟩ eadem re transitus esset, sententia esset,
schema esset, sed, ut Latroni placebat, schema quod 29M
vulnerat, non quod titillat: . . . Ex altera parte
transit a prooemio in narrationem Gallio et ipse per
sententiam sic: quidni filium mihi nolim cum isto
communem esse, cum quo utinam communem nec
patrem habuissem? Diocles Carystius illum sensum
a Latinis iactatum dixit brevissime, rarissimo genere,
quo duobus sententia verbis consummatur (nec
enim paucioribus potest): . . . Euctemon, levis
declamator sed dulcis, dixit nove et amabiliter
illum aeque ab omnibus vexatum sensum, quo re-
conciliatio fratrum temptatur: . . .

to give aid myself, you ought to have brought him to me, you ought to have sought to reconcile us, not tried to win a reputation for affection from our quarrel. Perhaps, when I was in need, I should have begged my brother if you had not existed. Perhaps he would have begged me if you had not existed. We can reach an agreement—if there isn't between us someone whom the wretched stubborn contenders prefer to beg."

In this *controversia* Hermagoras made an elegant 25 transition from proem to narration, one of a very rare kind indeed, combining transition, epigram and figure (but a figure, as Latro thought, that wounds rather than tickles): . . . On the other side, Gallio too passed from proem to narration by means of an epigram: " Why should I not prefer my son not to be shared with him?—would that I had never had to share a father with him." Diocles of Carystos gave very brief expression to a thought bandied about by the Latin declaimers, very unusually compressing the epigram into the minimum of two words: . . . Euctemon, a light-weight but agreeable declaimer, gave a nice new twist to the equally trite idea involving the attempt to reconcile the brothers: . . .

II

SACERDOS PROSTITUTA

Sacerdos casta e castis, pura e puris sit.

Quaedam virgo a piratis capta venit; empta a lenone et prostituta est. Venientes ad se exorabat stipem. Militem qui ad se venerat cum exorare non posset, conluctantem et vim inferentem occidit. Accusata et absoluta et remissa ad suos est. Petit sacerdotium.

1 PORCI LATRONIS. *Sacerdos vestra adhuc in lupanari viveret nisi hominem occidisset.* Inter barbaros quid passa sit nescio: quid pati potuerit scio. Sacerdoti 30M ne purus quidem contigit dominus. Absint ex hoc foro lenones, absint meretrices, ne quid parum sanctum occurrat dum sacerdos legitur. Si nihil aliud, certe osculatus est te quisquis puram putavit. O egregium pudicitiae patrocinium: "militem occidi"! At hercule lenonem non occidisti. Deducta es in lupanar, accepisti locum, pretium constitutum est, titulus inscriptus est: hactenus in te

---

[1] Compare the law in *C.* 4.2, with my note. This one is close to the practice with regard to Vestal Virgins in Rome, as described by Gell. 1.12—a priestess must not have any bodily defect, and her parents should not have been slaves or engaged in "negotia sordida." Bonner, 104.

[2] Petronius (1.3) makes fun of declamation pirates standing on the shore, chains in their hands (cf. below, §8). They had almost disappeared from the Mediterranean after being put

2

The Prostitute Priestess

A priestess must be chaste and of chaste [parents],
pure and of pure [parents].[1]

A virgin was captured by pirates [2] and sold;
she was bought by a pimp and made a prostitute.
When men came to her, she asked for alms.
When she failed to get alms from a soldier who
came to her, he struggled with her and tried to
use force; she killed him. She was accused,
acquitted and sent back to her family. She
seeks a priesthood.

Against the girl

Porcius Latro. Your priestess would still be 1
living in a brothel—if she hadn't killed a man.—I
don't know what she endured among barbarians, but
I know what she might have endured.—This priestess
did not even have a pure master.[3]—Let pimps and
harlots keep away from this forum, lest anything un-
holy obtrude during the choice of a priestess.—If
nothing else, you were at least *kissed* by all those who
believed you chaste.[4]—A marvellous defence of one's
chastity: " I killed a soldier." But you didn't kill
your pimp.—You were led to the brothel, took your
place; the price was fixed, the notice written; en-

down by Pompey, but Bonner (p. 34) points out that there had
been resurgences since. As often, we have a Greek situation
that does not altogether lack Roman point.

[3] She was a slave—and a pimp's (or pirate's) slave.

[4] i.e. those who respected your proclaimed virginity.

inquiri potest; cetera nescio. Quid in cellulam me
et obscenum lectulum vocas? de pudicitia sacerdotis
hic quaeritur. "Nemo" inquit "mihi virginitatem
eripuit": sed omnes quasi erepturi venerunt, sed
omnes quasi eripuissent recesserunt. *Quo mihi
sacerdotem cuius precaria est castitas?* Cum ex illo
lupanari cruenta fugeres, si qua tibi occurrisset . . .
Si mater tua prostitisset, tibi noceret: propter te
liberis tuis sacerdotium non darem.

2   FULVI SPARSI. Quid inclusa feceris nec quaerere
debemus nec scire possumus.

CORNELI HISPANI. Occidisti hominem. Quid
respondes? "Vim adferebat mihi." Etiam, puto.
Sacerdoti pro libertate vota facienda sunt: captivae
mandabitis? pro pudicitia vota facienda sunt: prosti-
tutae mandabitis? pro militibus vota facienda sunt:
isti mandabitis? *Id enim deerat, ut templa reciperent
quas aut carcer aut lupanar eiecit.*

MARULLI. Ut sciamus illam apud lenonem fuisse,
blanda est; ut sciamus apud piratas, cruenta est.
"Nemo" inquit "me attigit." Da mihi lenonis   31M
rationes: captura conveniet. Age, si quis venit pertinax? age, si quis hoc ipsum concupit, quod virgo
eras? age si quis, ne negare posses, ferrum attulit?

---

[1] i.e. require me to talk of.

[2] The epigram perhaps went: "if a priestess had met you,
she would have been defiled."

[3] Cf. Ov. *Met.* 3.266–8: "at, puto, furto est / contenta et
thalami brevis est iniuria nostri? / concipit—id deerat."

quiry can go so far against you—the rest is obscure.
Why do you summon me to [1] your room, to your
lecherous bed? The subject here is the chastity of a
priestess.—" Nobody took away my virginity." But
everyone came intending to take it away, everyone
went as though they had succeeded. What sort of a
priestess is it—I ask you—whose chastity is on
sufferance?—When you fled, stained with blood, from
that brothel, if anyone had met you[2] . . .—If your
mother had been a prostitute, it would go against
you; and because of you I should not grant your
children a priesthood.

FULVIUS SPARSUS. We should not ask, and cannot 2
know, what you did behind closed doors.

CORNELIUS HISPANUS. You killed a man. What is
your reply? " He was attacking me." Yes, I suppose he was.—Prayers for liberty have to be said by
the priestess: will you entrust that to a jail-bird?
Prayers have to be said for chastity: will you entrust
that to a prostitute? Prayers have to be said for
soldiers: will you entrust that to *this* woman?—All
that was left [3] was for temples to receive women
whom brothel and prison had rejected.

MARULLUS. We can tell she has been in a pimp's
house—she is a wheedler; we can tell she has lived
with pirates—she is stained with blood.—" Nobody
touched me." Give me the pimp's accounts: you
will find the entries balance.[4]—What if an obstinate
man visited you? Or someone who found your very
virginity an attraction? Or someone who brought a
sword to make sure you could not refuse?

---

[4] i.e. you brought in your proper share of money.

3 P. Vinici. Eam sacerdotem facite quae aut
honesta maneat, qualis semper fuit, aut poenam
sentiat si esse desierit. Cuius audaciae es, puella?
Etiamsi nos nobis non timeremus, tu tibi metuere
deberes. Aliter deorum numini subiecta uniuscuius-
que conscientia est, aliter nostrae aestimationi: nos
tantum quae palam feceras vidimus, illi etiam quae
secreta sunt. *Indignam te sacerdotio dicerem si
transisses per lupanar.* Praecedens hanc lictor
summovebit? huic praetor via cedet? summum
imperium consules cedent tibi? quaecumque meretrix
prostabit fugiet? Fas sacerdoti non esset ancillam
tibi similem habere: tene [1] fieri sacerdotem fas erit?
Nam quod ad sortem pertinet, ne reliquae virgines
contaminarentur haec segregata est. Castam te
putas quia invita meretrix es? Nuda in litore stetit
ad fastidium emptoris; omnes partes corporis et in-
spectae et contrectatae sunt. Vultis auctionis exitum audire? vendit pirata, emit leno, excipit fornix.[2]
Eo deducta es ubi tu aliud nihil honestius facere
potuisti quam mori. Inpensius stipem rogasti quam 32M
sacerdotium rogas. "*Fortuna*" inquit "haec me
coegit pati; misereri debent omnes mei." Et ego
misereor tui, puella; *sed non facimus miserandas sa-*

---

[1] tene *Otto, Gertz:* ne.
[2] excipit fornix *ed.:* excipitur nihil.

---

[1] Lictors were attendants on magistrates, and also on the
Flamen Dialis and the Vestal Virgins (Plut. *Num.* 10.3). For

Publius Vinicius. You must choose as priestess 3 someone who will either remain decent, as she always was, or would feel the punishment if she stopped being decent.—What sort of boldness is this, girl? Even if we didn't fear for ourselves, you ought to dread for yourself. Everyone's conscience is subject to the power of gods quite otherwise than to our judgement: we have seen only your overt actions, they the secret too.—I should call you unfit for the priesthood if you had merely passed through a brothel.—Will the lictor [1] ahead of her remove the crowd from *this* woman's path? Will the praetor give way to *her*? Will the highest power, the consuls, yield to *you*? Will any practising whore have to flee your sight? A priestess would not be allowed to have a maid like you: should *you* become a priestess? —As to the drawing of lots,[2] this woman has been kept apart, so as to avoid the other girls being polluted.—Do you regard yourself as chaste just because you are an unwilling whore?—She stood naked on the shore to meet the buyer's sneers; every part of her body was inspected—and handled. Do you want to hear the outcome of the sale? A pirate was the seller, a pimp the buyer, a brothel the place to which she was taken.—You were led off to a place where you could do nothing more upright than to die.—You asked for money more eagerly than you ask for a priesthood.—She says: "Fortune compelled me to suffer this; all must pity me." *I* pity you, girl, but we don't make priestesses of women who need pity.

their other privileges, see Roscher, *Lex. gr. u. röm. Myth.* 6.265 *seq.*
 [2] Vestal virgins were chosen by lot (Gell. 1.12.11).

*cerdotes.   Non est apud nos maximus honor ultimorum
malorum solacium.*

4   MENTONIS.   Honorem habitum aurium maiestatis-
que vestrae velim quod necesse est in hac causa
nominare lupanar, lenonem, meretricios quacstus,
homicidium. Quis credat? inter haec sacerdos
quaeritur. At mehercules futurae sacerdoti nihil
ex his audiendum erat. Sacerdotis vestrae summa
notitia est quod prostitit, summa virtus quod occidit, summa felicitas quod absoluta est. Non potest
in ea sperari sacerdos in qua sperari meretrix potest: aliis oculis virginem leno aestimat, aliis pontifex.

BLANDI. "Virgo sum" inquit; "interroga, si
dubitas, archipiratam, interroga gladiatorem, an
rogatus virginitati pepercerit." Non refello, dum
scias clausa esse testibus tuis templa. In auctione
nemo voluit liceri ut enotuit servisse piratis: non
videbatur iste virginis vultus, ista constantia et ne
armatum quidem timens audacia.

5   ARELLI FUSCI patris. Ne metue, puella: pudica es;
sed sic te viro lauda, non templo. Meretrix vocata
es, in communi loco stetisti, superpositus est cellae
tuae titulus, venientem recepisti: cetera, etiamsi
in communi loco essem, tamen potius silerem.

POMPEI SILONIS. Excipitur meretricium osculis,
docetur blanditias et in omnem corporis motum con- 33

64

We do not, in our city, make the greatest of honours into a solace for the most extreme of misfortunes.

MENTO. With all respect to the dignity of my 4 audience, I must in this case name a brothel, a pimp, the profits of a whore, a murder. Who would credit it? *This* the context for the investigation of a priestess' credentials! But surely a future priestess shouldn't hear any of these words!—Your priestess is very well-known: she was a prostitute. She is very virtuous: she has killed. She is very fortunate: she was acquitted.—There is no prospect of a priestess in a woman in whom there is prospect of a harlot.—A pimp and a high priest judge a virgin with different eyes.

BLANDUS. "I am a virgin," she says. "If you doubt it ask the chief pirate, ask the gladiator whether, when begged to do so, they spared my virginity." I don't try to refute you—so long as you realise that your witnesses are banned from entering temples.—At the sale no-one wanted to make a bid when it was known she had been a pirate's slave. They found nothing virginal in that face, that self-possession, that boldness that feared not even an armed man.

ARELLIUS FUSCUS SENIOR. Do not fear, girl. You 5 are chaste. But give yourself that sort of credit to a husand, not to a temple. You were called a whore, you offered yourself in a " public place," a notice was put above your door, you welcomed all comers. As for the rest, even if I were in a " public place " I should prefer to keep silence.

POMPEIUS SILO. She was welcomed by the kisses of the whores, taught to wheedle, shown how to make

fingitur. Avertite aures petiturae sacerdotium,
dum reliqua narro. Nihil ad vos deferam dubium,
nihil audietis nisi quod vicinitas [1] vidit. Tu sacerdos? Quid si tantum capta, quid si ⟨tantum⟩ prostituta, quid si tantum homicida, quid si tantum rea
fuisses?

6   ROMANI HISPONIS. Numquid hoc negas, conluc-
tatam te tamen cum viro, quem in illa volutatione
necesse est prius super te fuisse? Aiebat leno
merito occisum militem, plus ausum quam in prostitutam licebat. Exorasti populum: numquid et
lenonem? numquid et piratam illum, quem non
poteras occidere?

ARGENTARI. "Armatum" inquit "occidi." Quid
inermes? Gloriatur homicidio eius quem nescio
an sero occiderit.

7   CESTI PII narratio: *Ita domi custodita est ut rapi
posset; ita cara fuit suis ut rapta non redimeretur; ita
raptae pepercere piratae ut lenoni venderent; sic emit
leno ut prostitueret; sic venientes deprecata est ut ferro
opus esset.* Coniectum in urnam nomen eius non exit
sed eiectum est; tempus erat nunc [2] sortiri: urna pur-
gata est. Stetisti puella in lupanari: iam te ut
nemo violaverit, locus ipse violavit. Stetisti cum
meretricibus, stetisti sic ornata ut populo placere
posses, ea veste quam leno dederat; nomen tuum   34?

---

[1] vicinitas *C. F. W. Müller, Madvig:* uicina ciuitas.
[2] nunc *Haase, Bursian:* non.

all kinds of movement with her body. Turn away your ears, you others seeking the priesthood, while I narrate the rest. I shall tell you nothing that is uncertain, you will hear nothing that the whole neighbourhood did not see.—You a priestess? What if you had been *only* a captive, *only* a whore, *only* a murderer, *only* a defendant?

ROMANIUS HISPO. Do you deny that, all the same, 6 you struggled with the man? that as you rolled about with him, it is inevitable that he was, to begin with, on top of you?—The pimp said the soldier deserved to be killed, because he dared to do more than was permissible to a whore.—You won over the people [1]—did you win over the pimp? did you win over the pirate? —you couldn't kill *him*.

ARGENTARIUS. She says: "I killed an armed man." What about the ones who were unarmed?— She glories in the murder of a man whom she killed, maybe, too late.

Narration of Cestius Pius. She was guarded at 7 home—and she got kidnapped. She was dear to her family—and when she was kidnapped she was not ransomed. The pirates spared her after taking her— and sold her to a pimp. The pimp bought her—and made her a prostitute. She begged mercy of her visitors—and required a sword.—Her name, when tossed into the urn, did not come out—it was ejected. Now was the time to draw lots: the urn had been cleansed.—You offered yourself, a girl in a brothel. Even if nobody outraged you, the place itself did so. You offered yourself with harlots, beautified to please the populace, dressed in the clothes the pimp had

[1] Your clients.

pependit in fronte; pretia stupri accepisti, et manus,
quae dis datura erat sacra, capturas tulit; cum
deprecareris intrantis amplexus, ut alia omnia impe-
traris, osculum erogasti. Ancillae ex lupanaribus
sacerdoti non emuntur; coram sacerdote obscenis
homines abstinent. Non sine causa sacerdoti lictor
8 apparet: occurrenti [1] meretricem summovet.[2] Non
est credibile temperasse a libidine piratas omni crudelitate efferatos, quibus omne fas nefasque lusus est,
simul terras et maria latrocinantes, quibus in aliena
impetus per arma est; iam ipsa fronte crudeles et
humano sanguine adsuetos, praeferentes ante se
vincula et catenas, gravia captis onera, a stupris
removere potuisti, quibus inter tot tanto maiora
scelera virginem stuprare innocentia est? Sed
lupanar excepit. Omnis sordida iniuriosaque turba
huc influit, nec quisquam eo ut iudicet venit. At
omnes favere fabulis tuis? at omnibus persuasum
est? nemo in tanta euntium redeuntiumque turba
inventus est qui fortunae tuae vellet inludere?
Ergo tu, cum tam innocens quam dicis vixeris, ista
passa es ⟨et⟩ [3] credis deos esse? " Nihil " inquit
" passa sum." Hoc satis est nupturae, sacerdoti

---

[1] occurrenti *ed.*: occurrent (occurrenti *V*) tibi.
[2] summovet *ed.*: summouisset.
[3] *Supplied by Castiglioni.*

---

[1] For a similar description of life in a brothel, see Juv.
6.121 *seq.*

provided.[1] Your name hung at the door; you received the wages of sin, and the hand that aspired to sacrifice to the gods took immoral gains. When you begged to be excused the visitor's embraces, you may have got everything else you wanted—but you had to pay a kiss.—One doesn't buy a priestess' *maids* from a brothel: in a priestess' presence men abstain from obscenity.—It is not without reason that a lictor attends a priestess: he removes a prostitute from her way.—It is incredible that pirates abstained 8 from lust, men brutalised by every sort of cruel deed, for whom right and wrong are a jest, plunderers by land and sea, whose profession is to attack the property of others, in arms. Such men, cruel even to look at, used to human blood, carrying before them chains and bonds destined to weigh heavily on their captives—could you turn *them* aside from their desires? Amid so many greater crimes, the deflowering of a virgin is for them an act of innocence.[2] But the brothel took you in. To this place flows a crowd of all filthy and dangerous men: no-one comes there to play the judge.[3] Yet everyone sympathised with your tales? Everyone believed them? No-one was to be found in such a throng of comers and goers who wanted to make a joke of your ill-fortune?—Do *you*, having suffered such things, even if you have lived as innocently as you claim, believe the gods exist?—" I suffered nothing," she says. This is enough for a bride—but not enough for a priestess.

---

[2] Cf. Sen. *Thy.* 744–5: " hactenus si stat nefas, / pius est." Perhaps also Quintilian 7.2.33: " nec pro innocentia (encenia MSS.) ducendum scelus."

[3] i.e. prepared to weigh the girl's story calmly.

parum. Ubi adhuc fuisti? discede, ignota es. ⟨Ubi adhuc non fuisti?⟩ [1] discede, nimium nota es.

9 P. Asprenatis. Contradico non inimicitiis cuiusquam inpulsus; quod enim odium, quae inimicitiae 35M ⟨cum ea⟩ [2] cuiquam esse possunt quam nemo civium suorum norat antequam prostitit? *Movet me respectus omnium virginum*, de quibus gravis hodie fertur sententia *si in civitate nulla inveniri potest neque meretrice castior neque homicida purior*. Piratae te inviolatam servaverunt? a sacerdote se non abstinuisset pirata, leno, mango. De sacerdotis pudicitia his sponsoribus credendum est? Iacuisti in piratico myoparone; contrectata es alicuius manu, alicuius osculo, alicuius amplexu. An melius pirata servavit quam pater? Conversata es cruentis et humano sanguine delibutis: inde est profecto quod potes 10 hominem occidere. Proclama ingenuam esse te; quid expectas? cum in lupanar veneris, iam tibi omnia templa praeclusa sunt. Conservarum osculis inquinatur, inter ebriorum convivarum iocos iactatur, modo in puerilem, modo in muliebrem habitum composita: istinc ne patri quidem redimenda est. *Nulla satis pudica est de qua quaeritur.* Non legerem te sacerdotem etiamsi sacerdoti servisses. Virginem

[1] *Supplied by Müller.*
[2] *Supplied by Madvig.*

---

[1] Answer (apparently): abroad. Being " known " is made a qualification for priesthood in §4.
[2] Who had allowed her to be kidnapped (cf. §7).

Where have you been hitherto? [1] Go away, you are unknown. Where have you not been hitherto? Go away, you are too well-known.

PUBLIUS ASPRENAS. If I speak against her, it is not 9 because I am moved by hatred for anybody. What hatred, what enmity can be felt for a woman whom none of her fellow-citizens knew before she became a prostitute? I am swayed by regard for all the virgins on whom today a grave sentence is being passed if in this city no-one can be found who is chaster than a whore or purer than a murderess. The pirates kept you inviolate? A pirate, a pimp, a slave-trader would not have left even a priestess alone. Are these the sureties in whom we are to trust on the point of a priestess' virginity? You lay in a pirate junk; you were defiled by someone's hand, someone's kiss, someone's embrace. Did a pirate look after you better than your father? [2] You consorted with men who were murderers, smeared with human blood: hence, of course, your ability to kill a man.—Proclaim you are free-born. What are 10 you waiting for? [3] Once you enter a brothel, all temples are closed to you.—She is sullied by the kisses of her companions, bandied about amid the jests of drunken revellers, made to act now as a boy, now as a woman. From such a place not even her father can redeem her.—No woman is chaste enough if an enquiry has to be held about her.—I should not choose you as priestess even if you had been slave to a priestess.—Our priestess is a virgin: whom have we

---

[3] i.e. whatever your birth, your career leaves you no chance of a priesthood.

esse sacerdotem nostram cui credimus? meretrici,
lenoni, piratis: haec enim testium summa est. Casti-
gationem [ex][1] pontificis maximi meruerat sacerdos,
si te e lupanari redemisset. Convenit omnis libidin-
osorum turba et concurrit ad meretricem novam.
Illud certe fateberis, pudicitia tua precaria est; tot
intraverunt cellam tuam gladiatores, tot iuvenes, 36M
tot ebrii: et omnes ante militem inermes? Ego
illam dico prostitisse: illa se dicit etiam mendicasse.
Pudicitiam sacerdotis meae etiam carnifici debeo.

11 IUNI GALLIONIS. Ambitiosa lex est: ad sacerdotium [non][2] nullas ⟨nisi integrae⟩[3] non sanctitatis
tantum sed felicitatis admittit; inquirit in maiores,
in corpus, in vitam: videris quemadmodum tam
morosae legi satis facias. Capta es a piratis, inter
servos, inter homicidas in illis myoparonis angustiis
spatiata es. Viderimus quid in te audere potuerit feritas hostium, libido barbarorum, licentia
dominorum. Certum habeo, iudices, cum hanc
feritatem barbarorum audiatis, favetis illi, ut quam-
primum mutet servitutem ⟨sacerdotio⟩.[4] Sic istam
servaverunt piratae quamadmodum qui lenoni essent
vendituri, ⟨sic istam servavit leno quemadmodum
qui esset coacturus⟩[5] stare in illo ordine, ex eadem
vesci mensa, in eo loco vivere in quo etiamsi non

---

[1] *Deleted by Bursian.*　　　　　[2] *Deleted by Thomas.*
[3] *Supplied by Haase.*　　　　　[4] *Supplied by Gertz.*
[5] *Supplied by Haase and Müller.*

to believe on this point? A harlot, a pimp, some pirates? That is the sum total of the witnesses.—A priestess would have merited the reproach of the high priest if she had ransomed you out of a brothel.—All the mob of lechers throngs together and rushes to the new whore.—You will at least confess that your chastity is on sufferance: so many gladiators, so many young men, so many drunks entered your room; were they all unarmed, before the soldier came?—*I* say that she was a prostitute. She says she was a beggar [1] too.—I owe the chastity of my budding priestess to the fact that she is also a murderer.

JUNIUS GALLIO. The law is importunate. It admits 11 to the priesthood no woman not of inviolate good fortune—as well as chastity. It enquires into a woman's ancestors, her body, her life. *You* had better see to it how you can satisfy so pernickety a law. You were captured by pirates, you walked among slaves and murderers in the cramped quarters of the privateer. *We* shall see what liberties might have been taken with you by savage enemies, lustful barbarians, licentious owners. I am sure, judges, that, hearing of the savagery of these barbarians, you favour her, and hope that she may exchange her slavery for a priesthood as soon as possible.—The pirates looked after her as men would who proposed to sell her to a pimp. The pimp looked after her as a man would who proposed to force her to offer herself in those ranks, eat at the same table, live in a place where you see sex even if you do not experience it.—

---

[1] In asking for alms. I.e. her plea in defence merely aggravates her offence.

12 patiaris stuprum videas. Aliquis fortasse inventus est
quem hoc ipsum inritaret, quod rogabas. Ipse autem
leno pepercit? Ignoramus istos, quibus vel hoc in
eiusmodi quaestu praecipue placet, quod inlibatam
virginitatem decerpunt? Servavit te leno, quam
prostituturus erat in libidinem populi? Ita est? sic
leno⟨te⟩,[1] tamquam nos, castam e castis? "*Omnes*" 37M
inquit " *exorabam.*" *Si quis dubitabat an meretrix esset
audiat quam blanda sit.* Haesisti in conplexu, osculo
pacta es; ut felicissima fueris, pro pudicitia inpudice
rogasti. Quid faciam mulieri inter[2] crimina sua
delitiscenti? Cum dico: "vim passa es," "occidi"
inquit; cum dico: "hominem occidisti," "inferebat"
inquit "vim mihi." Sacerdos nostra stuprum homicidio, homicidium stupro defendit.

13 Divisio. Latro in has quaestiones divisit: an
per legem fieri sacerdos non possit; etiamsi lex illi
non obstat, an sacerdotio indigna sit. An lege pro-
hibeatur, in haec duo divisit: an casta sit, an pura
sit. An casta sit, in haec divisit: utrum castitas
tantum ad virginitatem referatur an ad omnium
turpium et obscenarum rerum abstinentiam. Puta
enim virginem quidem esse te, sed contrectatam
osculis omnium; etiamsi citra stuprum, cum viris
tamen volutata es: es[3] talis qualis videri potest cui

---

[1] *Supplied by Müller.*   [2] inter *Novák:* in.
[3] volutata es: es *ed.:* uoluntate es casta.

Perhaps someone turned up whose lust was provoked 12
by the very fact that you begged for mercy.—Did
even the pimp spare you? Are we unaware of the
character of such people, who regard it as a special
attraction of their profession that they have the opportunity to deflower virgins? Did a pimp keep you
safe when he was going to prostitute you to the lust
of the populace? Is it so? Did a pimp want you, as
we do, " chaste and of chaste parents "?—" I begged
them all off," she says. If anyone doubted whether
she was a whore, let him hear how wheedling she is.—
You clung to his embrace, you sealed your bargain
with a kiss: however lucky you were, you had to be
unchaste in begging for your chastity.—What is to be
done with a woman who looks for safety to her
crimes? When I say, You were outraged, she replies, I killed. When I say, You killed a man, she
says, He was raping me. Our budding priestess
defends her sin by confessing to murder, her murder
by confessing to sin.

Division

Latro made a division into the following points: 13
Can she, by law, become a priestess? Even if the
law does not stand in her way, is she worthy of the
priesthood? On, Is she forbidden by law, he made
two subdivisions: Is she chaste? Is she pure? On,
Is she chaste? he made the following division: Is
chastity to be judged merely by virginity or by
abstinence from all shameful and obscene things?
" Suppose you *are* a virgin, but sullied by everyone's
kisses: even if you haven't had sex, you've nevertheless rolled about with men; are you a woman of the

75

lex nocere vult matrem quoque incestam? Etiamsi
ad virginitatem tantum refertur castitas, an haec
14 virgo sit. Aiebat Apollodoreis quidem placere fixa
esse themata et tuta, sed hic non repugnare controversiam huic suspicioni; non enim ponitur adhuc
virginem ⟨esse⟩,[1] et multa sunt propter quae credibile sit non esse. Illud adiciebat: denique etiamsi
non effecero ut credant iudices non esse virginem, 38M
consequar tamen ut non putent dignam sacerdotio
de qua dubitari potest an virgo sit. An pura sit, in
haec divisit: an, etiamsi merito occidit hominem,
pura tamen non sit homicidio coinquinata; deinde:
an merito occiderit hominem innocentem uti corpore
prostituto volentem. Absoluta est: ostendit non
puram se esse sed tutam. An idonea sit, in tracta-
tiones quas quisque vult dividit: an idonea sit tam
infelix ut caperetur, ut veniret, ut lenoni potissimum,
ut prostitueretur, ⟨ut⟩ [2] occidere hominem cogere-
tur, ut causam diceret.
15   Cestius etiam altius petit, et obiecit quod tam
vilis suis fuisset ut non redimeretur.

Silo Pompeius, dum praeceptum sequitur quo iube-
mur ut, quotiens possumus, de omnibus legis verbis
controversiam faciamus, illam quaestionem movit:
" casta e castis." Lex, inquit, " e castis " cum

---

[1] *Supplied by Gronovius.*
[2] *Supplied by Bursian.*

sort who would, according to the law, be harmed even by having an unchaste mother?" Even if, on the other hand, chastity is to be judged solely by virginity, *is* she a virgin? He said that the followers of 14 Apollodorus [1] like fixed themes that cannot be tampered with; but here the terms of the *controversia* did not clash with such a suspicion. It is not stated that she is still a virgin, and there are many reasons to make it credible that she is not. He added: "Finally, even if I do not persuade the judges she is no virgin, I shall ensure they regard as unworthy of a priesthood one whose virginity is in doubt." On, Is she pure? he made this division: Even if she was justified in killing the man, is she pure once defiled by murder? Then: *Was* she justified in killing an innocent man who wanted to employ the body of a prostitute? "She was acquitted, it is objected. At her trial she showed not that she was pure but that the law could not touch her." The question, Is she suitable? everyone divides into the developments they wish: Is a woman suitable who is so unlucky as to be captured, sold, sold to a pimp of all people, prostituted, forced to kill a man, brought to trial?

Cestius went even further back, and reproached 15 her with being so worthless in the eyes of her family that she was not ransomed.

Pompeius Silo, following the advice that tells us to raise, whenever possible, a dispute about every word of the law, brought up a point about " chaste and from the chaste." [2] " When," he said, " the law

---

[1] See *C.* 2.1.36 n.

[2] *e castis* clearly implies " of chaste parents," as I have translated elsewhere.

dicit, hoc non tantum ad parentes refert sed ad omnes quibus conversata est virgo; non enim adicit "e castis parentibus," sed "e castis" cum dicit, vult illos a quibus venit virgo castos esse. Intellego, inquit, sub hoc verbo multa. "Castis" cum dicit, ⟨intellego castis⟩ [1] penatibus: tu ex incestis venis; intellego castis disciplinis: tu ex obscenissimis venis. Quid enim didicisti? et quaecumque hoc loco dici poterant. Idem et in illa parte fecit "pura e puris."

16   Hispo Romanius accusatoria usus pugnacitate negavit puram esse, non ad animum [2] hoc referens sed ad corpus: tractavit impuram esse quae osculum impuris dederit, quae cibum cum impuris ceperit.   39M

Albucius figura divisit controversiam; dixit enim: *putemus tres sacerdotium petere: unam quae capta est, alteram quae prostitit, tertiam quae hominem occidit: omnibus nego;* et sic causam contra singulas egit.

Fuscus Arellius sic divisit: probabo indignam sacerdotio primum etiamsi pudica sit; deinde quia nescimus an pudica sit; novissime quia non sit pudica.

17   Fuscus pro puella colorem hunc introduxit:

---

[1] *Supplied by Schultingh.*
[2] animum *Thomas:* eam.

says 'from the chaste,' it is referring not only to the
parents but to everyone with whom the girl had to do.
It does not go on to say 'from chaste *parents*': when
it says 'from the chaste,' it means that those from
whom the girl comes should be chaste. Under this
phrase," he went on, "I understand a lot. When it
says 'the chaste,' I understand 'a chaste household.' You come from an unchaste household. I
understand 'chaste upbringing.' You come from the
foulest of upbringings. For what did you learn
there?" And so on, with everything that could be
said on these lines. He did the same for the other
part, "pure and from the pure."

Romanius Hispo, using the vehemence that marks 16
an accuser,[1] said she was not pure. He asserted this
with reference not to her motivation but to her body.[2]
His treatment was that it made her impure that she
had given kisses to the impure, taken food with the
impure.

Albucius used a figure to divide up the *controversia*.
He said: "Let us suppose three women are seeking
the priesthood, one who has been a captive, one who
has been a prostitute, one who has killed a man. I
refuse it to them all." And in this way he conducted
the case against each in turn.

Arellius Fuscus' division was: "I shall prove her
unworthy of the priesthood first, even if she is chaste:
then, because we do not know if she is chaste: finally,
because she is not chaste."

For the girl, Fuscus used this *colour*: the immortal 17

---

[1] Hispo (for whom see Index of Names) was indeed a
notorious *delator*.
[2] For the contrast, see Sen. *Ep.* 88.8.

voluerunt di immortales in hac puella vires suas ostendere, ut appareret quam nulla vis humana divinae
resisteret maiestati: [1] putaverunt posse *miraculo*
esse in captiva libertatem, in prostituta pudicitiam, in
accusata innocentiam.

Latro dixit: aliqua capta felicior fuit, nulla fortior.

Marullus cum descripsisset dignationem puellae
magnam fuisse, altius quiddam superbiusque vultu
ipso praeferente, hanc adiecit sententiam quam
solebat mirari Latro, immo, ut ipse aiebat, exosculari:
narrate sane omnes tamquam ad prostitutam venisse,
dum tamquam a sacerdote discesserint.

18 Albucius dixit: Nescio quis feri et violenti animi
venit, ipsis credo dis illum impellentibus ut futurae
sacerdotis non violaret castitatem ⟨sed⟩ ostenderet.[2]
Praedixit illi abstineret a sacro corpore manum:
"non est quod audeas laedere pudicitiam quam 40M
homines servant, dii expectant"; [cruenti] [3] et in
perniciem ruenti suam " en " inquit " arma, quae
nescis ⟨te⟩ [4] tenere pro pudicitia," et raptum
gladium in pectus piratae sui torsit. Hoc factum
eius ne lateret eisdem dis immortalibus fuit curae:
accusator inventus est qui pudicitiae eius in foro
testimonium redderet. Nemo credebat occisum
virum a femina, iuvenem a puella, armatum ab
inermi: maior res videbatur quam ut posset credi
sine deorum immortalium adiutorio gesta.

[1] maiestati *Thomas:* macis *AB:* magis *V.*
[2] ostenderet *Thomas, Gertz:* uideret.
[3] *Deleted by Kiessling.*
[4] *Supplied here by C. F. W. Müller.*

gods wanted to show their power by means of this girl, to make it clear that no human strength could stand up to the majesty of the gods. They thought it would count as a miracle if freedom were seen in a captive, chastity in a prostitute, innocence in one accused.

Latro said: "There have been luckier captives—none braver."

Marullus described how great the girl's dignity was: her very face showed something lofty and proud. Then he added an epigram which Latro used to admire, even, as he himself put it, to " dote on ": " You may say that all came to her as to a prostitute —so long as you say that they went away as from a priestess."

Albucius said: " There came a man of fierce and 18 violent temperament, sent, I believe, by the gods themselves to put on display the chastity of one destined to be priestess, not to violate it. She told him to keep his hands off her holy body: ' You must not dare to harm chastity that men preserve and gods look forward to.' When he came rushing to his doom, she said: ' Look, your weapon—you do not realise that it is in the cause of chastity that you carry it.' And seizing the sword she drove it into her attacker's breast. Those same immortal gods took care that this deed of hers should not go unnoticed; an accuser turned up to bear witness to her chastity in the courts. No-one could believe a man had been killed by a woman, a youth by a girl, one armed by one unarmed. It was too great a feat for it to be supposed to have taken place without the aid of the immortal gods."

19   Cestius timuit se in narrationem demittere; sic illam transcucurrit: haec dixit in sacerdote futura maxime debere aestimari: pudicitiam, innocentiam, felicitatem. *Quam pudica sit, miles ostendit; quam innocens, iudex; quam felix, reditus.* Etiam habemus quandam praerogationem sacerdoti ab ipso numine datam, licet isti obiciant fuisse illam captivam, lenoni postea servisse, causam novissime dixisse: *inter tot pericula non servassent illam dii nisi sibi.*[1]

Argentarius illud in narratione dixit: accusator in hoc maxime premebat ream: aiebat occisum esse intra verba, antequam vim adferret.

20   Silo Pompeius hac figura narravit: eam vobis sacerdotem promitto quam incestam nulla facere possit fortuna. Potest aliquam servitus cogere: servit et barbaris et piratis, inviolata apud illos mansit. Potest aliquam corrumpere prolapsi in vitia saeculi 41M prava consuetudo (etiam matronarum multum in libidine magisterium): pudica permanebit. Licet illam ponatis in lupanari: et per hoc illi intactam pudicitiam efferre contigit. Fuit in loco turpi, probroso; leno illam prostituit, populus adoravit: *nemo non plus ad servandam pudicitiam contulit quam quod ad violandam attulerat.* Multum potest ad

---

[1] *After* sibi *E has* seruaturi fuissent, *V* seruata fuisset.

---

[1] The *centuria praerogativa* was the century chosen by lot that had the first and binding vote in the Roman popular assembly.

[2] This would go against the girl's innocence of murder, but would be in favour of her having preserved her chastity.

Cestius feared to let himself go in narrative. This 19
was how he skated over it. He said that three things
have particularly to be prized in an aspiring priestess:
chastity, innocence, luck. " The soldier showed how
chaste she is; the judge how innocent; her return
how lucky. Indeed, we have in a way an advance
choice [1] for the priesthood given by heaven itself,
however much these people reproach her with having
been a captive, then served a pimp, finally answered
an accusation. Amid so many dangers, she would
not have been preserved by the gods—except for their
own service."

Argentarius said, while narrating: " The accuser
pressed the defendant on this point especially: he
said the man was killed while he was still talking and
before he brought force to bear." [2]

Pompeius Silo used the following figure for his 20
narration: " I guarantee you a priestess whom no
bad fortune can make unchaste. Some women can
be forced to it by slavery: she served barbarians and
pirates, remaining inviolate in their hands. Some
women can be depraved by the evil habits of a decadent age [3] (even married women have much to teach
in the matter of lust): she will remain chaste to the
end. You may put her in a brothel: even through
this she managed to carry her chastity away untouched. She was in a shameful, vicious place; the
pimp set her up as a prostitute, the people venerated
her; each visitor paid more [4] to preserve her chastity
than he had brought along to violate it. An enemy

[3] See Index of Commonplaces, s.v. Age.
[4] In alms.

rectum quoque pudici animi propositum hostis
⟨cum⟩ [1] gladio: non succumbet, immo, si opus fuerit,
pudicitiam vindicabit.   Incredibilem videor in puella
rem promittere? iam praestitit: adulescentem
misericordis populi beneficium polluere temptantem
gladio reppulit.   Fuit qui illam accusaret caedis:
absoluta est.   Ne qua posset esse vobis dubitatio
quae ventura ad sacerdotium erat an pura esset, an
integra: iam iudicatum est.

21   Triarius dixit: negabat se puella fecisse; negabat
illum suis cecidisse manibus: Altior, inquit, humana
visa est circa me species eminere et puellares lacertos
supra virile robur attollere.   Quicumque estis, dii
immortales, qui pudicitiam ex illo infami loco cum
miraculo voluistis emergere, non ingratae puellae
opem tulistis: *vobis pudicitiam dedicat quibus debet.*

Alterius partis color nihil habet difficultatis: ad- 42M
paret ⟨ex sententiis⟩ [2] quas praeposui.   Dicendum
est in puellam vehementer, non sordide nec obscene.
Sordide, ut Bassus Iulius, qui dixit: " extra portam
hanc virginem " et: " ostende istam aeruginosam
manum," ⟨vel⟩ [3] Vibius Rufus, qui dixit: " redolet
adhuc fuliginem fornicis."   Obscene, quemadmodum
Murredius rhetor, qui dixit: " unde scimus an cum
venientibus pro virginitate alio libidinis genere

[1] *Supplied by Thomas.*
[2] *Supplied by Schultingh.*
[3] *Supplied by Müller.*

---

[1] Her chastity.   [2] At the murder trial.

with a sword has much power over the resolve of a chaste mind, however upright. *She* will not give way —if necessary, she will avenge her chastity. Is what I promise incredible in a girl? She has fulfilled that promise. She drove off with a sword a youth who tried to violate the privilege [1] accorded her by the pity of the populace. An accuser appeared, to charge her with manslaughter; she was acquitted. In case there should be any doubt in your minds whether the aspiring priestess is pure and intact: the judgement has already been made." [2]

Triarius said: " The girl said she had not done it. 21 She said he had not fallen by her hand. ' A form taller than human seemed to loom around me, raising my girlish muscles above a man's strength. Whoever you are, immortal gods, who wished chastity to emerge miraculously untouched from that ill-famed spot, the girl you helped is not ungrateful. She owes you her chastity—and she vows it to you.' "

The *colour* on the other side presents no problems: it is obvious from the epigrams that I placed earlier. One must speak with passion against the girl, but not vulgarly or obscenely: vulgarly like Julius Bassus, who said: " Outside the gate [3] with this virgin " and " Show us that rust-stained [4] hand," or Vibius Rufus, who said: " She still reeks of the soot of the brothel," or obscenely like the rhetor Murredius, who said: " How do we know that she did not bargain with her visitors to keep her virginity at the expense of some

---

[3] The Esquiline Gate, outside which lived the executioner and executions were carried out (cf. Plaut. *Pseud.* 331; Tac. *Ann.* 2.32).

[4] Stained with the small change of the customers.

22 deciderit?" Hoc genus sensus memini quendam
praetorium dicere, cum declamaret controversiam de
illa quae egit cum viro malae tractationis quod virgo
esset et damnavit: postea petit sacerdotium. No-
vimus, inquit, istam maritorum abstinentiam qui,
etiamsi primam virginibus timidis remisere noctem,
vicinis tamen locis ludunt. Audiebat illum Scaurus,
non tantum disertissimus homo sed venustissimus,
qui nullius umquam inpunitam stultitiam transire
passus est; statim Ovidianum illud: " inepta loci,"
et ille excidit nec ultra dixit. Hoc autem vitium
aiebat Scaurus a Graecis declamatoribus tractum,
qui nihil non et permiserint sibi et inpetraverint.[1]
23 Hybreas, inquit, cum diceret controversiam de illo
qui tribadas deprehendit et occidit, describere coepit
mariti adfectum, in quo non deberet exigi inhonesta   43]
inquisitio: ἐγὼ δ᾽ ἐσκόπησα[2] πρότερον τὸν ἄνδρα,
⟨εἰ⟩[3] ἐγγεγένηταί τις ἢ προσέρραπται.

Grandaus, Asianus aeque declamator, cum diceret
in eadem controversia: " non ideo occidi adulteros
[non][4] paterentur," dixit: εἰ δὲ φηλάρρενα μοιχὸν
ἔλαβον.

In hac controversia de sacerdote non minus obscene
dixit Murredius: fortasse dum repellit libidinem,
manibus excepit. *Longe recedendum est ab omni obs-*

---

[1] inpetraverint *Haase and Madvig:* penetrauerunt.
[2] ἐσκόπησα *Müller:* EZNCOΠHCa.
[3] *Supplied by Bursian.*
[4] *Deleted by the editor.*

other brand of lust?" I remember a certain ex- 22
praetor using this type of idea when he declaimed the
controversia on the woman who sued her husband for
maltreatment [1] because she was still a virgin, and got
him convicted: afterwards she seeks the priesthood.
"We know," he said, "the kind of abstinence displayed by husbands who, even if they don't insist on
the first night because the bride is frightened, nevertheless play about in the neighbourhood." Scaurus
was listening—he was a witty as well as eloquent man,
who allowed no folly to pass unpunished. At once he
came out with "Wrong place" from Ovid,[2] and the
other lost his thread and said no more. Scaurus used
to say this fault derived from the Greek declaimers,
who allowed themselves every licence—and got away
with it. Hybreas, he said, speaking the *controversia* 23
about the man who caught his wife and another
woman in bed and killed them both, proceeded to
describe the feelings of the husband (after all a husband ought not to be asked to carry out so shameful
an examination): "But I looked at the man first, to
see whether he was natural or artificial."

Grandaus, no less Asian [3] a declaimer, said in the
same *controversia*: "They would not tolerate the killing of male adulterers on these grounds"; then "But
if I had detected a pseudo-male adulterer..."

In this *controversia* about the priestess, Murredius
spoke no less obscenely. "Perhaps while she re-
pelled his lust, she took it in her hands." One should

---

[1] See *C.* 3.7 n.
[2] *Priap.* 3.7–8: "quod virgo prima cupido dat nocte marito,
/ dum timet alterius vulnus inepta loci."
[3] For Asian rhetoric, see Introduction, p. xv.

cenitate et verborum et sensuum: quaedam satius est
causae detrimento tacere quam verecundiae dicere.

Vibius Rufus videbatur cotidianis verbis usus non
male dixisse: ista sacerdos quantum mihi abstulit!

III

Incesta De Saxo

Incesta saxo deiciatur.

Incesti damnata, antequam deiceretur de
saxo, invocavit Vestam. Deiecta vixit. Repetitur
ad poenam.

1 ⟨Porci⟩ Latronis. Hoc expectastis, ut capite
demisso verecundia se ipsa antequam impelleretur
deiceret? *Id enim deerat, ut modestior in saxo esset*
quam in sacrario fuerat. Constitit et circumlatis in
frequentiam oculis sanctissimum numen, quasi parum violasset inter altaria, coepit in ipso quo vindica- 44M
batur violare supplicio: hoc alterum damnatae in-
cestum fuit. Damnata est quia incesta erat, deiecta

---

[1] The idiom lies in the " vulgar " ethic dative *mihi*.

[2] For the law, see Quintilian 7.8.3, 5–6, where this precise
case recurs. A man found guilty of incest with his daughter
was flung from the Tarpeian rock (on the Capitol in Rome) in
A.D. 33 (Tac. *Ann.* 6.19). But it is the declaimers who have
chosen to switch the meaning of *incesta* to " unchaste " and

keep well away from every obscenity of word or thought. Some things are better left unspoken, even if it costs you your case, rather than spoken at the cost of your shame.

Vibius Rufus was thought to have used everyday language quite well in saying: " What a profit our priestess made!"[1]

3

THE UNCHASTE WOMAN DOWN THE ROCK

An unchaste woman shall be thrown from the rock.[2]

A woman condemned for unchastity appealed to Vesta before being thrown from the rock. She was thrown down, and survived. She is sought to pay the penalty again.

Against the woman

PORCIUS LATRO. Were you waiting for modesty, head bowed, to throw itself off before it was pushed? For that was all that was left, that she should be more modest on the rock than she had been in the shrine.— She stood still, and casting her eyes round the crowd proceeded to profane that most holy divinity, in the midst of the punishment she was suffering, as though she had not profaned it sufficiently among the altars: this was a second act of unchastity on the part of the condemned girl.—She was condemned because she

apply the case to a Vestal Virgin (though this, it will be noticed, is not specified in the theme): for Vestals were buried alive for such offences. See Bonner, 92–3.

est quia damnata erat, repetenda est quia et incesta et damnata et deiecta est. *Dubitari potest quin usque eo deicienda sit donec efficiatur propter quod deiecta est? Patrocinium suum vocat pereundi infelicitatem. Quid* tibi, *inportuna mulier, precer nisi ut ne bis quidem deiecta pereas?* Veniet ad colendum Romani imperii pignus etiamsi non stupro, at certe carnificis manu incesta? " Invocavi " inquit " deos." Statuta in illo saxo deos nominasti—et miraris si te iterum deici volunt? Si nihil aliud, loco incestarum stetisti.

2 Cesti Pii narratio. Quid agam? *exponam quando stuprum commiserit, cum quo,* quibus consciis? *Ista quia probavi damnata est.* Quid postea accessit quod illam virginem faceret? quod iacuit in carcere, quod ducta est ad saxum, quod inde proiecta? Ait se innocentem quia perire non potuit. Ita lex de sacerdote inpura[1] in iudicio quaeri voluit, de iudicibus in supplicio? Ampliatur a iudicibus in poenam. Postulat ut, cum contra poenam causa tuta non fuerit, contra causam tuta poena sit. *Non putas legem*

---

[1] sacerdote inpura *Bursian:* sacerdotum iure.

---

[1] Vesta: cf. *C.* 4.2 n.

[2] That is, was the intention of the law that the validity of the trial of a priestess should be made to depend on the outcome of her execution? This is the point of the next epigram also.

[3] She claims that the outcome of the punishment (i.e. her being alive) should be upheld against the new court proceed-

was unchaste, cast down because she had been condemned, and she deserves to be led back for punishment because she is unchaste and has been condemned
and thrown off the rock.—Is there a doubt that she
should be thrown down again and again until the
purpose of her being thrown down is achieved?—She
summons to her defence her lack of success in dying.
—What prayer can I offer for you, obstinate woman,
except that you should not perish even when you are
thrown down a second time?—Shall a woman go to
worship the divinity guaranteeing the rule of Rome [1]
who has been made unchaste if not by an act of lust,
at least by the hand of the executioner?—" I called
on the gods," she says. Stood on that rock, you
named the gods—yet you wonder that they want you
cast down a second time? If nothing else, you have
stood where the unchaste stand.

Narration of Cestius Pius. What am I to do? Am 2
I to explain when she committed the act, with whom,
who were the accomplices? It is just because I
proved all that that she was condemned. What has
happened since to make her a virgin? That she lay
in prison, that she was led to the rock, that she was
thrown off it?—She says she is innocent because she
failed to die. Did then the law want enquiry to be
made into an unchaste priestess in court—and into
the judges at the time of the punishment? [2]—The
judges adjourn their decision until the punishment.—
She demands that, though the case was not safe
against the penalty, her penalty should be safe
against a case.[3]—Don't you think the law that took

ings, though the previous proceedings had been nullified by the
outcome of the punishment.

cavisse ut perires quae cavit quemadmodum perires?
Exoremus te, mulier, ut iterum absolvaris? Aut tu
sacerdotium violasti aut hi sacerdotem. *Male*
de diis existimas si sacerdoti suae tam sero succurrunt.
Lata est sententia; pronuntiatum est; damnata 45M
es: interrogo te hoc loco, mulier, responde mihi:
sunt dii?

3   ARELLI FUSCI patris. Iterum experiamur: quid
times propitios deos? " Erat " inquit " praeruptus
locus et inmensae altitudinis ⟨tristis aspectus⟩.[1]
Dicebam tibi: incestam lex mori voluit. Stat moles
abscisa in profundum, frequentibus exasperata saxis
quae aut elidant corpus aut de integro gravius im-
pellant; inhorrent scopulis enascentibus latera:
[et inmensae altitudinis tristis aspectus][2] electus
⟨is⟩[3] potissimum locus ne[4] damnati saepius deician-
tur.

FULVI SPARSI. A superis deiecta, ab inferis non
recepta, in cuius poenam saxum extruendum est.

4   IULI BASSI. Nihil putaram amplius adici posse
audaciae istius quam quod in illa rupe Vestam nomin-
averat: en,[5] ab ipso supplicio in templum usque re-
voluta quidquid secundum deos sanctissimum est
contactu suo polluit et, quam a saxo nusquam reverti fas est nisi ad saxum, †quanto minus quam†

---

[1] *Supplied by Konitzer from below.*
[2] *Deleted by Konitzer.*
[3] *Added by Schultingh.*
[4] ne *Summers:* ut.
[5] en *Gertz:* enim.

care how you should die also took care that you *should* die?—Do we have to beg you, woman, to be acquitted a second time?[1]—Either you profaned your office, or these men[2] profaned a priestess.—You think ill of the gods if you imagine they help their priestesses so late in the day.—The vote has been taken, the verdict given: you have been condemned. I ask you here, woman, give me your reply: Do gods exist?

ARELLIUS FUSCUS SENIOR. Let us try the experiment again: why are you afraid of the gods?—they are on your side.—" It was a sheer place, terrifying was the sight of that vast height." I told you: the law required the unchaste woman to die. It stands, a massy crag, cut away to a vast depth, spiky with rocks everywhere, ready to crush the body or send it on its way again more heavily. The sides bristle with projecting rocks. This was a spot chosen specially so that the condemned should not be cast down more than once.

FULVIUS SPARSUS. Thrown down by the gods above, rejected by the gods below: for *her* penalty one would have to construct a special rock.

JULIUS BASSUS. I had supposed that nothing more could accrue to this woman's audacity than that she named Vesta on that cliff. Yet, look, she went straight back from the very execution to the temple, and polluted by her touch all that is most sacred, after the gods. She should not return from the rock anywhere except to the rock—yet, still worse [?], she bounced back to her temple.—Does she come here,

---

[1] i.e. to submit yourself to the judgement of the rock again.
[2] The judges and their minions: cf. §5.

in templum resiluit? hoc potius venit ubi damnatur
quam illo ubi absolvitur?

ALBUCI SILI. Si quis adhuc dubitabat de deiecta,
veniat et sibi ipse credat. Haec inpudentia virginis
est? In urbe tam beata cum tot superfluant virgines, cum tot principum filiae sint, postulat ut praeteri- 46M
tis his potissimum ab inferis eruatis sacerdotem.
" Quare ergo, si incesta sum, vivo? " Nescio; hoc unum scio, nec fieri quod non potest nec portentum
esse quod potest. Absit nefas, te ut id saxum absol-
vat quod tantum damnatas accipit.

5 ARGENTARI narratio. Paene, iudices, narrare coepi
qualis esset rea; sed quid efficiam cum illam incestam probavero? Nempe ut de saxo deicienda
videatur? iam visa est. Non imitabor istius impuden-
tiam, ut repetendo iudicium quod factum est in-
probasse videar. Quod exigebatur probavi; quod
iudicastis exequor.

CORNELI HISPANI. Deos deasque invoco, quos
priore iudicio non frustra invocavi: incesta quam
tardissime pereat. " Invocavi " inquit " numina."
Quid invocas, mulier? Si innocens es, dii non sunt.
Videte quantum sacerdos peccaverit quae nec ab-

where the verdict on her is " guilty," rather than there,[1] where the verdict is " acquitted " ?

ALBUCIUS SILUS. If anyone still had any doubts about the girl who was thrown down the cliff, let him come and believe his own eyes. Is this the effrontery a virgin would show? In so fortunate a city, so full of virgins, so crowded with daughters of leading men, she asks that you should pass them over and prefer to dig up a priestess from the underworld.—" Why, then, if I am unchaste, am I still alive ? " I have no idea. But this I do know: the impossible does not happen, and the possible is no miracle.—Let us be rid of the impious idea that you have been acquitted by a rock which receives on it none but the condemned!

Narration of Argentarius. I was just about, judges, 5 to describe what sort of woman the defendant is. But what shall I accomplish if I prove her unchaste? That you should decide that she deserves to be flung down from the rock? You have already decided. I shall not emulate her impudence by seeming, in bringing it up again, to criticise a judgement that has already taken place. I have proved what was asked; I am carrying out what you judged.

CORNELIUS HISPANUS. I call on the gods and goddesses whom I called on—and not in vain—at the previous trial: let the unchaste woman die as slowly as may be.—" I called on the divine powers," she says. Why do you call on them, woman? If you are innocent, the gods do not exist.[2]—See the enormity of the sin of a priestess who could not be

---

[1] i.e. the rock, contrasted with the court room.
[2] Because they would have saved her earlier (cf. §2 " You think ill . . .").

solvi potuit nec mori. Aut tu sacerdotium violasti aut nos sacerdotem. Erras ⟨si⟩ satis ad sacerdotium putas perire non posse.

6 ROMANI HISPONIS. Ab Tarpeio ad Vestam, cuius vittam carnifex rupit, a templo ad saxum, a saxo ad templum: hac pudicae sacerdotis inter supplicia et vota discursus est. Inter superos inferosque iactata in novam poenam revixisti.

POMPEI SILONIS narratio. Quod ad rerum expositionem pertinet, iudices, non committam ut ultionem deorum immortalium morer. "Incesta saxo deiciatur." Lege damnata est: habetis iudicium. Deiecta est: habetis exemplum.

VIBI GALLI narratio. Brevis expositio rerum est: [1] adversariam incesti postulavi, accusavi, damnavi, carnifici tradidi: permittitis iam abire? Accusator recedo; eamus ad absolutionem tuam. *Ita dii damnatam maluerunt absolvere quam sacerdotem?* sero innocentiam damnata concupisti, vitam deiecta.

7 Ex altera parte. FULVI SPARSI. *Damnata deiecta est: absoluta descendit.*

---

[1] i.e. back to the rock.
[2] Again with the implication that divine intervention would have come earlier.

acquitted, and could not die.—Either you have profaned your priesthood—or we have profaned our priestess.—You are mistaken if you think it is sufficient qualification for a priesthood to be unable to die.

ROMANIUS HISPO. From the Tarpeian Rock to Vesta, whose fillet the executioner broke, from temple to rock, from rock to temple, this is the way our chaste priestess hurries between her prayers and her punishment.—Bandied about between gods above and gods below, you have lived again—to receive a new penalty. 6

Narration of Pompeius Silo. As for the narrative of events, judges, I shall not venture to delay the revenge of the immortal gods. " Let the unchaste woman be cast from the rock." She has been condemned according to the law; you have your judgement. She has been cast down: you have your precedent.

Narration of Vibius Gallus. My exposition of events is short. I arraigned my adversary for unchastity. I accused her, had her condemned, handed her to the executioner. Do you now permit me to retire? I, the accuser, withdraw: let us go to your acquittal.[1]—So the gods preferred to acquit a condemned woman rather than a priestess? [2]—You were too late in longing for innocence when you had already been condemned, for life when you had been flung down.

The other side

FULVIUS SPARSUS. Condemned, she was cast down; acquitted, she descended. 7

ARELLI FUSCI patris. *Putares puellam demitti, non deici.*

CESTI PII. Nullam habebat gratiam: in templo vixerat; itaque tantum deos invocabat. *Lex sacerdotem non usque ad saxum differret nisi expectaret deorum sententiam.*

Cornelius Hispanus descripsit *altitudinem montis etiam secure despicientibus horrendam,* et adiecit: Carnifex quoque recedens impellit. Nihil fecit tamquam rea; contumax est innocentia; turpe putabat sacerdos rogare nisi deos.

MARULLI. Mirandum est si oppressa est virgo sine gratia? Cuius enim genibus submisit manus? quem deprecata est, quae tarde rogavit etiam deos?

8 DIVISIO. Latro in has quaestiones divisit: utrum lex de incesta tantum sit, vel quae deiciatur nec pereat; an etiam damnata, si innocens post damnationem adparuit, deici non debeat. An haec innocens sit; an haec deorum adiutorio servata sit.

Cestius et illas subiunxit huic ultimae quaestioni: an dii inmortales rerum humanarum curam agant; 48M etiamsi agunt, an singulorum agant; si singulorum agunt, an huius egerint. Improbabat Albucium quod

ARELLIUS FUSCUS SENIOR. You would think the girl was being lowered down, not cast down.

CESTIUS PIUS. She had no influence. She had lived in the temple. That is why she could invoke only the gods.—The law would not put off the case of a priestess until she reached the rock unless it awaited the pronouncement of the gods.

Cornelius Hispanus described the height of the mountain, terrifying even for those who look down from it in safety, and added: " The executioner, even, recoils as he pushes."—She acted in no way like a guilty woman. Innocence is arrogant: she thought it shameful for a priestess to call on anyone but the gods.

MARULLUS. Is it surprising if a girl without influence was condemned? To whose knees did she lower her suppliant hands? To whom did she appeal?—she who was slow to appeal even to the gods.

Division

Latro divided so as to give the following questions: 8 Does the law relate to an unchaste woman without qualification, even one who is cast down without dying: or should even a condemned woman not be cast down if her innocence has been demonstrated after her condemnation? Is this woman innocent? Was she saved by the aid of the gods?

Cestius added the following to this last question: Do the immortal gods concern themselves with human affairs?[1] Even if they do, do they concern themselves with individuals? If so, had they been concerned with this girl? He criticised Albucius for

[1] As Epicureans denied.

haec non tamquam particulas incurrentes in quaestionem tractasset sed tamquam problemata philosophumena.

Fuscus Arellius pater sic divisit: utrum incestae poena sit deici an perire; utrum providentia deorum an casu servata sit; si voluntate deorum servata est, an in hoc, ut crudelius periret.

9 Hic color fere sententiis quas praeposui permixtus est; quid tamen Cestius senserit indicabo. Contra sacerdotem quidam dixerunt: videri deos infestos illi in hoc eam servasse, ut diutius torqueretur. Aiebat Cestius malle se casu videri factum quam deorum voluntate; nam si semel illos intervenire huic rei fatemur, manifestius erit ⟨contra⟩ [1] poenam servatam esse sacerdotem quam in poenam; itaque non probabat illud Triari: " remissam tibi poenam putas ? ampliata es." Ea ipsa, inquit, ampliatio, quae apud iudices fieri solet, ex qua verbum in sententiam petitum est, non est damnantis sed dubitantis.

10 Declamaverat apud illum hanc ipsam controversiam Varus Quintilius, tunc Germanici gener ut praetextatus. Cum descripsisset circumstantium ⟨indignationem⟩ [2] quod tam cito oculis poena subduceretur, dixit: exaudierunt dii immortales publica vota et preces: incestam ne cito supplicium transcurreret revocaverunt. Cestius multa contumeliose dixit

49M

[1] *Supplied by Gertz.*
[2] *Supplied by Kiessling.*

dealing with these matters not as small points affecting the issue but as philosophical problems.

Arellius Fuscus senior's division went like this: Is
the penalty for an unchaste woman to be thrown
down or to die? Was she saved by the foresight of
the gods or by chance? If she was saved by the will
of the gods, was it to ensure she died a more cruel
death?

This *colour* [1] is implied in most of the epigrams I 9
have placed earlier. But I will tell you Cestius' view.
Some used against the priestess the argument that
hostile gods seemed to have saved her for further
torment. Cestius said he preferred it to be made to
seem the result of chance, not the will of the gods.
For if we once agree that they are concerned in this
matter, it will be obvious that the priestess was
saved to thwart punishment rather than to suffer
punishment. And so he did not approve of Triarius':
" Do you think your penalty has been remitted?
You have been granted a stay." And he said that
that very " stay " that is part of legal procedure, and
from which the word was taken for the epigram, is
used not in condemnation but in doubt.

Quinctilius Varus, then son-in-law of Germanicus 10
and only a very young man, had declaimed this very
controversia before Cestius. After describing the indignation of those standing around because the
penalty was so swiftly snatched from before their
eyes, he said: " The immortal gods heard the prayers
and entreaties of the people. They called the unchaste woman back, so that she should not hurry
through her execution so quickly." Cestius had a

[1] That is, her being saved to suffer again.

in istam sententiam: Sic, inquit, quomodo quadrigas revocaverunt? Nam et ante posuisti ⟨istam⟩ [1] similitudinem, quia et haec de carcere exierat. Cum multa dixisset, novissime adiecit rem quam omnes improbavimus: "ista neglegentia pater tuus exercitum perdidit." Filium obiurgabat, patri male dixit.

11 Pastor Aietius hanc controversiam apud Cestium dixit iam senator, et hunc colorem optimum putavit: sic veneficiis corpus induruit ut saxa reverberet inultum. Cestius hunc corripuit et dixit: "Hoc est quare ego auditores meos invitem ad alios audiendos ire? Aeque male mihi facit ille qui aut athleta aut pthisicus[2] est." Dicebat autem in Albucium, qui illis diebus dixerat in hac controversia: "durius saxo," et in Bassum Iulium multa, qui dixerat: "virgo desultrix."[3] Othonem Iunium patrem memini colorem stultum inducere, quod eo minus ferendum est quod libros colorum edidit. "Fortasse" inquit "poenae se praeparavit, et ex quo peccare coepit cadere condidicit." 50

12 Silo Pompeius hunc colorem temptavit: praestatur, inquit, quaedam ⟨et⟩ [4] damnatis sacerdotibus verecundia: erubuimus quicquam ex damnatae veste detrahere.

---

[1] *Supplied by Müller.*
[2] phthisicus *Haase:* pthuicus.
[3] desultrix *Gertz:* desu(l)b saxo.
[4] *Supplied by Haase.*

lot of abuse for that epigram. " Did they call her back like a chariot-and-four? You used that image before, as well, by saying that she too had left the prison." [1] And after a lot more, he finally added something we all disapproved: " It was by that sort of carelessness that your father [2] lost his army." In telling off the son, he slandered the father.

Aietius Pastor spoke this *controversia* before Cestius 11 when he was already a senator. He thought this *colour* the best: her body had been made so hard by drugs that it bounced on the rocks without being harmed. Cestius picked on him, and said: " Is this why I encourage my audience to go and hear others? In my eyes an athlete and a consumptive are equally bad." [3] He also spoke against Albucius, who had at much the same time said in this *controversia* " harder than the rock," and a great deal against Julius Bassus, who had said: " a virgin good at leaps." I remember Junius Otho introducing a stupid *colour*, something the less tolerable because he published books of *colours*: " Perhaps she got ready for her punishment, and, from the start of her misbehaviour, took thorough lessons in falling."

Pompeius Silo also tried out this *colour*: " One 12 owes a certain respect to priestesses, even after condemnation. We blushed to remove any of the condemned girl's clothes."[4]

---

[1] This depends on the identity of the word (*carcer*) for " prison " and that for the starting-barrier on a racecourse.

[2] Consul of 13 B.C., who lost three legions in the German forests in A.D. 9.

[3] Point unclear.

[4] Which billowed out and acted as a parachute (cf. Apul. *Met.* 4.35).

Hispanus dixit: ita putaveras una te poena posse defungi, cum in saxo deos nominasses?

Triarius indignantium voces descripsit et dicentium: Quia non potes, vis mori.

Marullus dixit: Constitit in saxo, invocavit deos; publica indignatio exorta est: Audet ista nominare deos, audet hoc loco? quid autem habet iam quod illos roget, nisi bonam mortem?

Diocles Carystius dixit: καταπήδα[1] καὶ δεύτερον καὶ τρίτον καὶ μέχρι ἂν πέσῃς ἐφ' ὃ βέβλησαι.

IV

FORTIS SINE MANIBUS

Adulterum cum adultera qui deprehenderit, dum utrumque corpus interficiat, sine fraude sit.
Liceat adulterium in matre et filio vindicare.

Vir fortis in bello manus perdidit. Deprendit adulterum cum uxore, ex qua filium adulescentem habebat. Imperavit filio ut occideret; non occidit; adulter effugit. Abdicat filium.

---

[1] καταπήδα ed.: hal aaπιaa (or similar).

---

[1] Cf. §10. The text of the epigram is very doubtful.

[2] Or perhaps: until your fall effects the purpose of your being thrown (for which cf. §1 " Is there a doubt . . .").

[3] For this law, see Bonner, 119–21. Despite the allusions in Quintilian 5.10.104 and 7.1.7, it is not likely that it remained in force after the Lex Iulia de adulteriis (c. 17 B.C.).

Hispanus said: " Did you think you could get by with one punishment, just because you invoked the gods on the rock? "

Triarius described the words of the indignant[1] crowd, who said: " You are willing to die—because you cannot."

Marullus said: " She stood still on the rock, called on the gods; anger broke out among the spectators: Does this girl dare name the gods, does she dare name them *here*? But what has she now to ask from them except an easy death? "

Diocles of Carystos said: " Leap down a second time, a third time, and until your fall takes you to the place to which you are thrown." [2]

4

THE HERO WITHOUT HANDS

Whoever catches an adulterer with his mistress in the act, provided that he kills both, may go free.[3] A son too may punish adultery on the part of his mother.[4]

A hero lost his hands in war. He caught an adulterer with his wife, by whom he had a youthful son. He told the son to do the killing. The son refused. The adulterer fled. The husband now disinherits his son.

---

[4] It is clear from §8 that this is the meaning, despite Bornecque. The law was certainly valid for Greece, and Bonner (pp. 121–2) argues for its application in Rome also, at least under the Republic.

1   PORCI LATRONIS. Adulteros meos tantum excitavi.
Me miserum! quamdiu iacuerunt, postquam depre- 51M
henderam! Ego te non abdicem? vellem posse
occidere. O acerbam mihi virtutis meae recorda-
tionem! o tristem victoriae memoriam! ille onustus
modo hostilibus spoliis vir militaris adulteris meis
tantum male dixi: *solus ego ex omnibus maritis nec
dimisi adulteros nec occidi.* Quid ridetis? inquam;
habeo manus: vocavi filium. Tu viri fortis filius, qui
stringere ferrum non potes? Ne truncus quidem
capi potui nisi domi. Utcumque tamen potui obluc-
tatus sum et truncum corpus opposui. Exierunt
adulteri tantum meo sanguine cruenti.

    CORNELI HISPANI. O dignum cui aut pudica con-
tingat uxor, aut inpudica, dum armatus est! Te, res
publica, invoco, quae manus meas possides. *Quis non
putet aut me sine filio fuisse aut filium sine manibus?*

2   CESTI PII. *Conceptus est iste—ex quo, sciemus cum
adulteros deprehendero.* Numquam putavi futurum
salva re publica ut vir fortis sentiret se manus perdidisse.

    MARULLI. Adulteros meos usque ad limen prose-
cutus sum. Cucurri miser ad ferrum, quasi manus
haberem.

For the husband

PORCIUS LATRO. All I did was to wake up my de- 1
ceivers. Alas: how long they lay there after I had
caught them!—*I* not disinherit you? I wish I could
kill you.—O, bitter is the memory of my bravery!
Sad the recollection of my victory! I was once a
soldier, loaded with spoil from the enemy: but I
could only abuse those who had deceived me.—I am
the only husband who has ever failed both to let his
deceivers go [1] and to kill them.—" Why do you
laugh? " I said. " I have hands "—and I sent for
my son.—Are *you* a hero's son?—you cannot draw a
sword.—Even in my maimed state I could only be
taken—in at home.[2]—But as far as I could I struggled,
opposing my maimed body to them.—My deceivers
left stained with blood—but it was only mine.

CORNELIUS HISPANUS. O, here is someone who
deserves a chaste wife—or an unchaste one, so long
as he can hold arms!—I invoke you, Republic: *you*
have my hands.—Anyone might suppose either that
I had no son or that my son had no hands.

CESTIUS PIUS. He was conceived—we shall know 2
the identity of the father when I catch the adulterers.[3]—I never supposed that, while the republic was
not in danger, a hero could feel the loss of his hands.

MARULLUS. I chased my deceivers right to—the
threshold.—Alas, I ran to get my sword as though I
had hands.

---

[1] The son had done that (§2).
[2] The epigram (clumsily translated here) depends on the
double meaning of *capi*—" taken in battle " and " deceived ":
cf. §3 " He conquered . . ."
[3] The adulterer will be the father (cf. §4).

TRIARI. Deciderunt arma cum manibus: *tunc primum sensi me perdidisse.* DESCRIPTIO PUGNAN-TIS VIRI FORTIS. Dii boni, et has aliquis manus derisit?

P. ASPRENATIS. Arcessitus ut occideret adulteros, venit ut dimitteret. Ita ego manus etiam pro adulteris perdidi? Steti deprehensus ab adulteris meis; patris desertor, matris leno, quem, puto, iam creditis non esse filium viri fortis, tertius in cubiculo derisor 52M stetit.

3 FULVI SPARSI. *In bello suas, in domo etiam filii manus perdidit.* Processit in bellum hic unus omnium adul-escentis filii vicarius. In acie vicit, domi captus est. Spectat inter spolia viri fortis volutantes adulteros. "Adulescens, venit tempus militiae tuae." Indigna res: deceptus est; *tam frustra ad filium quam ad gladium cucurrit.* Ridebant adulteri truncas viri fortis manus, circa sua arma labentis.

ARGENTARI. *Ante patriae quam patri negavit manus.* Libenter causam eius suscepi; quis enim illum non vindicet? Quid hoc infelicius, quem adulteri tunc riserunt cum deberent mori? Vir fortis in civitate truncus integros adulteros spectat?

---

[1] And not only for my country.

[2] Instead of the other way round: Hagendahl compares *Decl.* p. 161.17 Ritter.

[3] The normal procedure would be the reverse of this. The declaimer invents a further point to blacken the youth (so also Argentarius just below).

TRIARIUS. My weapons were lost to me when I lost my hands. But this was the first time I felt my loss.—*Description of the hero fighting.* Good god, has someone been able to mock at *these* hands?

PUBLIUS ASPRENAS. Summoned to kill the adulterers, he arrived to let them go.—Was it then for the benefit of adulterers too [1] that I lost my hands?—I stood there, caught out by my deceivers; [2] deserter of his father, his mother's pimp, a boy you can surely no longer think the son of a hero, he stood there in the bedroom, making a third to mock me.

FULVIUS SPARSUS. He lost his own hands in war; he lost his son's too, at home.—This man, alone of all, went to war as a substitute for his youthful son.[3]—He conquered in the field, and was taken at home.—He watched the adulterers rolling about amid a hero's spoils.—" Son, now is the time for your military service."—A shocking thing—he was deceived: he ran to his son as vainly as to his sword.—The adulterers laughed to see the mutilated hands of the hero, as they fumbled over his weapons.

ARGENTARIUS. He denied the service of his hands to his fatherland before he denied them to his father. —I gladly took up this cause: who would not be ready to avenge him? [4]—Who could be more unlucky than this man—laughed at by adulterers at the moment when they should have been dying?—Does a maimed hero in this city look on at adulterers of sound limb?

---

[4] Argentarius makes an advocate speak for the father. The lawyer is prepared to stand up for the hero: the hero's son, however, had not been.

4 Iuli Bassi. Non est quod putetis puniri illum: ad suos dimittitur; ⟨dimittitur⟩,[1] inquam, ad matrem suam, nescio an et patrem. Meruit hereditatem illius quem occidere parricidium putavit. Nulli umquam plus debuistis viro forti: *usque eo pro vobis pugnavit ut pro se non posset. Adulescens, quos dimisisti sequere.*

5 Pars altera. Vibi Galli. " Matrem" inquit " non occidisti." Quem minus hoc crimine perdere debui quam patrem? Pater occidere iussit: lex vetat. Non comparassem patri legem, nisi cum illa lex fuisset. *Alterum putavi parricidium matrem coram patre occidere.*

Arelli Fusci patris. O misera pietas, inter quae parentum vota constitisti! *Non semper scelera nostri iuris sunt, et truces quoque animos misericors natura debilitat.*

6 Divisio. Latro hac usus est divisione: an licuerit 53M filio tunc vindicare; an oportuerit; an, si licuit et oportuit, ignoscendum sit illi si non potuit indulgentia repugnante. An licuerit, in illa divisit: an tunc liceat adulterium filio vindicare cum maritus non est; an tunc liceat ubi maritus in eo loco est quasi omnino non esset. An oportuerit, tractationis quidem est, quam

[1] *Supplied by Schultingh.*

JULIUS BASSUS. You should not think the boy is 4
being punished; he is being let go—to his relations.
He is going back, I say, to his mother—perhaps also
to his father.—He has deserved to inherit the property of a man whose murder he regarded as parricide.—You have never owed more to a hero: he
fought for you till he became incapable of fighting for
himself.—Young man, you let them go: follow them.

The other side

VIBIUS GALLUS. "You refused to kill your 5
mother." On this charge the last thing I should
have forfeited was my father.[1]—My father ordered
the killing: the law forbids it. I should not have
hesitated between the law and my father—except
that the law was on *her* side.—I thought it a second
parricide to kill my mother with my father there.

ARELLIUS FUSCUS SENIOR. Alas for filial affection,
look at the parental prayers you stood between!
Crimes are not always within our power, and even
savage tempers are weakened by a natural pity.

Division

This was the division used by Latro: Was the boy 6
permitted to kill at that point? Should he have
killed? If he could and should, ought he to be forgiven if he was prevented from doing so by the
rebellion of his better feelings? As to, Was he permitted, he subdivided thus: Is a son allowed to
punish an adultery when the husband is not there?
Is he when the husband is on the spot—but so placed
that it is as if he were not there? The question,

[1] By *abdicatio*.

ut quisque vult variat; Latro sic tamen ordinavit:
oportuit, etiamsi pater non iuberet, occidere adulteram viri fortis uxorem; oportuit iubente patre,
etiamsi ipse posset occidere; oportuit, cum et iuberet
et ipse non posset. Novi declamatores illam quaestionem temptaverunt ex verbo legis natam " adulterum cum adultera qui deprehenderit, dum utrumque
corpus interficiat, sine fraude sit ": an nemo possit
occidere nisi qui deprehenderit; temptaverunt et
illam: an non possit abdicari filius ob id quod illi
facere sua lege licuit.

7   Color pro adulescente unus ab omnibus qui decla-
maverunt introductus est: " non potui occidere," ex
illa Ciceronis sententia tractus quam in simili controversia dixit, cum abdicaretur is qui adulteram matrem
occidendam acceperat et dimiserat: Ter non . . .

Latro descripsit *stuporem totius corporis in tam in-
opinati flagitii spectaculo*, et dixit: *Pater, tibi manus
defuerunt, mihi omnia.* Et cum oculorum caliginem,
animi defectionem, membrorum omnium torporem 54M
descripsisset, adiecit: *antequam ad me redeo, exierunt.*
Gorgias inepto colore, sed dulci: . . . Pammenes ex
novis declamatoribus dixit: . . . Gorgias egregie
dixit: . . . Pammenes dixit: . . .

Should he have, is a point of development, which everyone varies as he so wishes. But Latro organised it thus: he ought, even without his father's orders, to have killed a hero's wife taken in adultery; he ought, seeing that his father *did* order him, even if the father was himself capable of killing; he ought, because his father ordered him and could not act himself. Recent declaimers have attempted a point arising from the letter of the law: Whoever catches an adulterer with his mistress in the act, provided that he kills both, may go free. They asked whether one can only kill if one has done the catching oneself. They also tried out the question whether a son could be disinherited for something which he was permitted to do by a law specifically relating to him.

One *colour* in favour of the youth was introduced 7 by all declaimers: " I could not kill." This was taken from an epigram of Cicero's, spoken [1] in a similar *controversia*, when someone was to be disinherited after being given the task of killing his mother when taken in adultery and then letting her go: " Three times . . . not . . ." [2]

Latro described the numbness of his whole body at the sight of so unexpected a scandal, and said: " Father, your hands failed *you*: everything failed *me*." He elaborated on the dimness of his eyes, his faintness, the paralysis of all his limbs, and added: " Before I came to, they had gone." Gorgias used a misplaced but pleasant colour: . . . Among the newer declaimers, Pammenes said: . . . Gorgias excellently said: . . . Pammenes said: . . .

---

[1] Yet see *C.* 1 pr. 12: Bonner, 30.
[2] That is, Three times I tried, but failed, to kill.

8 Fuscus Arellius dixit: *maius erat scelus quod imperabas quam quod deprehenderas.*

Albucius non narravit, sed hoc colore egit ab initio usque ad finem: ego me defendere debeo? Si quid mihi obiectum erit, aut negabo aut excusabo. *Si quid exegeris maius viribus meis, dicam: ignosce, non possum; ignoscit filio pater navigationem recusanti, si non fert mare; ignoscit non sequenti castra, si non potest, quamvis pater ipse militaris sit.* Non possum occidere. Agedum *ipsam legem recita: " liceat et marito,* liceat et patri, *liceat et filio."* Quare tam multos nominat, nisi quod putat aliquos esse qui non possint? Et in descriptione dixit: Cum me vocavit pater, " hoc " inquam " putavit supplicium futurum morte gravius, si adulteram filio ostenderit." Et illud dixit: *Exierunt adulteri inter patrem debilem et filium stupentem.*

Silo hoc colore narravit: non putavi mihi licere.

9 Blandus hoc colore: utrimque fili nomen audio; pater rem petit iustiorem, mater faciliorem. Et illud post descriptionem adiecit: fatebor vobis, parricidium coram patre facere non potui.

Cestius hoc colore egit: " Prosiluit " inquit " protinus mater et amplexu suo manus meas adligavit. Ago confusioni meae gratias quod nihil in illo cubiculo vidi praeter matrem et patrem: pater rogabat ut 55M occiderem, mater ut viveret; pater ne nocens in-

---

[1] The law does not, in fact, say this.
[2] i.e. for the wife.

Arellius Fuscus said: "The crime you ordered was 8 greater than the one you had detected."

Albucius did not narrate, but pleaded from start to finish with the *colour*: Need I defend myself? " If there is any charge against me, I shall either deny it or find an excuse for it. If you ask of me more than my strength permits, I shall say: Forgive me, I cannot. A father forgives a son who refuses to sail if he cannot stand the sea; he forgives him for not becoming a soldier if he lacks the ability, even though the father is himself a military man. *I* cannot kill. Come, recite the actual law:[1] The husband may, a father may, a son may. Why does it name so many unless it thinks there are some who could not bring themselves to do it?" And in his description he said: "When my father called me, I said to myself: He thought it would be a punishment[2] worse than death if he showed the adulteress to her son." He also said: "The adulterers left—between a feeble father and a paralysed son."

Silo's narration employed the *colour*: " I did not think it was allowed."

Blandus' *colour*: " From both sides I hear myself 9 called son. What my father asks is more just, what my mother asks more simple." After his description, he added: " I will confess it: I could not commit parricide in front of my father."

Cestius' plea used this *colour*: " Straightway my mother leapt forward and pinioned my hands in her embrace. I owe it to my confusion that I saw nothing in that bedroom except my father and my mother; my father asked me to kill, my mother asked to live. My father asked that the guilty should

punita esset, mater ut ego innocens essem; pater
recitabat legem de adulteriis, mater de parricidiis."
Et ultimam sententiam dixit: occidere matrem si
turpe est noluisse, non potui.

Argentarius dixit: non est quod me ex hoc habitu
aestimetis, quod manus habeo: tunc non habui.   Et
illud dixit: dat poenas tibi: perdidit virum, perdidit
filium; aegrotanti non adsidebo, egentem non alam;
omnia mihi libera sunt, iam vitam illi non debeo.

10   Ex altera parte multa sunt pulcherrime dicta; sed
nescio an Graecis nostri cessuri sint.   In hac controversia dixit Damas: . . . Habet aliquid corrupti haec
sententia.   Latro dixit: quantum ego tunc questus
sum cum fortuna mea, quod non et oculos perdi-
dissem!

Silo Pompeius dixit: fili, aut oculos erue aut manus
commoda.

Omnes aliquid belli dixerunt illo loco quo deprensi
sunt adulteri ⟨et⟩ dimissi.   Latro dixit: adulteros
meos tantum excitavi.   Fuscus Arellius illius sententiae [1] frigidius dixit contrariam [illi sententiam]: [2]
adulteros interventu meo ne excitavi quidem.
Vibius Rufus dixit: adulteri marito non adsur-
rexerunt.   Pompeius dixit: adulescens, denique

---

[1] illius sententiae *Vahlen:* inius senuntiae.
[2] *Deleted by Konitzer.*

---

[1] As a result of the stupefaction: cf. also §7 " Father, . . ."
[2] She gave me my life, I gave her hers: we are quits.

not go unpunished, my mother that *I* should preserve my innocence. My father recited the law on adultery, my mother that on parricide." His final epigram was: " If it is a disgrace not to have wanted to kill my mother, I *could* not do it."

Argentarius said: " You should not judge me from my present state; I have hands now—but then I had none." [1] He also said: " She has had her punishment at your hands: she has lost her husband and her son; I shall not sit by her bed when she is ill, I shall not support her if she is in need. I am quite free; I no longer owe my life to her." [2]

On the other side, there were many brilliant say- 10 ings. But our declaimers may perhaps have to yield to the Greeks. In this *controversia* Damas said: . . . This epigram has something decadent about it. Latro said: " How heartfelt at that moment my complaint to my fate, that I had not lost my eyes too! "

Pompeius Silo said: " Son, either tear out my eyes or lend me your hands."

Everybody had something nice to say at the point where the adulterers were caught and let go. Latro said: " All I did was to wake up my deceivers." [3] Arellius Fuscus turned Latro's epigram upside down, less pointfully: " My arrival did not even wake up the adulterers." Vibius Rufus said: " The adulterers did not get up to greet [4] the husband." Pompeius said: " Youth, wake up the adulterers at last. Since your arrival, they have been lying there

[3] See §1.
[4] A pun on *adsurgo* = " get up out of bed " and " rise as a mark of respect to."

adulteros excita; postquam tu venisti, securius iacent. Latro dixit: erratis qui me putatis manus 56M non habere: filium vocavi: ut intravit, ab adultero salutatus est.

11 Fuscus dixit: Fili, tuam fidem, ostende te integro manus me non perdidisse. Controversiam mihi de te facit adulter: veni et utrius sis filius indica.

P. Vinicius et pulchre dixit et nove (sumpsit ab omnibus bene dicta): inrupi in cubiculum adulterorum: quid mentior miser? aperto cubiculo expectabant adulteri.

Cestius dixit: vocavi filium; risit adulter tamquam qui diceret: meus est.

Vibius Rufus dixit: adulter meus exit—et commodo suo. Hybreas hunc sensum optime dixit: . . . Dionysius, filius eius Dionysii qui Ciceronis filium docuit, elegans magis declamator quam vehemens, hunc sensum et vehementer dixit et eleganter: . . .

12 Vibius Rufus dixit: quam otiosi, quam securi adulteri transierunt praeter oculos meos, praeter filii manus!

Latro cum exeuntis adulteros descripsisset adiecit: adulescens, parentes tuos sequere.

Nicetes illam sententiam pulcherrimam, qua nescio an nostros antecesserit: . . . Sed illud Albuci utique Graecos praeminet: cum pugnantem se acie descripsisset, dixit: me miserum, quas manus adulter

more relaxed." Latro said: "'You are wrong to suppose I have no hands.' I called my son.[1] When he came in, the adulterer greeted him."[2]

Fuscus said: "Son, I beg you, show me that I have **11** not lost my hands so long as *you* are whole. The adulterer disputes you with me; come and show which of us is your father."

Publius Vinicius said nicely, and also originally (usually he stole everyone else's witty sayings): "I burst into the adulterers' bedroom. Why should I lie, alas? The room was unlocked—they were waiting for me."[3]

Cestius said: "I called my son. The adulterer laughed, as though to say: He's *mine*."

Vibius Rufus said: "My deceiver left, and at his leisure." Hybreas put this idea very well: . . . Dionysius, son of the Dionysius who taught Cicero's son, an elegant rather than an impassioned declaimer, put this idea both elegantly and passionately: . . .

Vibius Rufus said: "How casually, how carelessly **12** the adulterers went past my eyes, past my son's hands!"

Latro, having described the departure of the lovers, added: "Youth, follow them—they are your parents."

Nicetes spoke this very pretty epigram, that perhaps outdid our declaimers: . . . But this one of Albucius' certainly outstrips the Greeks: having described himself fighting on the battlefield, he said: "Alas, what hands they were that the adulterer

---

[1] See §1.
[2] With a hint of their connivance: see §12.
[3] Knowing I could not harm them.

effugit! Et illud Albuci: *" Non potui "* *inquit* *" matrem occidere."* *Quo excusatior sis, adice:* *" et patrem."* Albucius sic narravit tamquam filio sciente factum esset adulterium; suspectum quasi conscium matri suae fecit.

P. Asprenas dixit: exit novissime maritus et dedit adulteris suis locum. Idem dixit: matrem occidere non potes? adulterum certe occide: an et iste pater est? 57

Dixerat Nicetes: . . . Murredius dum hanc sententiam imitari vult, stultissimam dixit: reliqui in acie pugnantes manus.

V

RAPTOR DUARUM

Rapta raptoris aut mortem aut indotatas nuptias optet.

Una nocte quidam duas rapuit; altera mortem optat, altera nuptias.

1 PORCI LATRONIS. Iam se parabat in tertiam, nisi nox defecisset. *Stuprum*[1] *accusatur, stuprum defendit;*

---

[1] stuprum *ed.:* stupro.

---

[1] Cf. Sen. *Agam.* 293: "natus Thyestae.—si parum est, adde et nepos."

[2] For this absurdity, see Bonner, *A.J.P.* 87 (1966), 281–2.

[3] It is rape that is in question, though occasionally I use

escaped!" Also: "I could not, he says, kill my mother. To merit pardon the more, add: Or my father."[1] Albucius' narrative was based on the supposition that the adultery took place with the connivance of the young man—he made him suspect as being in his mother's confidence.

Publius Asprenas said: "Finally, the husband left, and gave place to his deceivers." Also: "You cannot kill your mother? At least kill her lover. Or is *he* your father?"

Nicetes had said: ... Murredius, wishing to imitate this epigram, produced a very foolish one: "I left my hands behind fighting in battle."[2]

5

THE MAN WHO RAPED TWO GIRLS

A girl who has been raped may choose either marriage to her ravisher without a dowry or his death.[3]

On a single night a man raped two girls. One demands his death, the other marriage.[4]

Against the man

PORCIUS LATRO. He was just getting ready for a third—but the night was too short for him.—He is

---

" seduction " for the sake of variety. For the law, see Bonner, 89–90, who finds parallels to it in both Greek and Roman practice.

[4] The theme is classified under the *status* of " contrary laws " in *RLM* p. 383.32. In Calp. Flacc. 51 a similar situation leads to the magistrates choosing the humaner course.

cum altera rapta litigat, alteram advocat. Vindicate patres, vindicate fratres, vindicate mariti; *fortior publicae disciplinae severitas surgat: iam binae rapiuntur.*

MENTONIS.   Postero die erat in huius domo fletus, lamentatio matris spes suas deplorantis, cum interim ex alia domo alia vociferatio oritur, alius tumultus. *Coit populus velut publico metu exterritus, vix credit duos* tantum *fuisse raptores,* cum interim producitur publicus pudicitiae hostis, quem una nocte unius virginis iniuria non satiaverat.

CESTI PII.   *Alteram iniuriæ rapuit, alteram patrocinio.* Quantum suspicor, ne rapta quidem es. Quaeris argumentum? non irasceris. Quomodo istud fit? duabus iniuriam fecit, una queritur? " Misericors sum "inquit. Gaude; habes qui te vindicet. Vide 58M qualem habitura sis virum: non est una contentus.

Argentarius eundem sensum dixit hoc adiecto: non est una contentus, ⟨ne⟩ una quidem nocte.

2   POMPEI SILONIS.   At quam bene mimum egit, quomodo raptam se questa est, qua vociferatione! quam paene illi optione cessimus!

TRIARI.   *Perieras, raptor, nisi bis perire meruisses.*

IUNI GALLIONIS.   Sumatur de illo supplicium, con-

---

[1] The second victim is addressed: for her connivance, see §2 " But how well . . ." and §8.
[2] The other girl, in insisting on death.

accused of rape—and he makes rape his defence. He is at law with one of his victims, and is using the other as his counsel.—Revenge, fathers! Revenge, brothers! Revenge, husbands! Let the harshness of the state's legal system rise to new heights of rigour: now girls get raped in pairs.

MENTO. Next day there was wailing in this girl's home as her mother lamented her lost hopes: at the same time from another house there arose a second clamour, a second tumult. The people collected as though there was some public disaster to startle them: they could scarcely believe there had only been two ravishers—when suddenly there was led forth this enemy of the people's chastity, a man whom the wrong done to one virgin on one night had not satisfied.

CESTIUS PIUS. He raped one girl to do her wrong, the other to defend himself.—To my mind, you [1] were not even raped. You ask for proof? You show no anger. How is that? He wronged two, and only one complains? "I am prone to pity," she says. Rejoice—you have someone to avenge you.[2]—Look what a husband you're going to get—one woman is not enough for him.

Argentarius used the same idea, with this addition: "He is not satisfied with one woman—not even on one night."

POMPEIUS SILO. But how well she acted out the 2 farce, how she complained of rape, how she screamed! How near we came to letting her have her choice!

TRIARIUS. You would have died, rapist—but for the fact that you deserved to die twice over.

JUNIUS GALLIO. Let punishment be exacted from

stituatur in conspectu publico, caedatur diu, toto die pereat qui tota nocte peccavit. Subito fastidiosus raptor occurrit et ait: "iam nec nuptias volo." Stulta, deciperis; dicam, si vis, quid dixerit tibi; idem enim dixit et huic: "dum te peto, in illam incidi."

ARELLI FUSCI patris. Retro amnes fluant, sol contrario cursu orbem ducat, confugiat sacrilegus ad aras: raptorem rapta vindicat.

3 Ex altera parte. POMPEI SILONIS. Postero die cum illi narratus esset nocturnus error, dum putat se in unam incidisse, huic priori supplices summisit manus, hanc prius deprecatus est, exoravit: propter hoc, puto, ista magis raptori irascitur. Altera ex puellis raptorem mori vult, altera servari: reum alter iudex damnat, alter absolvit; *inter pares sententias mitior vincat.* Dicam quod sentio: magis irasceretur si unam tantum rapuisset; diceret: "ergo ego sola digna visa sum cui iniuriam faceret?"

ARGENTARI. *Refer* nunc *Verginiam, refer Lucretiam: plures tamen Sabinae sunt.* Ex tribunis potentior est 59M qui intercedit. Non est invidiosa potestas quae

---

[1] The result of over-mildness with the ravisher in this case.

[2] The so-called ἀδύνατον (impossibility) figure; cf. Eur. *Med.* 410–1: "The founts of holy rivers climb upwards, and justice and all things are turned upside down." For rivers and sun combined, see Ov. *Trist.* 1.8.1–2: "in caput alta suum labentur ab aequore retro / flumina, conversis solque

him, let him be placed in the public gaze, let him be killed slowly, let him take all day to die—he took all night to sin.—Suddenly we find a choosy rapist saying: "Now I don't even want marriage."[1]—Foolish girl, you are being tricked. If you like I'll tell you what he said to you—he said the same to this other girl: "While I was looking for you, I ran into her."

ARELLIUS FUSCUS SENIOR. Let rivers reverse their course,[2] let the sun trace his orbit in the opposite direction, let the sacrilegious flee to the altar: a girl who has been ravished is trying to save her ravisher.

The other side

POMPEIUS SILO. The day after, when he had his 3 error of the night before explained to him—he thought he'd only encountered one girl—he lowered his hands in supplication to this girl first; she was the first he implored and won over—hence, I suppose, the other's greater anger with her ravisher.—One of the girls wants the ravisher to die, the other wants him saved; one judge condemns the defendant, the other acquits him. The votes are equal—let the gentler prevail.[3]—I shall say what I feel: she would be more angry if he'd only raped one; she'd say: "So am I the only one he thought it worth wronging?"

ARGENTARIUS. Now tell of Verginia, of Lucretia: however, the Sabine women have greater numbers on their side.[4]—Among tribunes the one who proclaims

recurret equis," which may well be related to Fuscus' epigram.

[3] Cf. C. 2.3.3 and note.

[4] The Sabine women accepted marriage after their rape— and their greater numbers give them the decision in preference to Verginia and Lucretia, who did not.

misericordia vincit. Quid cessas, puella? pro marito
roga. (Haec sententia deridebatur a Cestio quasi in-
proba.)

4   DIVISIO.   In hac controversia de prima quaestione
nulli cum altero convenit. Latro primam fecit
quaestionem: non posse raptorem qui ab rapta mori
iussus esset servari. Si legatus, inquit, exire debet,
peribit; si militare debet, peribit; si ius[1] dicere
debet, peribit; si raptam ducere debet, aeque peribit.
Si is *te ante rapuisset et nuptias optasses,* interposito
deinde tempore *antequam nuberes hanc vitiasset, negares
illum debere mori rapta iubente?*   Atqui nil interest, nisi
quod dignior est raptor morte cuius inter duos raptus
ne una quidem nox interest. Si rapta nupsisses,
deinde post tertium diem rapuisset aliam, negares
illum mori debere? Atqui quid interest, nisi quod
honestius tunc maritum defenderes quam nunc raptorem defendis?

5   Alteram fecit: an rapta quae nuptias optat *nihil
amplius raptori praestare possit quam ne sua lege pereat,
contra alienam legem nullum ius habeat.* Optasti nuptias: non occidetur tamquam raptor tuus. At idem
eadem nocte qua te rapuit ⟨si⟩[2] stationem deseruit,

---

[1] ius *ed.* (lege ius *Müller*): lege.
  Added by Schott.

---

[1] The *tribuni plebis* had a right of veto (*intercessio*) against
acts of magistrates, laws, etc.   An individual tribune could
veto actions by his colleagues.

the veto is the one who prevails.[1]—A power that uses pity to accomplish its victory wins no unpopularity.— What are you waiting for, girl? Beg—for your husband. (This epigram was jeered at by Cestius as outrageous.)

Division

In this *controversia* there is no agreement on the 4 first question. Latro's was: A ravisher who is ordered by his victim to die cannot be saved. " If he has to go out on an embassy, he will die. If he has to serve as a soldier, he will die. If he has to administer the law, he will die. If he has to marry a girl he raped, he will die just the same. If he had raped you before and you had chosen marriage, then, in the interval before the wedding, had wronged this girl, would you say he ought not to die if the girl he raped demanded it? Yet there is no difference between the two cases—except that a seducer deserves to die the more when there is not even a single night to separate his two rapes. If you had married him after being raped, then two days later he had raped another, would you say he ought not to die? Yet what is the difference?—except that it would then be more honourable for you to defend your husband than it is for you to defend your ravisher now."

The second point he made was: Can a victim of 5 rape who chooses marriage grant her ravisher anything else but immunity under the law as far as she is concerned, having no power to thwart the law as it affects another? " You chose marriage; he will not die for seducing *you*. If, on the same night that he raped you, he deserted his post, he will be beaten to

fuste ferietur; si sacrilegium fecit, occidetur. Licet
tu dicas: " quid ergo ? ego non nubam ? " *tu raptori
praestas ut illum ipsa non occidas; non potes praestare ne
quis occidat.* Quomodo sacrilegus, quamvis a te   60Ī
servatus, periret, sic alterius puellae raptor, vel a te [1]
servatus, peribit.   Si rapuisset te, deinde in adulterio
deprehensus adservaretur in tormentum diutius pereundi, tu interim educta nuptias optasses—datur enim
optio et in absentem—, vetares illum occidi a marito ?
Quid interest qua lege pereat, nisi quod modestius
alienam legem interpellares quam tuam ?

6   Tertiam fecit: cum quod utraque optat fieri non
possit, an ea eligenda sit optio qua ultio ad utramque
perveniat.   Ait quae mortem optat: mea optio et te
vindicat, tua me non vindicat; nec hoc tibi mea optio
praestat quod mihi: ex occiso raptore invidiam.   Illa
respondet: Optio tua me non vindicat: vindictam tu
meam putas, non fieri quod volo, fieri quod nolo ?
Etiam *contumeliosum mihi erit te dignam videri in cuius
honorem homo occidatur, me dignam non videri in cuius*

---

[1] raptor vel a te *Gertz, Schott:* proteruitate.

---

[1] The so-called *fustuarium* (Liv. 5.6.14 with Ogilvie *ad loc.*):
see H. M. D. Parker, *The Roman Legions* (Oxford, 1928), 232–5.
[2] This was true of graver offences (Bonner, 106).
[3] Latro has to envisage this possibility, because if the
adulterer was killed at once (and this was the only way
sanctioned by law) there would have been no point in discuss-
ing whether the girl could save him.
[4] Cf. *Rhet. Gr.* 2.171.13–15 Spengel on the same theme:

death;[1] if he committed a sacrilege, he will be axed.[2] You may say: 'Well? Am I not to marry?' What you are granting your ravisher is that it is not you who are the cause of his death—what you cannot grant him is that he should not be killed. If he had committed sacrilege he would die however much *you* granted him his life: so will he as the ravisher of a second girl, even though *you* grant him his life. If he had raped you, then been caught in adultery and reserved to be tortured by having to wait longer for death,[3] and you meanwhile had been summoned to court and had chosen marriage (for the choice is available even when the man is not present), would you be able to prevent him being killed by the husband? What difference does it make which law he perishes by?—except that you would be acting more modestly in trying to hold up his death under a law not concerning you than under one concerning you."

His third question was: Since it is impossible for 6 the choice of both to be carried out, should the choice which gives both revenge be preferred? "The girl who chooses death says: 'My choice gets revenge for you too—but yours does not get it for me;[4] nor will my choice give *you* what it gives me—unpopularity as a result of the death of the ravisher.' The other replies: 'Your choice does *not* avenge me. Do you think revenge for me consists in what I want not happening, and what I do not want taking place? In fact, it will be an insult to me that you are thought to deserve the death of a man for your sake, while I

"The girl who insists on death will say that he will pay the penalty to both if he dies, but that if he marries the other girl one part of the law will be ineffective."

honorem servetur. Isto modo et mea te vindicat: nempe lex duas poenas scripsit vitiatori: alteram passurus est; non eris inulta, nam raptor non erit inpunitus: habebit poenam, indotatam uxorem. Respondet eodem modo: morietur ⟨utrique, tibi servabitur⟩ [1] sed non mihi.

Quartam fecit quaestionem: si non potest utrius- 61 que rata esse optio, utra quae valeat dignior sit. Ultimam non quaestionem sed tractationem ⟨fecit: neminem⟩ [2] non raptorem impunitum futurum si haec via impunitatis monstraretur, ut qui plures rapuisset tutior esset; neminem non inventurum aliquam humilem quae se in optionem commodaret.

7   Fuscus Arellius primam quaestionem hanc fecit: ⟨an⟩ [3] qui duas rapuit perire utique debeat. Lex, inquit, quae dicit: "rapta raptoris aut mortem optet aut nuptias," de eis loquitur qui singulas rapuerunt; non putavit quemquam futurum qui una nocte raperet duas. Non quaero quid optetis; quod severissime optare potestis occupo: necesse est raptorem mori. Quare? utrique raptae ultio debet contingere. Utramque non potest ducere, utrique mori potest. Una pars legis ad hunc raptorem pertinet, in qua mors est. Putate enim utramque nuptias optasse: quid futurum est? in raptoris matrimonium ambitus erit. Putate illum plures rapuisse quam duas: quid fiet? una nubet? nuptiae ad unam pertinebunt, mors ad omnes. Qui duas rapuit utique debet mori. Quare?

---

[1] *Supplied by the editor after Kiessling and Gertz.*
[2] fecit *supplied by Otto,* neminem *by Haase.*
[3] *Supplied by Haase.*

am not thought to deserve his reprieve for mine. Now looked at like *this*, my choice avenges you also. Look, the law prescribed two punishments for the ravisher. He will suffer one of the two. You will not go unavenged, for the ravisher will not go unpunished: he will have his penalty—a wife without a dowry.' The first girl replies as before: ' If he dies, he will die for both of us; if he is reprieved, he will be reprieved for you, but not for me.' "

He made the fourth question: If the choice of both cannot stand, which is the worthier to prevail? The last he made a development rather than a question: Every ravisher would go unpunished if this route to safety were signalled—the more girls raped, the safer the rapist. Everyone would find some lowclass girl who would lend herself to make a choice.

Arellius Fuscus made this his first question: Ought 7 someone who has raped two girls die in any case? " The law that says a raped girl may choose her ravisher's death or marriage to him is talking about ravishers of one girl. It did not imagine that there would be anyone who would seduce two girls on one night. I do not enquire what your choice is: I seize on the harshest choice open to you—the ravisher must die. Why? Both girls must have their revenge. He cannot marry both, but he can die for both. Only one part of the law applies to *this* ravisher—where it says ' death.' Suppose both have chosen marriage. What is to happen? Competition for marriage to a seducer. Suppose he had seduced more girls than two. What will happen? Will one marry him? Marriage will affect one girl; death all. The seducer of two girls should certainly die. Why? I will tell

dicam. Quod ⟨quaeque⟩[1] vult eligat: aut ⟨mortem
utraque aut⟩[2] nuptias optabunt aut altera mortem,
altera nuptias; si ⟨aut⟩[3] nuptias ⟨utraque aut altera
mortem, altera nuptias⟩[4] optaverint, non poterit fieri 62[?]
quod utraque volet; uno modo poterit fieri quod
utraque volet, si utraque mortem optaverit: ergo fiat
quo uno duae vindicari possunt.

8   Hic tractavit: ne exemplum quidem utile esse non
utique perire eum qui duas rapuerit; [ne][5] hunc
morem perniciosissimum civitati introduci, ut aliquis
propter hoc non pereat, quia perire saepius meruit.

Reliquam partem controversiae Fuscus in haec
divisit: utra optio honestior sit, utra iustior, utra
utilior.   Cestius hanc partem controversiae sic divisit:
utra optio[6] dignior sit quae valeat; utra optione
raptor dignior sit.

Cestius et coniecturalem quaestionem temptavit:
an haec cum raptore conluserit et in hoc rapta sit, ut
huic opponeretur.

9   Latro aiebat non quidquid spargi posset suspiciose,
id etiam indicandum:[7] colorem hunc esse, non quaestionem; eam quaestionem esse, quae impleri argumentis possit.   Cestius aiebat et hanc posse impleri
argumentis.

Hunc sensum a Latinis iactatum Nicetes dixit: ἐπὶ
τὴν τρίτην νὺξ ἔκλινεν.[8]   Glycon dixit: . . . Diocles

---

[1] *Supplied by the editor.*   [2] *Supplied by Gertz.*
[3] *Supplied by Gertz.*   [4] *Supplied by Schenkl.*
[5] *Deleted by Schott.*   [6] optio *Müller:* puella.
[7] indicandum *Kiessling:* uindicandum.
[8] ἔκλινεν *Thomas:* ΕΧΙΝΕΝ.

---

[1] i.e. the factual point.
[2] Second meaning: victim. Latro's epigram repeated

you. Let each choose what she wants. Either they will both choose either death or marriage, or one will choose death, one marriage. If both choose marriage, or one marriage and one death, it will be impossible for the wishes of both to be carried out. Only if both choose death will the wishes of both be able to be implemented. Let us therefore follow the only route by which both can be avenged."

Here his treatment was that it wasn't a good prece- 8 dent, either, that a man need not necessarily die after seducing two girls. That someone should not die just because he deserves to die more than once is a most pernicious custom to introduce into a state.

The rest of the *controversia* Fuscus divided thus: Which choice is more honourable, which more just, which more expedient? Cestius divided this part of the *controversia* thus: which choice deserves to prevail? Which choice does the ravisher deserve?

Cestius also had a try at the conjectural question,[1] Did one girl connive with her seducer and was seduced just in order that she could be pitted against the other?

Latro used to say that there was no need to make 9 an obvious show of everything that could be scattered about to arouse suspicion: this was a *colour*, not a question (a question being something that could be filled out with arguments). Cestius' view was that this too *could* be filled out with arguments.

An idea much bandied about by the Latin declaimers was expressed by Nicetes: " The night was verging towards the third [hour]." [2] Glycon said:
below is similar, but does not seem to have this double meaning.

Carystius dixit: . . . Hunc sensum Vibius Rufus subtiliter dixit: volo tibi malam gratiam cum sponso tuo
facere: habet amicam.

In hac controversia dixit Albucius: ambulet in 63M
masculos. Adeo nullum sine amatore vitium est ut
hoc quidam disertum putaverint; ego tamen magis
miror hoc potuisse Albucium dicere quam aliquos
potuisse laudare.

Ex Latinis dixit Triarius: gratulor vobis, virgines,
quod citius inluxit. Argentarius dixit: quaeritis
quid isti finem rapiendi fecerit? dies. Latro: iam se
parabat in tertiam, nisi nox defecisset.

VI

Archipiratae Filia

Captus a piratis scripsit patri de redemptione;
non redimebatur. Archipiratae filia iurare eum
coegit ut duceret se uxorem si dimissus esset;
iuravit. Relicto patre secuta est adulescentem.
Redit ad patrem, duxit illam. Orba incidit.
Pater imperat ut archipiratae filiam dimittat et
orbam ducat. Nolentem abdicat.

1 Porci Latronis. Pro di boni, et haec puella hos-
pitio patris excepta est? Prohibeo domo terra pro-

---

[1] The girl who chose marriage.
[2] See §1.

. . . Diocles of Carystos said: . . . This idea was cunningly put by Vibius Rufus: " I want to make bad blood for you [1] with your fiancé. He has a girl-friend."

In this *controversia* Albucius said: " Let him resort to males." Some thought even this clever, so true is it that no fault lacks its supporter. *I*, however, find it more surprising that Albucius was capable of saying it than that there were people capable of praising it.

Of the Latin speakers, Triarius said: " I congratulate you, virgins, that dawn came early." Argentarius said: " You ask what brought his rapes to a halt? Day." Latro: " He was just getting ready for a third—but the night was too short for him." [2]

6

The Pirate Chief's Daughter

A man captured by pirates wrote to his father about a ransom. He was not ransomed. The daughter of the pirate chief forced him to swear to marry her if he was let go. He swore. She left her father and followed the young man. He returned to his father, and married the girl. An orphan appeared on the scene; the father orders his son to divorce the daughter of the pirate chief and marry the orphan. He refuses. His father disinherits him.

For the father

Porcius Latro. Good God! Was *this* girl wel-[1] comed into his house by your father?—She should be

hibendam. *Bonae spei uxor, bonae spei nurus, quae amare potest vel captivum, odisse vel patrem.* "*Captus*" inquit "*in tenebris iacebam.*" *Narra, obsecro, soceri tui beneficia.* Possum, iudices, esse securus? Filius meus ait se uxori parricidium debere.

Cesti Pii. Quis interfuit nuptiis tuis? pater? denique puellae pater?

2 Ex altera parte. Iuli Bassi. Hodie captivus essem nisi haec archipiratae filia fuisset. Ut dixi: 6 "patrem habeo," inter bonos captivos sepositus sum. Archipiratae filia vocatur, puto ex aliqua nata captiva; certe animum eius natura a patre abduxerat: misericors erat, deprecabatur, flebat, movebatur periculis omnium; nihil in illa deprehendi poterat piraticum. Promisi nuptias, et quasi aliquam sacram testationem tuum nomen inserui. *Eo loco me non deseruit in quem venire etiam patres timuerunt.* Artius nos fortuna alligavit [nisi corpus omnia vinculis] quam ut orba posset divellere. *Vidisses* tectum pannis corpus, omnia *membra vinculis pressa, macie retractos introrsus oculos, obtritas catenis et inutiles manus: talem quis amare nisi* 3 *misericors posset?* Decepi te, puella, alia pollicitus:

---

[1] The answer (not at all) would demonstrate the unsuitability of the match.

[2] Hers had been to leave her father. His might be more literal.

banned from dry land—*I* ban her from my house.—
Here is a promising wife, a promising daughter-in-law
—she can love even a prisoner, hate even her father.
—He says: " I was a prisoner: I lay in darkness."
Tell me, I beseech you, how your father-in-law
helped you.[1]—Can I be safe, judges? My son says
he owes his wife a parricide.[2]

CESTIUS PIUS. Who was present at your wedding?
Your father? At least the girl's father?

The other side

JULIUS BASSUS. I should be a captive today but for 2
this daughter of a pirate chief.—When I said, " I have
a father," I was set apart, among the " good "
prisoners.[3]—She is called the daughter of a pirate
chief: but her mother, I think, was some captive.[4]
Certainly her character set her apart from her father:
she showed compassion, she made intercession, she
wept, was moved by everyone's perils. There was
nothing of the pirate detectable in her.—I promised
to marry her, and put in your name as a kind of holy
invocation.[5]—She did not let me down in a place to
which even fathers feared to come.—So Fortune has
bound us together too closely for an orphan to be able
to separate us.—You would have seen my body
clothed in rags, all my limbs burdened under chains,
my eyes sunken in my emaciated state, my hands
worn with shackles and useless. Who but a woman
who felt pity could love such a man?—I deceived you, 3
girl—this was not what I promised: " When you

---

[3] In hope of the ransom that never came.
[4] An inference from her pity for captives.
[5] Cf. below, §11.

137

cum veneris in patriam mecum, ibi tibi gratiam
referam; hic catenatus, egens, squalidus quid possum? Pater meus, socer tuus—hoc enim te iam
pridem vocabat—, socer, inquam, tibi tuus gratiam
referet.

Quidam avitas paternasque flagitiis obruerunt
imagines, quidam ignobiles nati fecere posteris genus:
in illis non servasse quod acceperant maximum
dedecus, in illis quod nemo dederat fecisse laudabile
est. Si possent homines facere sibi sortem nascendi,
nemo esset humilis, nemo egens, unusquisque felicem
domum invaderet; sed quamdiu non sumus, natura 65M
nos regit et in quemcumque vult casum quemque
mittit: hic sumus aestimandi, cum sumus nostri.
4 Quis fuit *Marius*, si illum suis inspexerimus maioribus? *in multis consulatibus* [1] *nihil habet clarius quam se
auctorem. Pompeium si hereditariae extulissent imagines,
nemo Magnum dixisset. Servium regem tulit Roma,* in
cuius virtutibus humilitate nominis nihil est clarius.
Quid tibi videntur illi ab aratro, qui paupertate sua beatam

----

[1] multis consulatibus *Haase* (tot c. E): mites consiliati.

----

[1] For this commonplace on ancestry, compare Juvenal 8,
Sen. *Ep.* 44. *Exempla* in both directions are supplied by Val.
Max. 3.4–5 (cf. Vell. Pat. 2.128).

[2] *Decl.* p. 438.24 Ritter: "We get our family by lot—we
do not choose it: and before we are born we have no control
over our destinies."

[3] Cf. Juv. 8.245 *seq.*

come with me to my country, I will show my gratitude there. Here, in chains, in need, filthy, what power have I? My father, your father-in-law " (she had been calling you that long since) " your father-in-law, I say, will repay you."—

Some have buried their grandfathers' and fathers' family portraits beneath shameful deeds—while some ill-born sons have given their posterity a family to be proud of.[1] In the former the greatest disgrace is not to have kept what they inherited; in the latter it is praiseworthy to have accomplished what none had given them. If men could construct their own lots at birth, no-one would be low-born, no-one poor, everyone would enter a prosperous house. But so long as we are unborn, it is nature that controls us, sending us each into the lot that she wishes.[2] We are to be assessed on this earth, now that we are our own masters. Who was Marius if we look at him 4 with his ancestors in mind?[3] Despite his many consulships, he has nothing that does him greater credit than that he was self-made. If busts of ancestors had carried Pompey to his peak,[4] no-one would have called him the Great. Rome had for king Servius, among whose virtues there is no greater distinction than the lack of distinction in his name.[5] What do you think of the men who came from the plough to enrich the republic with their poverty?[6]

[4] The Latin could mean " escorted Pompey to his grave." But the emphasis is on Pompey's glorious life, not his sordid death.

[5] His name implied his servile descent: see *C.* **3.9** n.

[6] Principally Cincinnatus (see *C.* 2.1.8 n.). Compare the plural in Val. Max. 4.4.4.

fecere rem publicam? Quemcumque volueris revolve nobilem: ad humilitatem pervenies. Quid recenseo singulos, cum hanc urbem possim tibi ostendere? Nudi ⟨hi⟩ [1] stetere colles, interque tam effusa moenia nihil est humili casa nobilius: fastigatis supra tectis auro puro fulgens praelucet Capitolium. Potes obiurgare Romanos quod humilitatem suam cum obscurare possint ostendunt, et haec non putant magna nisi apparuerit ex parvis surrexisse?

5 " Misereri illius oportet, quia orba est." Ista tamen habet propinquos, habet amicos paternos, habet te inbecillitatis suae tutorem fortissimum. Omnes uxores divites servitutem exigunt. Crede mihi, volet in suis regnare divitiis; et tamen aecum est †eam possidere domum quam me† [2] agnoverit. Si coeperimus esse magis liberi, si paulo speciosior animo eius adfulserit domus, si parum blande fecerimus, relinquet: et tunc est tormentum carere divitiis cum illas iam senseris. Vides quid inter duas uxores intersit: ista si nos reliquerit repetet sua, haec quod dedit dimissa non auferet. Multi uxores sine dotibus

66M

[1] *Supplied by Schultingh.*
[2] *The exact form of this passage is uncertain. I have translated the text as emended by Haase and Müller:* eam ⟨me⟩ possidere domum quae erum me.

---

[1] Juv. 8.272-3: " . . . ut longe repetas longeque revolvas / nomen, ab infami gentem deducis asylo"; Sen. *Ep.* 44.1: " omnes, si ad originem primam revocantur, a dis sunt."
[2] Cf. *C.* 2.1.5. A hut attributed to Romulus was preserved on the Capitol (Vitr. 2.1.5 and, e.g., Camps on Prop. 4.1.6).

Unroll the pedigree of any nobleman you like: you will arrive at low birth if you go back far enough.[1] Why should I detail individuals? I could point out the whole of this city to you. Once these hills stood bare; among such wide-flung walls there is nothing more distinguished than a low hut,[2] though above it shines out the Capitol with its sloping roofs, gleaming in pure gold. Can you reproach the Romans?—they might cover up their humble beginnings, but instead they make a show of them, and do not regard all this as great unless it is made obvious that it rose from a tiny start.—

"One must pity her—she is an orphan." But *she* 5 has relatives, she has friends of her father, she has you as the most valiant champion of her weakness.— All rich wives demand slavery;[3] believe me, she will want to be queen amid her riches; yet it is right that I should have a household that recognises *my* authority. If I start being a little too independent, if, to her mind, another's house has a rather more brilliant gleam, if I behave too roughly, she will go. And it is a torment to be without riches—when you have once got the feel of them. You see the difference between the two wives; if this one leaves me, she will want her money back; if I divorce the other, she will not deprive me of what she gave me.[4] Many

For the contrasting splendour of the temple of Jupiter on the Capitol, see Propertius *loc. cit.* and *C.* 2.1.1 n.

[3] Cf. Juv. 6.224: "imperat ergo viro, sed mox haec regna relinquit"; Sen. *Phoen.* 595–7: "A gift made over to my wife, shall I tolerate the harsh rule of a rich bridal chamber and follow the commands of my father-in-law like a lowly lackey?"; Philostr. *Vit. Soph.* 610; Jerome *Ep.* 127.3.

[4] My freedom.

habuere,[1] quidam dictas non accepere dotes, quidam etiam emptis contenti fuere mancipiis, et, cum possent accipere divitias, emere quibus libertatem 6 darent maluerunt quam suam vendere. Aliquis in adoptionem iuvenis petitur: si volet ire, quaerat senex ille qui petit quales et quot habeat maiores, quanta bona, an satis magno se possit addicere. Aliquis capere orbos senes vult et suas spes in alienas mortes diffundere: excutiat testamenta, scrutetur census. Ubi vero quaeret uxorem, videat an nuptias suas amet, an nil pluris faciat marito, an misericors sit, an fortis sit, an possit, si quid viro inciderit, mala una tolerare: si his bonis fuerit instructa, dotata est.

Non possumus una felices esse: quod solemus, una infelices erimus. Fac, inquit, quod imperat; nolo propter me patrem tuum offendas. Ibo, inquit, sola. Tu ibis? Quo, infelix? quas petitura regiones? 67M Est enim tibi aliquis locus? Pater tuus nobis maria praeclusit, meus terras.

7 CESTI PII. Solent qui coguntur a patribus ut uxores ducant illa dicere: "non sumus etiam nunc apti nuptiis." Ego contra refugio uxorem quia uxorius sum.

ARELLI FUSCI patris. Inpotens malum est beata uxor. Cum inmensum pondus auri orba attulerit, cum pecunia arcas nostras oneraverit, quid aliud quam

---

[1] uxores—habuere *Gertz:* duxere—haerem (aeram *V*).

have had wives without dowries, some have failed to
get the stated sum, some have been content with
bought slaves, and, though they might have received
riches, have preferred to buy women to whom they
could grant liberty rather than sell their own. A 6
youth is being requested for adoption. If he wants
to go, he should enquire how many ancestors the old
man who seeks him has, what rank they are, what the
old man's wealth—whether he can knock himself
down at a sufficient price. Another man wants to
make a prey of childless old men, to rest his hopes
widely on the deaths of others; he should pore over
wills, examine income returns. But when he is in
search of a wife, he should see whether she loves the
idea of marriage to him, whether she rates nothing
above her husband, whether she is prone to pity,
brave, able to tolerate with her husband any ills that
may afflict him. If she is equipped with these ad-
vantages, she has her dowry.—

We cannot be fortunate together; we shall be unfortunate together—we are used to it.—She says:
" Do what he asks. I don't want you to offend your
father for my sake. I will go, alone." *You* will
go? Where, unhappy girl? What direction will you
take? Have you a place to go to? Your father has
barred the seas to us, mine the land.

CESTIUS PIUS. Men who are compelled by their 7
fathers to marry often say: " I am not yet suited to
marriage." But *I* shun a wife because I love my wife.

ARELLIUS FUSCUS SENIOR. A rich wife is a disaster
that cannot be regulated. When the orphan brings
a vast weight of gold, when she weighs down my
coffers with money, what else shall I be but a rich

beati serviemus? Altera filium dat tibi, altera patrimonium: pater, utra magis dives est? Locuples est,
pater, quam mihi concilias: o si scires quam dives et
haec fuisset! "Orba" inquit "est": et haec orba
est; inter duas orbas ea mihi curanda est magis quam
orbam ego feci.

8   Divisio. In hac controversia nihil litium fuit:
fere omnes consentiunt. Latro primam quaestionem
fecit: an pater propter matrimonium abdicare filium
possit, cum liberum cuique huius rei arbitrium sit.
Gallio subiecit huic: etiamsi potest imperare filio ut
uxorem ducat, an ei qui iam habet. Latro secundam
fecit: si ius est patri etiam propter matrimonium
abdicandi, an huic liberum non fuerit parere cum
iurasset. Hoc in haec divisit: an nemo iureiurando
teneatur quo per necessitatem adactus est; an
expleverit iusiurandum ducendo illam uxorem; an,
etiamsi non explevit, non teneatur religione qui
coactus aliquid contra iusiurandum facit: hunc autem
cogi a patre. Si per iusiurandum [facit hunc] [1] potest
parere patri, an debeat. Hic de meritis puellae et
moribus.

9   Colore hoc usus est Latro pro patre: *puellam non* 68M
misericordia motam, sed libidine, et ideo non esse beneficium. In argumentis eleganter hanc partem trac-

---

[1] *Deleted by Kiessling.*

---

[1] In the moral sense of riches.
[2] By being the cause of her leaving her father.
[3] Cf. *Decl.* p. 50.5–6 Ritter. In fact, *abdicatio* not being a

slave?—One girl brings you a son, the other a fortune: which is the richer, father? The one you are trying to win for me is rich; if only you knew how rich *this* one would have been![1]—"She is an orphan." So is the other. Of the two orphan girls, I must take more care of the one whom *I* made an orphan.[2]

Division

In this *controversia* there was no dispute, and pretty 8 well all agree. Latro's first question was: Can a father disinherit a son because of his marriage?—this being within the free choice of all.[3] To this Gallio added: Even if he can order his son to marry, can he so order a son who already has a wife? Latro's second was: If a father has a right to disinherit even for a marriage, was *this* son free to obey, having given his word? This he subdivided: Is anyone bound by an oath to which he was constrained?[4] Did the son completely fulfil his oath by marrying this woman?[5] Even if he did not, can someone be held to his oath if he does something contrary to it under compulsion? —and the son *is* under compulsion from his father. If within the terms of the oath he can obey his father, should he? Here he spoke on the services and character of the girl.

Latro used for the father this *colour*: the girl was 9 motivated not by pity but by lust—so it was no service she did. In arguing this, he elegantly treated this

legal act, there were no limits on the father's exercise of it; and his *patria potestas* included the right to withhold consent to his son's marriage.

[4] Cf. *C*. 4.8.
[5] That is, having done so, can he now leave her?

tavit: etiamsi beneficium dedisset, non esse sic referendam gratiam; deinde beneficium esse quod iudicio detur, non quod furore aut morbo.

Hispo Romanius alio colore dixit illam non amore adulescentis, sed odio patris sui secutam; voluit illi et amoris commendationem detrahere.

Buteo longe arcessito colore usus est; voluit enim videri non invito patre, sed secreto suadente, palam dissimulante totum hoc gestum; arte [1] illa [2] honestam condicionem nuptiarum inventam, cum alio nullo modo posset; neque enim aliter effugere illos potuisse nisi patiente patre. Sed aiebat Latro non esse tanti detrahere illi commendationem soluti adulescentis ut detraheretur invidia relicti patris.

Fuscus Arellius egregie declamavit; non enim propter nuptias orbae dimitti illam, sed, quamvis orba non esset, eici iussit. Non aliam sibi magis placere sed illam displicere dixit, et hoc quod Latro transcurrerat pressit: timere se puellam temerariam, inter piratas natam, inter piratas educatam, inpiam in patrem.

Gallio illud quod omnes scholastici transierunt dixit: timere se ne haec speculatrix esset et piratis occasiones omnes indicaret, aut certe ne videretur; nolle se suspectum esse rei publicae.

69

---

[1] arte *Gertz:* re.
[2] illa *ed.* (illa filiae *Gertz*)*:* illæ (illam *V*).

---

[1] The pirate.

point: even if she had done a service, there was no
need to repay her in this way; further, a service is
something done as an act of judgement, not as a
result of madness or disease.

Romanius Hispo used a different *colour*, saying that
the girl had followed him not because she loved the
youth but because she hated her father. He wanted
to deprive her of the credit even for love.

Buteo used a far-fetched *colour*: he wanted it to
seem that everything had happened not against the
will of the father,[1] but at his secret instigation,
though on the surface he pretended not to. By this
artifice an honourable match had been made that
would have been impossible otherwise. They could
not have escaped if the father had not allowed it.
But Latro said that to deprive her of the credit for 10
freeing the youth was too great a price to pay for her
losing the unpopularity resulting from her abandoning her father.

Arellius Fuscus declaimed excellently: his orders
were that the girl should be divorced, but not because
of the marriage to the orphan—she should be got rid
of even if the orphan didn't exist. It wasn't that he
liked another girl more; he didn't like this one. He
pressed a point skated over by Latro, that he was
afraid of this impulsive girl, born and bred amidst
pirates, who felt no sense of duty towards her own
father.

Gallio said something that all the schoolmen left
out, that he was afraid she might be a spy ready to let
the pirates know of any opportunity for plunder—or
she might be thought to be: and he didn't propose to
be suspect in the eyes of the state.

⟨Iulius Bassus ex altera parte hoc pressit, se⟩ [1] illi
iurasse; timuit ne puella videretur improbe iusiurandum exegisse: ne quid liberi sibi esset, adiecit iurasse
se per patrem.

11 Triarius dum sententiam puerilem captat, inepte
dixit iurasse se et per orbam. Aiebat enim Cestius
male deseri hanc orbam ⟨si per eam⟩ [2] etiam iurasset.
Latro aiebat ⟨alterum⟩ [3] quoque iusiurandum inep-
tum esse; nihil enim minus convenire quam aliquem
per patrem iurare patrem relicturae.

Omnes honestam mentem puellae dederunt,
omnes dixerunt eam misericordia motam, non amore.
Solus Pollio iudicio fecisse vult eam [etiam misericordia discessisse];[4] dixit enim illam non potuisse
cum piratis vivere; ut primam honestam occasionem
invenerit discedendi, discessisse.

12 Q. Haterius a parte patris pulcherrimam imaginem
movit: coepit enim subito quo solebat cursu orationis
describere, quasi exaudiret aliquem tumultum, vastari
omnia ac rapi, conburi incendiis villas, fugas agres-
tium; et cum omnia implesset terrore, adiecit: quid
exhorruisti, adulescens? socer tuus venit.

Glyconis valde levis [et greca] [5] sententia est: 70
καταπόντωσον τὸν ἴδιον γενέτορα·[6] ἔχομεν πατέρα.
Tolerabilem dixit illam rem, cum iurisiurandi vim

---

[1] *Supplied by Gertz.*
[2] *Supplied by Müller.*
[3] *Supplied by Vahlen.*
[4] *Deleted by Kiessling.*
[5] *Deleted by the editor.*
[6] γενέτορα *Bursian:* ΤΕΝΕΝΟΝΠ.

Julius Bassus, on the other side, pressed the point that he had sworn to her. He was afraid the girl might be thought to have exacted the oath by unfair means; to show he had no freedom left now, he added that he had sworn by his father.

Triarius, in search of a childish epigram, absurdly 11 said that he had also sworn by the orphan. Cestius said that he was not acting honourably in deserting the orphan if he had gone so far as to swear an oath by her. Latro said the other oath was absurd too; nothing was less appropriate than for someone to swear by his father to a girl who proposed to leave her father.

Everybody credited the girl with good intentions, everybody said her motive was pity, not love. Only [1] Pollio wanted her to have done it on a calculation; for, he said, she could not stand living with the pirates, and she left on the first honourable opportunity for leaving.

Quintus Haterius, for the father, drew a beautiful 12 picture. He began, with his usual [2] sudden flood of oratory, to describe, as though he heard some disturbance, universal devastation and plunder, villas burnt, peasants fleeing. And when he had filled the scene with terrifying details, he added: " Why are you afraid, young man? It is only your father-in-law arriving."

Glycon's epigram is very feeble: " Drown the man who begot you: we *have* a father." [3] He said something tolerable when he was describing the force of

[1] But cf. §9 above.
[2] Cf. *C.* 4 pr. 7.
[3] The youth is persuading the girl to help him: cf. §3.

THE ELDER SENECA

describeret: hoc esse quod foedera sanciret, quo
astringerentur exercitus: ὅρκος ἐστὶν πεῖσμα καὶ
παρὰ πειραταῖς πεπιστευμένον.

Artemon circa eundem sensum versatus est a parte
adulescentis; cum dixisset relictum patrem, adiecit:
λοιδόρει νῦν τὸν ἀρχιπειρατήν, τὸν μιαιφόνον, τὸν
ἱερόσυλον · πρόσθες, εἰ θέλεις, καὶ τὸν ἐπίορκον.

VII

A PIRATIS TYRANNICIDA DIMISSUS

Liberi parentes alant aut vinciantur.

Quidam alterum fratrem tyrannum occidit,
alterum in adulterio deprehensum deprecante
patre interfecit.   A piratis captus scripsit patri
de redemptione.   Pater piratis epistulam scripsit: si praecidissent manus, duplam se daturum.
Piratae illum dimiserunt.   Patrem egentem non
alit.

1   PORCI LATRONIS.   Da mihi epistulam esurientis
istius.   "Manus" inquit "praecidantur."   In 71

---

[1] See Cic. *Off.* 3.106 *seq.* on the sanctity of oaths: but *he*
excepts oaths sworn to pirates.

[2] The girl had abandoned her father to follow the young
man.   The speaker hints that, as far as oath-breaking was
concerned, there was nothing to choose between the pirate
and a father who encouraged his son to leave a wife he had
sworn to marry.

[3] Cf. *C.* 1.1 n.

[4] Tyrants were a Greek phenomenon; but the career of
Caesar presented parallels to them (cf. Cic. *ad Att.* 9.4 for

an oath; it was this that ratified treaties and bound armies: " An oath is a tie that even pirates respect."[1]

Artemon dealt with the same idea on the side of the youth. He said the father had been abandoned, and added: " Now abuse the pirate chief, the murderer, the temple-robber; add, if you wish, the breaker of his oath."[2]

7

THE TYRANNICIDE THE PIRATES LET GO

Children must support their parents, or be imprisoned.[3]

A man killed one of his brothers, a tyrant.[4] The other brother he caught in adultery and killed despite the pleas of his father. Captured by pirates, he wrote to his father about a ransom. The father wrote a letter to the pirates, saying that he would give double if they cut off his hands. The pirates let him go. The father is in need; the son is not supporting him.[5]

For the son

PORCIUS LATRO. Give me the letter of this hungry father. He says: " Let his hands be cut off." May

declamations concerning tyrants that Cicero found relevant in 49 B.C.), and tyranny was a favourite subject in the schools under the Empire (satirised by Petr. 1.3). Seneca the younger gives us a stock tyrant in the Lycus of the *Herc. Fur.*, while Tacitus injected something of the schools into his portrait of Tiberius (see B. Walker, *The Annals of Tacitus* [Manchester U.P., 1952], 149 *seq.*, 204 *seq.*).

[5] A more complex version of this theme reappears in *Decl.* 5.

quamvis corporis partem potius saevitia incurrat:
cetera membra mea sunt, manus publicae sunt.
Numquid ⟨nimium⟩ [1] peto tyrannicida? Talem me
dimittite qualem a piratis recepistis. Non habeo
quod de fortuna queri possim mea: qui manus meas
⟨praecidi voluit ad manus meas⟩ [2] confugit. "*Si
praecideritis*" inquit "*manus*." *Si irasceris, scribe
potius: "si occideritis"*: *tyrannicida exitum tyranni
rogo. Non timeo ne quas manus piratae solverunt iudices*
2 *alligent.* Ex omnibus quae mihi fortuna terra
marique privatim mala publiceque congessit, [tyran-
num adulterumque piratas] [3] nihil expertus sum
durius quam patrem: tyrannus cum timeret manus
meas, non praecidit; iniuria matrimonii nihil abstulit
corpori; piratae, quasi beneficio meo viverent, gratis
miseriti sunt: unum hostem inexorabilem habui. O
felicem rem ⟨publicam⟩,[4] quod sublato inimico non
ante tyrannidem navigavi! "Genui" inquit
"⟨te⟩,[5] educavi": nempe istud beneficium et
tyranno praestitisti et adultero. Has manus si per
te redimere non potes, rem publicam appella. 72
Adulter cum manibus sepultus, tyrannus cum manibus proiectus est. ⟨In⟩ [6] magnis sceleribus iura
naturae intereunt: non magis tu pater es quam illi
fratres. Audite novam captivi vocem: tutus sum, si

[1] *Supplied by Gertz (after* num).
[2] *Supplied by Müller.*
[3] *Gloss enumerating the evils, deleted by Haase.*
[4] *Supplied by Bursian.*
[5] *Supplied by Gertz.*
[6] *Supplied by Rebling.*

his cruelty fall on any other part of my body than
that; the rest of my limbs belong to me—the hands
belong to the people.—Surely I don't ask too much—
after all I killed a tyrant: let me go in the state [1] you
received me in from the pirates.—I have no complaint
to make of my luck; the man who wanted my hands
cut off has taken refuge—with my hands.—" If you
cut off his hands," he writes. If you are angry, write
rather: " If you kill him "; I killed a tyrant—what I
ask is a tyrant's end.—I am not afraid that judges
will chain hands that pirates loosed.—Of all the evils 2
which fortune has heaped up for me on land and sea,
in public and in private, I have found nothing harsher
than my father. The tyrant was afraid of my hands,
but he did not cut them off; the injury done to my
marriage did not remove any part of my body; the
pirates—as though their life was due to my deed—
took pity on me, and made no charge; I only had
one inexorable enemy.—How happy for the commonwealth that, having rid myself of my enemy,[2] I did
not sail off before the tyrant came to power!—" I
begot you," he says, " and brought you up." That
was what you did for a tyrant and an adulterer.—If you
cannot ransom these hands by yourself, appeal to the
commonwealth.—The adulterer was buried with his
hands, the tyrant flung to the dogs with his.—In
great crimes the rights granted by nature perish;
you are no more my father than they were my
brothers.—Hear a strange utterance from a captive:

[1] i.e. unmutilated. The son addresses the judges (though
his hands are now menaced by chains rather than the knife).
[2] The adulterous brother. Latro assumes that this killing
came first, despite the implication of the theme.

pater meus nihil habet. Quidquid habes, pro redemptione filii mitte; non est quod timeas: non
deerunt tibi alimenta, cum dixeris ⟨te⟩ [1] tyrannicidae
patrem. *Pro adultero filio ⟨rogasti; pro tyrannicida
non⟩ [2] rogas: quaerite nunc quomodo tyranni fiant.*

3 CESTI PII. Cedo mihi epistulas patris: quaeris
unde habeam cum mihi nullas miseris? "*Duplam
dabo* pecuniam": *apparet, pro unico filio rogat.*
"*Duplam* pecuniam *dabo*": *unam* [pecuniam dabo
iam] [3] summam *pro filio, alteram pro tyrannicida.* "*Si
manus praecideritis*": *hoc ne* ⟨in⟩ [4] *adulteros quidem
licet.* "Non habui pecuniam." Sed rogare illos
potes et audacter roga: in misericordes piratas incidi.
Quare non alo? quia captum filium tuum—[agere] [5]
parum est si dixero non redemisti. Alere non possum, perdidi manus. Non credis? epistulas lege.
Duplam pecuniam dabas, avaris dabas, piratis dabas:
sic excusabant piratae ipsi se mihi cum praeciderent
manus: "pater iussit" aiebant: "magnum facinus
4 est, sed magno licet." "Egens sum" inquit. Mentiris. Cedo mihi patris mei censum. "Quid ergo?
ales patrem?" Dimissus fortasse promittam, cum 73M
rogaveris: nihil paciscor. *Etiamnunc manus meas
petis? Nega tuam esse epistulam, et habes argumentum*

---

[1] *Supplied by Bursian.*
[2] *Supplied by Müller after Schultingh.*
[3] *Deleted by Schultingh.*
[4] *Supplied by Haase and Bursian.*
[5] *Deleted by Thomas.*

" I am safe, so long as my father has no money."—
Whatever you have, send it to ransom your son; there
is nothing to be afraid of: you will not go short of
food if you say you are father of a tyrannicide.—You
put in a word then for an adulterer son, but you put
in none now for a tyrannicide: now ask how tyrants
are made!

CESTIUS PIUS. Give me my father's letter. Do 3
you ask where I got it?—for you sent me none.
" I will give twice the money." It's obvious—he's
begging for his only son. " I will give twice the
money." Half qua son, half qua tyrant slayer. " If
you cut his hands off." This is not permitted even as
a punishment for adulterers.—" I didn't have the
money." [1] But you can beg them—you can beg
them boldly: it is pirates prone to pity I have fallen
in with.—Why don't I support you? Because you—
it's insufficient if I say you did not ransom your son
when he was a prisoner. I cannot support you—I
have lost my hands. Don't you believe me? Read
your letter. You offered double the money, you
offered it to greedy men, you offered it to pirates.
This was the excuse the pirates themselves gave
when they came to cut off my hands. " Your father
ordered it," they said. " It is a great crime—but the
price is high."—" I am in need," he says. You lie. 4
Give me my father's income figure. " Well then? [2]
Will you support your father? " Perhaps if I were
loosed, I should promise at your request: I make no
bargain.—Are you still after my hands? [3]—Say it

---

[1] This seems a strange excuse, in view of the theme.
[2] The father speaks, after the son has seen the census-rating.
[3] This time to chain them.

—*dic: ego rogare etiam pro adultero soleo.* " Qui non aluit " inquit " patrem adligetur ": plus de manibus meis timui.

CORNELI HISPANI. Quid me rogarit pater nescio: publica vindicta cruentum gladium privato tyranno impressi. Captum me piratae nihil amplius quam alligaverunt. "Duplam pecuniam dabo." Quid? plus polliceris quam petitur? Unde tantas patrimoni vires habes? Etiamnunc tamquam ⟨de⟩[1] tyranni arca loqueris? Corrupit frater uxorem meam, quam nec tyrannus violaverat. Ut pretium piratae constituerunt, gavisus sum: " quam locuples est pater! poterat dare etiamsi duplam poposcissent." *Remiserunt me rei publicae cum manibus, patri cum epistulis.*

5 POMPEI SILONIS. Pactus sum de redemptione, scripsi patri: quicumque pro tyrannicida vestro pependistis, certum habeo, solliciti optastis ut hae litterae ad patrem pervenirent. "Egeo" inquit. Sic subito? quod ex toto emi non debet, duplo emit.

ARELLI FUSCI patris. Causam meam tenui apud eos qui nihil debebant manibus meis. Tunc primum

<hr>

¹ *Supplied by early editors.*

<hr>

¹ An argument supporting your denial of the authenticity of the letter, viz. that you normally beg for your sons when they're in trouble. ² When a captive of the pirates.

³ When he asked me not to kill my adulterous brother (the "private tyrant").

⁴ With the implication that the father profited by the power of his son.

⁵ Inconsistent with the last epigram but one. But, as Bornecque points out, Seneca may be quoting from declamations spoken on different occasions.

isn't your letter, and you have an argument [1]—say: "I am used to begging—even on behalf of adulterers."—He says: "Let him be bound who failed to support his father." I feared [2] more for my hands.

CORNELIUS HISPANUS. I don't know what my father begged me: [3] I plunged a sword bloody with a public punishment into a private tyrant.—When I was captured, the *pirates* merely bound me.—"I shall give twice the money." What? You promise more than is asked? Where do you get such vast hoards of wealth? Can it be that you speak as though you still controlled a tyrant's coffers? [4]—My brother violated my wife—whom even the tyrant had not violated.—When the pirates fixed the price, I rejoiced: "How rich my father is! [5] He could have given it even if they'd asked double."—They sent me back to the commonwealth with my hands—and to my father with his letter.

POMPEIUS SILO. I made a bargain about the 5 ransom, and wrote to my father. I am sure that all those of you who were in suspense for your tyrant-killer prayed anxiously that the letter should reach my father.—"I am in need," he said. So suddenly? —What he shouldn't buy at all, he is ready to buy at twice the cost.

ARELLIUS FUSCUS SENIOR. I won my case before people [6] who owed nothing to my hands.—My father complains he is in need only now he has seen my hands.[7]—What wonder if the pirates did not think it

---

[6] i.e. the pirates, whom the son persuaded to let him go. The present judges, in contrast, owe a lot to the son, and should be even more sympathetic.

[7] Seen, that is, that his previous plot has failed.

egere ⟨se⟩ [1] queritur iste cum manus meas vidit.
Quid mirum si non putaverunt turpe piratae accipere
mercedem quam pater dabat? Ades, pietas; si 74M
sancte vixi, si innocenter, effice ut iste manus meas
qui odit desideret. Tarde mihi epistula solvi videbatur. *Hoc* prorsus *ad fabulas* [2] repleto sceleribus
*nostris saeculo deerat ut narraretur aliquis solutus a
piratis, adligatus a patre.*

6 BLANDI. Hic, qui unde vivat non habet, quam care
tyrannicidas vestros emancat! Quid ais, pirata fili,
piratarum magister, *eius crudelitatis emptor cuius nec
pirata venditor* est?

ROMANI HISPONIS. " Pater piratis salutem ": hanc
eripis filio. *" Duplam dabo ": quid necesse est? potui
vilius solvi. " Ut praecidatis manus." Obstipuerunt
piratae, et* cum dimitterent *dixerunt: " indica patri* tuo
non omnia piratas vendere."

MENTONIS. Adhuc, iudices, tamquam pro meis
manibus egi; verum confitendum: vobis remissae
sunt. Exhibeo, res publica, piratarum depositum
tibi: manus hae tuae salvae ad te perlatae sunt.
Fac quod voles: illud unum rogo, si peccaverunt,
cuilibet alii vinciendas trade: si isti trades, sic alli-
gabit quomodo solvit: praecidet.

---

[1] *Supplied by Thomas.*
[2] ad fabulas *E :* fabulis.

dishonourable to receive a price that a father was willing to pay?—Stand by me, my sense of duty! If I have lived purely and innocently, ensure that this man who hates my hands should feel the need of them.—I thought the letter was being opened slowly.[1]—This is what was needed to complete the legends of an age packed with our crimes, that it should be told how someone released by pirates was imprisoned by his father.

BLANDUS. This man who has nothing to live on, 6 how much he pays for the mutilation of the man who killed your tyrant! What do you say, you plunderer of your son, you mentor of pirates, who are willing to buy a cruelty not even a pirate will sell?

ROMANIUS HISPO. " A father to the pirates, good health." That is just what you wrest from your son. " I will give double." What need? I could have got my release cheaper. " To cut off his hands." The pirates were staggered, and when they let me go they said: " Tell your father that pirates do not have everything for sale."

MENTO. Up to now, judges, I have pleaded as though for *my* hands. But I must confess it: it was for *your* sake they were spared. I show you, my country, what was put in safe keeping with the pirates; these are *your* hands, sent safe to you. Do what you will. All I ask is that if they sinned you should give them to any other to be bound. If you give them to *him*, he will bind them the way he freed them—he will cut them off.

[1] Or: " a long time was passing before the letter was opened." In either case a suspenseful extract from Fuscus' narrative.

7 ALFI FLAVI. Adhuc *qualem optem patrem nescio.*
Divitem? debilitat. Egentem? adligat. Neutrum mani-
bus meis expedit. " Duplam dabo ut manus praecidatis ": filium minus crudelem habuisti.

MARULLI. Ut adlata est epistula [qu(a)e],[1] coep- 75M
erunt iam me piratae solvere; ut recitata dupla in
epistula pecunia est, " hic est " inquam " pater quem
vobis laudaveram ".

TRIARI. *Ubi est patrimonium tuum* illud *quod tyran-*
nos instruit, quod adulteros facit? ubi est ? Certe in me
nil inpendisti.

8 Pars altera. IULI BASSI. Infelix futura est etiam
victoria mea: si non tenuero causam, fame moriar; si
tenuero, hoc tantum consequar, ne fame moriar.
Duxi uxorem nimium fecundam: *peperit mihi tria*
nescio quae *prodigia* variis generibus *inter se,* [et] [2]
iudices, *furentia: alium qui patriam posset opprimere,*
alium qui fratrem, alium qui patrem. Testor, iudices,
omnes cives meos: una servivimus, nemo tyrannidem
me uno sensit magis. Argumentum habeo maximum
quod vivo: non pepercissetis mihi si putassetis me
patrem tyranni. Dum inter se pugnant, vicit res

---

[1] *Omitted by early editors.*
[2] *Deleted by Novák. But the text is uncertain.*

ALFIUS FLAVUS. As yet I do not know what sort of 7
father to pray for. A rich one? He maims me. A
poor one? He chains me. Neither process is kind
to my hands.—" I will give double if you cut off his
hands." You had a son [1] who was less cruel.

MARULLUS. When the letter was brought, the
pirates at once set about freeing me. When the bit
about the doubled price was read out, I said: " This
is the father whose praises I sang to you."

TRIARIUS. Where is that fortune of yours that
equips tyrants, that makes adulterers? Where is it?
Certainly you spent nothing on me.

The other side

JULIUS BASSUS. Even my victory is going to turn 8
out unlucky. If I don't win my case, I shall die of
hunger. If I do, the only advantage will be that I
won't die of hunger. I married a wife who was all too
fertile: she bore me three indescribable monsters,
whose rage they directed in various ways at each
other—one capable of wronging his country, one his
brother, one his father. I call all my fellow-citizens
to witness, judges: we were all slaves together, but
no-one felt the tyranny more than I. My strongest
proof is that I live; you would not have spared me if
you had thought me the father of the tyrant.[2]—They
fought among themselves—and the commonwealth

---

[1] The tyrant!
[2] A vivid way of saying: If you thought I had profited
from my relationship with the tyrant or had any affection for
him.

publica. Reliqui duo, quia non poterant in nos, inter se tyrannidem exercuerunt. Habebat iste nescio quam uxorem, quam in arce cognoverat. Si alligare
9 te possem, proficiscentem alligassem. Non opus est tibi magna inpensa ad sustinendum patrem: magna mihi omnia sunt; tu mecum alimenta partire. Nolo 7ℓ me tam bene alas quam ego te alui; nolo ignoscas mihi: quidquid passus es, quidquid timuisti, patiar: posce flagella, scinde rugas. Ustus es? subice ignes, semimortuam hanc faciem, quae tantum in contumeliam suam spirat, quia extingui non potest, exure. Si parum est, fac quod ais ne piratas quidem fecisse, manus praecide. Exhibeo tibi. Hae sunt illae quae quidlibet scribunt. Ubi est gladius tuus? stringe. Tyranno licuit vulnere mori; adulter uno ictu breviter confectus est: pater te pro beneficio similem sortem rogo. Ne tu quidem apud piratas famem timuisti. Neminem tyrannus sic torsit.

10 PORCI LATRONIS. Fili, nihil amplius quam famem deprecor; si tamen inexorabilis es, illud pro beneficio peto, ut aut tamquam adulter moriar aut tamquam tyrannus. Par erat utriusque fortuna illo tempore: [ut] tu alligatus eras, ego in senectute immobilis et vincto simillimus; tu in solitudine mei, ego in omnium meorum solitudine; tu lucem non videbas, ego etiam oderam. Hoc unum inter nos interest, quod tu etiam a piratis cibum accepisti.

BLANDI. Deprecabar non pro adultero sed pro

---

1 For the tyrant's citadel see Mayor on Juv. 10.307.

won. The remaining two, not being able to lord it
over us, lorded it over each other.—This one had
some wife or other, whom he had got to know in the
castle.[1]—If I could bind you, I should have bound you
as you set off.—You don't need to spend a lot support- 9
ing your father; everything counts as a lot in my
eyes; share your food with me. I don't want you to
support me as well as I supported you. I don't want
you to forgive me. Whatever you have suffered,
whatever you have feared, *I* will endure. Call for
whips, tear my wrinkled flesh. Were you branded?
Bring fire to bear, use flames to finish off this half-
dead shape that breathes only to suffer insult—for it
cannot be snuffed out. If that is not enough, do
what you say that even the pirates did not do—cut
off my hands. Here they are—these are the hands
that will write *anything*. Where is your sword?
Draw it. The tyrant was allowed to die with a single
wound; the adulterer was swiftly despatched at
a single stroke; your father asks for the boon of a
like end. Not even you, among the pirates, had
starvation to fear. The tyrant tortured no-one like
this.

PORCIUS LATRO. Son, I protest at nothing beyond 10
my hunger. But if you are inexorable, I claim as a
boon that I should either die like an adulterer or like
a tyrant.—Both of us, at that time, had a like fate.
You were in chains, I immobile in my old age and very
similar to a chained man. You were without me, I
was without all my sons; you could not see the light,
I even hated it. The only difference between us is
that you got food—even from pirates.

BLANDUS. My prayers were not for the adulterer

domo, ne fratrem occideret, tyrannicidam inquinaret, patrem respergeret. Roganti mihi et has interponenti manus paene praecidit. Haec sententia deridebatur a Latrone tamquam puerilis: hoc ei provisum est, ut aliquem ex suis reliquisse videatur quem 7'
non occiderit.

VIBI RUFI. Hae nempe scripserunt epistulam manus: praebeo; praecide et ale.

POMPEI SILONIS. "Liberi parentes alant aut vinciantur." Ad te legem meam transfero: licet alliges, et alas.

11 DIVISIO. Fere ⟨omnes⟩ [1] hac usi sunt divisione: an lex causam nec patris nec filii aestimet, sed omnis pater a filio alendus sit. ⟨Latro⟩ [2] dixit *legem hanc pro malis patribus scriptam esse, bonos etiam sine lege ali.* Si non omnes alendi sunt, an hic alendus sit. Hanc quaestionem Latro in haec divisit: an alendus sit quod filium a piratis non redemit: hoc loco quaesit an non potuisset redimere, an noluisset; deinde: an alendus sit etiamsi praecidi filii manus voluit; novissime: an praecidi voluerit.

12 Hispo Romanius separatim quasi iuris quaestionem fecit: an qui non redemit filium non possit ab eo alimenta petere. Sed hoc utraque quaestio continet, ut aiebat Gallio, et prior, in qua quaeritur an omnis

---

[1] *Supplied here by Müller.*
[2] *Supplied by Haase.*

but for the family—that he should not kill his brother, spoil his record as killer of tyrants, stain his father's reputation. When I begged, raising these hands to stop him, he almost cut them off.—The following epigram was jeered at by Latro as childish: His object is to be seen to have left one of his family whom he has not killed.[1]

VIBIUS RUFUS. These hands wrote the letter: I stretch them out. Cut them off—and feed me.

POMPEIUS SILO. " Children must feed their parents or be bound." I transfer my rights to you; bind me, but feed me too.

Division

Almost everyone used this division: Does the law 11 insist that every father is fed by his son without taking into account the circumstances either of the father or of the son? Latro said this law was written with bad fathers in mind—good fathers get supported even without a law. If not all are to be fed, is this one? This point Latro subdivided thus: Should he be supported seeing that he did not ransom his son from pirates? Here he asked whether he was unable to ransom him, and whether he was unwilling to. Then: Should he be supported even if he wanted his son's hands cut off? Finally, *did* he want them cut off?

Romanius Hispo raised separately a sort of question 12 of the letter of the law: Can a man who does not ransom his son claim sustenance from him? But, as Gallio said, this is contained in both the previous

[1] That is, the son, in not supporting his father, was not positively killing him as he had killed his brothers.

pater alendus sit; dicitur enim: quid si quis filium excaecaverit? quid si quis non redemerit? et cum ad alteram quaestionem ventum est, in qua quaeritur an hic pater alendus sit, nihil aliud potest dici quare non alatur quam quod non redemit, quam quod duplam promisit ut manus praeciderentur. Graecorum improbam quaestionem satis erit in eiusmodi controversiis semel aut iterum adnotasse: an in tyrannicidam uti pater hac lege possit; quasi sacras et publicas manus esse in quas sibi ne piratae quidem licere quicquam putent. Nostri hoc genus quaestionis submoverunt.

13 Silo Pompeius non eis tantum usus est quibus ceteri, cum diceret non debere hunc patrem ali quod non redemisset filium et quod praecidi manus filio voluisset, sed a privatis causis transit ad publicam causam; dixit enim non debere ali hominem perniciosum rei publicae, qui tyrannum filium habuisset, qui non occidisset, qui desideraret amissum, qui vindicaret; et negavit ullam aliam illi causam esse persequendi tyrannicidam nisi libertatem publicam et descripsit mores hominis impii, cruenti, quia per liberos non posset per piratas tyrannidem exercentis: quae ut liberius diceret, patronum filio dedit.

Et illud in hac parte laudatum est [a] [1] Silone declamante: coeperat hoc tractare, non debere ali tyranni

---

[1] *Deleted by Bursian.*

points: the first in which enquiry is made whether every father is to be supported (for one says: What if a father has blinded his son? what if he has failed to ransom him?); and when one comes to the second point, whether *this* father is to be supported, no other reason for his not being supported can be given than that he did not ransom his son and promised double if his hands were cut off. An invalid point raised by the Greeks it will be sufficient to note once or twice in *controversiae* of this sort: Can a father use this law against a tyrant-killer? Those hands over which not even pirates think they have any power are (they say) as it were holy, the possession of the state. Our declaimers have got rid of this type of point.

Pompeius Silo did not limit himself to the points 13 used by the others, such as that this father should not be supported because he had not ransomed his son and because he had wanted his son's hands cut off, but passed from private reasons to a public one: he said that no support should be given to a man who was a danger to the state, who had had a tyrant for a son, who had failed to kill him, who regretted his loss, who tried to avenge him; and he said that he had no other reason for assailing the killer of the tyrant except his hatred for the people's liberty. He elaborated on the character of the man, impious, bloody, exerciser of a tyranny by means of pirates because he could not exercise it by means of his sons. In order to be able to put this more freely, he represented the son as having an advocate to speak for him.

There was applause at this part of Silo's declamation. He had begun to deal with the point that the father of a tyrant should not be supported—he should

patrem; omnibus faventibus illum fame necandum; et cum diu pressisset illum tyranni patrem esse, adiecit: aude postulare ut illud tibi prosit, quod tyrannicidae pater es. Blandus hunc sensum, cum postero die declamaret, in ironiam vertit, et, cum obiecisset quod tyranni pater esset, adiecit: nolite illum aversari; habet quod adponat: et adulteri pater est.

14 Colorem pro patre alius alium introduxit. Fuscus iratum se illi confessus est fuisse, quod fratrem in conspectu patris occidisset, et huic loco vehementer 7⁹ institit, quom nemo hoc tyrannus, nemo pirata fecisset. " Iratus " inquit " ob hoc ipsum fui, quod hoc scelere etiam tyrannicidium inquinaveras; adparet te morbo quodam adversus tuos furere." Et servavit hunc actionis tenorem: " iratus fui hodieque irascor nec queror ": nec se demisit in preces aut rogavit, sed iure patrio usus est. Illud ad excusandam epistulae crudelitatem adiciebat: scripsi piratis non eo animo ut manus tibi praeciderentur, sed ut exprobrarem tibi cruentatas in conspectu patris fraterno sanguine manus. Tuto autem scribebam; *sciebam* enim *piratas non facturos nisi pecuniam accepissent*, quam non mittebam: denique nec praeciderunt. *Et si sperassent, utique praecidissent:* sed apparuit illas epistulas irascentis esse, non promittentis. In ultimo descripsit quam miser futurus esset alimenta acci-

be starved off to everyone's satisfaction; and, after dwelling for some time on the fact that he was a tyrant's father, he said: " Dare to ask that your being father of a tyrannicide should stand you in good stead." When Blandus declaimed next day, he gave this idea an ironical twist, reproaching him with being the tyrant's father and adding: " Don't shrink from him. He has something to set against that: he is father of an adulterer also."

Different *colours* were advanced on the father's **14** behalf. Fuscus declared that he had been angry with his son, because he killed his brother in their father's sight; and he pressed strongly on the point, for no tyrant, no pirate would have behaved thus. " I grew angry," he said, " just because by this crime you had tainted even your killing of a tyrant; it is clear that your mad rage against your family is a sort of disease." And he preserved this course throughout his plea: " I was angry, and I am angry today, and I do not complain." He didn't lower himself to prayers or entreaties, but used his rights as a father. This was his excuse for the cruelty of his letter: " I did not write to the pirates with the intention that your hands should be cut off, but to reproach you with the hands that you had stained with the blood of your brother as your father looked on. I was quite safe to write thus: I knew the pirates would not do it if they did not get the money—and I wasn't sending it. In fact, they did not cut the hands off—and if they had had any hope of the money they would certainly have done it: but it was obviously the letter of an angry man—not a man who was making a promise." At the end he described how wretched he would be re-

piens ⟨ab⟩ [1] illis manibus quas paulo ante spectaverit fratrem occidentes, et adiecit, quod aiebat praeceptore suo dicente summa cum admiratione exceptum, illud Homeri ⟨in⟩ Priamo dictum: [2]

⟨καὶ κύσε χεῖρας
δεινάς, ἀνδροφόνους, αἵ οἱ πολέας ἀτάνον υἷας.⟩ [3]

15   Silo Pompeius et ipse iram fassus est: aiebat enim non habiturum fidem si negasset iratum fuisse; sed irae causam non dixit quam Fuscus; transeundas aiebat eas offensas quibus ille gloriaretur; hanc causam posuit, quod relictus esset ab unico filio, quod invito se navigasset, cum videret ⟨se⟩ [4] senem, orbum, iam paene egentem: iam tum illum fugisse ne aleret; et ad preces patrem deduxit et rogavit in epilogo filium.

Et *Sparsum* hoc colore declamasse *memini, hominem inter scholasticos sanum, inter sanos scholasticum.*

16   Cestius colore longe alio usus est; dixit *non iram fuisse illam patris, sed calliditatem:* " *Non habebam* " inquit " *unde redimerem. Quem rogarem* pecuniam *in tam avara civitate, in qua ne filii quidem patres alunt? Usus sum consilio: sciebam piratas non crudeles esse, sed avaros.* Volui *efficere ut* et *desperarent posse* illum *redimi* et propter hoc supervacuum [et cum] [5] futurum

---

1 *Supplied by Kiessling.*
2 in Priamo dictum *Thomas:* priamo aptum.
3 *Supplied by Faber.*
4 *Supplied by Gertz.*
5 *Deleted by Müller.*

ceiving support from the hands he had not long ago
seen killing a brother, and added what he said was
received with great admiration when his teacher declaimed them, the words of Homer on Priam:

> " And he kissed the terrible hands,
> Killers of men, which had slain so many of his sons." [1]

Pompeius Silo, too, declared that he had been 15
angry. He said he would not be believed if he said
he had not been. But he did not give the same
reason as Fuscus for his anger. He said that one
should set aside the causes for offence of which Fuscus
made so much. His own reason was that he had been
abandoned by his only son, that his son had gone to
sea against his wishes, though he saw that he was old,
bereaved, already approaching poverty. The motive
for his flight was even then to avoid supporting him.
He made the father beg, and in the epilogue he
appealed to the son.

I recall that Sparsus also declaimed with this
colour; among the schoolmen he ranked as sane,
though among the sane he ranked as a schoolman.

Cestius employed a quite different *colour*. He said 16
that the father had been not angry but cunning. " I
did not have," he said, " the money for the ransom.
Whom could I ask for money in so greedy a country—
where not even sons will support their fathers? I
acted with a purpose; I knew that the pirates were
not cruel but avaricious. I wanted to make sure they
despaired of getting a ransom for him, and so let him
go as useless for that purpose. Whether my plan was

---

[1] *Il.* 24.478–9. Priam is begging Achilles to allow the
ransom of the body of Priam's son, Hector.

dimitterent. *An prudenter cogitaverim nescio; interim feliciter cogitavi:* post epistulas illas quas accusat dimissus est.''

Latro totum se ab istis removit coloribus, et advocavit vires suas tanto totius actionis *impetu* ut attonitos homines tenuerit; hoc enim colore usus est: Nescio quid scripserim. Olim iam mihi *excussa mens est. Ex quo vidi filium unum in arce, alterum in adulterio, tertium in parricidio,* ex quo respersus sum fili morientis sanguine, ex quo *relictus* sum *solus, orbus, senex,* odi meos. *Hic color* illius viribus *adprobandus est; quanta enim vi opus est ut aliquis accusando se* 81M *miserabilem faciat!*

17 Albucius omnes colores miscuit, et, ut hoc liberum esset, patronum patri dedit nec voluit narrare. A propositione coepit: alimenta pater a filio petit; deinde cum ad defendendum venit quod scripsit duplam se daturum si manus praecidissent, primum Latroniano colore usus est: hoc, inquit, respondeo: nescit quid fecerit, ⟨in⟩ insaniam malis actus est. Hic philosophumenon locum introduxit quomodo animi magnis calamitatibus everterentur; deinde anthypophoran sumpsit: mentiris; ille vero iratus fuit. Cogis, inquit, me dicere iratum tibi merito fuisse. Exsecutus est omnia; hoc illi inter cetera obiecit, quod occupasse ⟨arcem⟩ fratrem suum ignorasset [aut dissimulavit], ut [1] tyrannicidio quoque

---

[1] occupasse arcem (*added by Faber*)—ut (*so Faber*) ed.: occupat—ait.

a sensible one, I don't know. However, my plan *did* turn out a lucky one; it was after the letter he accuses me of that he got released."

Latro kept quite clear of all these *colours*, and summoned up his powers in such a great flood throughout his speech that he kept his hearers in a state of astonishment. For this was the *colour* he used: " I don't know what I said in the letter. It is a long time since I went off my head. Since I saw one child in the castle, one an adulterer, the third a parricide, since I was spattered with the blood of a dying son, since I was left alone, childless, old, I have hated my family." This *colour* needs the support of all Latro's force to make it acceptable; for it requires a good deal of power for someone to make himself an object of pity by means of accusations.

Albucius mixed up all these *colours*, and, to make 17 this freely possible, gave the father an advocate, and decided against giving a narrative of the facts. He began from the statement: " A father seeks support from his son." Then, when he came to defending the fact that he wrote he would give double if the hands were cut off, he first used Latro's *colour*: " This is my reply. He does not know what it was he did. He has been driven mad by his misfortunes." Here he introduced a philosophical passage, on how minds are overthrown by great calamities. Then he posed an objection: " You lie. He was angry." His reply was: " You force me to say that he was justified in being angry with you "—and he went through all the details; among other things he charged him with not knowing that his brother had seized the castle: his idea was to deprive him of the credit even for his

eius commendationem detraheret.[1]   Deinde ad illum
colorem redit Cestianum: " Sed puto illum consilio
fecisse quae fecit.   Quid ergo ? quid iste tamen dicit ?
†quare scripsisse ?†   Nihil dicit; flet, mori vult, sed
non fame.''

18   In hac declamatione Albucius hanc sententiam
dixit dubiam inter admirantes et deridentes: panem
quem cani das patri non das ?

Glycon egregie dixit: ἐλεήσατε αὐτόν· υἱὸς[2]
κινδυνεύει πατέρα θρέψαι.

Gargonius fuit Buteonis auditor, postea scholae 82M
quoque successor, vocis obtusae sed pugnacissimae,
cui Barrus scurra rem venustissimam dixit: centum
raucorum vocem habes.   Hic putavit se vafrum
colorem excogitasse pro patre: Ego, inquit, dictavi:
" duplam dabo, si manus non praecideritis.''   Lib-
rario una syllaba excidit " non,'' et scripsit " si praecideritis.''   Digna res quae voce illa diceretur.

Artemon dixit: φιλότεκνε πάτερ, καὶ σοὶ τιμωρεῖν
ἀποκνεῖ τις;

Adaeus dixit: εἴδομεν ταχινὸν σκάφος. καὶ τίς
τῶν ἀντιώντων ἐν τούτῳ τῷ σκάφει πατήρ ἐστιν;[3]

Nicetes dixit: " διπλᾶ δώσω ἂν ἀποκόψητε τὰς
χεῖρας.'' ἐζήτουν οἱ πειραταί · μή τι ἐτυράννηαας: μή
τι ἐμοίχευσας;

---

[1] detraheret ed. after Haase: fratre.
[2] υἱὸς Gertz: MOC.
[3] The text of this epigram is very corrupt: Müller's version is
here printed.

tyrannicide. Then he came back to the *colour* used
by Cestius: " But I imagine he did what he did of set
purpose. Well then? But what does he say? Why
write?[1] He says nothing, he weeps, he wants to die
—but not of hunger."

In this declamation Albucius used an epigram dis-   18
puted between the admirers and the mockers:
" Don't you give your father the bread you give your
dog? "[2]

Glycon said, excellently: " Pity him—a son in
danger of having to support his father! "

Gargonius was a pupil of Buteo, and later successor
to his school, a man with a dim but combative voice
(the buffoon Barrus said a very pretty thing to him:
" You have the voice of a hundred hoarse men ").
This character imagined he'd thought up a crafty
colour on behalf of the father: " I was dictating: ' I
will give you double if don't cut off his hands.' The
scribe missed a syllable, and wrote: ' If you cut
. . .' " A thing worthy of being said by that *voice*!

Artemon said: " Father and lover of your children,
does someone hesitate to help even you?"[3]

Adaeus said: " We saw a swift ship. 'Which one
of those meeting us in this ship is your father?'"[4]

Nicetes said: " ' I will give double if you cut off his
hands.' The pirates enquired: ' Surely you haven't
been a tyrant? or an adulterer?'"

[1] This passage is corrupt.
[2] Cf. Quintilian 8.3.22: " In my youth there was praise for
the epigram ' Give a father bread,' and in the same case
' You feed even a dog.'"
[3] Presumably sarcastic.
[4] From the narrative: the father, of course, did not come.

VIII

TER FORTIS

Qui ter fortiter fecerit, militia vacet.

Ter fortem pater in aciem quarto volentem exire retinet; nolentem abdicat.

1 PORCI LATRONIS. Miserrimus pater, iam non viderem filium nisi abdicarem. Fortis plus quam legi 83M aut patri ⟨satis⟩ [1] est, tertio mihi non redit sed relatus est. *Quod patriae superest patri vindico.* Fugit me filius, et quidem ad hostem? Quousque pavidus proeliorum nuntios expectabo? Filii mihi vacationem peto.

CESTI PII. Abdico filium ut habeam. Non minus vacatio mea rei publicae profuit quam militia: duxi uxorem. (Sic descendit in narrationem.) Tertio audivi velut denuntiantes deos, faceret adulescens iam felicitatis suae finem. Ego advocationem in unam pugnam petii: accidat, inquam, quidquid timeo si illum amplius in aciem dimisero; cum diis pactus sum. "Non timeo" inquit: hoc est cur timeam. Obicitur mihi quod me filius oderit?

---

[1] *Supplied by Kiessling.*

---

[1] A declaimers' fiction (Bonner pp. 88–9), found also in Calp. Flacc. 15.

[2] He would be off at the war otherwise: cf. §3 Silo.

[3] Cf. Sen. *Agam.* 799: "victor timere quid potest?—quod non timet."

8

THREE TIMES A HERO

Anyone who has acted heroically three times
shall be exempt from military service.[1]

A father tries to stop a man who has acted
heroically three times and wants to go to fight a
fourth time. The son refuses; he disinherits
him.

For the father

PORCIUS LATRO. Unhappiest of fathers that I am, 1
I should not now be seeing my son were I not disinheriting him.[2]—Braver than the law or his father
requires, he did not return to me the third time: he
was brought back.—What his country has left I claim
for his father.—Does my son flee from me—and in the
direction of the enemy?—How much longer must I
await the news of battles with fear in my heart? I
seek leave for my son—for *my* sake.

CESTIUS PIUS. I disinherit my son in order not to
lose him.—*My* exemption profited the state as much
as my military service: I married a wife. (Thus he
passed to narrative.)—The third time I heard the
gods, apparently warning that my son should not
push his good luck any further. *I* sought a respite
for just one fight; " let whatever I fear take place,"
I said, " if I allow him to go to war after that." I
made a bargain with the gods.—" I am not afraid,"
he said. That is why *I* am afraid.[3]—Am *I* reproached
with my son hating me?

2   Arelli Fusci patris. *O me filio pugnante iam lassum!* Magna omina sunt: nihil hoc putas, quod viri fortis pater timeat? Miserum me: iam hosti nimis notus es, *iam pro te nescio quid etiam lex timet. Miraris si quod legi satis est patri nimis est?* " Numquid luxuriam " inquit " obicis? " Ego vero te etiam hortari possum in voluptates. Quousque duro castrorum iacebis cubiculo? quousque somnum classico rumpes? quousque cruentus vives? Simus hilares: trium victoriarum vota solvenda sunt. Tot acies sustinuisti, tot vulnera; possum cum re publica queri: sero dimitteris. Subinde audio te dicentem: 84¹ " malo gloriam quam vitam "; hoc ergo me exanimat, quod mori tibi tam facile est. Denique uno quiesce bello.

3   Pompei Silonis. *Causa mihi abdicandi est, ne sine filio vivam,* quem tam diu non viderem nisi abdicarem. *Abdicatio mea in potestate abdicati est.*

Romani Hisponis. Quid fatigante felicitatem molestius est? quid expectas donec castris eiciaris?

Mentonis. Erubescit res publica tam cicatricoso milite uti. Non oportet tantam virtutem sine successore concidere: ducenda uxor est²; sed iam nunc te admoneo ne unum tollas.³

Corneli Hispani. Non ante te retinere coepi quam dimisit res publica. Nullum iam tibi vulnus

---

¹ Cf. §16 and *C.* 7.3.10.
² As a body.
³ Or he might turn out to be a soldier too.

ARELLIUS FUSCUS SENIOR. O, how tired *I* am of my 2
son fighting!—The omens are portentous: do you
think it nothing that the father of a hero is afraid?—
Alas, now you are all too well-known to the enemy.
Now even the law feels a fear for you.—Are you
surprised if what is enough for the law is too much for
a father?—" Do you charge me with debauchery? "
he says. No, I am ready even to encourage you to
indulge in pleasures. How much longer will you lie
on that comfortless camp bed? How much longer
will the trumpet break into your sleep? How much
longer will you live stained with blood? Let us be
merry. The vows for three victories need paying.
You have endured so many fights, so many wounds.
I have a just complaint to the state—you are being
demobilised too late.—I often hear you say: " I
prefer glory to life." This then is what frightens me,
that you find death so easy.—At last—lie low in *one*
campaign.

POMPEIUS SILO. My reason for disinheriting is that 3
I want to avoid living without a son—whom I should
not have seen for so long a time if I were not disinheriting him.—Whether I disinherit is up to the
one I disinherit.

ROMANIUS HISPO. What is more troublesome than
someone who wearies his good fortune?[1] Why wait
till you are thrown out of the camp?[2]

MENTO. The state is ashamed to employ a soldier
who has so many scars.—Such virtue should not fall
without an heir. You must marry. But I warn you
here and now: don't raise a single son.[3]

CORNELIUS HISPANUS. I did not begin to keep you
back until the state released you.—No wound can

nisi per cicatricem inprimi potest. Adhuc diutius
fuisti cum hoste quam apud patrem: domi tantum
sanatus es.

IUNI OTHONIS patris. *Optimus virtutis finis est, antequam deficias desinere.*

4   Ex altera parte. . . . ter fortiter . . . *Certe pugnare abdicatis licet.*

ALBUCI SILI. Quis hic subitus insonuit tumultus?
Numquid imperator vocat? Venio. Plurimum in
prima acie laboravi. *Pudet me: ter victi militant.*

P. ASPRENATIS. Quousque, inquit, periclitaberis?
Bene habet, iudices: pater me putat dignum esse qui
salvus sim. *Senator post sexagesimum et quintum
annum in curiam venire non cogitur, non vetatur.* Prae-   85
torio licet praetexta toga uti festis aut sollemnibus
diebus: numquid necesse est? *Quidquid aut praemii
aut honoris nomine datur, in utramque partem licet;
alioqui desinit praemium esse, cui necessitas iungitur.*
Pareo tibi, pater, qui gloria nos inmortales fieri
5 dicebas, qui ex acie redeuntis vulnera osculabaris: ad
haec nova et diversa imperia subito me circumagi

---

[1] Cf. Sen. *Helv.* 15.4: " per ipsas cicatrices percussa es ";
Prov. 4.11.

[2] So Quintilian 12.11.3. It was said that Afer " malle . . .
deficere quam desinere."

[3] Particular point unclear.

[4] For the topic cf. *Decl.* p. 203.1 Ritter. For the age
contrast Sen. *Brev.* 20.4: " lex . . . a sexagesimo senatorem

mark you except through a scar.[1]—Up to now you have spent longer with the enemy than in your father's house. My house was a mere convalescent home for you.

JUNIUS OTHO SENIOR. The best end for virtue is to stop before you have to give up.[2]

The other side

. . . three times bravely . . . At least the dis- 4 inherited are allowed to fight.

ALBUCIUS SILUS. What is this sudden clamour? Isn't it the general calling? I am coming.—I have laboured much in the front rank.[3]—I am ashamed: men who have been *defeated* three times go on soldiering.

PUBLIUS ASPRENAS. " How much longer," he says, " will you endanger your life? " All is well, judges— my father thinks I deserve to survive.—A senator after his sixty-fifth year is not forced to come to the House—but he is not barred.[4] Someone of prae- torian rank may wear the *toga praetexta* [5] on holidays or feast-days: does he *have* to? Whatever is given as reward or honour allows a choice: otherwise, if com- pulsion attaches to it, it stops being a reward.—It is you I obey, father, you who used to say we become immortal by the glory we win, you who used to kiss my wounds when I came back from battle. Do you 5 think that I can suddenly switch to obeying these new

non citat " (see Mommsen, *Röm. Staatsrecht* 3.ii [1888] 917 n. 2).

[5] Toga with purple border worn by high magistrates and others (see Mommsen, *op. cit.* 1³[1887] 418 *seq.*, who seems to overlook this privilege for the ex-praetor).

putas posse? Non ita est: ille in nos dominatur affectus qui animum primus intravit. Luxuria, avaritia, desidia, invidia,[1] timor non dediscuntur, et cotidie omnia haec aut castigantur aut puniuntur: tam etiam vitiorum tenaces sumus. Crede mihi, pater: non sum mei iuris cum ille proelii clamor exortus est: invadere hostes libet, obstantis cuneos gladiis diducere; hic impetus, hic ardor animi domum tuam trinis hostium spoliis adornavit, huic supplicationes illas debes, propter hunc me etiam cum abdicas diligis. Non animus, non lingua constat; in alieno opere conprehensus sum; toga ipsa umeris 6 non sedet. Ad obsidendum hostem, ad occupandum castris locum, ad intercipiendos hostium commeatus ire iusseris: non animo⟨siorem videbis militem⟩;[2] 86 *otium imperas animo non otioso.* Quotienscumque *tumultus aliquis exortus est, in me omnium civium deriguntur oculi,* meas spectant manus; *et adhuc—verum dicendum est—nihil patria debet mihi: numquam pugnavi nisi coactus.* Credisne quicquam referre ubi simus, quem vitae cursum agamus? eadem pericula nos ubique circumstant et totidem ad mortem viae sunt. Interdum continuatus labor firmiores facit: saepe quod corroboraverat, desidia consumpsit.

---

[1] invidia *Müller:* iu(s)titia.
[2] *Supplied by Gertz and Müller.*

and different precepts? It is not so. The emotion that was the first to enter our minds is the one that holds sway over us. Luxury, avarice, sloth, envy, fear cannot be unlearned—and every day all these things are either reproved or punished, so tenacious are we even of our vices. Believe me, father, I cannot control myself when the familiar noise of battle has burst out. It thrills me to attack the enemy, to scatter the opposing ranks with the sword. It is this energy, this spirit that has decorated your house with three sets of spoils from the enemy. It is to this you owe those supplications;[1] it is because of this that, even as you disinherit me, you love me.— My mind, my tongue are disturbed; I am caught in a task that is foreign to me; the very toga does not sit well on my shoulder.[2] Order me to go and besiege 6 the enemy, seize a place for a camp, cut off the enemy supplies: you will see no soldier more spirited. You are enjoining leisure on a mind that is not suited for leisure.—Whenever some trouble has broken out, all the citizens look at me, look at my hands. And up to now (I must tell the truth) the state owes me nothing; I have never fought except under duress.— Do you believe it makes any difference where we are, what course of life we follow? The same dangers encompass us everywhere, and as many routes to death.[3]—Sometimes we are made stronger by continual hardship; often what labour has hardened sloth has undone.

---

[1] Days of celebration voted to victorious generals.

[2] i.e. speaking in court does not suit him.

[3] Cf. *C.* 7.1.9 and often elsewhere, e.g. Sen. *Ep.* 70.14, *Phaedr.* 475.

MARULLI. Sine me aliquod meritum in patriam conferre: *adhuc militia mea legis munus est.* Pugnabo et abdicatus, nec verebor ne inutilis sit opera mea patriae. *Athenienses abdicato vicerunt duce: quantum* inter me et illum *interest! ille abdicationem virtute delevit, ego merui.*

7 DIVISIO. Prima quaestio illa ab omnibus facta est vulgaris: an filius ob id quod sui iuris sit abdicari possit; deinde: an debeat; haec tota tractationis est.

Graeci illam quaestionem primam solent temptare, quam Romanae aures non ferunt: an vir fortis abdicari possit. Non video autem quid adlaturi sint quare non possit: nam quod et vir fortis est et totiens fortiter fecit non plus iuris illi adfert sed plus commendationis.

8 Colorem a parte patris quidam duriorem fecerunt; voluerunt enim videri invisum filio patrem: itaque illum malle cum hostibus vivere quam cum patre. 87M Paene omnes: esse adulescentem insatiabilem gloriae et propter ⟨id⟩ [1] ipsum patri et moderandum et continendum. Quidam ex toto ad patris indulgentiam refugerunt, et non disputaverunt hoc modo quo Silo Pompeius disputavit, qui sic divisit ut diceret: etiamsi patrem non haberes, desinere debebas; quia 9 patrem habes, desinere debes, quia pater vetat; aut illo modo quo Gallio, qui sic divisit hanc partem: hoc

---

[1] *Supplied by Haase and Bursian.*

---

[1] The story of the disinheritance of Themistocles is told, e.g., by Val. Max. 6.9 ext. 2 and Nepos *Them.* 1, denied by Plut. *Them.* 2 (Busolt, *Gr. Gesch.* 2.640 n. 2).

[2] They appealed entirely to emotion: see below, §11.

Marullus. Allow me to do some service to the state. Up to now my campaigning has been a duty owed to the law.—I will fight even if I am disinherited, without being afraid that my action is profitless to the state. The Athenians conquered with a leader who had been disinherited.[1] What a gulf between him and me! He cancelled disinheritance by his courage, I merited it by mine.

Division

The first question put by everyone is the common 7 one: Can a son be disinherited for something that is within his rights? Then: Should he be? This is wholly a matter of treatment.

The Greeks tend to attempt first a question not tolerable to Roman ears: Can a brave man be disinherited? But I don't see what they can adduce in favour of his not being. The fact that he is a brave man and acted bravely so often does not bring him greater rights—merely greater credit.

Some produced a rather stern *colour* on the father's 8 side; they wanted it to look as though the son hates his father and so prefers to live with the enemy rather than with his father. Almost all said that the son is insatiable for fame, and for that very reason must be restrained and controlled by his father. Some resorted entirely to the father's indulgent attitude towards his son,[2] and did not argue in the way employed by Pompeius Silo (whose division was: Even if you had no father, you ought to have stopped fighting; because you have a father and he forbids you, you ought to stop), nor in that used by Gallio, whose 9 division of this side was: I order this for the state's

impero rei publicae causa, tua causa, mea causa.
Sequentia duo videtis quemadmodum potuerit im-
plere: illud, rei publicae causa se imperasse, sic
tractavit: primum, ut pluribus iuvenibus pateat ad
virtutem aditus, non debere omnem occasionem
fortiter faciendi ab uno occupari. Deinde: expedire
rei publicae non videri tantum ex uno pendere;
futurum ut animi et hostium crescerent et suorum
frangerentur si casu ter fortis occidisset. Ad ultimum: utile esse rei publicae ter fortem servari ut sit
qui ostendatur iuventuti; iam illum magis posse ornamentum esse quam praesidium. Illum sensum
veterem: " iam pro viro forti nescio quid etiam *lex*
timet " hoc loco Gallio posuit: " haec *quoque*" inquit
" *ter viro forti aut diffidit aut consulit.*"

10   Ne illam quidem secuti sunt tractationem qua usus
est Blandus, qui dixit: Militia tibi supervacua est,
invidiosa est, periculosa est. Supervacua est quia
non cogeris, immo verecunde vetaris. Gloriae causa
aliquis militat: consecutus es gloriam; vacationis 88M
causa: consecutus es; praemii ⟨causa⟩:[1] tria domi
praemia sunt; et sic transit ut diceret invidiosum esse
unum hominem totiens optare omnes honores inter-
cipere; quam periculosa res esset invidia, quam
magnos viros oppressisset. Hic exempla. Periculosam esse militiam eodem modo collegit quo
ceteri; illud unum [non][2] adiecit de lege, non posse

---

[1] praemii causa *Bursian:* praemium.
[2] *Deleted by Novák.*

sake, for your sake, for my sake. You can see how
he was able to develop the last two of these. His
treatment of the point that he had given the order for
the sake of the state went like this: first, so that more
youths should find the way open to heroism, every
opportunity for brave action should not be mono-
polised by one man. Second, it was in the interests
of the state that so much should not seem to depend
on a single man; the spirit of the enemy would grow,
that of their own men would be shattered, if by some
chance the triple hero should fall. Finally, it was
advantageous for the state that the triple hero should
be kept safe, as a model for youth. By now his forte
was to be a decoration rather than a shield. Gallio
placed here the old idea: " Now even the law feels
fear for the hero ";[1] he said: " The law too either
lacks confidence in the triple hero, or takes pre-
cautions for his safety."

Nor did they follow the treatment employed by 10
Blandus, who said: " Military service for you is
superfluous, invidious, dangerous. Superfluous because you are not being forced to go, indeed you are
being tactfully forbidden.[2] A man serves as a soldier
for the sake of glory; you have won it. Or for leave;
you have won it. Or for a prize: you have three at
home." In this way he passed to saying that it is invidious for one man to wish to grab all the honours so
often; he showed how dangerous envy is, and what
great men it has overthrown. Here he gave instances. He proved that military service was
dangerous just as the others did, but he had a point

[1] Cf. §2.
[2] By appeal to the law.

iam illum fortiter facere quia omnes illum hostes
peterent: " et [adiecit] [1] ideo lex ter fortem dimisit;
scit illum iam observari ab hoste."

11   His ergo omissis illi qui amantem patrem induxerunt hoc genere egerunt: " non possum pati,
non possum desiderium tui sustinere." Hoc loco
Aeschines ex novis declamatoribus, cum diceret: non
me gloria cupidiorem tui fecit, non omnibus ad-
miranda virtus;" confitebor "inquit" adfectus patris,
quos ut quisque volet interpretetur: οὕτως ἂν καὶ
δειλὸν ἐφίλουν." Videbatur hic, dum indulgentiam
exprimit, non servasse dignitatem patris.

Placebat autem Latroni potius ratione retinere [2]
patrem quam adfectu, cum in ratione habeat aliquem
locum et adfectus.

12   Asprenas colorem secutus est longe alium; dixit
enim se non negare rei publicae viri fortis opera, sed
ad necessarios casus reservare. Si magnum aliquod
bellum incidat, tunc et veteranos vocari ad arma. Et
illa sententia eius hoc loco valde laudata est: " nunc
illi militent quibus necesse est; tu militabis si erit 89M
necesse." Sic venisse populum Romanum ad Scipio-
nem Aemilianum cum maius bellum Numantinum
apparuisset quam quod sustinere alii duces possent;
magnum intervallum inter Carthaginem et Numan-
tiam Scipioni datum. Sic ad Pompeium cum piratae

---

[1] *Deleted by Müller.*
[2] retinere *Schultingh:* retineri.

to add about the law, that he could not now act heroically because all the enemy made straight for him: "That is why the law demobilised the triple hero. It knows the enemy now keep their eyes on him."

So those who introduced an affectionate father left 11 all this out, and pleaded after this manner: "I cannot endure, I cannot bear the lack of you." In this passage, Aeschines, one of the new declaimers, said: "Your fame did not make me more fond of you, nor your virtue that is the wonder of all. I will confess what a father feels—let each take it as he likes: I should love even a coward as much." He was thought in his portrayal of the father's indulgence not to have maintained his dignity.

Latro, however, wanted the father to hold his son back because of reason rather than emotion, though emotion too has some place in reason.

Asprenas pursued a quite different *colour*. He said 12 he did not deny to the state the services of a brave man, but was reserving them for critical circumstances. Should some great war arise, then even veterans got called to arms. And his epigram here was highly praised: "Now let those who must do their service; you will do yours if the time comes when *you* must." That was how the Roman people resorted to Scipio Aemilianus when it became clear that the Numantine war was too great to be borne by other leaders. Between Carthage and Numantia Scipio was given a long break.[1] So, too, the Romans had resort to Pompey when the pirates had closed the

---

[1] Between 146 and 134 B.C. (though he was by no means inactive).

maria clausissent. Magna praesidia non esse consumenda. Hoc loco Asprenas de lege dixit et ipse sententiam: videlicet ad hos casus lex ter fortem seposuit.

13 A parte filii colorem induxerunt quidam ut illum cupidum gloriae et bellicosum facerent. Nicetes quidem hoc usus est verbo: παραστήσομεν αὐτὸν τοῖς δικασταῖς ἀρειμάνιον, et sic egit ut quereretur quod cessarent manus suae, quod inermes essent. Latroni non placebat hic color: malebat adulescentem iudicio quam morbo militare. Hoc est, inquit, quod pater efficaciter dicat, detrahere illum operibus suis gloriam temerarium,[1] sanguinarium, quem nec pater possit retinere nec lex dimittere.

14 Quidam pacti sunt cum patre, tamquam Mento, qui dixit semel tantum militare se velle ut aliquid videretur rei publicae supra legem praestitisse. Quidam perpetuam denuntiaverunt militiam: quamdiu vires fuissent, non defuturum rei publicae virum fortem. Non probabat hunc colorem Latro; negabat patri abscidendam spem filii in perpetuum. Vibius Rufus hoc colore egit quo Mento, sed illud adiecit: pervenire ad se voces invidentium illas: "numquid amplius pugnavit quam quantum[2] necesse illi fuit?" Quidam hoc quoque compositum et simulatum inter 90M nos putaverunt, ut ego militare vellem, tu vetares.

15 Latro vehementer egit a parte patris, et adiecit:

---

[1] gloriam temerarium *Faber:* glomerarium.
[2] quantum *Kiessling:* dum.

seas.[1] Great safeguards should not be squandered. Here Asprenas too spoke an epigram on the law: "Surely it was for such emergencies that the law set aside the triple hero."

On the son's side, some introduced the *colour* of 13 making him greedy for fame, and war-like. Nicetes indeed used the phrase: "We shall present him to the judges as full of fury for battle," and pleaded by complaining that his hands were unemployed and unarmed. Latro disliked this *colour*; he preferred the youth to be a soldier as a result of sound judgement and not madness. He said: "Something the father can say effectively is that his son is detracting from the fame of his own services: he is rash, bloodthirsty, a man whom his father cannot hold back nor the law release."

Some struck a bargain with the father, like Mento, 14 who said he wanted to go on just one more campaign, so as to be seen to have done something for the republic beyond what the law required. Some proclaimed that he would serve for ever: so long as he had the strength, the hero would not fail the republic. Latro did not approve of this *colour*. He said the father should not have his hopes for his son destroyed for ever. Vibius Rufus' speech used the same *colour* as Mento's, but he added: "The voices of the envious reach my ears: 'Did he not fight longer than he needed to?' Some people even thought that this was an arrangement, a pretence cooked up between the two of us—*I* should want to fight, *you* would refuse permission."

Latro pleaded forcefully on the father's side, add- 15

[1] 67 B.C.

THE ELDER SENECA

abdicato quoque non permittam exire, iniciam manus, tenebo, novissime ante limen exeuntis cadaver hoc sternam: ut ad hostem pervenias, patrem calca.

Putabat Plancus, summus amator Latronis, hunc sensum a Latrone fortius dictum, a Lesbocle Graeco tenerius, qui dixit sic: κείσομαι· ὡς τεῖχος, ⟨ὡς⟩[1] τάφρον ὑπέρβηθι καὶ πατέρα.

Fuscus Arellius religiosum patrem induxit ominibus territum; aiebat praeceptorem suum in hac controversia describentem pericula futuri proelii ab hoc Homeri versu coepisse:[2] δαιμόνιε, φθίσει σε τὸ σὸν μένος.

Glycon dixit: ὄψεσθε πῶς θανάτου καταφρονῶ. τούτου πατήρ εἰμι.

Diocles Carystius dixit: ἂν ἐπιτύχῃς, μίαν προσθήσεις ἀριστείαν· ἂν ἀποτύχῃς, τρεῖς ἀριστείας ἀπολέσεις.

16   Glycon dixit: οὐκ ἔστιν εὐοιωνιστὸν ὑπὸ κλαίοντος προπέμπεσθαι.

Aeschines, non ille orator—tunc enim non declamandi studium erat—, sed hic ex declamatoribus   91M novis dixit, cum denuntiaret filio periculum et praesagiis tangi se diceret: ἔστιν τι πατὴρ εἰς υἱοῦ τύχην μαντικώτατον.

---

[1] *Supplied by Gertz.*
[2] ab—versu coepisse *C. F. W. Müller:* ob—uersus ed(id)isse.

ing: " Even when I have disinherited him, I shall not
let him go out to fight, I shall lay my hands on him,
hold him, and at the last let my dead body fall on the
threshold as he goes. To get to the enemy you must
trample over your father." [1]

Plancus, a great admirer of Latro, thought that
Latro put this idea too strongly, but that Lesbocles
the Greek put it too feebly, thus: " I shall lie in
your path: pass over your father too—as over a wall
or a ditch."

Arellius Fuscus made the father superstitious,
terrified of omens. He said his teacher, when he
described in this *controversia* the dangers of the
battle to come, began with the Homeric verse: [2]
" Good sir, your strength will consume you."

Glycon said: " You will see how I despise death.
I am this man's father." [3]

Diocles of Carystos said: " If you are successful
you will merely add one feat of arms. If you fail, you
will forfeit three."

Glycon said: " It is no good omen to be seen off by 16
one who weeps."

Aeschines—not the orator, for in his day the vogue
for declamation did not exist, but the recent declaimer—said, while warning the son of the danger
and saying he was being troubled by omens: " A
father is the best of seers with regard to the fate of a
son."

[1] Cf. Jerome *Ep*. 14.2: " licet in limine pater iaceat, per
calcatum perge patrem."

[2] *Il*. 6.407.

[3] And therefore brave (cf. §2 " The omens . . ."). But it
is not clear why the father alludes to his own death (perhaps
as did Latro just above?).

THE ELDER SENECA

Diocles Carystius dixit sententiam quae non in declamatione tantum posset placere sed etiam in solidiore aliquo scripti genere, cum de fortunae varietate locum diceret: μία γάρ ἐστιν πρὸς τύχην ἀσφάλεια τὸ μὴ πολλάκις αὐτὴν πειρᾶσαι.

Dorion dixit rem paulo quidem elatiorem quam pressa et civilis oratio recipit, sed qua egregie attonitos patris adfectus exprimeret: τίς ἐπιθυμία, τέκνον, ἠμαγμένα πιεῖν, ἠμαγμένα φαγεῖν; φοβοῦμαι μή που παράταξις, μή που λοιμός,[1] μή που πάθη σ' ἔλῃ. φοβοῦμαι περὶ τῆς οἰκουμένης.[2] τί, τέκνον, θρυλῶ;[3]

---

[1] λοιμός Haase: ΛΕΤΜΟΣ.
[2] οἰκουμένης ed.: ΟΙΚΟΥ ΜΕΝΕ.
[3] θρυλῶ ed.: ΕΡΥΛΣ AB: ΘΡΨαC V.

Diocles of Carystos spoke an epigram that could give pleasure not only in a declamation but even in some more solid type of writing, when he was speaking the commonplace on the mutability of fortune: "There is one safeguard against chance—not to make trial of it too often."

Dorion said something rather too exalted to be tolerated by concise forensic oratory, but which excellently portrayed the stupefaction of the father: "What longing is this, my child, to eat and drink blood? I fear you may be a prey to battle, disease, suffering. I fear for the whole world. What, child, am I babbling about?"

LIBER SECUNDUS

Seneca Novato, Senecae, Melae filiis salutem.

1 Cum repeterem quos umquam bene declamantes audissem, occurrit mihi inter alios Fabianus philosophus, qui adulescens admodum tantae opinionis in declamando quantae postea in disputando fuit. Exercebatur apud Arellium Fuscum, cuius genus dicendi imitatus plus deinde laboris impendit ut similitudinem eius effugeret quam inpenderat ut exprimeret. Erat explicatio Fusci Arelli splendida quidem sed operosa et implicata, cultus nimis adquisitus, conpositio verborum mollior quam ut illam tam sanctis fortibusque praeceptis praeparans se 103M animus pati posset; summa inaequalitas orationis, quae modo exilis erat, modo nimia licentia vaga et effusa: principia, argumenta, narrationes aride dicebantur, in descriptionibus extra legem omnibus verbis dummodo niterent permissa libertas; nihil

BOOK 2

PREFACE

Seneca to his sons Novatus, Seneca and Mela
greetings

When I went over in my mind all the good de- 1
claimers I had ever heard, I came among others on
the philosopher Fabianus, who as quite a youth was
no less famous for his declaiming than he was later for
his dialectic. He trained with Arellius Fuscus.
And having imitated Fuscus' style of speech, he had
then to spend on avoiding being like him more trouble
than he had spent on becoming like him. Arellius
Fuscus' developments [1] were brilliant, but elaborate
and involved, his ornament too contrived, his word
arrangement more effeminate [2] than could be
tolerated by a mind in training for such chaste and
rigorous precepts. His oratory was highly uneven,
sometimes bare, sometimes because of its over-
freedom wandering and discursive. Proems, arguments and narrations he spoke dryly, while in descriptions words were always granted a licence that

[1] See especially *S.* 2.23 and extracts in succeeding *suasoriae.*
[2] Such use of moral terms in connection with style is frequent in ancient criticism; see especially Sen. *Ep.* 114.

acre, nihil solidum, nihil horridum; splendida oratio et magis lasciva quam laeta.

2   Ab hac cito se Fabianus separavit, et luxuriam quidem cum voluit abiecit, obscuritatem non potuit evadere; haec illum usque in philosophiam prosecuta est.   Saepe minus quam audienti satis est eloquitur, et in summa eius ac simplicissima facultate dicendi antiquorum tamen vitiorum remanent vestigia. Quaedam tam subito desinunt ut non brevia sint sed abrupta.   Dicebat autem Fabianus fere dulces sententias, et, quotiens inciderat aliqua materia quae convicium saeculi reciperet, inspirabat magno magis quam acri animo.   Deerat illi oratorium robur et ille pugnatorius mucro, splendor vero velut voluntarius non elaboratae orationi aderat.   Vultus dicentis lenis et pro tranquillitate morum remissus; vocis nulla contentio, nulla corporis adseveratio, cum verba velut iniussa fluerent.   Iam videlicet conpositus et pacatus animus; cum veros conpressisset adfectus et iram doloremque procul expulisset, parum bene imitari 104M

3 poterat quae effugerat. Suasoriis aptior erat; locorum habitus fluminumque decursus et urbium situs moresque populorum nemo descripsit abun-

---

¹ Seneca *Ep.* 40.12 speaks of his *facilitas*.   He discusses his style generally in *Ep.* 100.

² See Index of Commonplaces s.v. Age (and cf. especially *C.* 2.1.10 *seq.*).

³ Cf. Sen. *Ep.* 100.8: " He lacks the vigour of an orator."

went beyond the rules—the only requirement was that they should shine. There was nothing sharp, hard or jagged. The style was brilliant, wanton rather than luxuriant.

Fabianus rapidly disassociated himself from this, 2 and cast off the lavishness at will. But he couldn't escape the obscurity, which dogged him right into his philosophy. He often expresses less than the hearer needs; and amid his extreme simplicity and fluency [1] of style there remain traces of early weaknesses. Some sentences stop so suddenly as to be abrupt rather than concise. But Fabianus often spoke agreeable epigrams, and whenever a theme cropped up that allowed criticism of the age,[2] he was inspired, to greatness of mind rather than asperity. He lacked the toughness of the orator,[3] the fighter's edge, but a sort of unselfconscious sheen played upon his unaffected style. As he spoke, his expression was gentle, and, like his calm character, relaxed. He did not strain his voice or exaggerate his movements as the words flowed out, so it seemed, unbidden. Of course, the fact was that his character was by now placid and peaceful.[4] He had suppressed genuine feelings, banished afar anger and grief, and was no good at pretending to feel what he had escaped from.[5] He was better suited to *suasoriae*. No-one 3 described more lovingly the characteristics of places, the courses of rivers, the positions of cities, the

[4] Cf. Sen. *Ep.* 100.8: "sunt . . . illa . . . placida et ad animi tenorem quietum compositumque formata."

[5] In accordance with Stoic ethics, which the followers of Sextius approved. Anger was regarded as temporary madness, grief as an error.

dantius. Numquam inopia verbi substitit, sed velocissimo ac facillimo cursu omnes res beata circumfluebat oratio.

Haec eo libentius, Mela, fili carissime, refero quia video animum tuum a civilibus officiis abhorrentem et ab omni ambitu aversum hoc unum concupiscentem, nihil concupiscere. Tu [1] eloquentiae tamen studeas: facilis ab hac in omnes artes discursus est; instruit etiam quos non sibi exercet. Nec est quod insidias tibi putes fieri, quasi id agam ut te bene cedentis studii favor teneat. Ego vero non sum bonae mentis impedimentum: perge quo inclinat animus, et paterno contentus ordine subduc fortunae magnam tui partem.

4   Erat quidem tibi maius ingenium quam fratribus tuis, omnium bonarum artium capacissimum: est et hoc ipsum melioris ingenii pignus, non corrumpi bonitate eius ut illo male utaris. Sed quoniam fratribus tuis ambitiosa curae sunt foroque se et honoribus parant, in quibus ipsa quae sperantur timenda sunt, ego quoque eius alioqui processus avidus et hortator laudatorque vel periculosae dum honestae modo industriae duobus filiis navigantibus te in portu retineo. 10

Sed proderit tibi in illa quae tota mente agitas declamandi exercitatio, sicut Fabiano profuit: qui

---

[1] tu *Thomas:* ut.

character of peoples. He never stopped for lack of a word: a generous flood of speech flowed round everything in a swift and easy stream.

I am the more happy to relate this, my dear son Mela, because I see that your mind, shrinking from political office and averse from all ambition, has only one desire—to have no desires.[1] But *do* study eloquence. You can easily pass from this art to all others; it equips even those whom it does not train for its own ends. There is no reason for you to think plots are being laid for you, as if I were planning that you should be held tight by enthusiasm for a study that goes well. No, *I* am no obstacle to a good mind; go where your inclination takes you, and, content with your father's rank,[2] withdraw a great part of yourself from the reach of fortune.

You had a greater intellect than your brothers, 4 completely capable of grasping all honourable arts. And this is in itself the guarantee of a superior mind, not to be corrupted by its good quality into using it ill. But since your brothers care for ambitious goals and set themselves for the forum and a political career, where even what one hopes for is to be feared, even I, who otherwise am eager for such advancement and encourage and praise such efforts (their dangers don't matter, provided they are honourable), even I keep you in port while your two brothers voyage out.

But the practice of declamation will help you in those pursuits to which you are whole-heartedly

[1] Like a good Stoic: cf. Sen. *Ep.* 87.3: " fecit sibi divitias nihil concupiscendo."
[2] Equestrian (cf. Tac. *Ann.* 14.53). Mela took this advice (Sen. *Helv.* 18.2: " honores . . . sapienter contempsit ").

aliquando cum Sextium audiret nihilominus decla-
mitabat, et tam diligenter ut putares illum illi studio
5 parari, non per illud alteri praeparari.   Habuit et
Blandum rhetorem praeceptorem, qui ⟨primus⟩ [1]
eques Romanus Romae docuit; ante illum intra
libertinos praeceptores pulcherrimae disciplinae con-
tinebantur, et minime probabili more turpe erat
docere quod honestum erat discere.   Nam primus
omnium Latinus rhetor Romae fuit puero Cicerone
Plotius.   Apud Blandum diutius quam apud Fuscum
Arellium studuit, sed cum iam transfugisset, eo
tempore quo eloquentiae studebat non eloquentiae
causa.   Scio futurum ut auditis eius sententiis
cupiatis multas audire.   Sed nec ille diu declamationibus vacavit et ego tanto minorem natu quam
ipse eram audiebam quotiens inciderat, non quotiens
volueram.   In hunc ergo libellum quaecumque ab
illo dicta teneo conferam.

I

106 M

ADOPTANDUS POST TRES ABDICATOS

Dives tres filios abdicavit.   Petit a paupere
unicum filium in adoptionem.   Pauper dare vult;
nolentem ire abdicat.

[1] *Supplied by Haase.*

---

[1] Reminiscent of Cic. *Orat.* 145.
[2] The emphasis is on this word, freedmen normally being
Greek.   Seneca stresses how late in Roman history this event

devoted, just as they helped Fabianus. At one time, though he was pupil of Sextius, nevertheless Fabianus went on declaiming, and so enthusiastically that you might have supposed he was preparing for that—not being prepared by that for something else. He also 5 had the rhetorician Blandus for his teacher, the first Roman knight to teach in Rome. Before his time, the teaching of the most noble of subjects was restricted to freedmen, and by a quite unsatisfactory custom it was accounted disgraceful to teach what it was honourable to learn.[1] For the first Latin[2] rhetorician of all in Rome was Plotius, in Cicero's boyhood. Fabianus studied longer under Blandus than under Fuscus, but after he'd become a deserter and was studying eloquence not for its own sake. I know that when you hear his epigrams you will want to hear many. But he didn't find time for declamation for very long, and, as he was so much younger than I, I used to hear him as often as chance permitted rather than as often as I should have liked. Such sayings of his as I remember, then, I will collect for this book.

1

The Man faced with Adoption after the Disinheritance of Three Sons

A rich man disinherited his three sons. He asks a poor man for his only son to adopt. The poor man is ready to comply; when his son refuses to go, he disinherits him.

came. For Plotius, see Suet. *Gr. Rhet.* 26, with Brugnoli's notes.

THE ELDER SENECA

1   PORCI LATRONIS. Hancine meam esse fortunam?
eodem tempore et abdicor et adoptor. Ista videlicet
domus adulescentem me non capit, quae te senem
fecit. Quietiora tempora pauperes habuimus; bella
civilia aurato Capitolio gessimus. Divitias putas
aurum et argentum, ludibria fortunae, quae interim
cum ipsis dominis veneunt? Denuntio tibi, dives:
etiamsi venero, dabo operam, quod in tua domo facil-
limum est, ut abdicer. Etiamsi multa contra expectationem accidunt, *numquam tamen futurum putavi
ut aut pater meus liberos odisset aut dives concupisceret.*
Non desidero patrimonium; fragilis et caduca felicitas
est, et omnis blandientis fortunae speciosus cum periculo nitor: et sine causa saepe fovit et sine ratione
destituit. Vidi ego magni exercitus ducem sine
comite fugientem; vidi ⟨ab⟩ [1] ambitiosa turba clien-
tium limina deserta sub domino sectore venalia.
Nam quid ex summis opibus ad egestatem devolutos
loquar? Multa tibi succurrent exempla, etiamsi in
una domo quaeras.

    [1] *Supplied by C. F. W. Müller.*

---

    [1] The standard line of the Roman historians (e.g. Sall. *Cat.*
10 *seq.*) was that riches brought corruption to Rome. The
turning point was placed in the middle of the second century
B.C.: and it was after the fall of Carthage in 146 that the
ceilings in the temple of Jupiter on the Capitol were first
gilded (Plin. *N.H.* 33.57: we know from this same passage
that the gilding was extended when the temple was rebuilt

For the son

Porcius Latro. So *this* is my luck! At one and 1
the same moment I am disinherited—and adopted.—
It seems there is no room for me, a young man, in the
house in which *you* have grown old.—When we were
poor, times were quieter; it was when the Capitol
was gilded that we fought civil wars.[1] Do you regard
as riches such playthings of fortune [2] as gold and
silver, which sometimes get sold along with their
owners?—I warn you, rich man: even if I come, I
will aim at something that is very easily obtained
in your house—disinheritance.—Many unexpected
things happen; but I never thought my father would
come to hate his children or a rich man come to covet
them.—I feel no need of an estate. Happiness is
vulnerable and perishable, and all good fortune's
flattering glitter has danger mingled with its lures;
often it has cosseted men for no reason, often deserted
them without a cause. I have seen the leader of a
great army in flight and companionless; I have seen
the threshold deserted by its mob of hopeful clients,
and put up for sale, its owner the auctioneer.[3] No
need to tell of those who have toppled from supreme
wealth to poverty. You will come across many
precedents—even if you restrict your enquiries to
one house.[4]

after being burnt down in 83 B.C., and this brings us more
exactly to the period of the Civil Wars.

[2] Fortune and Riches naturally play a large part in this
declamation: see Index of Commonplaces s. vv.

[3] *sub* suggests this meaning. But *sector* should = "bid-
der"; and Latro perhaps meant: "the former owner's master
bidding for it."

[4] That of this rich man.

2 RUFI VIBI. Habendos esse liberos is quoque iudicat qui non libentissime habet. Ego illos in frivola invitavi nostra: qui illis meam promisi domum, suam eripiam? Quid faciam? si paruero abdicabor, si non paruero abdicabor. Patrem amo: haec est contumacia mea. Dives filium non habet: me dabis; dives reduxerit suos: me recipies; ita non adoptari sed commodari recuso.

3 CESTI PII. Accipe vitae meae testem, quod magni aestimas, divitem, cui placere difficile est. Vultis scire quare patrem non relinquam? quia genuit me, quia educavit, quia abdicavit. *Diu dubitavi ille amicum temptaret an hic filium.* " Abdico " inquit. Hoc pater verus! quid ab eo qui adoptabit sperare possum?

Narratio CESTI PII. Dives sustulit unum filium: non fuit contentus; quid enim erat diviti unus? tres sustulit; poterat unum in adoptionem dare: abdicavit unum, alterum, tertium. Iam nihil diviti putatis superesse? quartum addet.

4 ARELLI FUSCI patris. Quisquis es avarus pecuniae custos inmensique cultor soli: cum multa quaesieris,

---

[1] The young man thinks his adoption will remove the possibility of the rich man letting his own sons come home: cf. §9 " Why turn down . . ."

[2] By his future father: cf. §9 " People who hear . . ."

VIBIUS RUFUS. Even the man who is loath to keep 2 children judges them indispensable.—I invited them to come to our shack, I promised them my home—am I to deprive them of theirs? [1]—What am I to do? If I obey I shall be disinherited,[2] if I disobey I shall be disinherited.—I love my father: that is where my obstinacy [3] lies.—The rich man has no son; you propose to donate me. Suppose the rich man recalls his own; you will take me back. I refuse to be—I can't say adopted—to be lent around like this.

CESTIUS PIUS. Take as a witness to my way of 3 life [4] this rich man, since you rate him so high: after all, he is difficult to please.—You want to know why I am not leaving my father? Because he begot me, because he brought me up, because he disinherited me.—I spent a long time wondering whether the rich man was testing out his friend or the poor man his son.—" I disinherit you," he says. This from my real father! What can I hope for from my adoptive father-to-be?

Narration of Cestius Pius. The rich man raised one son. He was not satisfied: what was one to a rich man? He raised three. He could have given one away to be adopted. He disinherited the first, the second, the third. Do you suppose the rich man has by now nothing in reserve? He will add a fourth.

ARELLIUS FUSCUS SENIOR. If you are a greedy 4 saver of money, a cultivator of measureless lands, I ask you: you will acquire much, but will you be able

[3] Obstinacy being a normal reason for disinheritance.
[4] To prove I do not deserve to be disinherited: cf. §7 " I have no accuser . . ."

poterisne omnibus frui? Filium quaeris: ecce turba
iuvenum sine patre. Impera quod vis: navigabo,
militabo, dummodo ubicumque fuero tuus sim. *Ita
nos pauperes sumus, qui habemus quod divites rogent?*
Unde talem patrem? non irasceris nisi ut ames.
Quid porro? ista patrimonia, in quae male sani [1] 108M
ruitis, gaudia dominorum an onera sunt? Mille cor-
ruentium inter divitias suas exempla referebas, et
inter illa ponebas et divitis domum. Merito abdicasti an inmerito? *si inmerito abdicasti, odi patrem tot
eicientem innocentes: si merito, odi domum tot facientem
nocentes.* Aliquid in domo locupleti non agendum
agam. Quae apud nos frugalitas est, apud illos
5 humilitas est. Petis iterum potius filios quam recipis.
Colit etiamnunc in Capitolio casam victor omnium
gentium populus, cuius tantam felicitatem nemo
miratur; merito potens est: nempe ab eius origine
est qui non reliquit patrem. Egredientem te certe
domo redeuntemque comitabor nec nisi in limine
deseram: ero in publico filius. *Amo aeque paupertatem quam patrem: utrique consuevi.* Non possum
agere in domo divitis filium. Si carum tibi servum
venderes, quaereres numquid saevus emptor esset.

---

[1] sani *V:* insani *AB.*

---

[1] The three disinherited sons.
[2] Cf. Sen. *Ep.* 71.23: "luxurioso frugalitas poena est."
[3] A reason for the youth not letting himself be adopted: he
doesn't want to deprive the three of their patrimony. Cf.
above, p. 206 n. 1.

to enjoy it all?—You are in search of a son: look, here is a flock of young men with no father.[1]—Give what orders you will. I will sail the seas, serve as a soldier, so long as I can be your son, wherever I am.— Can we be poor if we have something that rich men ask for?—Where find such a father? You show anger only to show your love.—What then? Those inherited millions after which you fools chase, are they a joy to their owners or a burden?—You used to give me a thousand instances of men collapsing amid their riches: among them this rich man's house.— Were you justified in disinheriting them or not? If unjustified, I hate a father who throws out so many innocent sons. If justified, I hate a household that makes so many guilty.—I shall do something that one ought not to do in a rich man's house. What in our house is frugality counts as meanness there.[2]— You are more liable to look elsewhere for sons a 5 second time than to take your own back.[3]—Even now on the Capitol the people that has conquered the world venerates a hut.[4] Nobody is surprised at that people's great success. It is right that it has power: for it derives its origin from one who did not abandon his father.[5]—I shall at least accompany you as you go out of the house and return to it, and I shall only leave you on the doorstep [6]—in public I shall be your son.— I love poverty as much as I love my father; I have got used to both.—I cannot act the son in the house of a rich man.—If you were selling a favourite slave, you would enquire if the buyer was cruel.—Indeed, I

[4] Cf. *C.* 1.6.4 n.
[5] Aeneas, who saved Anchises from Troy.
[6] Not being allowed, qua disinherited, to enter: cf. *C.* 3.3.

Unam mehercule horam qua tibi irato satis faciam ter
pluris omni patrimonio puto. Hoc solum omnium,
quod sic me amittere cupis, satis amare non possum.
Quid faciam adoptatus? loquar de filiis eius bene?
6 de abdicatione? Ego in domum vestram intrabo
tamquam ego vos eiecerim? ego ornamenta vestra
occupabo, ut me, si illic quid commisero, ⟨et vester 10
eiciat⟩ [1] nec meus recipiat pater? Quid est quod aut
negandum mihi aut excusandum sit? Non insanis-
simum dispendiorum malum, non erubescendos
amores neque luxuriantem habitum neque potatus
obicis filio. Haec si non potes, aliqua saltem ex com-
mentariis amici tui describe: madentem unguentis
externis, convulneratum libidinibus, incedentem ut
feminis placeat femina mollius, et cetera quae morbi
7 non iudici sunt: abdicatio loquax est. Quam te,
paupertas, amo, si beneficio tuo innocens sum! Accusatorem non habeo; immo, me miserum, etiam
laudatorem habeo et eum cui non omnes placent—
hoc enim malo dicere quam " omnes non placent."
Non tibi per multos fulta liberos domus est neque turba
lateri circumerrat nec multus intra limen heres est nec
post me alius quem retineas: *quamquam ne sic quidem
debuisti dare,* quom etiam [2] deos cum votis patris

___

[1] *Supplied by Müller.*
[2] quom etiam *Otto after Kiessling:* quam enim.

---

[1] Or: " Shall I speak well."
[2] The three sons: see above, p. 208 n. 3.
[3] That is, when one disinherits one gives elaborate reasons,
of the kind given by the rich man. The poor man has made

regard a single hour spent in mollifying your anger
as worth three times any inheritance.—That you want
to be rid of me in this manner is the sole thing in you
that I cannot love as I should.—What am I to do
when I am adopted? Shall I do well to speak [1] of his
sons? Of the disinheriting?—Shall *I* enter your 6
house as though *I* had driven you [2] out? Shall *I* take
over your fineries, with the prospect that, if I mis-
behave myself there, your father will throw me out
without mine taking me back?—What is there for me
either to deny or to excuse? You are not reproaching your son with madly reckless expenditure, shameful amours, luxurious clothing, or tippling. If you
can't accuse him of these things, take some hints
from your friend's notebook: " sodden with exotic
perfumes, crippled by lusts, to please women step-
ping along more delicately than a woman," and all the
other things that point to madness rather than sound
judgement. Disinheriting is a talkative business.[3]—
How I love you, poverty—it is thanks to you that I 7
am innocent. I have no accuser: in fact, unluckily I
even have someone to praise me, and a man whom not
everyone pleases (I prefer that to saying: " everyone
displeases him ").—Your house has no abundance of
sons to lean on, no crowd hovers at your side; you [4]
have no plenitude of heirs behind your front-door,
nor is there another after me for you to keep for
yourself. And even if there had been, you ought not
to have given me away—you had seen even the gods

no such accusations, and his son would be innocent of them
(cf. §§14 and 15), because his poverty has made luxury impossible (cf. the next epigram).

[4] The poor father.

vidisses certantis. Et *tutior adversus fortunam est cui aliquid post damnum superest,* et habemus exemplum posse aliquem tres filios perdere. Ille Croesus inter reges opulentissimus, memento, post terga vinctis manibus ductus est. Tu, Crasse, post evestigata illa fugitivorum arma urbis Romanae divitissimus civis,[1]

8 nunc apud Parthos eges sepulchro quoque. [dicta 110 praeterea illia corruentium][2] Non refero quotiens [enim inter divitias suas exemplo] ⟨inter illa⟩ [3] istam posueris [4] domum meliores perdentem divitiis suis liberos. Hoc ⟨animo⟩ [5] scio nostros fuisse maiores, hoc illum Aelium Tuberonem, cuius paupertas virtus fuit, hoc Fabricium Samnitium non accipientem munera, hoc ceteros patres nostros, quos apud aratra ipsa mirantes decora sua circumsteterunt lictores. Surgite, surgite, miserrimi iuvenes, et meum rogando patrem vestrum rogare discite.

9 BLANDI. Tres genuit, quattuor abdicat. " *Abdico* " inquit: *apparet unde venias.*

GALLI VIBI. Si quis me audit adoptari, iam putat abdicatum. " Quare ⟨respuis divitias? "⟩ [6] Respon-

---

[1] civis *C. F. W. Müller:* qui.
[2] *Deleted, along with* enim—exemplo, *by the editor after Wiles as a corrupted marginal note alluding to the parallel passage in §4.*
[3] *Supplied by the ed. after Gertz.*
[4] posueris *Ribbeck, Gertz:* posueritis.
[5] *Supplied by Müller.*
[6] *Supplied by Thomas.*

quarrelling with a father's prayers.[1]—One is better protected against fortune if one has something in reserve after a loss: after all, we have an instance of the possibility of losing *three* sons.—Remember: the Croesus who was richest among kings was taken to his death, his hands bound behind his back. Crassus, richest citizen of Rome after the tracking down of those rebel runaways, now lies in Parthia, without even a tomb. I will not say how often you added to these instances [2] this case of a household losing sons more precious than its own wealth. I know that this was the spirit of our ancestors, of the Aelius Tubero whose poverty was a virtue, of Fabricius who rejected the presents of the Samnites,[3] of the rest of our forebears,[4] who stood at the very plough in awe of the symbols of authority of the lictors who surrounded them.—Rise, rise, wretched youths, and by imploring my father learn how to implore your own.[5]

BLANDUS. He begot three, he disinherits four.— 9 " I disinherit you," he says. It is obvious whom you have been visiting.[6]

VIBIUS GALLUS. People who hear I am being adopted regard me as already disinherited.—" Why

---

[1] The rich man's.

[2] Cf. §1 " You will come across . . . ," and especially §4.

[3] The Samnites were grateful for Fabricius' services: see Val. Max. 4.3.6; Gell. 1.14.

[4] Absurd generalisation from the case of Cincinnatus, who was summoned from the plough to dictatorship (Liv. 3.26.7–10; Flor. 1.5.13).

[5] Help me to persuade my father to keep me: it will be good practice for persuading your father to take you back.

[6] The father had been taking lessons from his rich friend. Cf. §21.

deo: ne auferam patri filium, filiis patrem. Nec tam
vicino exemplo emendaris? qui abdicat suos, quaerit
alienos. Nulla certa felicitas est: paulo ante ego
divitis filiis invidebam, modo illi mihi. Laudat me
pater, cum abdicet, laudo ego patrem, cum abdicer;
haec *una inter nos disputatio est: iste me dignum putat
beato patre,* ego me *meo.*

10 FABIANI PAPIRI. Ecce instructi exercitus saepe 111M
civium cognatorumque conserturi [praelium] [1] manus
constiterunt et colles equis utrimque complentur et
subinde omnis regio trucidatorum corporibus con-
sternitur; illa tum in multitudine cadaverum vel
spoliantium sic quaesierit aliquis: quae causa hominem adversus hominem in facinus coegit?—nam
neque feris inter se bella sunt nec, si forent, eadem
hominem deceant, placidum proximumque divino
genus; quae tanta vos pestis, cum una stirps
idemque sanguis sitis, quaeve furiae in mutuum san-
11 guinem egere? quod tantum malum ⟨huic⟩ [2] uni
generi vel fato vel forte iniunctum? An, ut convivia
populis instruantur et tecta auro fulgeant, parricidium
tanti fuit? Magna enim vero et lauta [3] sunt propter
quae mensam et lacunaria sua ⟨nocentes⟩ [4] potius
quam lucem innocentes intueri maluerint. An, ne

---

[1] *Deleted in the editio Romana (1585).*
[2] *Supplied by Otto.*
[3] et lauta *Müller:* laucia *AB:* et laudanda *V.*
[4] *Supplied by Novák.*

---

[1] For this topic cf. Sen. *Ir.* 2.8.3 and passages cited by
Mayor on Juv. 15.159.
[2] Cf. Sen. *N.Q.* 5.18.6.

turn down wealth?" I reply: so as not to take a son away from his father, a father from his sons.—Are you not set right by an instance so close at hand? He who disinherits his own sons looks for someone else's.—No good fortune is secure; not long ago *I* envied the rich man's sons, now *they* envy me.—My father praises me even while disinheriting me; I praise my father, even while I am being disinherited. This is the sole dispute between us: he thinks I deserve a rich father, I think I deserve my own.

PAPIRIUS FABIANUS. Look: often have armies of citizens and relatives taken their stand, drawn up to join battle; the hills on either side are filled with cavalry; and suddenly the whole terrain is strewn with the bodies of the slaughtered. Suppose someone amid that mass of corpses and looters should ask: What was it that compelled man to commit crime against man? Beasts do not war among themselves,[1] and even if beasts did wars would be unworthy of man, a quiet species, and nearest to the divine. What is this hideous disease, this fury that drove you to shed each other's blood [2]—though you are of one stock, one blood? What is this appalling evil that fate or chance has inflicted on this species alone? Was the setting out of banquets for whole peoples, the gilding of roofs, worth parricide? They must indeed be great and glorious objectives for which men preferred to look at their tables [3] and ceilings in guilt rather than at the sunlight in innocence. So that

---

[3] Brilliantly polished tables must clearly be meant (cf. Sen. *Ir.* 3.35.5, a fine attack on private luxury and public squalor), to match the brilliant ceilings (Sen. *Ep.* 90.9: " lacunaria auro gravia ").

quid ventri negetur libidinique, orbis servitium ex-
petendum est? In quid tandem sic pestiferae istae
divitiae expetuntur si ne in hoc quidem, ut liberis
relinquantur? Quid tandem est quod non divitiae
corruperint? Primum, si inde incipere velis, aedes 11
ipsas, quas in tantum extruxere ut, cum domus ad
usum ac munimentum paratae sint, nunc periculo,
non praesidio ⟨sint⟩ [1]: tanta altitudo aedificiorum est
tantaeque viarum angustiae ut neque adversus ignem
praesidium nec ex ruinis ullam [villam] [2] in partem
effugium sit.

12   Ad delicias dementis luxuriae lapis omnis eruitur,
caeduntur ubique gentium silvae; aeris ferrique usus,
iam auri quoque, in extruendis et decorandis domibus,
nempe ut anxii et interdiu et nocte ruinam ignemque
metuant; qui sive tectis iniectus est ⟨sive⟩ [3] fortuitus,
ruinae et incendia [4] illa urbium excidia sunt; quippe
non defendunt sua, sed in communi periculo ad prae-
dandum ⟨ut⟩ [5] hostes ⟨discurrunt appetunt⟩[6]que
aliena, et in suis domini a validioribus [7] caeduntur,
⟨accenduntur⟩ [8] alia ipsaque cum maxume flagrantia
spolium ex alienis ruinis feruntur. In hos ergo exitus

1 *Supplied here by Müller.*
2 *Deleted by Müller.*
3 *Supplied by Haase and Madvig.*
4 ruinae et incendia *Müller:* quae et beuna. *This sentence
and those following are highly uncertain.*
5 *Supplied by Gronovius.*
6 *Supplied by Müller.*
7 validioribus *Müller:* ualidiora.
8 *Supplied by Müller.*

our bellies and our lust may want nothing must we
seek to subdue the entire world? Why on earth
do we covet as we do those vicious riches if not even
to leave them to our children?[1] What is there
that riches have not corrupted? First, if you wish to
start there, the very buildings: these they have
raised to such a height that though houses are meant
for use and protection they are now sources of
danger, not of safety; such is the height of the
structures, so narrow are the roads that there is no
guarding against fire—and no escape in any direction
from collapsing buildings.[2]

To meet the whims of crazy luxury every stone is 12
quarried, forests are felled throughout the world.
Bronze and iron, and now gold too, are set to building
and decorating houses—I suppose so that their
owners may be able to worry day and night over the
risks of fire and collapse.[3] Whether fire seizes on
buildings by arson or accident, these collapses and
these blazes are the ruin of cities. For men do not
defend their own property, but amid the communal
danger hurry like enemies to the loot, and make for
what belongs to others. In their own homes owners
are killed by those stronger than they. Other things
are purposely set alight, and, still blazing, are carried
as booty from the ruins of others' houses. Is it to

[1] Fabianus for a moment glances at the theme of the declamation: cf. the end of §13.
[2] Cf. Sen. Const. 12.2: " tectis moliendis occupati tutelae
corporum inventa in periculum verterunt " (also Ep. 90. 43).
The dangers of fire and collapse are joined also by Juv. 3.190
seq.; Sen. Ben. 4.6.2.
[3] For the anxieties of wealth see Juv. 14.303 seq., with
Mayor ad loc.

varius ille secatur lapis et tenui fronte parietem tegit? 113M
[quam umetis seuere]¹ in hoc pavimentum tessela-
tum² et infusum tectis aurum?

13 O paupertas, quam ignotum bonum es! Quin
etiam montes silvasque in domibus marcidis et in
umbra fumoque viridia aut maria amnesque imi-
tantur. Vix possum credere quemquam eorum
vidisse silvas virentisque gramine³ campos, quos
rapidus amnis ex praecipitio vel, cum per plana in-
fusus est, placidus interfluit; non maria umquam ex
colle vidisse lenta,⁴ aut hiberna cum ventis penitus
agitata sunt: quis enim tam pravis oblectare animum 114M
imitamentis⁵ possit si vera cognoverit? Videlicet
⟨haec illis placent⟩⁶ ut infantibus quae tangi con-
prehendique manibus aut sinu possunt; nam magna
non capit exigua mens. Ex hoc litoribus quoque
moles iniungunt⁷ congestisque in alto terris exag-
gerant sinus; alii fossis inducunt mare: adeo nullis
gaudere veris sciunt, sed adversum naturam alieno
loco aut terra aut mare mentita aegris oblectamenta
sunt. Et miraris ⟨si⟩⁸ fastidio rerum naturae
laborantibus iam ne liberi quidem nisi alieni placent?

¹ *Deleted by Müller.*
² tesselatum *Schultingh:* leuatum.
³ virentisque gramine *Müller:* patentisque eamme *AB:*
patentisque *V.*
⁴ lenta *Thomas:* lata.
⁵ imitamentis *Vahlen:* (in)uita.
⁶ *Supplied by Gertz.*
⁷ iniungunt *Müller:* inuehuntur.
⁸ *Supplied by Kiessling.*

meet this end that mottled stone is cut to cover walls with its thin veneer?[1] Is it for this that the floor is covered with mosaic and gold poured on the roofs?

Poverty, how little known a good are you! Men [13] even ape[2] mountains and woods in their rotting houses, green fields, seas and rivers amid the gloom and smoke. I can scarcely believe any of these people have seen forests, or green, grassy plains, with a stream flowing through, turbulent in steep ground, calm in flat: or ever seen from a cliff the seas either sluggish or, when winds stir them to their depths, stormy. For who could delight his mind with such debased imitations if he knew the reality? I suppose they love these things as children love things they can touch, take in their hands and clutch to their laps. Small minds have no room for great things. So they pile up masses of masonry even on the sea-shore, stop up bays by heaping earth in the depth of the ocean. Others let the sea into the land by means of ditches. For truly they do not know how to enjoy anything real, but in their sickness they need un-natural fakes of sea or land out of their proper places[3] to delight them. Do you still wonder that, in their disdain for the natural, they now don't even like children—except those of others?

---

[1] Sen. *Ep.* 115.9: "parietes tenui marmore inductos"; cf. *Ben.* 4.6.2.

[2] For imitation of the countryside, cf. *C.* 5.5; *Decl.* p. 179.12 *seq.* Ritter; Sen. *Ep.* 122.8 (woods on roofs, buildings in the sea).

[3] Cf. Petr. 120.88–9: "expelluntur aquae saxis, mare nascitur arvis, / et permutata rerum statione rebellant"; Vell. Pat. 2.33.4 (of Lucullus); and, of course, such Horatian passages as *Od.* 3.1.33 *seq.*

14   HISPANI CORNELI. Solus omnium abdicor quia me
meus pater diligit, alienus adpetit. Quid mihi obicit?
meretricis amo? aes alienum feci? Dic, dives audiat.
" *Divitem* " *inquit* " *esse te volo* ": *o me abdicandum si*
talem patrem relinquo! Laudabat mihi pater paupertatem, narrabat divitum incommoda, aiebat multos
divites accusatos; ego certe memini abdicatos.
" Abdico " non est patris mei verbum.

15   TRIARI. Quare abdicas? Numquid dies noctesque
inpendo turpibus conviviis? plurimum vivo in lupanari? Si nescis quae crimina obiciantur, ab amico
disce. Si omnes mali sunt, quid isto patre ⟨miserius? 11
si omnes boni sunt, quid isto patre⟩ [1] furentius?

  ROMANI HISPONIS. In hanc ego domum ibo, in qua
aut totiens insanitur a patre aut totiens peccatur in
patrem? Cum prodiero repente dives, dicent
omnes: " Quis est iste quem magna fortuna non
decet? Haec est divitis quarta abdicatio."

16   SILONIS POMPEI. Quantumcumque est ⟨tibi⟩,[2] satis
mihi est; unicus [3] sum. Fortiter fortunam meam
feram; hoc non mihi primum accidit. Unicus sum
filius et tamen abdicor. *Quid videri me velis, nescio:*

[1] *Supplied by Müller after Bursian and early editors.*
[2] est tibi *Gertz:* et.
[3] unicus *Vahlen:* dictus.

CORNELIUS HISPANUS. I am absolutely the only 14
man to be disinherited because my father loves me
and someone else's father covets me.—What does he
reproach me with? Do I run after whores? Have I
got into debt? Say—and make sure the rich man
hears.[1]—"I want you to be rich," he says. O, I
should deserve disinheritance if I leave such a father!
—My father used to sing the praises of poverty to me,
tell me of the disadvantages of being rich, say that
many rich men have been accused. Certainly I recall
that they get disinherited.[2]—"I disinherit" is not a
word *my* father has in his vocabulary.

TRIARIUS. Why do you disinherit me? Do I 15
spend night and day in disgusting banquets? Do I
spend much time in the brothel? If you don't know
the charges that are normally made, take a tip from
your friend.[3]—If all his children are bad, who more
unhappy than this father? If all are good, who more
demented than this father?

ROMANIUS HISPO. Shall I then enter this house,
where the father is so often out of his mind—or so
often sinned against?—When I go out, suddenly
grown rich, everybody will say: "Who is this man?
Wealth doesn't suit him. This is the rich man's
fourth case of disinheritance."

POMPEIUS SILO. Whatever you have is enough for 16
me; I am the only son.—I shall bear my luck bravely;
I'm not the first this has happened to.[4]—I am the
only child—yet I get disinherited.—I don't know

---

[1] Otherwise *he* will disinherit him too.
[2] For example, the three sons.
[3] Cf. §6.
[4] Compare the three sons.

innocentem? sed abdicor; nocentem? sed adoptor. Utcumque tamen abdicatio tolerabilior est: unum abdicat; adoptio tres ⟨abdicavit, quartum⟩ [1] abdicatura est. *Non potest mihi dici quod ceteris abdicatis: " in tua potestate fuit; si paruisses patri, non perdidisses patrem ";* etiamsi non abdicarer, perditurus fui.*

17 Pars altera. Latronis Porci. *Si nescirem quid mali esset paupertas, nunc intellegerem: abdicationem filius* meus *non timet.* Fabriciorum imagines Metellis patuerunt; Aemiliorum et Scipionum familias [1] adoptio miscuit; etiam abolita saeculis nomina per successores novos fulgent. Sic illa patriciorum nobilitas ⟨a⟩ [2] fundamentis urbis [habet] [3] usque in haec tempora constitit: adoptio fortunae remedium est. Non ignoro ego quorum inopia per otium in angulis divitiarum convictos carpit accusandoque insequi non desinit.[4] Sed nulla materia in rebus humanis virtutes clarius ostendit: *census senatorium gradum ascendit, census equitem Romanum a plebe secernit, census in castris ordinem promovet, census iudices*

---

[1] *Supplied by Schultingh.*
[2] *Added by Schott.*
[3] *Deleted by Schott.*
[4] carpit—non desinit *Müller after Novák and others:* (s)trepit accusatioque cum sequi neque sunt.

---

[1] By adoption.
[2] Part of a commonplace on adoption (cf. *C.* 2.4.13). The names chosen have caused difficulties, as no connection of Fabricii and Metelli is known. The other allusion will be to the younger Scipio, son of L. Aemilius Paullus Macedonicus, who was adopted by the elder son of Scipio Africanus.

what you want me to appear. Innocent?—yet I am being disinherited. Guilty?—yet I am being adopted.—However it may be, disinheritance is the easier to bear. It disinherits only one, while adoption has disinherited three—and will disinherit a fourth.— What is said to all other disinherited sons cannot be said to me: " It was up to you. If you had obeyed your father, you would not have lost him." Even if I were not being disinherited, I was fated to lose him.[1]

The other side

PORCIUS LATRO. If I did not already know what a 17 misfortune poverty is, I should understand now: my son is not afraid of being disinherited.—The family portraits of the Fabricii found room for the Metelli. Adoption merged the families of the Aemilii and the Scipios. Even names that age has blotted out shine in the person of new heirs. That is how the nobility of the patricians has survived to this day from the founding of the city. Adoption is the remedy for Chance.[2]—I am well aware there are those who, because of their poverty, in corners and at leisure criticise those convicted of being rich, and never stop harrying them with accusations. But nothing in human affairs more clearly shows up virtue. It is income that raises to the rank of senator, income that separates the Roman knight from the plebs, income that wins promotion in the camp, income that chooses the judges in the forum.[3] Have I failed to persuade

[3] See the parallels cited by Mayor on Juv. 3.143, especially Plin. *N.H.* 14.5: " senator censu legi coeptus, iudex fieri censu, magistratum ducemque nihil exornare quam census . . ."

in foro legit. Non persuasi tibi? i ergo ad illos quos mavis sequi quam reducere.

18 Fusci Arelli patris. *Facilius possum paupertatem laudare quam ferre.* Quid mihi Phocionem loqueris, quid Aristiden? tunc paupertas erat saeculi. Quid loqueris Fabricios, quid Coruncanios? pompae ista exempla; ⟨tunc⟩ fictiles [1] fuerunt dii. Facile est ubi non noveris divitias esse pauperem. Quod vos liberis vestris optatis, ego meo impero.

19 Divisio. Non puto vos quaerere quomodo haec 117 controversia divisa sit, cum habeat negotii nihil; Fuscus tamen sic divisit: dico licuisse mihi adoptari, dico licuisse mihi recusare adoptionem; dico, ut non licuerit, recte tamen recusasse: et quod iure fit [verum est] [2] et quod sine iure, quod quidem rationem habeat, recte fit. Cum de iure diceret, dixit: " Sub arbitrio " inquit " patris es." Si ob hoc subicior patri quia filius sum, in hoc sine dubio, ut filius sim; et ad manum argumentum est: nempe abdicanti respondeo. Quid ita? qui [3] respondeo, scilicet id ago ne desinam filius esse; atque idem ago cum respondeo

---

[1] tunc fictiles *Drechsler:* fictilibus.
[2] *Deleted by the editor.*
[3] qui *ed.* (qui ei *Gertz*): que *B:* et *A:* quia *V.*

---

[1] That is, go and ask your friends, the disinherited sons, whom you prefer to join in their misfortune than to try to reconcile with their father (for this *colour* of Latro, see §30): *they* will tell you what a good idea wealth is.
[2] For pottery gods as a sign of antique poverty, cf. Juv.

you? Go and ask those whom you prefer to follow rather than to restore to their home.[1]

ARELLIUS FUSCUS SENIOR. I find it easier to praise 18 poverty than to put up with it. Don't tell me about Phocion, about Aristides. Poverty was fashionable in those days. Why talk of men like Fabricius and Coruncanius? Those are instances merely for show; that was a time when the gods were made of terracotta.[2]—It's easy to be poor when you haven't become acquainted with riches.—What you[3] make a prayer for your sons I make a command to mine.

Division

I cannot imagine you want to know how this *controversia* was divided—for it has no complications. 19 However, Fuscus' division went like this: I say it was legal for me to be adopted; I say it was legal for me to refuse adoption; I say that even if it was illegal, I nevertheless acted rightly in refusing. Both what is done according to the law and what is done against the law, so long as it is reasonable, is rightly done. On the topic of the law he said: " He says: You are under your father's control. Now if I am subject to my father just because I am his son, there is no doubt that the object is that I should *be* his son. And a proof is to hand. Am I not replying to one who is disinheriting me? Well, if I reply, I am surely acting in order that I should not cease to be his son. And I do the same thing when I reply to one who wants to

11.116 and Mayor *ad loc.* Plin. *N.H.* 34.34 remarks that statues were of wood or pottery down to the conquest of Asia Minor, " unde luxuria " (cf. p. 204 n. 1).
[3] The judges. The command is: Get rich.

emancipanti. *Quid* enim ad amittendum patrem *interest utrum eiciar an transferar?* Si non licet recusare, cur potius abdicas me quam tradis? Cum de officio diceret, in haec divisit: dico non fuisse dandum sine magna causa filium in adoptionem; dico multo minus a te; dico minime illi.

20 Silo Pompeius sic divisit: coepit a vetere et explosa quaestione, an in omnia *patri parendum sit; etiamsi in omnia, an ibi* tamen *non sit parendum quo efficitur ne pater sit;* deinde quaesit an invitus filius dari in adoptionem possit: si non potest, an ob id abdicari possit, 118 quod arbitrio suo usus est; an, ut possit, ⟨possit⟩ [1] non cum contra voluntatem patris, sed cum male arbitrio suo utitur. Hic subiecit an hic bene usus sit. Deinde officii partem tractavit, et ita divisit: turpem esse adoptionem, inutilem esse, periculosam esse. Cum diceret turpem, dixit: aliena bona invadere et trium filiorum subsessorem esse et liberis spem reconciliationis paternae eripere quam inhumanum est! Cum inutilem diceret, dixit patri inutilem esse, adoptanti inutilem esse, ⟨sibi inutilem esse⟩.[2] Cum patri inutilem diceret, tractavit quam *grave esset* filio *carere*

[1] *Added here by the ed.*
[2] *Supplied by Gronovius.*

---

[1] *Emancipatio* released a son from *patria potestas*, and could be the preliminary to adoption by another. The son argues that he can object both to disinheritance and to adoption by another, because in each case he is in fact not disobeying his father, but, in wanting to remain his son, supporting his authority.

release me from his control:[1] for what difference does it make, so far as losing one's father is concerned, whether I am thrown out or handed over? If I have no legal right to refuse, why are you disinheriting me rather than delivering me over to this man?"[2] On the topic of morality, he subdivided thus: I say that a son should not have been given away for adoption without a compelling motive—much less by you, and least of all to him.

Pompeius Silo's division went like this. He started 20 from an old and discredited topic: Is a father to be obeyed in everything? Even if he is, is he to be obeyed in something which means him no longer being a father? Then he asked if a son can be given away for adoption against his will. If he cannot, can he be disinherited for exercising his free will? Even if he can, can he be disinherited not when he exercises it against his father's wishes, but when he exercises it badly?[3] Here he added the question: *Did* the boy exercise it well? Then he dealt with the topic of morality, dividing it thus: Adoption in these circumstances is shameful, unprofitable, dangerous. On its being shameful, he said: "How cruel it is to invade the property of others, to lie in wait to ensnare three sons, to deprive children of the hope of reconciliation with their father!" On its being disadvantageous, he said it was so for the father, for the adopter and for himself. On its disadvantages for the father, he dealt with the point of how serious a matter it was to

[2] i.e. you could have had me adopted forcibly rather than disinherit me for refusing to be adopted.
[3] i.e. can he be disinherited for making a bad decision irrespective of its being a decision opposed by his father?

unico, ⟨quanto⟩ [1] *gravius eo quem alius concupisceret,* et
cum diceret divitem ipsum quoque, qui tot haberet
solacia, filium quaerere, dixit: tibi non erit facile
adoptare. Cum inutilem [rem] [2] diviti diceret, sic
tractavit: futurum ut ad suos rediret si non adoptas-
21 set. Hoc loco belle videbatur dixisse: si animum
patris intellegis, dat tibi notam reconciliandi suos:
negat se solitudinem pati posse. Cum inutilem esse
sibi diceret, paupertatem laudavit, in divitias invectus 11
est; dixit se posse divitiis corrumpi, quibus corrumpi
possent exercitus. Cum in divitias inveheretur,
dixit: Aiunt multa vitia divites habere istos et hoc
gravissimum: suos non amant. Nec est quod quisquam se putet satis firmum ad repellenda vitia: contactu ipso nocent transeunti. Timeo ne peccare
discam: ecce tu quam cito abdicare didicisti! Dixit
futurum ut diviti displiceret propius inspectus; ipsum
amorem paupertatis ab illis fastidiri; dixit futurum
ut abdicaretur si adoptatus ⟨non⟩ placuerit: [3] ego
nec meo placeo. Adiecit et periculosam sibi futuram
adoptionem in domo suos dominos desiderante, tota

---

[1] *Supplied by Müller.*
[2] *Deleted by Bursian.*
[3] non placuerit *Otto:* placuerunt.

---

[1] If the poor man takes the hint from what the rich man
says, he will realise he should try to reunite the rich man with
his children (rather than provide him with an adopted son).
Cf. §27 " It is true . . ."
[2] Bornecque refers to the corruption by luxury of the
Carthaginians in Campania in 216 B.C. (Liv. 23.18.10 *seq.*).

be without an only son, and even worse one whom another coveted. Remarking that even the rich man, equipped with so many comforts, was in search of a son, he said: " It will not be easy for *you* to adopt." On the disadvantages to the rich man, his treatment was that if he didn't adopt he would be free to return to his own sons. At this point he was 21 credited with a pretty *mot*: " If you[1] understand this father's mind, you will remark that he gives you the hint to reconcile his children to him: he says he cannot bear solitude." On the disadvantages to the son, he praised poverty, attacked riches. He said he might be corrupted by riches—which can corrupt whole armies.[2] While inveighing against wealth, he said: " They say those rich men have many vices, and worst of all they don't love their children. No-one should think he is strong enough to fend off vices: by the merest touch they infect the passer-by.[3] I am afraid I may learn to do wrong; look how soon *you*[4] learned how to disinherit! " He said the rich man would dislike him on closer inspection; the very love of poverty was an object of scorn to the rich; he would get disinherited if he found no favour after adoption—" Even my own father *I* do not please." He added that his adoption would be positively dangerous to himself in a house that missed its young masters, and that the household would be united in

But the reference is surely to mutinies and changing of sides caused by bribery: cf. *Decl.* p. 262.24 Ritter.

[3] Cf. Sen. *Tranq.* 7.3: " serpunt enim vitia et in proximum quemque transiliunt et contactu nocent."

[4] The poor man, on the example of his friend the rich man (above, p. 213 n. 6).

familia expellere insitivum heredem cupiente.

22 Latro ultimam quaestionem posuit quam fere solebat: etiamsi non recte fecit quod adoptari a divite
noluit, an tamen, ⟨si⟩[1] id bono adversus patrem
animo fecit, non ignoscendum sit; deinde: an bono
adversus patrem animo fecerit. In hac quaestione
bona pars adulescentis est patrem amantis et opibus
praeferentis; Latro tamen negabat patrem daturum
manus bono adversus se animo factum, sed consensum
filiorum adversus patres dicturum. †tacitum nescio 120]
quam†

23 . . . Brocco cuidam non malo rhetori visum erat, qui
dixerat adulescentem videri sibi habere operta[2]
quaedam vitia; male de se existimare eum qui ire ad
iudicem strictum innocentiae nollet.

Argentarius omnes priores transit partes, statim ad
hoc venit: debueritne patri parere an non debuerit;
et in figuram contulit declamationem. "Volo" inquit "aliquis filium abdicet qui petit a patre paupere
ut in adoptionem diviti daretur; quam bonam"
inquit "causam pater habebit! dicet hic . . .,"
deinde sic transit, cum declamasset eam controversiam quae posita non erat: "si ille filius malam
causam habet, ego bonam habeo." Contulit suam
causam cum illo.

[1] *Supplied by Bursian.*
[2] operta *Gertz:* capita.

its desire to get rid of the heir that had been foisted on it.

Latro made the last question his usual one: Even 22 if he was wrong to refuse to be adopted by a rich man, should he not be forgiven if he acted in a good spirit towards his father? Then: *Had* he acted in a good spirit towards his father? In this question the good role is that of the young man who loves his father and prefers him to wealth. But Latro said that the father would not concede that the action was done in a good spirit towards himself, but would say that it was the result of a conspiracy of the sons against their fathers.

. . . it had seemed to one Broccus, a tolerable 23 rhetor, who had said the youth appeared to him to have some hidden faults. If you refuse to join the family of a rigorous judge of innocence, you must have a bad opinion of yourself.

Argentarius passed over all the earlier sections, and came straight to this: Ought he to have obeyed his father or not? He gave the form of a figure [1] to his declamation. " I want to consider a case where someone disinherits a son who has asked his poverty-stricken father to let him be given for adoption to a rich man. What a good case such a father will have! He will say . . ." Then—having in this manner de-claimed a *controversia* that had *not* been set—he made his transition thus: " If *that* son has a bad case, *I* have a good one ": and he proceeded to compare his own case with the other.

[1] i.e. the *controversia* was given a special and artificial form (of a comparison), reminiscent of the familiar " figures " of word and thought. Cf. 1.1.15 n.

24   De colore magis quaesitum est: an adulescens
debeat in divitem aliquid dicere. Quid enim faciet?
dicet in eum qui tantum honoris illi habet, et in amicum paternum, non dicet in eum quem fugit? Et
illi tamen qui sibi abstinentiam conviciorum impera-
verant non bene praestiterunt; *aliquos sententiae dul-
cedo subrepsit,* cui non potuerunt obsistere. *Aridi
declamatores fidelius quos proposuerunt colores tuentur:*
nihil enim illos *sollicitat, nullum schema,* nulla sententia. 121
*Sic quae malam faciem habent saepius pudicae sunt: non
animus illis deest, sed corruptor.*

25   Fabianus philosophus hoc colore usus est ut diceret:
etiamsi sustinerem alicui tradi, at diviti nollem, et in
divitias dixit, non in divitem: illas esse quae frugali-
tatem, quae pietatem expugnassent, quae malos
patres, malos filios facerent.

*Gallus Vibius fuit tam magnae olim eloquentiae quam
postea insaniae, cui hoc accidisse uni scio, ut in insaniam
non casu incideret, sed iudicio perveniret; nam dum in-
sanos imitatur, dum lenocinium ingeni furorem putat, quod
simulabat ad verum redegit.* Hic controversiam postero

26 die quam erat a Fabiano dicta declamavit; solebat
autem sic ad locos pervenire, ut amorem descripturus
paene cantantis modo diceret: " amorem describere
volo " sic tamquam " bacchari volo "; deinde de-

---

[1] Than about the division (cf. §19).
[2] i.e. the poor father.
[3] Sen. *Ben.* 3.16.3: " Chastity is a proof of ugliness ";
Juv. 10.296–8.

There was more discussion about the *colour*.[1] 24
Ought the youth to criticise the rich man? Think
what that means. Is he to reproach one who is doing
him so signal an honour, his father's friend, while
saying nothing against the man he is having to flee?[2]
Yet even those declaimers who committed themselves to abstaining from abuse did not keep to their
promises very well; some were lured on by the
delights of epigram, and could not resist. It is the
dry declaimers who keep more faithfully to the *colours*
they have laid down. There is nothing to bother
them, no figure, no epigram. In just the same way it
is the ugly women who are more frequently chaste;[3]
it's not the motive they lack—it's the seducer.

The philosopher Fabianus' *colour* led him to say: 25
" Even if I could stand being handed over to another,
I should not want to be handed over to a rich man ":
and he inveighed, not against the rich man but
against wealth. It was wealth that had taken frugality and natural affection by storm, wealth that
made bad fathers and bad sons.

Vibius Gallus was once as eloquent as he was later
crazed. He was the one man of my acquaintance not
to have fallen into madness by chance but to have come
to it by an act of judgement. He aped the mad,
thought insanity would be a good pander to his
genius—and so made a reality of what he pretended.
He declaimed this *controversia* the day after Fabianus.
Now he used to approach his commonplaces in the 26
following manner. If he was going to describe love,
he would say, in a tone almost like a singer's: " I wish
to describe love," rather as if he were saying: " I
wish to rave like a bacchant." Then he would pro-

scribebat et ⟨ut⟩ [1] totiens coepturus repetebat: "amorem describere volo." In hac controversia plane quod voluit consecutus est, ut divitias nobis in odium adduceret: saepe enim ingessit: "divitias describere volo," et multa facunde explicuit, corruptius quam Fabianus sed dulcius. Hoc unum 122 occurrit in quo pusillum inest insaniae: "*non me delectant ignoti servorum domino greges nec sonantia laxi ruris ergastula: patrem gratis amo.*"

27 Fuscus Arellius [et] [2] hunc colorem dixit: Ominibus offendor. Cum primum de adoptione ista cogitarem, occurrerunt mihi tres abdicati, et audio in ista domo tres fuisse filios nec esse. *Timeo infelicem liberis domum.* Et alias causas dixit—licet enim plura abdicato dicere propter quae non ablegetur [3]—, sed nunc refero cui rei quisque maxime institerit.

Latro illo colore usus est, sodalem se tribus divitis filiis fuisse: "Semper" inquit "illos colui, immo adhuc colo. Cum abdicati essent, ego illis suasi ut tacerent et patrem cedendo mitigarent; dixi: cum primum tempestivum putabitis, patrem vestrum rogabit meus. Ecce admonent me aptissimum esse

---

[1] *Supplied by Müller.*
[2] *Deleted by Müller.*
[3] ablegetur *Müller:* leget.

ceed with his description; and, as though making
repeated fresh starts, he would keep saying: " I
wish to describe love." In this *controversia* he completely attained his objective of making us hate
wealth. For he kept dinning into us: " I wish to
describe wealth," and made many eloquent developments, in worse taste than Fabianus but more at-
tractively. I only remember one thing involving a
tiny bit of madness: " I do not like gangs of slaves
whom their master does not know,[1] slave-camps filling
the countryside with their din for miles around. I
love my father—free of charge."

Arellius Fuscus used this *colour*: " I am put off by 27
omens. When I was first pondering on this adoption, I met three disinherited sons; now I hear that
there were once three sons in that household—but
they aren't there now. I am afraid of a house that
bodes no good to children." And he gave further
reasons—disinherited sons are allowed to give several
reasons why they should not be thrown out; but
now I am noting what each declaimer particularly
stressed.

Latro used the *colour* that he had been the companion of the rich man's three sons. " I always kept
up with them—in fact I still do. When they were
disinherited, *I* advised them to keep quiet and try to
soothe their father by giving in to him. I said: ' As
soon as you think the time is ripe, my father will try
to persuade yours.' Well, here they come to let me
know the time is exactly right. It is true—my

---

[1] For slaves so numerous their master does not know them,
cf. Sen. *Beat. Vit.* 17.2; Petr. 37.9 (and 47.12); *Decl.* 13.13
and p. 33.21 Ritter.

tempus. Verum est; *non potest pater invenire recon-*
ciliationis aptius tempus: dives filios quaerit."

28 Cestius illo colore: Quos abdicatione non potuit
terrere, putat se castigaturum adoptione. Non ille
tuum filium concupiscit: suos corrigit. Cum illos
correctos putaverit, me satis minatum abdicabit.
" Non faciet "inquit. Atqui neminem adhuc habuit
in quo hoc aut facilius aut iustius faceret.

Fabianus hoc colore, ut dixi, egit: nolo dives esse.

Rufus Vibius hoc: nescio dives esse. Haec in hoc 123
oco cum diceret excepta sunt: non est quod putes
omnibus divitias convenire; nihil est indecentius [1]
novicio divite. Et illud dixit: alius animose loquatur
et ex contemptu divitiarum gloriam petat; ego non
dico: " dives esse nolo," sed " nescio."

29 Albucius et ipse divitias insecutus est, et dixit
pulchram de Fabricio sententiam: " munera "inquit
"regia respuit: cum auro dominum noluit [2] accipere." Et illum locum egregie tractavit: Omnes
cibos habebo suspectos, omnes potiones; trium pae-
dagogi illic ⟨sunt⟩; [3] occidere me volet quisquis
frugalissimus fuerit. Non venenum pauperes timent,
non heredem; adhuc nec abdicationem timebamus.

30 Silo Pompeius illo colore egit: nemo illi placere

---

[1] indecentius *Thomas:* innocentius.
[2] noluit *Müller:* et.
[3] illic (*Bursian*) sunt *Kiessling:* illis.

---

[1] His disinheritance of his own sons having been harder
and less just.

father can find no apter time for his task of reconciliation: the rich man is in search of sons."

Cestius' *colour*: " He thinks he can punish by adop- 28 tion those he failed to frighten by disinheritance. It's not that he wants your son—he's trying to mend the ways of his own children. When he thinks they're reformed, he will disinherit me, my job of threatening complete. ' He won't do that.' Yet up to now he has had no-one to whom he could do it more easily or more justly." [1]

Fabianus, as I said,[2] used the *colour*: " I don't want to be rich."

Vibius Rufus' *colour*: " I don't know how to be rich." These remarks of his on the topic were popular: " You shouldn't imagine riches suit everybody. Nothing is more indecent than a *nouveau riche*." He also said: " Others may talk big, and try to win a reputation by scorning riches. *I* do not say: ' I don't want to be rich,' but ' I don't know how to be rich.' "

Albucius, too, inveighed against wealth, and spoke 29 a fine epigram on Fabricius: " He rejected a king's [3] presents: he didn't want to get a master along with the gold." And he treated the following topic excellently: " Every meal, every drink will be suspect for me; the slave attendants of the three are there—and the most honest of them will long to be my murderer. The poor have neither poison nor an heir to fear; [4] up to now I didn't even fear disinheritance."

Pompeius Silo used this *colour*: " Nobody can 30

2 §25.
3 Pyrrhus': cf. *C.* 5.2.
4 Cf. Juv. 10.25–7.

potest; ne in hoc quidem aliquem retinuit, ut non omnes abdicaret. "Ecce nunc" inquit "invenit novam abdicationem, ne quid de reditu sperare possent." Et cum multa dixisset in divitem, dixit: non est quod mireris si te odi; amo quos abdicasti.

Color a parte patris aliquid curae desiderat. Quidam induxerunt patrem cupidum divitiarum, quod invidiosum est in hoc visum, quia ita divitias filio dare vult ut filiis eripiat. Itaque Latro optimo colore usus est: in hoc, inquit, te in adoptionem volo dare, ut facilius per te abdicati reconcilientur. 124

Cestius: "timeo" inquit "ne abdicer": vellem timeres.

31 Albucius hoc colore usus est: summam sibi amicitiam cum divite fuisse; dixisse illum sibi dubitanti an filium tolleret: "tolle" inquit "in meum patrimonium; ego istum fratrem liberorum ⟨meorum⟩ [1] iudicabo." Itaque cum et tertium abdicaret, dixit: quid sic mihi illudis tamquam unicus? etiamnunc filium habeo. Venit ad me et ait: redde quem educasti mihi: *si emendati fuerint liberi mei, habebo hunc cum illis; si perseveraverint* furere, *habebo* hunc *pro illis.* Temptavi statim reducere illum in gratiam cum filiis:

---

[1] *Supplied by Jahn.*

---

[1] i.e. by the rich man. The father's reply alludes to the disinheritance he has himself inflicted.

please him. He didn't even keep one of his sons to avoid disinheriting them all. Look, now he has found a novel type of disinheritance—depriving them of any hope of return." After much invective against the rich man, he said: " You shouldn't be surprised if I hate you; I love those you disinherited."

The *colour* on the father's side needs some care. Some introduced a father who was greedy for wealth; but this was thought to reflect badly on the father, because he wants to give his son riches in such a way as to deprive other sons of them. And so Latro used the best *colour*: " I want to give you for adoption in order that through you the disinherited sons may be the more easily reconciled with their father."

Cestius: " 'I am afraid I may be disinherited,'[1] he says. I could wish you *were* afraid."[2]

Albucius employed this *colour*: He had been on the best of terms with the rich man, who had said to him when he was hesitating to acknowledge his son: " Acknowledge him—to inherit my estate. I shall regard him as brother to my children." So when he was disinheriting his third, he said: " Why do you[3] jeer at me like this, as though you were the only one left? I still have a child." " He came to me and said: ' Give me the boy you have raised for me. If my children reform, I will have this one as well as them; if they continue in their folly, I will have this one instead of them.' I tried straight away to bring him back to terms with his sons, but the time was not

[2] The son took disinheritance calmly, having nothing to lose: cf. §17.
[3] The third son.

intempestivum erat. Temptavi cogere subtrahendo meum: respondit, tamquam non posset diviti deesse filius.

32 Silo dixit: " amicus " inquit " abdicatorum sum." Quid ergo? mavis inimicum adoptet? Si intraveris domum, videbis an aliqui animum patris a filiis avertant. " Si reduxerit " inquit " illos, quid me [1] fiet? " Capit divitis domus et quattuor liberos. Si te illi fratrem gravabuntur, libentissime recipiam. Sic de me dives meruit, ut illi ⟨et⟩ [2] dare filium paratus sim 125 et commodare.

Blandus hoc colore egit, ut diceret divitem inexorabilem liberis esse. Omnia se fecisse ut illum placaret; videri esse magnas causas et graves; itaque certam futuram adoptionem.

33 *Otho Iunius pater* solebat difficiles controversias belle dicere, eas in quibus inter silentium et detectionem [3] medio temperamento opus erat. *Edidit* quidem *quattuor libros colorum, quos belle Gallio noster Antiphontis libros vocabat: tantum in illis somniorum est.* Et hoc vitium ab antiquis qui artem dicendi tradebant duxerat; illi enim colores probabant qui non possunt coargui, non ut somnia, sed ut non essent aliquo nomine offensui. Sed ridiculum est adfectari quod falsum probari non possit. Non multum interest in

---

[1] quid me *Müller:* et quid.
[2] *Supplied by Bursian.*
[3] detectionem *Gertz:* actionem.

ripe. I tried to force his hand by refusing my son; the tone of his reply suggested that a rich man could never be without a son."[1]

Silo said: "'I am the friend of the sons he dis-inherited,' he says. What of it? Do you prefer him to adopt an enemy? If you become part of his house, you will be able to find out if people are alienating the father from his sons.[2] 'If he brings them back, what will become of me?' A rich man's house has room even for four sons. If they find you annoying to have as a brother, I will most gladly take you back. The rich man has done so well by me that I am ready to give him my son—or to lend him." **32**

Blandus' *colour* was to say that the rich man was irreconcilable to his sons. He had done everything to soothe the rich man; it was clear that the reasons for the disinheritance were good and compelling, so the adoption would be secure.

Junius Otho senior used to declaim difficult *contro-versiae* very prettily—I mean those where one needed a blend half-way between silence and bald statement. He published four books of *colours*, which my friend Gallio wittily used to call "the books of Antiphon," so full are they of dreams. He had picked up this fault from the ancient preceptors of oratory, who used to recommend irrefutable *colours*—not dreams necessarily, but such as would give no offence under some circumstances. But it is laughable to make a point of something that cannot be proved false. It makes little difference whether you put up a false **33**

---

[1] The rich man could always get another by adoption, and so could not be blackmailed by the poor man.

[2] And so be able to help your friends.

causa sua falsum aliquis testem det an se: alteri enim
credi non debet, alteri non solet.

34   Otho tamen Iunius bene dicebat has controversias
quae suspiciose dicendae erant. Itaque memini
optime illum dicere pro †hac re ne† adulteri reo, in
quem [1] Syriacus Vallius, homo disertus, [ad] [2] calum- 12(
niam iuraverat. Erat genus iudici tale: speciosum
iuvenem dominus suus deprehendisse cum uxore in
cubiculo testatus est et ob hoc uxorem suam dimisit;
hoc nomine servum adulteri postulatum dominus non
defendebat, mulier, in quam petebatur praeiudicium,
tuebatur. Opus erat aliquo colore, cum in cubiculo
35   visa esset cum servo et marito. Otho Iunius nullam
rem certam posuit, sed tantum circumventam a viro
mulierem egregie tractavit; cuius actio quam utilis
fuisset, statim adparuit Nigro Bruttedio dicente, qui
hoc colore usus est: arcessitum a domino servum ut
inter se medius et dominam recumberet; illam non
esse passam; maritum indignatum prosiluisse quasi
in corruptorem. ⟨Verbo in hac re aeque corrupto⟩ [3]
usus est quam colore: dixit enim arcessitum servum

---

[1] quem *ed.:* quam.
[2] *Deleted by Opsopoeus.*
[3] *Supplied by Müller after Gertz.*

---

[1] i.e. if your *colour* depends on an alleged dream, you cannot
prove you ever dreamt it: cf. Quintilian 4.2.94 (such colours
are too easy to carry weight).

[2] This was presumably a real case; but the speakers behave
as though still in the school.

[3] An accuser had to swear his accusation was not malicious
(*RE* s.v. calumnia col. 1415).

[4] A slave would usually be defended by his master (here the

witness or yourself where your own case is concerned:
the liar is to be disbelieved—and you yourself
generally are.[1]

However, Junius Otho was good at declaiming 34
controversiae which needed to be spoken allusively.
And so I recall that he shone particularly on behalf
of the slave (?) charged with adultery,[2] against
whom the eloquent Vallius Syriacus had sworn he
brought no false charge.[3] The case was like this: a
man attested that he had caught an attractive youth,
a slave of his, with his wife in her bedroom, and on
this pretext divorced his wife. The slave was therefore prosecuted for adultery. His master did not
speak in his defence, but the woman did, a pre-
judgement being sought against her.[4] There was
need of some *colour*, since she had been seen in the
bedroom with the slave and her husband. Junius 35
Otho made no definite statement, but put up an excellent show of the woman having merely been trapped
by her husband. How useful this speech had been
was immediately made clear during that of Bruttedius
Niger, who used this *colour*: The slave had been sent
for by his master to lie between him and his mistress.
She had not tolerated it; the husband had got angry,
and threw himself on the slave as though he were a
seducer. On this topic he made use of a word in as
bad taste as his *colour*: he said the servant was sent
for to give a " sop " to his master's lust.[5] When

prosecutor). But if he were convicted, that would prove the
wife guilty in advance (*praeiudicium*), and so she defends him.
[5] For a discussion of this obscure passage, see O. Immisch,
Glotta 15 (1927), 150-3, answered by Th. Birt, *ibid.* 17 (1929),
71-5.

ut dominicae libidini paparium faceret. Syriacus, cum secunda actione hunc colorem urgueret, diserte multa dixit, inter quae et hoc: " adulterum accusator in cubiculum usque perduxit, patronus in lectum," et paene causam abstulit. [et] [1] Illud autem tum *Syriacus* vafre fecit et belle respondit: cum prima 12 actione diceret, non posuit causam, sed argumentatus est; dixit probaturum se deprehensam in cubiculo 36 cum servo. Niger Bruttedius, cum ageret, obiecit Syriaco quod causam non posuisset, et [non] [2] institit adsidue quare non appareret quomodo servus sollicitatus esset, quomodo perductus in cubiculum. Cum responderet Syriacus, ait: Primum non apud eundem praeceptorem studuimus: tu Apollodorum habuisti, cui semper narrari placet, ego Theodorum, cui non semper. Deinde ⟨quod⟩ [3] quaeris, Niger, quare ego non narraverim: ut tu ista narrares feci. Et *contra Maximum Stertinium, a quo premebatur, cum comes eius fuisset, dixit: Per annos duodecim in officio tuo fui; dic quid* in domo tua *peccaverim? Sed haec est consuetudo vestra: iniuriam vocatis finem servitutis;* tamdiu vobis cordi sumus quamdiu usui. Haec a Syriaco dicta et magnis excepta clamoribus cum occurrerent mihi, praeterire non potui.

[1] *Deleted by Sander.*
[2] *Omitted by the early editors.*
[3] *Supplied by Gertz.*

Syriacus was attacking this *colour* in a second speech, he said a good many clever things, including this: "The adulterer was taken into the bedroom by prosecuting counsel, and into bed by defence counsel."[1] And he pretty well walked off with the case. Here is an example of Syriacus' clever devices and pretty repartee in the same case; in the first speech he did not give a narration of the facts, but merely argued, saying he would prove that the woman had been surprised in the bedroom with a slave. Brut- 36 tedius Niger in his speech reproached Syriacus with not having explained the case, and kept on pressing the point why it was unclear how the slave had been seduced and brought to the bedroom. When Syriacus replied, he said: "First of all, we did not study under the same teachers. You had Apollodorus, who likes always to have a narration. I had Theodorus, who doesn't always insist on one.[2] Then as to your complaint, Niger, that I didn't narrate: I made *you* do it." And against Stertinius Maximus, who had attacked him despite their being old friends, he said: "For twelve years I was in your circle: tell me what I did wrong in your house. But this is typical of your type. You call the ending of slavery an insult. We are to your liking as long as we are of use to you." I couldn't leave out these witticisms of Syriacus, received as they were with great applause, once I recalled them.

[1] i.e. the defence counsel's *colour* had (quite unnecessarily) conceded the presence of the slave in the bed; the prosecuting counsel merely claimed he had been in the room.

[2] For the differences between the rigorous Apollodorus and the more easy-going Theodorus, see G. M. A. Grube, *A.J.P.* 80 (1959), 337 *seq.*

37   Ad Othonem redeo, a quo longius aberravi. Solebat hos colores qui silentium et significationem
desiderant bene ⟨dicere⟩;[1] itaque et hanc controversiam hoc colore dixit, tamquam in emendationem
abdicatorum et reconciliationis causa faceret. Hoc
non detegebat, sed omnibus sententiis utebatur ad
hoc tendentibus, tamquam: " Non possum " inquit 128
" pati sine patre." Me autem sine te putas pati
posse? quemquam autem patrem putas pati sine
liberis posse? Et illud: credite mihi, impium nihil
de liberis duo patres cogitant. Et illud: " Recipiat "
inquit " suos; non possum sine te pati." Hoc fortasse illi placebit, quod ad tuum patrem reverti voles.
Et illud: Non amas abdicatos? domum illorum oc-
38 cupa. Amas? serva. Dixit et illud: " libenter "
inquit " pauper sum ": et ego. Dicet aliquis:
" quare ergo in adoptionem diviti filium? " Recipiet
excusationem si dixero: filii mei causa facio; honestius autem nunc facio quam si filii mei ⟨causa⟩[2]
facerem. Et illud: hoc aut meum consilium est aut
illius aut commune; consentiatis licet: duos senes
iungitis. Et illud: O temerariam adulescentiae et
incautam contumaciam! Fortasse iam supervacua
esset adoptio si non repugnasset. ⟨Et⟩ illud: non

[1] *Supplied by Otto.*
[2] *Supplied by Haase.*

---

[1] i.e. the poor son's love for his natural father might win over
the rich man to get reconciled with his natural sons.
[2] i.e. I do it for the other three.
[3] The rich man's. The two are in league over the adoption,

I have strayed a long way from Otho: let me return 37
to him. He was usually very good at *colours* which
required silence and hints. So he spoke on *this* theme
with a *colour* which represented the poor man as aim-
ing to reform the disinherited sons and reconcile them
to their father. He didn't reveal this, but all the
epigrams he used tended in this direction, for
example: " ' I cannot endure without my father,' he
says. But do you think *I* can endure without *you*?
Do you think *any* father can endure without his children? " Also: " Believe me, these two fathers have
no unnatural plots in mind for their children " and:
" ' Let him take his own back,' he says. ' I cannot
endure without you.' Perhaps this will please the
rich man—your wanting to return to your father."[1]
And: " You dislike the disinherited sons? Take
over their home. You like them? Then look after
it for them." He also said: " ' I am glad to be poor,' 38
says he. So am I. Someone will object: ' Why then
do you give your son to be adopted by a rich man? '
He will accept my excuse if I say: ' I do it for the
sake of my son.' But in fact I am acting more uprightly than if I did it for the sake of my son."[2]
This too: " This is either my idea or his[3] or a joint
one. You[4] may consent: you are joining two old
men." This also: " O, the rash and thoughtless
stubbornness of youth! Adoption might by now be
superfluous if he had not rebelled."[5] And: " I will

and they have "no unnatural plots in mind " because the
poor man is planning a reconciliation.

[4] The judges.

[5] That is, if the son had agreed to the adoption, the reconciliation might have taken place before the actual ceremony.

recipio; omnia licet facias, non ego ero pater orbo divite. Et illud in ultimo: Scis et me non invitum esse pauperem; ego te genui, ego divitias docui contemnere; sequere auctoritatem meam. Nihil turpiter suadeo, nihil sordide concupisco; crede fidei meae, hoc fieri expedit. " Quoi? " inquit: mihi, tibi, diviti; nihil amplius dico.

39 Totam [inquit] bene dixit controversiam, sed hoc genere ut putares illo dicente sic esse dicendam, deinde mirareris quid illi suspiciosa actione opus 129 fuisset cum aperta uti liceret. Belle de hoc vitio illius Scaurus aiebat illum acta in aurem legere.

Glycon Spyridion ex altera parte satis dulcem dixit sententiam: ἀγνωμόνως[1] ἀποκηρύττεις ὁμολογῶν ὅτι ἐφίλησας. Artemon dixit: οὐκ ἔστιν, πάτερ, τῶν βεβαίων κτημάτων πλοῦτος· ἑνὸς πλουσίου[2] τρεῖς ἀπόρρητοι ὑπαντῶσιν. Hermagoras dixit: περιελευσόμεθα τέσσαρες ἑνὸς ἀπόρρητοι.

II

IUSIURANDUM MARITI ET UXORIS

Vir et uxor iuraverunt ut, si quid alteri obtigisset, alter moreretur. Vir peregre profectus misit nuntium ad uxorem qui diceret decessisse

---

[1] ἀγνωμόνως *Müller:* OTΙOMONCYC.
[2] ἑνὸς πλουσίου *Gertz:* ΕΝΟΕΙΤαΟΙϹΙΟ.

not take you back. You may do what you like, but *I* will not be a father while the rich man is without children."[1] And, at the end: "You know that I too am happy to be poor. It was I who begot you, I who taught you to despise wealth. Follow my authority. I am advising nothing shameful, desiring nothing base. Trust in my good faith: this is expedient. 'For whom?' he asks. For me, for you, for the rich man. I say nothing more."

He spoke the whole *controversia* well, but in such a 39 way that while he was speaking you would think that that was the only way to speak it—afterwards you would wonder what need there had been for that allusive manner when it was possible to be open. Scaurus said nicely of this fault of his that he "reads the newspaper into your ear."

Glycon Spyridion, on the other side, said a quite agreeable epigram: "You are senseless to disinherit him when you agree that you loved him."[2] Artemon said: "Riches, father, are no secure possession, seeing that you come across three sons of one rich man— disinherited." Hermagoras said: "We will go around begging, the four disinherited by one."

2

The Oath Sworn by Husband and Wife

A husband and wife took an oath that if anything should happen to either of them the other would die. The husband went off on a trip abroad, and sent a message to his wife to say

---

[1] But after the reconciliation I will have you back.
[2] Cf. §14 "I am absolutely . . ."

virum. Uxor se praecipitavit. Recreata iube-
tur a patre relinquere virum; non vult. Abdicatur.

1   PORCI LATRONIS. *Dii inmortales, qua debetis providentia humanum genus regitis: effecistis ut illud non
periculum esset amantis sed experimentum.*

CESTI PII. Antequam iuraremus, diu haec inter
nos tacita lex erat. Si abdicata fuerit, non vivet.
Hoc illi pater non credit. Non est novum; nec vir
credidit. Quaeris quod iusiurandum fuerit? " ita
patri placeam."

FUSCI ARELLI patris. Iam, uxor, non navigabo, 130
non peregrinabor. Fides tua me timidum fecit.
" Mentitus ⟨es⟩ " [1] inquit; hoc sollemne est amantibus; ideo non nisi iurantibus credimus. *Hos dividere
vult socer quos ne mors quidem dividet?* " Moriar "
inquit; " habeo et causam et exemplum: quaedam ardenti-
bus rogis se maritorum miscuerunt, quaedam* vicaria
maritorum salutem anima redemerunt. Quam magna
gloria *brevi sollicitudine* pensata est! " O te felicem,
uxor! *inter has viva numeraris.*

----

[1] *Supplied by Otto.*

----

[1] An advocate would speak for her; where she is represented
as speaking (as in Cestius' first epigram), this is the report of
the advocate.

[2] Cf. Hispo's last epigram in §2.

[3] In this and the following epigram (cf. §3 " Father-in-
law . . .") the husband is represented as speaking.

that he had died. The wife threw herself off a
cliff. Revived, she is told by her father to leave
her husband. She does not want to, and is disinherited.

For the woman [1]

PORCIUS LATRO. Immortal gods, it is with proper 1
forethought that you rule the human race: you have
caused this to be for a loving wife not a peril but a
test.

CESTIUS PIUS. Before we swore, this had for long
been an unspoken rule for us.—If she is disinherited,
she will not live.[2] Her father does not believe this.
That is nothing new—her husband did not believe it
either.—You ask what the oath was by? "So may I
please my father."

ARELLIUS FUSCUS SENIOR. From now on, my wife,
I [3] shall not sail the seas, I shall not go abroad.
Your loyalty has made me cautious.—"You lied,"
she says. This is the way of lovers; that is why we
only believe statements on oath.—Does a father-in-
law propose to sever a couple whom even death will
not sever?—"I shall die," she says. "I have a
motive, and a precedent. Some have joined their
husbands on their blazing pyres,[4] some have bought
their husband's safety at the cost of a life in exchange.[5] What immense glory won by a short
agony!" How lucky you are, wife! You are num-
bered among women like these—while you are still
alive.

[4] Cf. §11; *C.* 2.5.8; 10.3.2. The Romans were aware of
Indian suttee (e.g. Val. Max. 2.6.14).
[5] Most notably Alcestis, who died to save her husband
Admetus.

2   MARULLI.   *Adsiduae contentiones erant:* " ego magis amo ": " immo ego "; " *sine te vivere non possum* ": " *immo ego sine te* ";   *qui solet exitus esse certaminum*, *iuravimus*.   Respexistis nos, di, quos numquam violavimus.

HISPONIS ROMANI.   Difficile est, iudices, eorum secretorum causas reddere quae amantibus etiam sine ratione iucunda sunt.   Nec est quod putetis de abdicatione hodie tantum illius agi: de spiritu agitur.   Scitis quemadmodum suos amet: non magis sine patre vivere potest quam sine viro.

3   IUNI GALLIONIS.   Socer—hoc enim te appellabo, quamdiu vixero—, quid sibi volunt altiores gemitus et fortiora inter lacrimas suspiria?   Nescio quid videris fortius, puella, promittere.   Non sum tanti ut bis pro me pericliteris.

ARGENTARI.   Nocet illi indulgentia suorum.   In duo pericula mulier incidit, quorum neutrum esset 13 experta si aut minus amaret virum aut minus amaret patrem.

ALFI FLAVI.   Nec est quod putetis illi facilius istius esse desiderium: et patrem amat, tamquam mori iuraverit.

4   Pars altera.   P. ASPRENATIS.   Nempe, si quid acciderit viro, uxor peritura est; et, si bene filiam

MARULLUS. There were continual disputes: " I 2 love more." " No, *I* do." [1] " I can't live without you." " Nor I without you." We swore an oath—the usual end to such disputes.—You looked favourably on us, gods—we never wronged you.[2]

ROMANIUS HISPO. It is hard, judges, to explain those private arrangements that lovers find sweet even for no reason.—Nor should you imagine that today we are concerned solely with her being disinherited: it is her life that is at stake. You know how she loves her dear ones; she cannot live without her father any more than without her husband.

JUNIUS GALLIO. Father-in-law (for I shall call you 3 that as long as I live), what is the meaning of those deep groans, those heavy sighs, those tears? You look, girl, as though you propose some too drastic course.[3] I am not worth your endangering yourself for me twice.

ARGENTARIUS. She is the victim of her affection for those dear to her. The poor woman has run two dangers, neither of which would she have had to face if she loved her husband or her father less.

ALFIUS FLAVUS. You should not think that she would find the loss of her father any less a grief: she loves him too—as much as if she had sworn to die.[4]

The other side

PUBLIUS ASPRENAS. In fact, if anything happens to 4 the husband, the wife is to die. And, if I know my

---

[1] Cf. the protestations of Acme and Septimius in Catullus 45.

[2] The woman kept her oath, and the gods made sure she did not die (cf. §9 " Spare me . . .").

[3] i.e. suicide.

[4] " If anything happened "—in this case disinheritance.

meam novi, [peritura est] [1] si quid genero meo acciderit filia mea moritura est; adiciam quod sit
indignum: si quid filiae meae acciderit, vir eius vic-
turus est. Vide qua te lege constrinxeris: si parueris
⟨non vives, si non parueris⟩ [2] vives.

BLANDI. O condicionem aequam! alteri vitam
debet, alteri devovet.

PAPIRI FABIANI. *" Non possum " inquit " relinquere
virum." Quicquam non potes quae mori potes? Paene
qui falsae mortis nuntium miserat verae recepit.* Vir,
dum nimis amat uxorem, paene causa periculi fuit;
uxor, dum nimis amat virum, paene causa luctus fuit;
pater, dum nimis amat filiam, abdicat. Servate,
⟨di⟩,[3] totam domum amore mutuo laborantem.
" Moriar " inquit: hoc patri minaris, viro promittis.
Potes sine viro pati; peregrinationem eius tulisti. Facilius potest carere eo cui spiritum debet quam eo cui
inpendit.

5   Et haec controversia non eget divisione; nam
praeter illam quaestionem, an pater abdicare possit 132
propter matrimonium, reliqua, cum ad aequitatem
pertineant, tractationis sunt. Optimam tamen
quaestionem coniecturalem Latro [fecit] [4] proposuit
illam: an, etiamsi non malo adversus uxorem animo

---

[1] *Deleted by Thomas.*
[2] *Supplied by Faber.*
[3] *Supplied by Schultingh.*
[4] *Deleted by Thomas.*

daughter, she *will* die if anything happens to my son-in-law. I shall add something that will shock: if anything happens to my daughter, her husband will go on living.—See what a rule you have tied yourself with! If you obey it you will die, if you disobey you will live.

BLANDUS. What a fair offer! She owes her life to the one, and is ready to sacrifice it for the other.

PAPIRIUS FABIANUS. "I cannot leave my husband." Is there anything you are not capable of doing if you are capable of dying?—The man who sent news of a pretence death all but received news of a real one.—A husband, too dearly loving his wife, was almost a cause of danger to her. A wife, too dearly loving her husband, was almost a cause of mourning to him. A father, too dearly loving his daughter, disinherits her. Gods, save the whole family—its trouble is its mutual affection.—"I shall die." This is a threat to your father, a promise to your husband.—You can endure without your husband; you put up with him being away abroad.—She can do without the man to whom she owes her life more easily than the man on whom she throws it away.

This *controversia*, too,[1] does not require a division. 5 For apart from the question, Can a father disinherit because of a marriage, everything else, being concerned with equity, is a matter of development.[2] However Latro brought up the following excellent conjectural point:[3] Even if the husband did not act

[1] Cf. *C.* 2.1.19.
[2] See Introduction, p. xviii.
[3] A point, that is, of *fact*, as opposed to equity and morality: cf. *C.* 2.1.22.

[fuit] [1] maritus fecit, tamen tam temerarius et in-
consultus relinquendus sit; deinde: an etiam malo
adversus uxorem animo fecerit. Fuscus Arellius
iuris quaestioni subiecit, non posse illam discedere a
viro: nam et hoc illam iureiurando obligavit. *Hunc*
enim *animum sine dubio fuisse iurantium, ut vivi non
diducerentur, cum illud quoque caverint, ne morte divi-*
6 *derentur.* Latroni contrarium videbatur onerari
iurisiurandi invidiam, cum extenuari deberet; ait:
illud iusiurandum contra fortunam videtur, hoc etiam
contra patrem.

Cestius contra fecit: ex toto dixit *iureiurando illam
liberatam illo casu;* solutos ipsos vinculo religionis et
ideo non futurum periculum uxori si quid accidisset
viro.

Silo Pompeius contra dixit illam teneri iureiurando,
et adiecit, etiamsi repudio diducta fuerit, non tamen
solvi foederis pactionem; " et ideo " inquit " honestum morti nostrae titulum vindico, ne, si quid acciderit, aut ego pro aliena uxore moriar aut illa pro
alieno viro."

7 Hispo Romanius hoc colore usus est: iusiurandum
iocosum fuisse; sicut multa cotidie iurarent amantes,
et ipsum iurasse; itaque oblitum se eam iurasse, 13
misisse nuntium ut experiretur ⟨an⟩ [2] affectus uxoris

---

[1] *Deleted by Kiessling.*
[2] *Supplied by Madvig.*

maliciously towards his wife, should she not leave so impulsive and imprudent a partner? Then: *Did* he act maliciously towards his wife? Arellius Fuscus added to the question of law the point that she could not leave her husband, for he had bound her to this too by the oath—it had undoubtedly been their intention when they swore that they should not be separated while still alive, for they had taken this step to ensure they were not separated in death either. Latro thought it unhelpful to increase the 6 unpopularity [1] arising from the oath when it ought to be lessened. "That oath seems to be directed against fortune; this one against the father as well."

Cestius did the opposite, saying she had been altogether freed from the oath by that circumstance; they were liberated from the constraint of scruple, and so there would be no danger to the wife if anything happened to the husband.

Pompeius Silo, on the other hand, said she was still bound by the oath, and added that even if she were separated from him by divorce the terms of the pact remained in force. "That is why I claim an honourable title for our death,[2] in case, should anything happen, I should have to die for someone else's wife—or she for someone else's husband."

Romanius Hispo used this *colour*: the oath had been 7 a joke—the man had sworn as lovers constantly swear every day. So he had forgotten the oath she had taken, and had sent a message to try out whether his

---

[1] Affecting the husband. "That oath" is the oath as ordinarily interpreted, "this one" the oath as construed by Fuscus.

[2] Meaning uncertain.

permaneret.[1] Uxorem intellexisse falsum nuntium
esse et ex eo se loco praecipitasse ex quo praecipitata
perire non posset, " ut, quomodo ego illam " inquit
" falso nuntio terrueram, sic illa " inquit " me falso
periculo terreret."

Marullus praeceptor noster licenter verbo usus est
satis sensum exprimente, cum diceret uxorem intellexisse mariti mendacium: et ipsa adversus temer-
arios mariti iocos relusit.

8   *Hanc controversiam memini ab Ovidio Nasone declamari apud* rhetorem *Arellium Fuscum, cuius auditor fuit;
nam Latronis admirator erat,* cum diversum sequeretur
dicendi genus.   Habebat ille comptum et decens et
amabile ingenium.   Oratio eius iam tum nihil aliud
poterat videri quam solutum carmen.   Adeo autem
studiose Latronem audit ut multas illius sententias in
versus suos transtulerit.   In armorum iudicio dixerat
Latro: mittamus arma in hostis et petamus.   Naso
dixit:

> arma viri fortis medios mittantur in hostis;
> inde iubete peti.

Et alium ex illa suasoria sensum aeque a Latrone 13
mutuatus est. *Memini Latronem in praefatione*

---

[1] permaneret *Madvig:* perueniret *AB:* non perimeret *V.*

---

[1] Apparently meaning Latro's and Seneca's (cf. *C.* 1 pr. 22,
24).

[2] *reludo* is used, in a different sense, by Manilius 5.170.

[3] The sentence is discussed, with over-rigorous logic, by
K. Büchner, *Mus. Helv.* 13 (1956), 180–4; see also T. F.
Higham, *Ovidiana* (ed. N. I. Herescu, Paris, 1958), 33–7.

wife's love remained constant. The wife had realised
the message was a trick, and had flung herself from a
place where a fall could not be fatal, in order (he said)
that " just as I had frightened her by a false report
she could frighten me by a fictitious danger."

Our [1] teacher Marullus made a bold use of a word [2]
that got his meaning over well. He said that the wife
saw through the husband's lie: she had "joked
back " in reply to her husband's rash jest.

I remember this *controversia* being declaimed by 8
Ovidius Naso at the school of the rhetor Arellius
Fuscus—Ovid being his pupil. He *was* an admirer of
Latro, though his style of speech was different.[3] He
had a neat, seemly and attractive talent. Even in
those days his speech could be regarded as simply
poetry put into prose.[4] However, he was so keen a
student of Latro that he transferred many epigrams
of his to his own verse. On the Judgement of Arms,[5]
Latro had said: " Let us hurl the arms at the enemy
—and go to fetch them." Ovid wrote:

" Let the hero's arms be hurled into the enemy's
    midst;
Order them to be fetched—from there." [6]

And he similarly borrowed from Latro another idea
in the same *suasoria*. I recall that, in a prefatory

More generally on Ovid and declamation, Bonner, 143–4,
149–56: L. P. Wilkinson, *Ovid Recalled* (Cambridge, 1955),
5–10: H. Fränkel, *Ovid* (Berkeley, 1945), 5–8.
    [4] Ovid himself says everything he tried to compose in prose
turned to verse (*Trist.* 4.10.23–6).
    [5] Between Ajax and Ulysses over Achilles' weapons, a stock
suasoria theme (see Duff on Juv. 7.115).
    [6] *Met.* 13.121–2.

quadam dicere quod scholastici quasi carmen didi-
cerunt: *Non vides ut immota fax torpeat, ut exagitata*
reddat ignes? Mollit viros otium, ferrum situ carpitur et
rubiginem ducit, desidia dedocet. *Naso dixit:*

> *vidi ego iactatas mota face crescere flammas*
> *et rursus nullo concutiente mori.*

9   Tunc autem cum studeret habebatur bonus declamator. Hanc certe controversiam ante Arellium
Fuscum declamavit, ut mihi videbatur, longe in-
geniosius, excepto eo quod sine certo ordine per locos
discurrebat. Haec *illo dicente* excepta memini: *Quid-*
quid laboris est in hoc est, ut uxori virum et uxorem viro
diligere concedas; necesse est deinde iurare permittas si
amare permiseris. Quod habuisse nos iusiurandum
putas? Tu nobis religiosum nomen fuisti; si men-
tiremur, illa sibi iratum patrem invocavit, ego
socerum. Parce, pater: non peieravimus. Ecce
obiurgator nostri quam effrenato amore fertur!
queritur quemquam esse filiae praeter se carum.
Quid est quod illam ab indulgentia sua avocet? di 13§
10 boni, quomodo hic amavit uxorem? Amat filiam et
abdicat; dolet periclitatam esse, et ab eo abducit sine
quo negat se posse vivere; queritur periculum eius

260

remark,[1] Latro said something the schoolmen learnt off as a sort of intoned tag: "Do you not see how a torch unbrandished is dim, but when shaken it gives out its fires? Men are softened by leisure, iron is eaten away by disuse, and takes on rust. Sloth brings forgetfulness." Ovid wrote:

" I have seen flames grow as a torch is shaken,
And again die when no-one brandishes it." [2]

Well, while a student, Ovid was held to be a good 9 declaimer. At any rate he declaimed this *controversia* before Arellius Fuscus far more cleverly,[3] to my mind, except that he ran through the commonplaces in no fixed order. I remember that the following sayings of his were applauded: "The whole trouble is getting you [4] to let husband and wife love each other. You *must* allow them to swear once you allow them to love.—What do you think our oath was by? It was *you* whose name aroused our awe. In case of perjury, she called down on herself an angry father, I an angry father-in-law. Spare me, father: we were not forsworn.—Look at the unbridled passion that sweeps our censor away! His complaint is that anyone apart from himself is dear to his daughter. Why is it that he summons her away from her fondness? Good god, how did *he* love *his* wife?—He loves 10 his daughter—and disinherits her. He is grieved that she should have been in danger—and takes her away from the man she says she cannot live without.

---

[1] Cf. Introduction, p. xvii.
[2] *Am.* 1.2.11–12.
[3] Apparently than Fuscus himself.
[4] The angry father.

qua paene caruit, hic qui amare caute iubet. Facilius in amore finem inpetres quam modum. Tu hoc obtinebis, ut terminos quasi adprobaturi custodiant, ut nihil faciant nisi considerate, nihil promittant nisi ut iure [1] pacturi, omnia verba ratione et fide ponderent? senes sic amant. *Pauca nosti, pater, crimina: et litigavimus aliquando et decidimus [2] et, quod fortasse non putas, peieravimus.* Quid ad patrem pertinet quod amantes iurant? si vis credere, nec ad deos pertinet.

11 Non est quod tibi placeas, uxor, tamquam prima peccaveris: perit aliqua cum viro, perit aliqua pro viro; illas tamen omnis aetas honorabit, omne celebrabit ingenium. Fer, socer, felicitatem tuam: magnum tibi quam parvo constat exemplum! In reliquum, ut iubes, diligentiores facti sumus; errorem nostrum confitemur; exciderat iurantibus esse tertium qui magis amaret: sic, di, sit semper. Perseveras, socer? recipe filiam: ego, qui peccavi, poena dignus 13 sum; quare uxori notae causa sim, socero orbitatis? Discedam e civitate, fugiam, exulabo, utcumque potero desiderium misera et crudeli patientia perferam. Morerer, si solus moriturus essem.

---

[1] ut iure *Müller:* utius.
[2] decidimus *Gronovius:* ceci(di)mus.

---

[1] For "Iuppiter ex alto periuria ridet amantum" (Ovid *Ars Am.* 1.633). For parallels, see Otto, *Sprichwörter,* 17–18.
[2] In attempting suicide: not all the ancients agreed with the younger Seneca on the merit of suicide (see J. M. Rist, *Stoic Philosophy* [Cambridge, 1969], c. 13).
[3] Cf. Quintilian 8.5.15: "rogant te, Caesar, Galliae tuae ut

He complains of the peril to one he almost lost—this man who preaches cautious love.—Where love is concerned, a parting is easier to come by than restraint. Will you get lovers to observe limits as though they have to answer for them, do nothing without forethought, promise nothing except as though by legal covenant, weigh up all their words rationally and conscientiously? That is the way old people love.—Father, you know of few of our crimes. We have, at times, quarrelled, been reconciled, and—though you may not think it—perjured ourselves. What is it to do with a father if lovers swear? If you will believe it, it is nothing to do even with the gods.[1]—There is 11 no need, wife, for you to pride yourself on being the first to sin [2] thus. Women have perished with their husbands, women have perished for them: *they* will be honoured by every age, sung by every genius. Contrive, father, to endure your good fortune.[3] What a small price *you* have to pay for so glorious an instance!—For the future, as you instruct us, we have become more cautious. We acknowledge our mistake. We forgot, when we swore, that there was a third party—who loved more; may it always be so, ye gods.—Do you persist, father-in-law? Take your daughter back; *I* was the sinner, and *I* deserve punishment. Why should I be the cause of censure to my wife, of childlessness to her father? I shall leave the city, flee, go into exile, endure my loss as best I may with a miserable and heartless endurance. I should kill myself—if I could die alone."

felicitatem tuam fortiter feras " (Africanus to Nero after his mother's death). The " instance," of course, is the rhetorical *exemplum* the wife would become.

12 Declamabat autem Naso raro controversias et non
nisi ethicas; libentius dicebat suasorias: molesta illi
erat omnis argumentatio. Verbis minime licenter
usus est nisi in carminibus, in quibus non ignoravit
vitia sua sed amavit. Manifestum potest esse, quod
rogatus aliquando ab amicis suis ut tolleret tres versus,
invicem petit ut ipse *tres exciperet in quos nihil illis liceret.*
Aequa lex visa est; *scripserunt illi quos tolli vellent*
secreto, hic quos tutos esse vellet: in utrisque codicillis
idem versus erant, ex quibus primum fuisse narrabat
Albinovanus Pedo, qui inter arbitros fuit:

     semibovemque virum semivirumque bovem;

secundum:

     et gelidum Borean egelidumque Notum.

Ex quo adparet summi ingenii viro non iudicium defuisse
ad compescendam licentiam carminum suorum sed ani-
mum. Aiebat interim decentiorem faciem esse in qua
aliquis naevos esset.

However, Ovid rarely declaimed *controversiae*, and 12 only ones involving portrayal of character. He preferred *suasoriae*, finding all argumentation tiresome. He used language by no means over-freely except in his poetry, where he was well aware of his faults—and enjoyed them.[1] What can make this clear is that once, when he was asked by his friends to suppress three of his lines, he asked in return to be allowed to make an exception of three over which they should have no rights. This seemed a fair condition. They wrote in private the lines they wanted removed, while he wrote the ones he wanted saved. The sheets of both contained the same verses. Albinovanus Pedo, who was among those present, tells that the first of them was:

" Half-bull man and half-man bull," [2]

the second

" Freezing north wind and de-freezing south." [3]

It is clear from this that the great man lacked not the judgement but the will to restrain the licence of his poetry. He used sometimes to say that a face is the more beautiful for some mole.[4]

[1] Cf. *C.* 9.6.11; Sen. *Ep.* 114.11; and Quintilian's judgements on Ovid (10.1.98) and the younger Seneca (10.1.130).
[2] *Ars Am.* 2.24.
[3] *Am.* 2.11.10. The third may not have been known to Seneca, or the manuscripts may have omitted it accidentally.
[4] For appreciation of moles, see Cic. *Nat. Deor.* 1.79.

III

RAPTOR PATREM NON EXORANS

Raptor, nisi et suum et raptae patrem intra dies
triginta exoraverit, pereat.

Raptor raptae patrem exoravit, suum non
exorat. Accusat dementiae.

1 PORCI LATRONIS. " Moriar," inquit " moriar."
Dic ergo verum; non fleo. *Quid contremescis, pectus?
quid, lingua, trepidas? quid, oculi, obtorpuistis? nondum
est tricesimus dies.* Vitam rogas? dedi et perdidisti.
" Mori " inquit " filium vis." Ego te mori volo?
immo furor tuus, illa caeca et temeraria cupiditas, et
inter haec pater illius, qui *nimis cito exoratus est.*

---

[1] Doubtless a complete fiction. The delay in the penalty
appears also in Calp. Flacc. 25.—Some of the declaimers
assume that marriage is the alternative to death (§§4, 20), as
in the more usual law used, e.g., in *C.* 1.5.

[2] For the *actio dementiae*, see Bonner, 93–4. There was no
such action in Rome, but Quintilian (7.4.11) tells us what
Seneca here confirms (§13), that the declamatory action is
parallel to a request in the courts for a *curator* in cases of real
mental derangement (cf. what Fabianus says in §12).—This
particular theme reappears in Quintilian 9.2.90 and *Decl.* 349:
details are given in later notes.

[3] This epigram is repeated in §18 without the words " non
fleo." Its import is not clear: perhaps it is parallel to
Diocles' in §23: " ' I am young and near to death.' Die then."

3

THE RAVISHER WHO FAILED TO WIN OVER
HIS FATHER

A ravisher shall die unless he wins over his own
father and the girl's within thirty days.[1]

A ravisher won over the father of the girl he
had raped; he is unable to win over his own,
and accuses him of insanity.[2]

For the father

PORCIUS LATRO. " I shall die, I shall die." Then 1
tell the truth:[3] I am not weeping.—Why do you
tremble, heart? Why stutter, tongue? Why be
dimmed, eyes? The thirtieth day has not yet
arrived.[4]—You ask for life. I gave it you—and you
have lost it.—" You want your own son to die." *I*
want you to die? No, it is your madness, your blind
and impulsive passion—and, as well, the girl's father,

Or perhaps *dic verum* means " tell the truth about your plot
with the girl's father " (cf. Vibius Rufus in §18); in that case
the words *non fleo* should be attached to the next epigram.
   [4] As both Quintilian (9.2.91) and the *sermo* to *Decl.* 349
point out, the father cannot (without seeming unduly harsh)
hold out no hope for his son. On the other hand, he
cannot promise to forgive him, because that would spoil the
controversia (cf. §11). Many of the declaimers therefore hint
at the father's real feelings, while making him persist in his
refusal. Quintilian cites another of Latro's epigrams of this
kind: " ' Will you kill me, then? ' Yes, if I prove capable of
it " (cf. *Decl.* p. 375.21 *seq.* Ritter), as well as one of Gallio's
from §6.

Quare tam cito senex ille remisit iniuriam? *Ne
tristiore quidem vultu expugnatam filiae pudicitiam tulit.*
Timeo ne verum sit quod audio, ne novo inauditoque
more de nuptiis puellae vitiator exoratus sit.

2 CESTI PII. Quo melius de sene iudicare possitis,
narrabo me iuvenem. Habui patrem sanae mentis 138
nec tam severum ut crudelis esset, nec tam indul-
gentem ut incautus. Duxi uxorem quam pater ius-
serat, nec tamen nuptiarum mearum me paenitet.
Fili, nonne saepe excandui, saepe reconciliatus sum,
saepe quod negaveram dedi? Ipse dispensasti triginta
dies, ut haberet primos soceer, medios reus, novissimos
pater. *Ne omnia vitia a* prima *adulescentia repetam,
virginem rapuit, patrem accusat: haec intra dies triginta.
Putas me accusatori promissurum quod filio negavi?*
" Impetravi " inquit " ab illo ": alii aiunt illum a te.
Mediis me diebus accusas. Rapuisti virginem, cum
tam libenter viveres?

3 ARELLI FUSCI patris. " Moriar " inquit: etiamnunc minaris? nondum rogas? " Quousque " inquit

---

[1] Cf. *Decl.* p. 375.14 Ritter: " I should be persuaded more
easily if *he* were angry Is it possible for a man whose daughter
has been raped to have been won over so soon? . . . What is
this great agreement of yours? "

[2] The second, that is, for accusing his father, the third for
trying to persuade him. The order suggests that Cestius is
accepting the view of Latro (§11) that the son didn't even try
to win his father over before accusing him. But this is not
consistent with the previous epigram, and can hardly be
extracted from the terms of the declamation.

[3] i.e. the son says: " I managed to persuade the girl's

who gave in too soon.[1]   Why did the old man forgive
the wrong so quickly?   He tolerated the outrage of
his daughter's chastity—and didn't even look cast
down.   I fear that what I hear is true, that something
new and extraordinary has happened: it is the
ravisher who has been won over—to marry the girl.

CESTIUS PIUS.   So that you can the better judge an 2
old man, I will describe my youth.   I had a father of
sound mind, not so stern as to be cruel, not so indulgent as to be foolish.   I married the wife my
father told me to—but I do not regret my marriage.—
My son, haven't I often flared up, often been reconciled, often given you what I had at first refused?—It
is you who divided out the thirty days—the first ten
for your father-in-law, the second for the defendant,
the third for your father.[2]—Not to list all his faults
since his earliest youth, he has raped a girl and is
accusing his father—all in thirty days.—Do you
imagine that I will promise my accuser what I have
denied to my son?—" I got it from *him*."   Others say
that *he* got it from *you*.[3]—You are accusing me in the
middle days.[4]—You raped a virgin—and yet you were
so fond of life.[5]

ARELLIUS FUSCUS SENIOR.   " I shall die."   Are you 3
still threatening me?   Aren't you yet imploring me?

father."   The father replies: " Others say he managed to
persuade you."   Cf. §1 " I fear . . ."
   [4] " Pendant ces jours ⟨où tu es suspendu entre la vie et la
mort⟩ " (Bornecque).   But there seems to be an allusion to
the division of time discussed in n. 2: and this " epigram "
may even be a gloss on that.
   [5] i.e. you can't expect to continue your *dolce vita* after
committing a capital offence.

" rogabo ? " Iam lassus es nec adhuc ullum rogasti.
" Non possum " inquit " exorare tam diu." Novo
more obicit dementi constantiam. " Quid ergo ? tu
poteris videre morientem filium ? " Fortasse non
potero et ideo irascor dum licet.

POMPEI SILONIS. Haec audacia eius ex parte culpae meae est: nimium indulgenter nutritus est,
omnia sibi putat licere, nihil umquam me rogavit.
" *Ignovit* " inquit. *Ita aliquis ante me rogatus est?*
Non nosti condicionem legis tuae: in hac culpa ⟨qui⟩
pares [1] sententias habent pereunt. Ipse se ad
alienam misit, lex illum misit ad meam. " Raptor, 139
nisi et suum et raptae patrem exoraverit, pereat."
Vis scire lex utrum maluerit ? non exorari : irascitur.
Ex duobus patribus eum raptor accusat qui legem
sequitur.

4 ARELLI FUSCI. *Miraris me dubitare? ipsa lex inter
mortem et nuptias dubia est.* Quid me intempestivae
proditis lacrimae ? nondum erat tempus fatendi.
Non est quod tibi quicquam promisisse lacrimas putes :
fleo quod necesse mihi est filium spectare morientem.
Quid facturus sim adhuc nescio; utique tu ante tricesimum diem nescies. " Exoravi " inquit " ⟨rap-

---

[1] qui pares *early editors :* res.

---

[1] With a hint that he had had no need to ask the other
father, because of their collusion.

[2] i.e. if one father is won over, the other not, the youth
must die. In the courts a tie in the votes led to acquittal
(cf. *C.* 3.2): see Cic. *Cluent.* 74; Sen. *Ep.* 81.26; A. H. J.

" How long shall I have to go on asking? " You are
already tired—yet you haven't asked anyone yet.[1]
" I cannot win you over after all this time." Here's
a new idea—to reproach a madman with consistency!
" What—will you tolerate seeing your son die? "
Perhaps I will not; that is why I am angry now, while
I have the chance.

POMPEIUS SILO. This brashness of his is partly my
fault: he was too indulgently brought up; he thinks
he may do anything; he has never *asked* me anything.—" *He* forgave me." So you asked someone
else before me?—You don't know the terms of the
law covering your case: for this offence those who
receive equal votes must die.[2] He sent himself off to
get the vote of another: now the law has sent him to
canvass mine.—" A ravisher shall die unless he wins
over his own father and the girl's." Do you want to
know which outcome the law prefers?—that they are
impossible to win over: it is an angry law. Of the
two fathers the ravisher is accusing the one who is
following the intention of the law.[3]

ARELLIUS FUSCUS. Are you surprised at my hesita- 4
tion? The law itself hesitates between death and
marriage.—Why do you betray me, unseasonable
tears? It was not yet time to confess. You should
not suppose that these tears made any promises to
you; I weep because I must watch my son die.—I
don't yet know what I am going to do: in fact, *you*
will not know—before the thirtieth day.—" I won

Greenidge, *The Legal Procedure of Cicero's Time* (Oxford, 1901),
498.

[3] By not giving in: an appeal to the supposed *voluntas* of
the law-giver.

tae⟩[1] patrem." Quid ergo mihi molestus es si hoc
tibi satis est?

MOSCHI. Effregit fores et identidem leges in-
vocantem coegit pati stuprum: nisi tam facile puellam exoravit quam patrem. Mortem vitiatione
meruit, accusatione deprecatur. Consumuntur interim dies: uter nostrum illos consumit? "Rogo"
inquit: non est fortunae meae rogari; nunc ego
rogare debueram, qui periclitor.

5 PAPIRI FABIANI. *Demens sum. Vides enim, turpiter
vivo*, meretricem amo, *legem ignoro, dies tuos non
numero*. Ad iudices vocat iudicem suum. "Ergo
moriar" inquit. Hoc si reo dicis, non curo; si iudici,
videbo; si dementi, non intellego. *Demens, inquit,* 140
es: et huic aliquis ignoscere potest qui sic rogat? Vos
mei iudices estis, iste habet suum iudicem, nec potest
inexorabilem queri quem nondum expertus est.

6 IUNI GALLIONIS. "Rogo" inquit. Nunc? hic?
sic? Si volebas rogare, admovisses propinquos, amicos, maiorum imagines, lacrimas, repetitos alte
gemitus. Testor deos, sic rogaturus fui puellae
patrem. "Quando" inquit ⟨"misereberis?"⟩
Cum⟩[2] vultum in supplicis habitum summiseris,

---

[1] *Supplied by Faber.*
[2] *Supplied by Thomas.*

---

[1] You—wasting them in accusation. The first sentence
of the epigram may be the words of the son.
[2] All these assertions are ironical, the intention being to
make it clear the father *is* counting the days—and proposes
to let his son off.

over the girl's father." Why then are you bothering me, if *that* is enough for you?

MOSCHUS. He broke down the doors, and, while she repeatedly invoked the laws, forced her to submit to his lust: or perhaps he won the girl over as easily as her father.—By a rape he has deserved death, by an accusation he is begging to avoid it.—Meanwhile the days go by. Which of us is it that makes them go by? [1]—"I beg you." I am not in a plight suitable for requests; *I* ought to be begging now—it is *I* who am in danger.

PAPIRIUS FABIANUS. I am mad. You can see—I live disgustingly, love a whore, lack acquaintance with the law, refuse to count the days that remain to you.[2]—He summons his judge [3] before the judges.— "Then I shall die." If you are saying this to the man you are accusing, I do not care: if to your judge, I will see about it: if to a madman, I do not understand.—"You are mad." Is it possible to forgive someone who makes requests like this?—You are *my* judges—he has a judge of his own; and one that he cannot complain to be inexorable, for he hasn't yet had experience of him.[4]

JUNIUS GALLIO. "I beg you." Now? Here? Thus? If you wanted to beg, you should have deployed relatives, friends, family portraits, tears, deep groans. I call the gods to witness: that is how I was going to beg the girl's father.[5] "When will you pity me?" When you set your face in the lines of a

---

[3] i.e. his father: so too "your judge" just below.

[4] Again his father, who has not yet made his final decision.

[5] If you had asked me first, I should have helped persuade him.

cum dixeris: " paenitet quod rapui, quod te priorem
non rogavi," cum dixeris te dementem fuisse, *de-*
liberabo cum amicis, deliberabo cum propinquis, deliberabo cum tua matre. *Me miserum, quam paene*
promisi! ⟨Dura⟩,[1] anime, dura; here fortior eras.
Et multum habeo quod deliberem: diversi me adfectus distringunt, inter reum et patrem distrahor;
hinc iniuria est, hinc natura. Quid properas? nemo
tibi praeter me rogandus est. " Ergo " inquit
" misereberis? " Nihil promittam ante tricesimum
diem. *O me miserum, quod tantum triginta diebus irasci*
7 *possum!* longiore tempore opus erat. Audi a de-
mente exempla huic crimini. Denis vicenisque annis
inter bella iuventus consenuit; nos dies triginta ferre
non possumus! Deliberabo: lex nihil vult temere
fieri; magna res est, inquit: delibera, cogita, tempus
accipe. Effregisti domum civis, ut dicis etiam misericordis; morere: non est hoc nocenti grave; ego nihil 141
peccavi: propter te mori cupio. Ratio a me exigitur
alienae culpae, meae potestatis. " Quid ergo facturus es? " Non pronuntiabo ante supremam.
Quid miraris si illum citius exorasti? Facilius est
iniuriam donare quam crimen. Agedum, *procede in*

---

[1] *Omitted by the manuscripts, but supplied from Quintilian*
9.2.91.

---

[1] For this family council, cf. *Decl.* p. 375.4 Ritter. It is
the usual form for a father exercising his *potestas* (e.g. Val.
Max. 2.9.2, 5.8.2).

[2] Cited by Quintilian 9.2.91.

suppliant, when you say: " I repent my rape, I am
sorry I didn't ask your forgiveness first," when you
say *you* were mad, then I will take counsel [1] with my
friends and relations and your mother. Oh dear,
how near I came to promising! Be strong, my mind,
be strong—you were stronger yesterday! [2] And I
have much to discuss; different emotions divide me,
I am split between my roles of defendant and father.
On one side is the wrong you did, on the other nature.
—Why hurry? You have no-one to beg except me.
" Then you will pity me? " I will make no promises
before the thirtieth day. How unhappy I am—I can
be angry only for thirty days! I needed a longer
time.—The madman will give you parallels for this 7
" crime." [3]—For ten or twenty years apiece young
Romans grow old in war: [4] to think that *I* cannot wait
for thirty days!—I will deliberate. The law depre-
cates precipitate action; it says: " This is a serious
matter. Consider, ponder, take your time."—You
have broken into the house of a citizen, even, you say,
of a compassionate one; die—it is not too much for a
guilty man. *I* have done no wrong—yet, thanks to
you, *I* long to die.—I am asked to pay for the crime
of another, and for the exercise of my own power.—
" What are you going to do, then? " I will not give
my decision before the last day. Why are you surprised that you won *him* over quicker? It is easier to
forgive an injury than an accusation.—Come on,

[3] The point, such as it is, lies in the use of the word madman
by the speaker of himself. The *exempla* are not given: but
cf. *C.* 2.4.4 " No-one . . ."
[4] If they can be patient, so can I.—Augustus fixed the
period of legionary service at twenty years.

medium, senex, cuius misericordia crudelis sum: non putasti mecum deliberandum? Unde scis qualem filium habeam? ego certe adhuc nescio qualem filiam habeas. " *Iam* " inquit " *angustum tempus est* ": *et tibi vacat accusare?* Nullum tempus uni verbo angustum est.

8 VIBI RVFI. Quis umquam praeter me ignoscere iussus est? " Iam " inquit " tempus angustum est." Ita non putas me subducere quantum supersit? " Iam " inquit " tempus angustum est." Angustum erat si duos rogare deberes. " Angustum tempus est " exclamat; " nescio quando rogem." Ergo me priorem rogare debuisti: non dico quia dignior sum qui prius roger quia pater tuus; id quod minimum est, propius habito. Hoc videlicet illa pars legis pertinebat: " et suum patrem exoret."

P. ASPRENATIS. *Sic aliquis exorat? sic deprecatur? Apparet nunc te primum rogare.* Demens sum: immo si vis argumentum dabo tibi: filius meus moriturus est, et nondum testamentum meum mutavi.

CORNELI HISPANI. Multi me adfectus diducunt: 142 necesse est de aliis querar, de aliis erubescam, de aliis timeam, de omnibus etiamnunc deliberem. Ne ille quidem, quamvis dicatur nimis exorabilis, ignovisset si sic rogatus esset.

---

[1] Cf. *Decl.* p. 373.26 Ritter: " The madness in this case is the sort that can be put right by a single word." The word would be *ignosco*.

[2] This absurdity perhaps qualifies as the silliest epigram in the whole collection.

come into the open, old man: it is because of your
pity that I am called cruel: didn't you think you
should discuss the matter with me? How do you
know what sort of a son I have? *I* certainly don't
know yet what sort of a daughter *you* have.—" Time
is getting short now." Yet you still have leisure to
accuse me? No time is too short for a single word.[1]

VIBIUS RUFUS. Who in the world has ever been 8
told to forgive, apart from me?—" Time is short
now." Do you think me incapable of working out
how much there is left? " Time is short now." It
would be short if you had two to win over. " Time is
short," he cries. " I don't know when I can ask
him." Well, you should have asked me first, then.
I don't say that because I deserve to be asked first,
because I am your father, but—a very small point—
because I live nearer.[2]—Surely this is the point of the
clause in the law that says:[3] " let him win over both
his own father . . ."

PUBLIUS ASPRENAS. Is this how to win favour?
How to beg pardon? This is obviously the first time
you have had to beg.[4]—I am mad: in fact, if you
wish, I will give you a proof: my son is about to die,
and I haven't yet changed my will.

CORNELIUS HISPANUS. Many emotions divide me.
I must complain of some, blush for others, fear others,
deliberate, even now, on all.—Not even *he*, however
complaisant he may be called, would have granted his
forgiveness if he had been begged like *this*.

---

[3] The point is the *order* of the names: " his own father "
is put first.

[4] Either because the other father begged him (cf. p. 270 n. 1)
or because the spoilt youth never had to ask for anything (§3).

9 Pars altera. ARELLI FUSCI patris. *Me miserum, pater! irae tuae detractum est nihil,* at *tempori multum. Infelicior sum quam si neutrum exorassem;* mortem timeo postquam mihi omnes gratulati sunt. Quid tibi, optime socer, pro ista misericordia tua, qua mihi et patri meo pepercisti, precer nisi superstitem filiam?

PAPIRI FABIANI. Non possum dissimulare, pater: quod illum exoravi, tuum beneficium est; certe cum exoratus est, hoc dixit: Aliud quidem suadebat dolor meus, sed quid faciam? Patris tui misereor. Miserere,[1] pater: scis quam brevis sit advocatio mea. " Misereor " inquit (vis verum dicam, quid dixerit?) " patris tui." Unde ego miser ab hoc patre veniens timerem patrem?

10 CESTI PII. Timeo mortem nec iam habeo cui peream.

MARULLI. Si tibi tam pertinax adversus me odium est, audacter quid sis facturus pronuntia; dic exorari te non posse. Quid me incerta mortis expectatione suspendis? Sollicitus inter somnos quoque velut admotam cervicibus meis securem expavesco. Si non inpetro ut vivam, hoc certe inpetrem, ne diu moriar. Non est quod putetis legem in numero dierum

---

[1] *Perhaps* misereor. ⟨Mei⟩ miserere (*E.H.W.*).

The other side

ARELLIUS FUSCUS SENIOR. How unhappy I am, 9 father. There has been no reduction in your anger— much in the time.—I am more unfortunate than if I had won over neither of them; I am in fear of death after everyone had congratulated me on my escape.— Best of fathers-in-law, what can I pray for you, in return for your pity, with which you have spared both me and my father, except a daughter to survive you?

PAPIRIUS FABIANUS. I cannot pretend, father: that I won him over is thanks to you. At least, when he had given his assent, he said: " My grief suggested otherwise. But what am I to do? I feel pity for your father." Feel pity yourself, father. You know how brief my respite is. " I pity," he said (you want me to tell you precisely what he said?) " your father." How can I, in my wretchedness, fear my father, coming as I do from hers? [1]

CESTIUS PIUS. I fear death—and now I have 10 no-one to die for.[2]

MARULLUS. If your hatred of me is so unrelenting, be bold and pronounce your intention; say you cannot be won over. Why keep me in suspense, in doubtful expectation of death? Worried as I am, even in my sleep I shudder at an axe that seems to approach my neck. If I do not succeed in winning life, may I at least win a quick death. You should not think that the law was stingy in the number of

---

[1] The son—to influence his father to clemency—says he cannot fear a father after having had such a good experience with the girl's.

[2] Estranged as he is from his father. But the text is uncertain.

angustam fuisse: ⟨est⟩ [1] lex illius diu mori. Responde, pater: *si servaturus es filium, iam tempus fuit; si
occisurus, iam tempus est.* Non possum metum sustinere ultra nec tormenta ⟨tot⟩ [2] diebus pati: et in me
mihi aliquid licet.

BLANDI. Ita parum tibi contigit quod solus pericli-
tante filio non rogas?

11   Latro sic divisit: an intra tricesimum diem raptor
cum alio agere possit, sicut non potest qui in custodia
est, qui in carcere. Etiamsi cum alio potest, an cum
patre possit, quoi vitae mortisque arbitrium datum
est, an illi accusare eum liberum sit quem mortiferum
est non exorasse? Etiamsi cum patre potest agere,
an ob id possit cuius faciendi potestatem lex patri
dedit: " ista enim ratione nihil licet si aut exorari aut
accusari ei necesse est." Deinde si potest agere, an
debeat. Irascendi causas tractavit, quod rapuit,
quod alium prius rogavit, quod patrem [3] non rogavit,
quod etiam accusat. Si non exorari ⟨a⟩ [4] filio dementia est, an tamen damnari dementiae non possit
cum adhuc an exoretur incertum sit. Hic paternos
adfectus tractavit spem facientis. Non probabat
Fuscum, qui paulo apertius agebat: Est, ⟨inquit,

---

[1] *Supplied by Bursian.*
[2] *Supplied by Schenkl.*
[3] patrem *Müller:* me.
[4] *Supplied by Bursian.*

days it allowed; it is *his* law that I should die slowly. Answer, father; if you are going to save your son, the time has passed. If you are going to kill him, the time has come. I cannot endure my fear any longer, suffer agonies for so many days. I too have some control over my destiny.[1]

BLANDUS. Wasn't it enough for you to be the only one to ask nothing when your son's life is in danger?

Latro's division was like this: Can a ravisher, 11 within the thirty days, go to law with another (for a captive [2] or a prisoner cannot)? Even if he can, can he with his father, who has powers of life and death over him? [3] Is he free to bring an accusation against one whom it is fatal not to have won over? Even if he can go to law with his father, can he do it because of an act in which the law has granted freedom of action to the father? " For on that principle the father has no choice—if he must be either persuaded or accused." Next, if he can go to law, should he? He dealt with the motives for anger, that he had raped the girl, begged the other father first, not begged his own (and is now even accusing him). If it is a sign of madness not to be won over by a son, can he be convicted of insanity while it is still uncertain whether he *will* be won over? Here he handled the hopes arising from the father's natural feelings. He didn't approve of Fuscus, who pleaded rather more openly. " It is against the terms of the *controversia*

---

[1] He hints he will commit suicide.

[2] Not having access to a magistrate.

[3] A son could not in fact normally sue or accuse his father (see F. Schulz, *Classical Roman Law* [Oxford, 1951], 160).

contra⟩ [1] controversiam promittere. Potest nihilominus et bonus agi pater et non exoratus.

12   Fabianus hanc quaestionem fecit et in ea multum moratus est: dementiae non posse agi nisi cum eo qui 144 morbo fureret; in hoc enim latam esse legem, ut pater a filio sanari deberet, non ut regi.

Latro eleganter dicebat quasdam esse quaestiones quae deberent inter res iudicatas referri, tamquam an quidquid optaverit vir fortis aut tyrannicida accipere debeat: quasi iam pronuntiatum sit non debere, nemo iam hanc quaestionem tractat, sicut ne illam quidem, an quidquid pater imperat faciendum sit. Inter has putabat et hanc esse, an pater ob dementiam quae morbo fieret tantum accusari a filio debeat; aiebat enim manifestum esse e lege et de officio patris quaeri et fingi quasdam controversias in quibus pater furiosus probari non possit, ⟨nec⟩ [2] absolvi tamen propter impietatem nimiam, libidinem foedam. Quid ergo? aiebat; numquam utar hac quaestione? utar cum aliis deficiar.

13   Pollio Asinius aiebat hoc Latronem videri tamquam forensem facere, ut ineptas quaestiones circumcideret, ⟨sed⟩ [3] in nulla magis illum re scholasticum

[1] *Supplied by Müller after Kiessling.*
[2] *Supplied in the ed. Hervageniana (1557).*
[3] *Supplied by Kiessling.*

to make any promises," said Latro. " Nevertheless, he may be represented as a good father—who hasn't been won over."

Fabianus produced this question, spending some 12 time over it: There can be no action for insanity except with someone who is mad as a result of illness. The law had been passed in order that the father should be cured by his son—not dictated to by him.

Latro wittily said that there were some questions that should be counted as things already decided, such as: Should everything a hero or a tyrannicide wishes be granted? No-one now handles this question, as though it has by now been settled that he should *not*.[1] So also with the question, Should every order given by a father be obeyed? Latro thought that in this category came also the question whether a father ought to be accused by a son of insanity only when it is the result of disease. He said it was clear from the law that there was scope for enquiry also into the duties of the father,[2] and that *controversiae* were sometimes contrived where the father could not be proved physically mad, yet could not be absolved either because of excessive disregard of natural affection or because of disgraceful passions. " Well then," he said, " shall I never use this question? Yes—when I have no others available."

Asinius Pollio used to say that Latro's pruning of 13 foolish questions was regarded as the sign of a true lawyer—but that in fact he was nowhere more clearly

---

[1] Not, e.g., marriage to someone else's wife (Quintilian 7.1.24).

[2] i.e. a declaimer could discuss a father's actions, without restricting himself to evidence of physical madness.

deprehendi. "Remittit" inquit "eam quaestionem quae semper pro patribus valentissima est." Ego [semper] [1] scio nulli a praetore curatorem dari quia inicus pater sit aut impius, sed quia furiosus; hoc autem in foro esse curatorem petere quod in scholas- 145 tica dementiae agere.

14 Gallio et superiore usus est quaestione et illam adiecit: an agi cum patre dementiae possit ob id quod fecerit, non ob id quod facturus sit. Neminem iniuriarum accusari quod iniuriam facturus sit, nec adulteri quod adulterium commissurus sit; ⟨sic ne⟩ [2] dementiae quidem quod demens futurus sit. Atqui tu non, inquit, mecum agis quod non exoravisti, sed quod non exoraturus es; puta enim hodie me exorari: demens non ero. Demens videor qui uno verbo sanari possum? Lex triginta dies dedit quia iudicavit aliquem duriorem futurum. Etiamsi demens est qui non exoratur a filio ⟨tricensimo die⟩,[3] numquid et qui vicensimo? Ergo non potes hoc nomine dam-

---

[1] *Deleted by Schultingh.*
[2] *Supplied by Bursian.*
[3] *Supplied by C. F. W. Müller.*

---

[1] This is normally taken as part of Pollio's criticism of Latro; but it goes against his argument, and it seems better to suppose that Seneca here chips in with a statement of the true facts. Pollio now merely says that Latro shows himself

betrayed as a true schoolman. " He is here abandoning a question which is peculiarly effective in defence of fathers." I [1] am of course aware that a praetor never grants a guardian on the grounds that a father is unfair or lacks affection—only because he is physically mad. And the seeking of a guardian in the courts is the equivalent of an action for insanity in a school-declamation.

Gallio employed the previous question, adding 14 another: Can an action be brought against a father for insanity in respect of something he is going to do and not in respect of something he has already done? [2] No-one is sued for injuries in respect of an injury he has yet to inflict, nor of adultery for an adultery he has yet to commit. So he could not be accused of insanity on the grounds that he is going to become mad. " Yet here you are, going to court with me not because you have failed to win me over, but because you are not going to win me over. For suppose I am won over today: then I shall cease to be mad.[3] Am I to be thought mad when I can be cured—by uttering a single word? The law gave thirty days because it judged that someone would be overharsh. Even if a man is mad because he is not won over by his son on the thirtieth day, surely he is not because he is not won over on the twentieth? So you cannot

up as no real lawyer because he abandons a very effective argument.

[2] Quintilian seems to assume this is possible (7.4.29–30); cf. also Seneca *Ir.* 1.3.1: " iniuriam qui facturus est iam facit."

[3] Cf. *Decl.* p. 374.6 Ritter: " si exoratus fuero, statim non modo sanus verum etiam bonus pater et indulgens ero."

nare me quod exoratus non sim; etiamnunc enim
exorari possum. Ita, si vis verum, agere mecum hoc
crimine non potes; utique ⟨intra⟩ [1] triginta dies
exorari possum, post triginta queri non potes: aut
crimen non habeo aut accusatorem.

15 Silo Pompeius fecit quaestionem qua Gallio usus est
⟨et illam adiecit⟩: [2] nihil acturum adulescentem
etiamsi damnaverit patrem; nihilominus enim peri-
turum quia lex nullam aliam salutis viam dedit raptori
quam si exoraverit patrem.

Latro haec omnia quasi membra in aliquam quaes- 146
tionem incurrentia tractabat, non ut quaestiones;
tamquam hoc ipsum in illam aiebat quaestionem incurrere in qua quaeritur an raptor possit accusare
patrem intra tricesimum diem. "Nam cum dico:
non potes accusare eum in cuius arbitrio positum est
moriaris an vivas, non magis quam magistratum in ius
vocare, quam de iudicibus tuis ferre sententiam, non
magis quam miles in imperatorem suum animadver-
tere, adicio: non opus est accusare; nihil enim tibi
proderit; etiamsi damnaveris, morieris; lex enim, si
non exoraveris, perire te vult; non exoras autem
etiamsi damnas." Quare hoc non in quaestionis loco
ponebat? Inbecillum putabat.

16 Adparet enim ⟨non⟩ [3] exigere legem ab eo ut
exoret patrem qui non habet quem exoret. Puta
enim patrem alicuius esse tam palam furiosum ut

---

[1] *Supplied by Müller.*
[2] *Supplied by Müller after Schultingh.*
[3] *Supplied by Jahn.*

condemn me on the grounds that I have not been won over. Even now I *can* be persuaded. So, if you want to be told the truth, you cannot prosecute me on this charge. At any rate within the thirty days I am still capable of being won over; after thirty days you are not capable of going to law. Either there is no charge—or there is no accuser."

Pompeius Silo used the question raised by Gallio, 15 adding this one: The youth would accomplish nothing if he did get his father condemned; for he would die none the less, the law giving a ravisher no chance of life if he did not win over his father.

Latro treated all these matters as parts to be subsumed under a question rather than as separate questions. For instance, this particular one came under the question, Can a ravisher accuse his father before the thirtieth day? " For when I say, You cannot accuse a man who has powers of life and death over you, any more than sue a magistrate,[1] pass judgement on your judges, punish your general if you are a soldier—when I say this, I add: There is no need to accuse him—for it will do you no good. Even if you get him condemned, you will die. For the law insists on your death if you fail to win him over: and you aren't winning him over even if you get him condemned." You may ask why he didn't make this a question: he regarded it as too weak.

[For it is clear that the law does not insist on his 16 father being won over by someone who has no father to win over. Suppose a father is too obviously mad to understand anything; does the law require *him* to

---

[1] Cf. Gell. 13.13; *Dig.* 2.4.2.

nihil intellegat: hunc exorari a filio vult? atqui eodem
loco est manifestus inclemens. [1]

Fuscus parum hoc putabat valens esse tamquam
quaestionem, satis valens tamquam argumentum; et
illam alteram quaestionem [satis valens questionem],[2]
non posse cum patre agi eo nomine quod non peccaverit sed peccaturus sit, in aequitatis tractatione
ponebat, cum diceret: Agere mecum dementiae,
etiamsi potes, ⟨non debes⟩.[3] *Numquid enim peccavi?*
Non sum exoratus: nondum transit tempus, etiamnunc
exorari possum. Quam iniquum est nondum esse me
nocentem et iam reum!

147

17 Omnes infamaverunt raptae patrem quasi cum
raptore conludentem. Gallio dixit: ingenuam virginem rapuit, si tamen rapuit. Silo Pompeius
eandem suspicionem in omnia contulit: " Exoravi "
inquit " raptae patrem." Immo tu, cum exorabilem
haberet patrem, rapuisti.

Hispanus dixit: Omnia cito facta sunt: iste cito
rapuit, ille cito ignovit. Nisi demens sum, aliquid
suspicandum.

Argentarius dixit: Rapta est et statim exorata;
immo nescio an exorata, deinde rapta. Spero te in-
nocentiorem fuisse quam vis videri. Tu exorasse te
dicis, ego te exoratum puto. Dic, quid tibi cum
18 socero convenit? Rufus Vibius dixit: Dic mihi quid
tibi ⟨cum socero⟩ [4] convenerit, quanto tibi nuptias

---

[1] inclemens *Walter:* demens.
[2] *Deleted by Kiessling.*
[3] *Supplied by Gertz.*
[4] *Supplied by Gertz.*

be won over by the son? Yet one who is undoubtedly unkind is in the same position.] [1]

Fuscus thought this too weak as a question, but effective enough as an argument. As to that other question—that the father cannot have an action brought against him because he has not yet done the crime, but is only going to do it—Fuscus put this in his treatment of equity, saying: " You should not sue me for madness even if you are allowed to. Have I done anything wrong? I have not been won over. The time has not yet passed—even now I may be persuaded. How unfair it is that I should already be accused—without being guilty yet! "

Everybody abused the father of the raped girl as 17 being in collusion with the seducer. Gallio said: " He raped a free-born girl—if it *was* rape." Pompeius Silo brought this same implication in everywhere. " He says, I won over the girl's father. Put it rather that you chose to rape her because she had a father who was easy to win over."

Hispanus said: " Everything happened quickly. The one raped quickly, the other forgave quickly. Unless I *am* mad, there is room for suspicion."

Argentarius said: " She was raped and immediately won over—or rather perhaps won over and then raped. I hope you were more innocent than you want to be thought to be. You say you had to do the winning over. *I* think *you* were won over. Tell me, what was your arrangement with your father-in-law? " Vibius Rufus: " Tell me, what was 18 your arrangement with your father-in-law? How

---

[1] This paragraph is either misplaced or (more probably) a commentator's gloss.

promiserit. Non vis? tum hercules fateberis cum dies venerit.

Asprenas dixit: " iam " inquit " non multum reliquum est ex triginta diebus "; si ex illo dies numerarem cum primum exorasti, aiunt iam triginta dies praeterisse.

Latro dixit, id quod inter sententias scriptum est: 148 " moriar "; dic ergo verum.

Cestius hac figura declamavit, ut rogaret patrem, tamquam ⟨non⟩ [1] exoratus esset raptae pater; deinde ad hanc sententiam transit: numquid peiorem causam habeo si apud alterum iudicem vici?

Eadem figura declamavit et Hispo Romanius, sed transit mollius: scio quid responderi possit mihi: facile est domestico iudici satis facere; videro ⟨de⟩ [2] te cum ab raptae patre [3] veneris.

19   In hac controversia Triarius dixerat: non scies an exores nisi ultimus dies venerit; et tum quamdiu licebit perseverabo. Deinde cum scholasticorum summo fragore: at tu quisquis es carnifex, cum strictam sustuleris securem, antequam ferias, patrem respice.

Belle deridebat hoc Asinius Pollio: filius, inquit, cervicem porrigat, carnifex manum tollat, deinde

---

[1] *Supplied by Bursian.*
[2] *Supplied by Thomas.*
[3] ab raptae patre *Thomas:* ad rapt(a)e patrem.

much did he promise the marriage for? Don't you want to tell? By heaven, you will confess when the day comes."

Asprenas said: "'There is not much left of the thirty days.' If I were to count the days since you were first successful in winning over, then they say the thirty days are up already."[1]

Latro said something I have placed among the epigrams:[2] "'I shall die.' Then tell the truth."

Cestius' declamation was based on the figure of begging his father as though the girl's father had not consented. Then he made the transition on this epigram: "Surely I don't have a worse case if I have been victorious in the opinion of the other judge?"

Romanius Hispo's declamation also used this same figure, but his transition was smoother: "I know what the reply to me might be: It is easy to satisfy a judge from one's own family; I shall see about you when you get back from the girl's father."[3]

In this *controversia* Triarius had said: "You will 19 not know whether you are to win me over before the last day comes. Even then, I shall hang on as long as I can." Then—amid thunderous applause from the schoolmen: "But do you, executioner, whoever you may be, when you raise the bare axe, before you strike look round at the father."

Asinius Pollio mocked this nicely: "Let the son stretch out his neck, let the executioner raise his

---

[1] i.e. according to report (cf. §2) the agreement came before the rape (so too Argentarius §17).

[2] §1.

[3] To which the son would reply: But I have already been to see him—and he has consented.

respiciat ad patrem et dicat: agon? (quod fieri solet victumis).   Sed ioco quoque remoto aiebat rem verissimam, non posse carnificem venire nisi eo tempore quo iam exorari pater non posset.

20   Cestius ex altera parte hoc colore usus est quare priorem rogasset raptae patrem: suspensum esse ⟨nolui patrem meum⟩,[1] volui statim illum securum esse de me; queritur quod illum potius cogitare de 14 matrimonio fili quam de periculo volui.

Latro hoc colore usus est: Scitis periclitantes alieno arbitrio agere.   Illi qui circa erant sodales, qui occurrerant amici paterni, aiebant: eamus statim ad raptae patrem; in eiusmodi casu hi rogantur; nam raptorum patres—rogant.

21   Silo Pompeius diversum colorem huic secutus est: nota erat, inquit, duritia patris mei; itaque amici suaserunt, ad raptae patrem iremus, ne noceret apud illum, tarde meum exorari patrem.

Hispo Romanius bello idiotismo usus est.   Dixerunt,[2] inquit, amici: eamus ad raptae patrem; hoc curemus, illud domi est.

Fuscus Arellius dixit: *prior rogatus est qui magis timebatur.*

Triarius a parte adulescentis dixit: timeo ne

---

[1] *Supplied by Gertz.*
[2] dixerunt *Otto:* uixit.

---

[1] When sacrificing the attendant asked " agone " and received the answer " hoc age ": see, e.g., Ov. *Fast.* 1.322.
[2] i.e. the thirty days up, he would no longer have a choice.
[3] The decision of the other father being favourable.
[4] i.e. his unreasonable complaint.

hand, then look round at the father and say: Am I to go ahead ? " [1] (the usual formula for victims). But, joking apart, he said what was perfectly true, that the executioner could not be sent for except when the father could no longer be won over.[2]

Cestius, for the other side, used this *colour* to 20 explain why he had asked the girl's father first: " I didn't want my father to be in suspense. I wanted him to have no worries for me right from the start.[3] His complaint [4] is that I wanted him to have to think about his son's marriage rather than his son's danger."

Latro employed this *colour*: " You know that those in danger act on the initiative of others. His companions round about, the family friends who had forgathered, were saying: ' Let us go to the girl's father at once. In cases of this kind it is they who are asked. As for the fathers of the ravishers—they do the asking.' " [5]

Pompeius Silo pursued a different *colour*: " Every- 21 one knew how harsh my father is. So my friends advised me that we should go to the girl's father, in case it harmed me in *his* eyes that I was taking a long time to win over mine."

Romanius Hispo employed a nice vulgarism. " My friends said: ' Let's go to the girl's father. Let us see to that—the other is in the bag.' " [6]

Arellius Fuscus said: " He asked first the one he feared more."

Triarius, for the youth, said: " I am afraid he [7]

---

[5] They help beg off the other father (cf. §6).

[6] For *domi est*, cf., e.g., Cic. *ad Att.* 10.14.2.

[7] Apparently the youth's father. The *colour* explains that the youth's father was fickle and so was left till last.

mutetur etiamsi exoratus est. Hunc sensum non inprudenter Silo Pompeius inprobabat; aiebat enim non posse mutari semel latam sententiam.

22 Quidam voluerunt videri cito exoratum raptae patrem, quidam tarde. Fuscus Arellius dixit: magnam partem legis consumpsi nec de mora queror: raptae pater rogabatur. Cestius non probabat, et hac sententia usus est cum hunc colorem argueret: dum vult videri rogatum diu raptae patrem, efficit ut videatur suum diu non rogasse; malo autem videri 15 huius [1] patrem tarde exorari quam tarde rogari.

Hermagoras solebat interdum diu schemata prosequi, interdum breviter et fortius attingere, sicut in hac sententia fecit, cum suspicionem facere vellet inter raptae patrem et raptorem collusionis: "πέπεισταί, φησιν, ὁ τῆς φθαρείσης πατήρ'. οὕτως ταχέως; μονονοὺ πρὸ τῆς φθορᾶς.

23 Artemon dixit: λέγε, ἐς τί σὺ πρὸς τὸν πατέρα τῆς ἐφθαρμένης συμπεφώνηκας; λέγε, πῶς πέπεικας; σιωπᾷς; †ΙѠΡΙΟ.†

Glycon dixit: βραδέως [2] ἐλεεῖς με · κηρὸς ῥύσις [3] οὐκ ἔστι. φθίνω κρυεροτέραν [4] θανάτου μέριμναν· οὐ περιμενῶ σου τὸν ἔλεον.

Hunc sensum commodius dixit Lepidus, Neronis

---

[1] huius *Kiessling:* hoc.
[2] βραδέως ed. (εἰ β. *Bursian*): NaaaUDℇaC *or similar.*
[3] κηρὸς ῥύσις *Thomas:* KNC PYCIIC.
[4] φθίνω κρυεροτέραν *Kiessling and Thomas:* ΦΤ ΙΝΜ ΚΡΥΟΤℇΡαΝ.

may change his mind even after consenting." Pompeius Silo, not unreasonably, did not like this idea; he said a verdict once given could not be altered.

Some wanted it to seem that the girl's father had 22 been won over slowly, some quickly. Arellius Fuscus said: " I have used up a great deal of the time allotted by the law, but I am not complaining of the delay: after all it was the *girl's* father I was trying to persuade." Cestius disapproved; attacking this *colour*, he used the epigram: " In his efforts to make it seem that he spent a long time asking the girl's father, he makes it look as if he spent a long time before asking his own. But I should rather the boy's father was slow to pardon than that the boy was slow to ask."

Hermagoras used sometimes to follow his figures [1] up for a long time, sometimes to touch on them concisely and effectively—as he did in this epigram, when he wanted to hint at collusion between the seducer and the girl's father: " ' The father of the girl has been persuaded.' So soon? All but before the seduction."

Artemon said: " Tell us what you agreed on with 23 the girl's father. Tell us, how did you persuade him? You are silent? ..."

Glycon said: " Your pity for me is slow to come. There is no deliverance from death. I waste away with an anxiety chiller than death—I will not wait for your pity."

This idea was put more suitably by Nero's teacher,

---

[1] In the sense of " figured " *controversia*: Hermagoras' hint is something he does not say outright, that it was a put-up job.

praeceptor: non misereberis nisi ultimo die? ego mei ante miserebor.

Diocles Carystius a parte patris ethicos dixit: " ἡβῶ θανάσιμος." [1] ἀπόθανε · εἰς τί γὰρ ἥρπαζες; εἰς τί γὰρ ἐφέρου; [2] εἰς τί γὰρ ἐμαίνου; [3] καὶ ταῦτα   151 δὴ ποήσας ἐνέδρας ἤ τι ὅμοιον.

IV

NEPOS EX MERETRICE SUSCEPTUS

Abdicavit quidam filium; abdicatus se contulit ad meretricem; ex illa sustulit filium. Aeger ad patrem misit: cum venisset, commendavit ei filium suum et decessit. Pater post mortem illius adoptavit puerum; ab altero [pater] [4] filio accusatur dementiae.

1 PORCI LATRONIS. Qualem vidi! ipsa fungebatur officiis, sedula circa aegrotantis lectum in omnia discurrebat ministeria, non incultis [5] tantum sed laniatis capillis. Ubi est, inquam, meretrix? Venit ad me subito qui diceret: filius antequam moriatur rogat venias. Non expectavi dum iste permitteret: amens

---

[1] ἡβῶ θανάσιμος ed.: ΕΒΩ ΟΝαΤΙΟC B: -αCΙΟC AV.
[2] ἐφέρου Thomas: ΕΟΕΟΥ.
[3] ἐμαίνου Bursian: ΕΝαΙΝΕΤΟ.
[4] Deleted in the editio Romana (1585).
[5] incultis Gertz: inpulsis BV: inpulsus A.

Lepidus: " Will you not pity me, except on the last day ? I shall pity myself before then." [1]

Diocles of Carystos, for the father, said, in character: " ' I am young and near to death.' Die then. Why did you rape her ? Why carry her off ? Why go mad ? And that after having set a trap, or something of the sort."

4

The Taking In of the Grandchild Born of a Prostitute

A man disinherited his son; the disinherited son betook himself to a prostitute, and acknowledged a son by her. He fell ill and sent for his father. When his father came, he entrusted his son to him and died. After his death the father adopted the boy. He is accused of insanity by his other son. [2]

For the father

Porcius Latro. What a woman I saw! She was [1] herself attending to what had to be done; attentive at the sick man's bedside, she ran to do every service, her hair not merely dishevelled but torn out. " Where is the prostitute ? " I said to myself.—I suddenly had a message to say : " Your son implores you to come before he dies." I didn't wait till *he* [3]

---

[1] Both the last epigrams hint at the possibility of suicide (cf. p. 281 n. 1).

[2] For the *actio dementiae*, see *C.* 2.3 n.—The theme recurs in Calp. Flacc. 30. Two parallels are noted below.

[3] The second son.

cucurri. Cetera quemadmodum narrem nescio: steterim an sederim, quid locutus sim, quid audierim, nescio; hoc unum scio, iacuisse me inter duos filios. Accede hoc, puer, depositum, crimen meum; non habeo miser cui te moriturus commendem.

2 CESTI PII. Recepi in sinum nepotem: vultis et 15: hunc abdicem? Duos filios sustuli; huic numero iam adsuevi. Patrem accusat, fratrem infamat, infantem persequitur: rogo vos, non satius est meretricem amare quam neminem? *In me novi generis dementia arguitur: sanus eram si non agnoscerem meos.* Tradidit infantem, expiravit; non habui cui redderem. Offerebam me propinquis, *expectabam ut aliquis pro abdicato rogaret: nemo audebat propinquorum fratre cessante;* illi videlicet in hac cogitatione tacebant: nos rogabimus cum frater non audeat? " Meretricis " inquit " filium recepisti ": nempe eius quae meum receperat. Fateor aliquando me insanum fuisse: nescii quis esset abdicandus, meliorem expuli.

3 PAPIRI FABIANI. Quam nihil in illa domo meretriciae vitae[1] vidi! Adsidebat mulier tristi vultu,

---

[1] meretriciae vitae *Madvig:* meretricia fide.

should give his permission: I ran all the way, out of
my mind.[1] I don't know how to tell the rest; I don't
know if I stood or sat, what I said, what I heard; all I
know is that I lay between two sons.[2]—Come here,
child, my responsibility, my guilt; unhappily if I die
I have no-one [3] to commend you to.

CESTIUS PIUS. I have taken my grandson to my 2
heart. Do you want me to disinherit him too?—I
acknowledged two sons; I've got used to this
number by now.—He accuses his father, abuses his
brother, persecutes the child; I ask you, isn't it
better to love a whore than to love nobody?—I am
charged with a new variety of madness; I should
count as sane if I refused to recognise my family.—
He handed me the baby and expired: I had no-one
to give him to.—I presented myself to our relations,
expecting that one of them would beg for the son I
had disinherited—but none of the relations dared,
for the brother hung back. Presumably they kept
silent because they thought: Are *we* to beg when the
brother does not dare? [4]—" You took in the son of a
whore." Yes, the whore who had taken in my son.—
I agree that I was mad—once upon a time; I did not
know which deserved to be disinherited—I drove out
the better of the two.

PAPIRIUS FABIANUS. How true it is that I saw 3
nothing of a prostitute's way of life in that house!
At the bedside sat a woman, sad-faced, ailing, herself

---

[1] An allusion to the present charge.
[2] His natural son and his (future) adopted son.
[3] His other son being estranged.
[4] For further criticism of the brother for not taking his
brother's part after the disinheritance, see §3 " ' Father . . .";
" I had entrusted . . ."; §4 " To sum up . . ."

adfecta, aegro simillima ipsa, demissis in terram
oculis. " Pater," inquit " nihil tecum frater locutus
est?" *In sinu meo et filium et animam deposuit.*
Domum pertuli. Dementiam vocat quod infantem
adoptavi.[1] Quid facerem? negarem aliquid filio cum
ille rogaret pro filio? Ignosco tibi quod tam durus
es: aegrum fratrem non vidisti. Ille magni modo
successor patrimoni natus in lectulo precario morie-
batur; non servorum turba circumstabat, non ami-
corum; inter infantem et mulierculam *deficientis* 153
adulescentis spiritus in adventum meum sustinebatur.
Ut *intravi, cadentes iam oculos ad nomen meum erexit,*
fugientemque animam retinuit. " Pater," inquit " quod
adhuc nihil deprecatus sum, non contumacia feci;
fratri mandaveram." Indico tibi crimina mea: ex-
pirantem coheredem tuum ad vitam volui revocare;
ut salvus esset rogavi deos et, licet dementiam voces,
si vixisset, recepissem.

4   Arelli Fusci patris. Securior eram, quoniam
putaveram illi omnia praestare fratrem, cum subito
nuntiatum est in ultimis esse filium, nec hoc a fratre. O
me miserum, quod solum nepotem recepi!

    Albuci Sili. Ut vidit uxorem, vidit patrem, cir-
cumspiciebat et fratrem.

---

  [1] adoptavi *Gertz:* abdicaui,

much like the patient, eyes cast down.—" Father,"
he said, " did my brother say nothing to you? "—He
entrusted to my keeping his son and his last breath.
I carried him home.—He calls it madness to adopt the
baby. What was I to do? Was I to deny my son
when he begged for *his* son?—I pardon you [1] for
being so harsh. For you didn't see your brother on
his bed of sickness. There he was, only the other day
the natural successor to a vast patrimony, dying on a
bed he had had to beg for. No crowd of slaves or
friends stood round; between the baby and a feeble
woman the dying youth continued to breathe till I
arrived. As I entered, he raised his already drooping
eyes at the sound of my name,[2] and held back his
departing life. " Father," he said, " it is not the
result of obstinacy that till now I have not begged
your pardon: I had entrusted that task to my
brother."—I will reveal my crimes: I wanted to
recall to life the dying man who was joint-heir with
you, I prayed to the gods that he might be spared,
and, though you may call it madness, I should have
taken him back had he lived.

ARELLIUS FUSCUS SENIOR. I was not worried, be- 4
cause I thought his brother was providing him with
everything he needed: but then suddenly I heard
that my son was on his death-bed—and it was not
from his brother I learned it.—Alas that it was only
my grandson I could take back!

ALBUCIUS SILUS. When he saw his wife and his
father there, he kept looking round for his brother too.

[1] The second son.
[2] Cf. Ovid *Met.* 4.145-6: " ad nomen Thisbes oculos in
morte gravatos / Pyramus erexit."

IULI BASSI. Tibi debeo, mulier, quod habuit filius meus in qua domo aegrotaret. Pudet dicere: ut nepotem agnoscerem rogatus sum. Non potest ⟨ex⟩[1] uno crimine dementia intellegi. Nemo sine vitio est: in Catone ⟨deerat⟩[2] moderatio, in Cicerone constantia, in Sulla clementia. Ad summam, tres fuimus, omnes peccavimus: ego quod abdicavi, frater quod tacuit, tu quod pro fratre non rogasti. Non sum uno herede contentus, duos habere volo: et, quo magis concupiscam, habui. Misit ad me adfectus, aeger. Non ibo? Mihi crede, aliter tu audis de coherede. Cogitate quis roget, pro quo roget, quem roget; videbitis neminem negare [non][3] posse nisi qui accusare possit et patrem.

5   Altera pars. PORCI LATRONIS. Quem honestius 154 subiecit meretrix quam peperit. *Pater istius incertus est; bene cum ipso ageretur si et mater.*

FUSCI ARELLI patris. Errat si quis [sit][4] me putat pecunia moveri. Primum adsuevi coheredem habere; deinde olim iam cum puero isto paterna divisi, quia multo illi pater donavit plus quam suam partem.

---

[1] *Supplied by Otto.*
[2] *Supplied by Otto.*
[3] negare *Schultingh:* rogare non.
[4] *Deleted by Bursian.*

---

[1] In not challenging the disinheritance and not begging his father's pardon (cf. §3).
[2] Meaning: you (the second son) have a financial interest in rejoicing in your brother's illness.
[3] i.e. in the view of the rest of the family; in either case the child was unworthy of adoption.

JULIUS BASSUS. I owe it to you, woman, that my son had a home to fall ill in.—I am ashamed to say it: I had to be begged to acknowledge my own grandson. —Madness cannot be diagnosed from a single fault. No-one is faultless: Cato lacked moderation, Cicero firmness, Sulla clemency.—To sum up, there were three of us—and we all acted wrongly: I in disinheriting, your brother in saying nothing,[1] you in not begging for your brother.—I am not satisfied with one heir, I want to have two: and—to make my desire greater—I did once have two.—He has sent to me, ill and sick. Shall I not go? Believe me, *you* react differently to news of your co-heir.[2]—Consider who is asking, whom he is asking and on whose behalf: you will see that no-one could refuse—except one capable of accusing his own father.

The other side

PORCIUS LATRO. A child whom it would have been 5 more honourable [3] for the prostitute to have pretended to be her own than to have borne.—His father is not certainly known; it would go better with him if his mother were too.[4]

ARELLIUS FUSCUS SENIOR. Anyone who thinks I am influenced by money is mistaken. First of all, I have got used to having an heir joint with me. Then, I have long since divided my father's estate with this child, because my father has given him much more than his share.[5]

[4] Cf. Calp. Flacc. 30: "nescio quid sit indignius, utrum patris origo, quod est dubia, an matris origo, quod certa est."

[5] i.e. while he was still in the house, the first son received far more money than his brother, and the second son regards this as having passed to the grandson.

ROMANI HISPONIS. *Incidit in meretricem inter omnia mala etiam fecundam.* Vere mimicae nuptiae ⟨in⟩ [1] quibus ante in cubiculum rivalis venit quam maritus.

ARGENTARI. Cum abdicaret, aiebat: hoc scilicet expectabo, donec e meretrice liberos tollas? *Mulier, nescio an adversus patrem iniuriosior quod abstulisti illi heredem an quod dedisti.*

6   ALBUCI SILI. Sine veniant illuc amici, sine propinqui: nolunt,[2] erubescunt in domum meretricis accedere. Mulier, quae sine praefatione honeste nominari non potes, cedo istum puerum nulli agnoscendum si mater adserat. Severissimus pater abdicavit etiam quem sciebat suum. Erat in domo puer, qui omnes vocabat patres. *Adoptavit eius filium propter quam* etiam *suum eiecerat.*

CESTI PII. Nullum genus iudicum recuso: si severi erunt, nocebit isti quod recepit meretricis filium; si 15 clementes, quod abdicavit suum. Clamavit pater: in domum ergo meam meretrix veniet aut, quod turpius est, filius ad illam ibit? Misit in domum nostram publicum puerum. Quis illis nuptiis interfuit nisi abdicatus aut abdicandus?

7   Latro sic divisit: an pater ob ullam adoptionem accusari possit, an ob hanc debeat.

---

[1] nuptiae in *Madvig:* nustis *AB:* nustus *V.*
[2] nolunt *Novák, Gertz:* nunc.

---

[1] That is, the whore was the son's mistress before becoming his wife.
[2] It is not clear who is meant to say these words.

ROMANIUS HISPO. He chanced upon a whore who, amidst all her other disadvantages, was also fertile.— Truly this was like a stage-marriage, where the lover came into the bedroom before the husband.[1]

ARGENTARIUS. As he disinherited, he said: " Am I supposed to wait until you raise children by a whore ? "—Woman, I'm not sure whether you do my father more injury by depriving him of an heir or providing him with one.

ALBUCIUS SILUS. Let the friends and relatives 6 come there:[2] they refuse, they blush to approach the house of a prostitute.—Woman—I cannot decently name you without asking my hearers' pardon first— give me this boy who can be acknowledged by no-one if his mother claims him.—My scrupulous father disinherited even one whom he knew to be his own son.[3]—There was a boy in the house,[4] who used to call everybody father.—He adopted the son of a woman who had caused him to throw out even his own.

CESTIUS PIUS. There is no type of judge I refuse. If the judges are harsh, it will go against him that he took in the son of a whore. If they are clement, that he disinherited his own.—My father cried: " Shall a whore then come to my house—or, what is more shameful, shall my son go to her ? "—He has sent into our house a child who belongs to everyone.—Who took part in a wedding like that except a disinherited son—or one who deserved to be ?

Latro's division was: Can a father be accused on 7 account of any adoption ? Should he be for this one ?

---

[3] Yet now he adopts a dubious grandson.
[4] i.e. the brothel.

Omnes infamaverunt adulescentem, quasi illius criminationibus factum sit ut frater abdicaretur; et ideo sententia laudatur Fabiani: nihil tecum locutus [sum] [1] est? Cum hoc unum puero noceat, quod ex meretrice natus est, omnes operam dederunt ut, quantum ⟨in hac⟩ [2] controversia licebat, huic vitio mederentur, efficerentque ne quicquam in illa videretur meretricis fuisse nisi nomen.

Marullus decenter hoc dixit, simul obiciens fratri impietatem: nihil, inquit, in illa domo meretricium fuit: scires, si mecum fuisses.

8 Albucius ethicos, ut multi putant, dixit—certe laudatum est cum diceret—: exeuntem ⟨me⟩ [3] puer secutus est. Non probabat hanc Messala sententiam: non habet, inquit, fiduciam si mavult videri recepisse puerum quam adduxisse; et sine [4] ratione est adoptatum esse non quia debuerit sed quia secutus sit. Fuit autem Messala exactissimi ingenii quidem 156 in omni studiorum parte, sed Latini utique sermonis observator diligentissimus; itaque cum audisset Latronem declamantem, dixit: sua lingua disertus est. Ingenium illi concessit, sermonem obiecit. Non tulit hanc contumeliam Latro, et pro Pythodoro Messalae orationem disertissimam recitavit, [que]

---

[1] *Deleted by Gertz.*
[2] *Supplied by Müller.*
[3] *Supplied by Bursian.*
[4] sine *Müller:* qua.

Everybody abused the son, representing it as due to his accusations that his brother came to be disinherited. Hence the praise for Fabianus' epigram: "Did he say nothing to you?"[1] Since the only objection to the boy is that he is the son of a whore, everyone endeavoured to remove this blot as far as they could within the terms of this declamation, and to make it seem that she had nothing of the whore about her except the name.

Marullus aptly said this (with the further effect of reproaching the brother with lack of affection): "There was nothing of the harlot in that house; you would know—if you had come with me."

Albucius' remark was in character, as many think 8 (at least it was praised when he uttered it): "As I went out the boy followed me." This epigram was disliked by Messala, who said: "He lacks self-assurance if he wants to give the impression that he let the child come rather than brought it. And it is unreasonable that the child should have been adopted not because of the rights of the matter but because he tagged along." Messala was of the nicest judgement in every branch of study, but above all he was the most careful precisian in the Latin language.[2] When he heard Latro declaim, he said: "He is eloquent—in his own language." He thus agreed that he was clever while criticising his expression. Latro could not abide this insult, and he recited Messala's very eloquent speech for Pythodorus, and for three days declaimed a specially pre-

[1] See above, §3.
[2] He wrote, for instance, a book on the letter s (Quintilian 1.7.23).

conpositamque [1] suasoriam ⟨de⟩ [2] Theodoto declamavit per triduum. Quae dixerit suo loco reddam,
cum ad suasorias venero.

9   A parte adulescentis non unus omnibus color
placuit. Quidam personam eius qualem acceperant
introduxerunt duram et asperam, ex quibus fuit et
Hispo Romanius: hoc unum aiebat efficiendum, ut
non durus videretur sed severus. In hac parte dixit
nobilem illam sententiam quam Fabius Maximus
circumferebat: venit adsidue in domum meretrix,
non recedit, paulum abest quin noverca sit.

Cestius bella figura egit: " Dementia " inquit " res
est sanitati contraria. Non quaeram extra exemplar
sani hominis ad quod patris mei ⟨mentem⟩ [3] exigam: [4]
ipsum sibi comparabo. Fuit aliquando sanus: tunc 15
quid faciebat? Oderat luxuriam, vitia castigabat.
Hunc tam severum senem putabitis sanum si vobis in
lupanari ostendero? " Sic declamavit ut patri accusatorem patrem daret et illum argueret sibi ipsum
conparando.

10   Latro patri pepercit; puerum pressit et dixit fratris
filium non esse et ne fratrem quidem hoc fateri
voluisse; illa verba aegro imperata.

---

[1] conpositamque *ed.:* que (quam *V*) conpositam quem
(quam *V*).
[2] *Supplied by Faber.*
[3] *Supplied by Ribbeck.*
[4] exigam *Kiessling:* gat.

pared *suasoria* on Theodotus.[1]   I shall record what he
said in the proper place, when I come to *suasoriae*.[2]

On the side of the youth not everybody chose the 9
same *colour*. Some kept the character they were
given for him, harsh and cruel: among them Romanius
Hispo, who said there was only one thing to be done—
to make him not harsh but severe.   In this passage
he spoke the well-known epigram publicised by
Fabius Maximus: " The whore constantly comes to
the house, she won't go away, she is virtually my
step-mother."

Cestius found a nice figure for his speech: " Madness is the opposite of sanity. I shall not look elsewhere for an example of a sane man against which to
measure my father's attitude: I shall compare him
with himself. He once was sane: what did he do in
those days ? He used to hate extravagance, castigate
vice. Will you think this stern father sane if I show
him to you in a brothel ? "   He declaimed in such a
way as to make the father his own accuser, proving
him guilty by comparing him with his former self.

Latro spared the father and attacked the boy, 10
saying he was not his brother's son—and that not
even his brother had wished to claim he was; what
he said was what he was told to say, during his illness.[3]

---

[1] Apparently for purposes of comparison: but the text is
corrupt. For the *suasoria* on Theodotus, see Quintilian
3.8.55–6.

[2] This passage proves the priority of the *Controversiae*, and
perhaps the incompleteness of the *Suasoriae* as we have them.

[3] Cf. Calp. Flacc. 30: "He called him his son—but he
spoke as a lover, he spoke as one who was scarcely by now
sane himself."

Fabianus ex omnibus istis colorem secutus est optimum, quo aiebat Messala posse non tantum bonam partem adulescentis fieri sed etiam honestam: obiecit patri quod fratrem abdicasset, non schemate, sed derecto: "Nihil" inquit "peccaverat; amat meretricem; solet fieri: adulescens est, expecta, emendabitur, ducet uxorem. Quare ergo tunc non egisti dementiae? Tuam expectabam paenitentiam; aiebam: iam recipiet. Hoc per transitum obicere coepit, quod non recepisset quom vidisset in lupanari habitantem. "Abdicasti" inquit "ut emendares? Vitia augeri vides. Nullum illius vitium: aetatis est, 158 amoris est; recipe, antequam aliquid faciat cuius 11 mox pudore moriatur." Ad ultumum obiecit illi quod aegrum non secum tulisset. "Potest" inquit "convalescere si viderit penates suos, ⟨si⟩[1] minus, certe morietur ⟨in⟩ solo paterno, suo, puro. Quare, inquit, tu apud fratrem non fuisti? Et ego queror. Ille, cum ad te mitteret, putavit se ad duos mittere. Utinam tecum fuissem, pater; redisses illinc cum filio, sed tuo." De adoptione novissime questus est et hac figura: Abstulisti mihi fratrem cum quo natus sum, cum quo educatus sum,

[1] *Supplied by Kiessling.*

---

[1] In what follows, Fabianus reports the youth's criticisms of the father at different stages of the affair ("He had done ... Did you ... He may ... "), and also two exchanges between

Fabianus pursued the best *colour* of all these, one
by which, according to Messala, the youth's role could
be made to seem both good and honourable; he
accused the father of disinheriting his brother—not
by means of a figure but directly.[1] " ' He had done
nothing wrong. He loves a whore—something that
often happens. He is a youth;[2] wait, he will reform
and marry.' ' Why didn't you accuse me of insanity
then? ' I was waiting for you to repent. I kept saying to myself: He will take him back yet." By a
transition he proceeded to reproach him with failing
to take him back when he had seen him living in a
brothel. " ' Did you disinherit him to reform him?
You see his faults are growing. There is no vice in
him; it is the fault of his age, of love. Take him
back, before he does something for shame of which he
may soon die.' " Finally, he reproached him for not 11
taking the sick man with him. " ' He may get
better if he sees his home: if not, he will at least die
on his father's ground, on his own ground, on un-
tainted ground.' ' Why were *you* not at your
brother's side? ' I too have a complaint over this.
When he sent to you, he thought his message would
reach both of us. Would that I *had* been with you,
father. You would have come back from there with
a son—your own." [3] Finally, he complained of the
adoption using the following figure: " You took
away from me the brother with whom I was born and

father and son in court ("Why didn't... Why were...").
Punctuation presents difficulty here.
   [2] This is the *locus indulgentiae*: cf. *C.* 2.6.11; Juv. 8.163;
Cic. *Cael.* 39 *seq.*
   [3] My brother—not merely your grandson.

ut quem dares? istum. Indignor hanc ⟨fieri⟩ [1] fratri
meo contumeliam, ut huius vocetur pater.

Sed ut aliquid iocemur, Fabius Maximus nobilis-
simus vir fuit, qui primus foro Romano hunc novicium
morbum quo nunc laborat intulit; de quo Severus
Cassius, antequam ab illo reus ageretur, dixerat:
quasi disertus es, quasi formonsus es, quasi dives es;
12 unum tantum es non quasi, vappa.[2] Hanc controversiam cum declamaret, Maximus dixit [quasi][3]
tricolum tale qualia sunt quae basilicani sectantur.
Dicebat autem a parte patris: [4] Omnes aliquid ad vos
inbecilli, alter alterius onera, detulimus: accusatur 159M
pater in ultimis annis, nepos in primis †abdicatur
nullus†. Haec autem subinde refero quod aeque
vitandarum rerum exempla ponenda sunt quam
sequendarum.

In hac controversia Latro contrariam rem ⟨non⟩ [5]
controversiae dixit sed sibi. Declamabat illam
Caesare Augusto audiente et M. Agrippa, cuius filios,
nepotes suos, Caesar [Lucium et Gaium] [6] adoptaturus

---

[1] *Supplied by Schultingh.*
[2] vappa *Gronovius:* alapam.
[3] *Deleted by Schott.*
[4] parte patris *Bursian:* patre.
[5] *Supplied by Schultingh.*
[6] *Deleted by Gertz.*

bred in order to give me—whom? This boy. I am indignant that my brother should be insulted by being called this boy's father."

But, to introduce a lighter note, Fabius Maximus was a very well-born man; he was the first to introduce to the Roman court the new evil that now afflicts it. Of him Cassius Severus, before being prosecuted by him,[1] had said: "You are as it were eloquent, as it were handsome, as it were rich: the only thing you are not as it were is a good-for-nothing." Now when Maximus was declaiming this 12 *controversia*, he uttered one of the tricola [2] of the type affected by habitués of the basilica; [3] he said (on the father's side): "We have all of us weak ones brought you [4] something to decide, one bringing the burdens of another. A father is accused in his last years, a grandson in his first, †no-one is being disinherited†." I often record these things, because I ought to give you examples of things to avoid as well as things to imitate.

In this *controversia* Latro said something that was harmful to himself rather than to his declamation. He was declaiming it in the presence of Augustus and Marcus Agrippa, whose sons [5]—the emperor's grand-

---

[1] Occasion unknown: for Cassius' trial for *maiestas*, see *C*. 3 pr. 5.

[2] Sentences constructed of three parallel *cola* or clauses: here the structure is spoiled by corruption. This trick is what Seneca means by "the new evil"; Cassius parodies it.

[3] Doubtless the Basilica Julia, home of the centumviral court.

[4] The judges.

[5] Gaius and Lucius, as the gloss here tells us. The time would be round 17 B.C.

diebus illis videbatur. Erat M. Agrippa inter eos qui
13 non nati sunt nobiles sed facti. Cum diceret partem
adulescentis Latro et tractaret adoptionis locum,
dixit: " iam iste ex imo per adoptionem nobilitati
inseritur " [1] ⟨et⟩ [2] alia in hanc summam. Maecenas
innuit Latroni festinare Caesarem; finiret iam
declamationem. Quidam putabant hanc maligni-
tatem Maecenatis esse; effecisse enim illum [3] non ne
audiret quae dicta erant Caesar, sed ut notaret.
Tanta autem sub divo Augusto libertas fuit ut prae- 160
potenti tunc M. Agrippae non defuerint qui ignobili-
tatem exprobrarent. Vipsanius Agrippa fuerat,
⟨at⟩ [4] Vipsani nomen quasi argumentum paternae
humilitatis sustulerat et M. Agrippa dicebatur. Cum
defenderet reum, fuit accusator qui diceret: " Agrippa
Marce et quod in medio est "—volebat Vipsanium
intellegi—; fuit qui diceret: " concurrite! Agrippa
malum habebit.[5] Responde sis, Marce [6] uterque."
Mihi videtur admiratione dignus divus Augustus,
sub quo tantum licuit, sed horum non possum
misereri qui tanti putant caput potius quam dictum
perdere. Latro dignus fuit miseratione, qui ne excusare quidem errorem suum potuit. Nihil est autem
crudelius quam sic offendere ut magis sis offensurus si
satis feceris.

---

[1] inseritur *Madvig:* ferunt.   [2] *Supplied by Kiessling.*
[3] illum *Madvig:* nibilum *AB:* nobilem *V.*
[4] *Supplied by Bursian.*
[5] habebit *Gronovius:* habebis.
[6] responde sis, Marce *ed. (after Ribbeck):* respondi (*om. A:*
-dis *V*) diis eam arce.

sons—the emperor seemed to be proposing to adopt
at that time. Agrippa was one of those who were
made noble, not born noble. Taking the part of the 13
youth and handling the topic of adoption, Latro said:
" Now he is by adoption being raised from the depths
and grafted on to the nobility "—and more to this
effect. Maecenas signed to Latro that the emperor
was in a hurry and that he should finish the declamation off now. Some thought this mere malice on the
part of Maecenas; he made sure not that Caesar
failed to hear what was said but that he noticed it.
However, in the reign of the blessed Augustus there
was such freedom of speech that, pre-eminent though
Agrippa then was, he did not lack critics of his low
birth. He had been Vipsanius Agrippa, but the name
Vipsanius, being a sign of his father's humble origin,[1]
he had got rid of, and he was now called merely
Marcus Agrippa. When he was defending a client
once, an accuser said: " Marcus Agrippa—and what
comes between "—he meant Vipsanius to be understood. And someone also said: " Hurry round!
Agrippa is in for a beating. Reply please—both
Marcuses." [2] The blessed Augustus, I feel, deserves
admiration if such licence was permitted in his reign;
but I cannot feel any sympathy for those who think it
worth losing their head rather than lose a jest.
Latro *did* deserve sympathy—he couldn't even excuse
himself for his slip: nothing is crueller than to offend
in such a way that apology will give even greater
offence.

[1] It is certainly a very rare name.
[2] Marcus Vipsanius and Marcus Agrippa.

THE ELDER SENECA

V

TORTA A TYRANNO PRO MARITO

Torta a tyranno uxor numquid de viri tyrannicidio sciret, perseveravit negare; postea
maritus eius tyrannum occidit. Illam sterilitatis nomine dimisit intra quinquennium non
parientem. Ingrati actio est.

1 PORCI LATRONIS. Si cum liberis torta esset, in-
dicasset. "Escende," inquit "occide tyrannum;
nisi occideris, indicabo." Subito iniecta manu
satelles "quid moraris?" inquit; "iam exposita
tormenta sunt." "Bene est," inquit mulier, "ad
stuprum non vocor." Instabat cotidie viro uxor,
exigebat tyrannicidium: "tempus est; escende; si
nihil aliud, ut liberos habeas: in tyrannide ¹ paritura
non sum." "Miraris si eo tempore ⟨parere non

¹ tyrannide *Gertz:* tyrannicide (-ida *V*).

---

¹ The law here implied is stated in *Decl.* 251 and discussed
by Bonner, 122–4, who argues that it was by no means inconsistent with Roman practice (for the famous divorce of
Spurius Carvilius Ruga, see Gell. 4.3).
² Bonner, 87–8. Sen. *Ben.* 3.6.1–2 shows clearly that the
law was not in force in Rome (add the implication of *C.* 3 pr.
17), though Bonner mentions some limited parallels. For the

5

THE WOMAN WHO WAS TORTURED BY THE TYRANT FOR HER HUSBAND'S SAKE

A wife, tortured by a tyrant to find out if she knew anything about her husband's plot to kill him, persisted in saying she did not. Later her husband killed the tyrant. He divorced her on the grounds of her barrenness when she bore no child within five years of marriage.[1] She sues him for ingratitude.[2]

For the woman

PORCIUS LATRO. If she had had children to be tortured along with her, she would have given the game away.—" Go up,"[3] she said, " and kill the tyrant: if you don't kill him, I will betray you."—Suddenly one of the tyrant's minions put his hand on her and said: " What are you waiting for? The tortures are all ready." " All is well," said the woman, " it is not to dishonour that I am summoned."[4]—The wife kept pressing her husband every day, demanding that he kill the tyrant. " The time has come: go up; if nothing else, so that you can have children—I don't propose to bear a child during a tyranny."—Are you surprised that I could not bear a child at a time when a married woman

Greek δίκη ἀχαριστίας (again only of limited application) add to Bonner's references Luc. 'Αποκηρ. 19.

[3] To the castle, where tyrants always live.

[4] Tyrants were notable for their womanising.

potui quo a tyranno torqueri⟩ [1] matrona potuit? "
"Escende, occide tyrannum; comes sequerer nisi
me inutilem dimisisset tyrannus. Escende: ego iam
feci tyrannicidium meum." *Eas nuptias tyrannicidium
diduxit quas non diduxit tyrannus.*

2 Cesti Pii. [Subito infelicis nuptias tyrannus oppressit.] [2] *Trahebantur matronae, rapiebantur virgines;*
nihil tutum erat; *nullae feliciores tunc videbantur quam
quae liberos non habebant.* Quaedam itaque elisere
conceptos, quaedam fecunditatem suam moratae
sunt. Quod ad hanc pertinet, agat sane [3] Fortunae
gratias quod illo tempore nihil peperit. *Tyrannus
suspicatus est nescio quid istum de tyrannicidio cogitare,
sive isti aliquid excidit, sive magna consilia non bene* 162
voltus texit.[4] *Utique de uxoris garrulitate queri non
potes, cum scias quemadmodum taceat.* Misit satellites:
"attrahite" inquit "uxorem, et" adiecit "si quos
3 filios habet." Veniunt in domum crudelissimi carni-
fices, in quorum vultibus tormenta erant: iactatur
misera inter satellitum manus, et toto itinere non
ducitur sed trahitur. Hanc aliquis, etiamsi torta non
sit, mirabitur non peperisse cum cogitaret [5] iste de
tyrannicidio? Audacter iam consilium indicamus,
iam enim, puto, licet. Nupsit isti propter liberos, sed
infelices nuptias cito tyrannus oppressit; hoc pub-

---

[1] *Supplied by Müller, following Bursian.*
[2] *Deleted by Gertz as an intrusion from §3.*
[3] agat sane *Müller:* ac sine.
[4] texit *Kiessling:* exigunt *AB:* exibuit *V:* tegit *E.*
[5] cogitaret *ed.* (cogitaverit *Schultingh*)*:* cogitur.

could be tortured by a tyrant?—" Climb up there—
and kill the tyrant; I would accompany you if the
tyrant hadn't incapacitated me before he let me go.
Climb: I have already done *my* tyrannicide."—The
marriage which a tyrant failed to sever has been
severed by his killing.

CESTIUS PIUS. [Suddenly the unhappy marriage 2
was utterly shattered by the tyrant.]—Matrons
were dragged to jail, virgins raped. Nothing was
safe. No women at that period were regarded as
luckier than those who had had no children. And so
some aborted children they had conceived, others put
a check on their own fertility. As for this woman,
she should thank her lucky stars that she bore no
child at that time.—The tyrant suspected that this
man had some thought of tyrannicide: perhaps because some word escaped him, perhaps because his
countenance did not well conceal his great plans.[1]—
At least you cannot complain that your wife is
garrulous: you know how she can keep silent.—He
sent his hirelings: " Bring in the wife. And " (he
added)" any sons she may have." There came to the 3
house the cruellest of executioners, torture in their
eyes. Flung about between the minions, the poor
thing was not led but dragged the whole way.—Will
anyone be surprised she did not bear children, even
before her tortures, seeing that her husband was plotting tyrannicide? I give away the plan now without
fear—for now, I think, I may.—She married him for
children—but all too soon the unhappy marriage was
shattered by the tyrant. This was a divorce for the

[1] Cf. Sen. *Thy.* 330–2: " multa sed trepidus solet / detegere
vultus, magna nolentem quoque / consilia produnt."

licum divortium fuit. Rapitur in arcem mulier, inter satellitum manus vexatur atque distrahitur. Hanc aliquis, etiamsi non torqueatur, non parere miretur? *Inposita in eculeum saepius ad absentem virum respexit quam ad praesentem tyrannum.* Quam multas matres audivi illo tempore: quid mihi[1] volui quae peperi?

4   ARELLI FUSCI. *Explicatur crudelitatis adversus infelicem feminam adparatus et illa instrumenta virorum quoque animos ipso visu frangentia ad excutiendam muliebris pectoris conscientiam proponuntur;* instat ante denuntiationibus quam tormentis tyrannus et minando torquet: tacet. Videt intentum tyranni vultum, videt oculos minaces: [et][2] tacet. Plus tibi praestare non potuit si de te liberos sustulisset. Flagellis caeduntur artus, *verberibus corpus abrumpitur* exprimiturque ⟨sanguis⟩[3] *ipsis vitalibus:* tacet. *Res publica, an sit tibi ista datura liberos nescio; tyrannicidam dedit.* Ita tu, mulier, non vis parere? delicata es, cruciatus puerperi times? Fremebat indignatione captae civitatis maritus et consilio suo et uxoris adiutorio fortior. " Quomodo occidam tyrannum? quae pars accedenti maxime vacat? ubi custodiae cessant? ubi natura loci minore munimento virtutem non summovet? " Sic vir et uxor noctes exercebant: *miraris si transit quinquennium inter*

10

---

[1] quid mihi *Gertz:* quidam.
[2] *Deleted by Kiessling.*
[3] *Supplied by Gertz.*

people's sake. The woman was dragged to the castle, maltreated by hirelings, torn apart. Is anyone surprised she does not bear children, quite apart from her tortures?—Placed on the rack, she thought more of the husband who was not there than of the tyrant who was.—How many mothers did I hear saying at that time: " What did I think I was doing when I had a child ? "

ARELLIUS FUSCUS. The apparatus of cruelty is de- 4 ployed against a miserable woman; the instruments that break the spirit even of men by their very look are set forth to extract the secrets in a woman's breast. The tyrant attacks with intimidation before torture—racks her with threats: she is silent. She sees the tyrant's set face, his threatening eyes: she is silent. She could have done you no greater service had she borne you children. Her limbs are cut by whips, her body broken by lashings, the blood forced out of her very vitals:[1] she is silent. I don't know whether she will give children to the state: she has given it a tyrannicide.—So don't you want to have children, woman? Are you squeamish, do you fear the agonies of childbirth?—The husband seethed with indignation for the city in servitude, strengthened by his own plans and his wife's help. " How am I to kill the tyrant? Which direction is most open to approach? Where are the guards lazy? Where does the lie of the land fail to ward off a brave man because of its feebler fortification? " *That* is how husband and wife spent their nights; do you wonder if five years passed, what with a wife who had been tortured and

[1] For other relished tortures, see e.g. *Decl.* 338; Sen. *Ep.* 14.5; Tac. *Ann.* 15.57; Curt. 6.11.15 *seq.*; Jerome *Ep.* 1.3 *seq.*

uxorem tortam et occupatum virum? Saeviebat etiamnunc tyrannus; torquebantur in conspectu maritorum
uxores; paenitebat matres fecunditatis suae.

5   HISPONIS ROMANI. In quid desideras liberos? ut
sint quibus relinquas patrimonium? Ingrate, ita tu
hac salva heredem non habes? Nullum tormenti
genus omisit; omnia membra laniata, omnes artus
convolsi [1] sunt, *scissum corpus flagellis, igne exustum,* 164
convulsum tormentis. Ignoscetis puto mulierculae si
dixero: fessa est.

HISPANI CORNELI. Cunctabatur ille nec ullis ad-
hortationibus in tyrannicidium poterat inpelli;
prorsus, cum uxorem vidisses, posses timenti ignoscere. Adsidue tormenta variantur; accenduntur
extincti ignes; tortor vocatur sub quo mariti uxores
prodiderant. Pacisci me tecum puta: ut taceam,
donas quinquennium? *Quid gloriaris tamquam non*
facilius sit occidere tyrannum quam sustinere? Duplici
beneficio uxoris suae obligatus ⟨est⟩: [2] et quod non
est occisus et quod occidit. Fastidit sterilem qui
fecit.

6   IUNI GALLIONIS. Instabat tyrannus: torque: illa
pars etiam potest; subice ignes: in illa parte iam
exaruit cruor; seca, verbera, oculos lancina, fac iam
ne viro placeat matrix.

---

[1] artus convolsi *Müller:* partes conuols(a)e.
[2] *Supplied by Schultingh.*

a husband who had such preoccupations?—Still the tyrant raged: wives were being tortured in the sight of their husbands, mothers were regretting their fertility.

ROMANIUS HISPO. What do you want children *for*? 5 So that you can have someone to leave your estate to? Ungrateful man, surely you *have* an heir while this woman lives?—He left out no variety of torture; all her limbs were mangled, all her joints wrenched; her body was torn with whips, burnt with fire, twisted by rackings. Surely you will pardon a poor feeble woman if I say: "She is worn out."

CORNELIUS HISPANUS. He hesitated—no exhortation could spur him on to kill the tyrant. When you had seen his wife, you could surely forgive his fears.—Constantly the tortures are varied. Fires that had been extinguished are relit. They call for the torturer whose attentions have made husbands betray wives.—"Suppose I make a bargain with you. If I give nothing away, will you make me a present of the five years?" [1]—Why do you boast?—as though it weren't easier to kill a tyrant than to endure his tortures.—He is bound to his wife by a double service: he was not killed, and he did the killing.—He scorns the barren woman: it was he who made her barren.

JUNIUS GALLIO. The tyrant pressed on. "Rack 6 her. That part is still available. Apply the fire. The blood is already dry *there*. Cut her, whip her, tear her eyes—make sure she no longer pleases her husband as a breeder of his children."

---

[1] i.e. do you agree not to insist on children within five years?

PAPIRI FABIANI. Describam nunc ego cruciatus et miram corporis patientiam inter tyrannica tormenta saevientia: extincti sanguine refovebantur ignes; in hoc desinebatur torqueri aliquando ut saepius posset. Exquisita *verbera, lamnae, eculeus, quidquid antiqua saevitia invenerat, quidquid* et *nova adiecerat—quid amplius dicam? et tyrannus torquebat et cum de tyrannicidio quaereret.* O nos felices quod nullis exhausta 16? puerperiis fuit! Tacuit ac silentio tyrannicidium fecit, certe tyrannicidam. Convolsis laceratisque membris nec adhuc sufficientibus non dimissa est ex 7 arce sed proiecta. Quid est quare uxorem dimiseris? *Numquid premit censum onerosa sumptibus? et, ut saeculi mos est, in deterius luxu fluente muliebris ambitio certamine mutuo usque in publica damna privatis insanit. Numquid gemmas et ex alieno litore petitos lapillos* et aurem vestemque nihil in matrona tecturam concupivit? Si talis esset, facile illam corrupisset tyrannus. *Expecta, potest parere; non respondet* ad propositum nec *ad certam diem fecunditas; sui iuris rerum natura est* nec ad leges humanas conponitur: modo properat et vota praecurrit, modo lenta est et [1] demoratur. Expecta, pariet. Quid dicis? "Non

[1] et *Vahlen:* modo.

---

[1] Cf. *C.* 2.7.3 *seq.*
[2] For extravagances in pearls, cf., e.g., Sen. *Ben.* 7.9.4; *N.Q.* 1.17.8; Petr. 55.6. For see-through dresses, Sen. *Ben.* 7.9.5, *Helv.* 16.4, *Ep.* 90.20; Jerome *Ep.* 127.3.

PAPIRIUS FABIANUS. Now I come to describe the torments, the extraordinary physical endurance she showed amid the raging of the tortures the tyrant applied. Fires that her blood had put out kept being rekindled; her tortures were halted occasionally— just so that they could be reapplied the more often. They looked out whips, plates, the rack, all the inventions of ancient sadism, all the innovations of modern sadism—what more need I say? A tyrant was the torturer—and the topic of his enquiry was a plot to kill him. How lucky we are that she had had no child-bearing to wear her out! She kept silence, and by her silence caused a tyrant's death—or activated his killer. Her limbs wrenched and mangled, and unable now to support her body, she was not let go from the castle: she was thrown out of it.—Why is it that you have cast out your wife? Is 7 she burdensome in her expenditure, does she weigh hard on your income? Certainly that is what the age is like—luxury spreads from bad to worse, and the ambitions of women,[1] competing with each other, bring madness to private households—and harm to the state. Surely *she* has never coveted pearls and precious stones sought on foreign beaches, gold, and clothes that will hide nothing of a married woman's body?[2] If she were like that, the tyrant would easily have corrupted her.—Wait: she is capable of bearing children. Fertility does not answer according to plan, follow a fixed timetable; nature is subject to its own laws, and does not adapt to fit human rules. Sometimes it hurries and runs ahead of our prayers, sometimes it lingers and holds them up. Wait: she will bear a child. What do you say? " It cannot

potest fieri." Quare? quod torta est. Imputat tibi quod †publica† est; imputat tibi quod torta est; imputat tibi quod sterilis est.

IULI BASSI. Aiebat tyrannus: ure, caede ventrem.

ARGENTARI. Caede ventrem, ne tyrannicidas pariat.

8   TRIARI. Non ex formula natura respondet nec ad praescriptum casus obsequitur; semper expectari fortuna mavult quam regi. Aliubi effunditur[1] inprovisa segetum maturitas, aliubi sera magno fenore 16 moram redemit. Licet lex dies finiat, natura non recipit. Aiebat tyrannus: " indica; nulla tua culpa est ": ⟨tacet.⟩[2] Caeditur: tacet; uritur: tacet. *Utrum putas mirandum esse, tuum tyrannicidium an huius silentium?* Expectasse aliqua per longum tempus maritum dicitur: quanta laus est servasse cum expectasse tanta sit? Alia desiderio viri attonita in ardentem rogum se misisse: haec non cum viro arsisset, quae pro viro arsit? Alia pro incolumitate mariti vicaria morte decidit: creditisne hanc in tormentis oppressam ⟨horruisse⟩[3] mortem? amplius pro viro praestitisset si quid amplius exegisset tyrannus.

9   MARCELLI. Si quid tamen[4] peccasset in partu, ignosci ei posset; nupserat enim isti occupato.

---

[1] effunditur *Gertz:* offenditur.
[2] *Supplied by Konitzer and Ribbeck.*
[3] *Supplied by the editor.*
[4] si quid tamen *Novák:* qui tamen qui.

be." Why? Because she was tortured. She has you to blame for her ..., her tortures and her barrenness.

JULIUS BASSUS. The tyrant said: "Burn her, beat her belly."[1]

ARGENTARIUS. "Beat her belly: make sure she bears no tyrant-killers."

TRIARIUS. Nature does not answer by rote, chance 8 does not obey a predetermined pattern. Fortune always prefers being waited for to being dictated to. In one place the corn springs up and ripens before it is expected, in another it comes late—and pays for the delay with great interest. Law may fix dates— nature takes no notice of them.—The tyrant said: " Give me the information. No fault rests with you." She is silent. She is beaten: she is silent. She is burnt: she is silent. Which do you think deserves admiration, your killing or her silence?—They say a woman[2] waited for her husband a long time: if it is a distinction to have waited, what distinction to have saved! Another, crazed for loss of her husband, pro- jected herself on to his burning pyre: *this* woman would have been prepared to burn with her husband —she burnt *for* him. Another settled to save her husband by dying in his stead: do you believe *this* woman, amid her torments, shrank from death?[3] She would have given more for her husband—if the tyrant had asked for more.

MARCELLUS. But if any fault was to be found with 9 her in her child-bearing, she deserved forgiveness—

---

[1] Cf. the last words of Agrippina (Tac. *Ann.* 14.8).
[2] Penelope for Ulysses.
[3] For these *exempla*, see *C.* 2.2.1 n.

Crudelior es etiam illo quem occidisti tyranno: ille
torsit, sed dimisit ad virum.

ALBUCI SILI. Vicerat saevitiam patientia; deerat
iam sanguis, supererat fides. Aliquando proiecta
est; deserebatur distortis manibus, emotis articulis;
nondum in sua membra artus redierant. Talem
uxorem tortor dimisit ad partum. Ingratus voca-
batur quod in praemio nullam uxoris fecerat mentionem. "Res tuas tibi habe." Inicere debuit
manum et ipsum te inter res suas trahere; nihil 167
amplius patri debes quam uxori. Mihi crede, maius
fuit tyrannicidium pati quam facere.

10 Pars altera. ARGENTARI. "*Ego* tamen *torta sum.*"
Merito obiceres nisi te vindicassem.

FULVI SPARSI. Vobiscum, iudices, loquor; quid
faciam? Non agam gratias quod ⟨non⟩ [1] indicavit
uxor? timeo ne vobis ingrati iam [2] ⟨teneri videar;
agam gratias? liberorum expers manebo . . .

DIVISIO. * * voluit in tali⟩ [3] controversia hanc
reum facere primam, si materia patitur: "non

[1] *Supplied in the ed. Hervageniana (1557).*
[2] *quid faciam—iam* appear in the MSS after recipit *in §8:
the words were transferred by Vahlen, who also supplied (exempli
gratia) what follows down to* manebo.
[3] *Supplied by Müller.*

---

[1] i.e. by thoughts of the tyrannicide. But there is a secondary hint at another meaning of *occupatus*, for which cf.
Decl. p. 417.16 Ritter: "sed vacuis indicere nuptias, non
occupatis."
[2] Whereas the husband divorced her. There is a play on
two senses of *dimitto.*

when she married him he was already preoccupied.[1]— You are crueller even than the tyrant you killed. He tortured her; but he sent her away [2]—to her husband.

ALBUCIUS SILUS. Endurance had overcome cruelty. Blood was running short now, but there was no shortage of loyalty. At last she was thrown out; she was abandoned, her hands twisted, her fingers displaced; her joints had not yet returned to their proper limbs. Such was the state of the woman when the tyrant let her go—to bear children.—They called him ungrateful because in asking for the reward [3] he made no mention of his wife.—"Take your goods." [4] She should have taken hold of you and dragged you along as part of her goods. You owe your wife as much as you owe your father.—Believe me, it was a greater deed of assassination to suffer than to act.

The other side

ARGENTARIUS. "But *I* was tortured." Your reproach would be justified—were it not that *I* avenged you.

FULVIUS SPARSUS. I ask you, judges: what am I to do? Am I *not* to thank my wife for giving no information? I fear I may already seem in your eyes to be guilty of ingratitude. *Am* I to thank her? I shall go on having no children . . .

Division

** wished in a *controversia* of this kind that the defendant's first question (if the theme allows) should

---

[3] For killing the tyrant.
[4] Based on the formula for *repudium*: "tuas res tibi habeto" (*Dig.* 24.2.2.1): cf. P. E. Corbett, *The Roman Law of Marriage* (Oxford, 1930), 224.

accepi ⟨beneficium," aut "accepi⟩ [1] quidem sed reddidi" aut "accepi quidem sed non potui reddere," aut isto novissime confugere: "non quisquis non reddidit beneficium ingrati tenetur; animus aestimandus est non reddentis."

Pollio Asinius aiebat numquam temptandam esse quaestionem primam, nisi manifesto obtineri posset, qua negamus nos beneficium accepisse; perit tota causa nisi in hoc vicit; apparet enim ingratum esse qui ne fatetur quidem se accepisse beneficium.

11 Gallio noster putat, quotiens possit, hoc auferendum 168 adversario; quotiens non possit, concutiendum; quotiens ne hoc quidem possit, ita transeundum quasi donemus et possimus quidem facere controversiam sed nolimus.

Idem Attico Dionysio, Apollodori discipulo, placuit. Hoc ille amplius: quotiens non potuerimus, aiebat, an beneficium acceperimus controversiam facere, de modo faciamus: non esse tam magnum quam ille dicat, sicut in criminibus facimus; quotiens negare non possumus, esse quidem crimen illud fatemur, sed leviore poena dignum quam accusator arguat.

12 Latro in hac controversia non dubitabat facere primam quaestionem, an beneficium dederit. Hoc in haec divisit: *etiamsi scisti de tyrannicidio viri nec indicasti, non est beneficium scelus non facere; deinde ne*

---

[1] *Supplied by Bursian, Kiessling.*

---

[1] Or perhaps: "never attempt the first question—that in which . . ."

[2] i.e. we should claim to have received no service.

be: " I received no benefit," or " I did receive a benefit—but I repaid it," or " I did receive a benefit, but I was unable to repay it," or in the last resort refuge should be found in this: " Not everyone who has failed to repay a benefit is guilty of ingratitude. One has to weigh up the intentions of the person who fails to repay."

Asinius Pollio used to say we should never attempt as the first question that in which [1] we claim we have received no benefit—unless it is obviously possible to carry the point: if it fails here the case is lost, for it is obvious that someone who doesn't even acknowledge that he has received a benefit is ungrateful. My 11 friend Gallio thinks that whenever possible we should deprive our opponent of this point,[2] and when it is impossible we should weaken it; and whenever even this is impossible, it should be passed over in such a way that we appear to be letting the point go and to be unwilling to make an issue of it even though we could.

The same view was held by a pupil of Apollodorus, Dionysius Atticus. He added this: whenever we cannot make an issue of whether we have received a benefit, we should dispute its *degree*, saying that it is not so great a benefit as is alleged—as we do in criminal charges: whenever we cannot deny a charge we concede it, but say it deserves a lighter penalty than the accuser claims.

In the present *controversia* Latro with no hesitation 12 made the first question: Did she confer a benefit? This he subdivided: " Even if you knew of your husband's plan to kill the tyrant and did not inform on him, it is no benefit to refrain from a crime ";

331

scisti quidem; non enim tibi indicavi nec tam magnum consilium, virilibus quoque animis grave, commisi muliebri garrulitati, quae id solum potest tacere quod nescit. ⟨Alteram fecit:⟩ [1] etiamsi dedit beneficium, an receperit. Occidi tyrannum, libertatem tibi reddidi, ultionem plenissimam persecutus sum, nefarium hostem illic occidi ubi torserat. Dices me rei publicae causa fecisse: et tu rei publicae causa tacuisti. ⟨Tertiam: an ob id⟩ [2] tutus sit quod lege fecerit. 169M Deinde ultima aequitatis tractatio: an quod fecit 13 facere debuerit. Hoc divisit in duo: an iam certam sterilitatem uxoris tam bonae ferre debuerit; an ne sterilis quidem pro certo sit.

Novi declamatores post Moschum Apollodoreum, qui reus veneficii fuit et a Pollione Asinio defensus damnatus Massiliae docuit, et hanc quaestionem in hac controversia fecerunt: an inter viros et uxores data beneficia ingrati lege teneantur. Non est beneficium sed officium facere quod debeas: sic filius patri se dicat beneficium dare. Hanc quaestionem fecit et Gallio noster.

Blandus in ultima parte controversiae, qua de re publica disputatur, quaestionem fecit an quinquennium numerari debeat excepta tyrannide. Illud

---

[1] *Supplied by Müller.*
[2] *Supplied by Müller after Bursian.*

---

[1] Cf. Hor. *Ep.* 1.5.9 and Porphyr. *ad loc.*

next: " You didn't even know about it. I gave you no information; I was not prepared to entrust so important a plan, a burden even on a man's spirit, to the garrulity of a woman, who is only capable of keeping something quiet if she knows nothing of it." The second point he made was: Even if she did confer a benefit on him, did she receive one from him? " I killed the tyrant, I gave you back your liberty, I executed the most complete revenge, I killed a most wicked enemy on the spot where he had carried out his tortures. You will say that I did it for the state; well, it was for the state that *you* kept quiet." The third question was: Is he safe from accusation in respect of something he did according to the law? Last came the handling of equity: *Should* he have done what he did? This he divided into two: Should 13 he have borne with the barrenness of so good a wife even if it was already beyond question? *Is* she certainly barren?

Recent declaimers, following the lead of Moschus the Apollodorean, who was tried for poisoning, defended by Asinius Pollio and convicted, and then taught at Marseille,[1] also made an issue in this *controversia* of the following point: Are benefits between husband and wife covered by the law on ingratitude? It is no benefit but a duty to do what you ought to do. On this basis, a son might say he conferred a benefit on a father. This question was also raised by my friend, Gallio.

Blandus, in the last part of the *controversia*, where dispute arises over the state, raised the question whether in reckoning the five years the period of the tyrant's rule ought to be excluded. A woman ought

tempus non debet inputari quasi sterili quo matres
etiam editos partus abominatae sunt: illud tempus
imputetur feminis quo rei publicae [1] pariunt, non
illud [2] quo tyranno. Huic subiecit an, etiamsi aliis
imputari tempus tyrannidis solet, huic non debeat.

14   Latro ex suo more has non quaestiones putabat, sed
membra illius ultimae partis ex aequitatis quaestione
pendentis. An ⟨ne⟩ [3] sterilis quidem, altius repetit: 170M
" Non [4] quaecumque quinquennio non peperit sterilis
est. Quid enim si vir alicuius afuerit toto paene
quinquennio peregrinatione, utri imputabitur? quid
si vir aegrotaverit? Si hic maritus a tyranno tortus
inutilis in concubitu suae uxoris iacuisset, ⟨utri⟩ imputari debuit [5] quinquennium? Quaeris quare non
pepererit? Tyrannis erat; nemo non cum parentibus suis querebatur quod natus esset. Adice [6] quod
torta est haec, quod maritus occupatus tyrannicidio
non vacavit in uxoris voluptates."

15   Buteo, aridus quidem declamator, sed prudens
divisor controversiarum, contra Latronem sentiebat,
Blando accedebat. Aliud enim esse aiebat: " quae
intra quinquennium non peperit, non utique sterilis
est "; aliud: " quae intra quinquennium non peperit,
non statim dimitti potest sterilitatis nomine "; hic

---

[1] quo rei publicae *Bursian:* in re publica.
[2] illud *Bursian:* plus.
[3] *Supplied by Schultingh.*
[4] non *Bursian:* anon *AB:* an non *V.*
[5] utri—debuit *Müller:* imputarit fuit *AB:* imputaturus
fuit *V.*
[6] adice *Gertz:* hic.

334

not to be reproached for barrenness in respect of a time when mothers grew to loathe even their previously born offspring. Women should be confronted with the time in which their children are born for the state, not for a tyrant. He added to this the point whether, even if others have to have the time of the tyrant's rule included, *she* ought to.

Latro, as usual, did not regard these as questions, 14 but as aspects of the last part, that depending on the question of equity. On the point: *Is* she in fact barren, he went into greater detail: " Not everyone who has failed to bear children within five years is barren. What if a woman's husband has been away travelling for almost the whole period, whose is the fault then? What if the husband has been ill? If this husband had been tortured by the tyrant, and had been unable to have intercourse with his wife, which of the two ought to have been blamed for the five years? Do you ask why she bore no children? There was a tyranny; everybody complained to their parents for having borne them. Moreover, the woman had been tortured, while the husband was preoccupied with his plan to kill the tyrant and had no time for the pleasures of matrimony."

Buteo, who was a dry declaimer, but skilful at 15 dividing *controversiae*, voted against Latro and in favour of Blandus. He said there is a difference between " She who has not borne children within five years is not certainly barren " [1] and " She who has not borne children within five years cannot automatically be divorced for barrenness." In one case

[1] Latro's assertion, contrasted with straightforward rejection of the law.

quaeri de condicione iuris, illic de spe fecunditatis.
Sed Blandum quoque arguebat; aiebat enim ⟨non⟩ [1]
sic fuisse quaerendum, an tyrannidis tempus excipi
deberet, deinde, [an] etiamsi non in aliis, an ⟨in hac,
tamquam⟩ [2] inter has gradus essent. Ipse sic hanc 171
partem ⟨vel⟩ [3] quaestionem dividebat: an, quaecumque quinquennio non peperit, tamquam sterilis
16 dimitti possit. ⟨Puta⟩ [4] accidere, quod Atheniensi-
bus in bello accidit, ut liberi et coniuges in aliquo
tutiore loco deponantur: inputabitur hoc tempus
feminis, quo viros non destituunt, sed non habent?
Si tyrannus non vetuisset istam parere, quin intra
⟨quinquennium parere potuerit, quis dubitet?⟩ [5] Et
cum hoc vehementer implevisset et probasset, non
omnes posse dimitti si quinquennio non peperissent,
tunc illo transit: an haec posset; et hic etiamnunc
non hoc quaerebat, an deberet dimitti, sed an posset,
et hoc contra Latronem dicebat: quomodo istam
quaestionem putas in aequitatis tractationem cadere,
cum quid liceat quaeratur, non quid oporteat? Hoc
enim, an haec possit, per illa impleo: non potest quia
⟨in⟩ tyrannide non conceperat. Aliquod tempus im-
mune a legibus miseriae faciunt. Non dico: ⟨non

---

[1] *Supplied by Otto after Gronovius.*
[2] *Supplied by Thomas.*
[3] *Supplied by Müller.*
[4] *Supplied by Novák.*
[5] *Supplied by Schenkl.*

the enquiry concerns the terms of the law, in the other it concerns the hope of fertility. But he also criticised Blandus, saying that he shouldn't have made a question of whether the time of the tyranny ought to be excluded, and then, even if it shouldn't in other cases, whether it should here, as if there were degrees of women. He himself divided this part (or question) thus: Can every woman who has not borne children within five years be divorced as barren? Suppose it happens—as with the Athenians in war-time [1]—that wives and children are sent away for safety to a more secure spot: will women have marked up against them a period in which they do not abandon their husbands—but do not have access to them? If the tyrant had not prevented this woman from having children, who would doubt that she could have had them within the five years? After forcefully developing and proving that not every woman could be divorced if she hadn't borne children within five years, he came on to the point: Could *this* woman? And here he still did not ask whether she ought to be divorced, but whether she *could* be. And in reply to Latro he said: " How can you suppose that this question falls under the treatment of equity when what is under discussion is not what ought to be the case but what is allowed? For as to the point whether she can be, I develop it thus: She cannot be, because her failure to conceive fell under a tyranny. Some periods are exempted from the operation of the laws by their misfortunes. I

---

[1] During Xerxes' invasion when women and children were evacuated to Salamis, Aegina and Troezen (Herodotus 8.41.1).

peperit⟩ [1] quia torta est—hoc adhuc praetereo et
aequitatis tractationi reservo—, sed quia tu maximae 17:
rei cogitatione occupatus nihil de liberis cogitasti.

17 Passienus, vir eloquentissimus et temporis sui
primus orator, hanc subtilitatem Buteonis non probabat: Latroni se adsentiri dicebat ideo ⟨quod
istae⟩ [2] quaestiones tractandae per se essent si haec
mulier iniusti repudi ageret; nunc ingrati agit: ita
non quaeritur an legitime sed an ingrate dimissa sit;
itaque in aequitatis tractationem cadunt etiam quae
iuris sunt. Nam cum quaeratur an non oportuerit
hanc dimitti etiamsi licuit, apparet quam utique non
oportuerit si ne licuit quidem.

Albucius itaque decentissime fecit—solebat enim
fere in aliquas figuras declamationem discribere—et
prius egit iniusti repudii, deinde ingrati: †inquit
putat emet an ullum beneficium a quo tamquam ini-
quae dimissa.†[3] Hinc omnes quaestiones ad sterilitatem et aestimationem quinquenni pertinentis libere
tractavit; deinde transit in ingrati accusationem.

18 Cestius pro viro ⟨hunc⟩ [4] introduxit colorem: *quo
tempore uxor torta est, nihil adhuc de tyrannicidio cogi-* 17:
tabam; postea cogitavi et haec ipsa mihi causa cogitandi

---

[1] *Supplied by Gertz.*
[2] *Supplied by Gertz and Thomas.*
[3] *I have translated my own hesitant reconstruction of this
sentence:* quis putet te ab ea ullum beneficium ⟨accepisse⟩ a
quo tam inique est dimissa?
[4] *Supplied by Gertz.*

don't say: She did not have children because she was tortured—this I still pass over, reserving it for the treatment of equity—but: She did not because *you* were occupied by thoughts of a highly important matter and had no thought of children."

Passienus, a most eloquent speaker and the fore- 17 most orator of his time, disapproved of this subtlety of Buteo's. He said he agreed with Latro, because these questions would have to be dealt with in their own right if the woman were suing for wrongful divorce: in fact she is suing for ingratitude. So the question is not whether she has been rightfully divorced but whether her divorce shows ingratitude. And so into the treatment of equity fall even matters pertaining to the law. For when one asks whether she ought not to have been put away even if it was allowed, it is obvious that she certainly ought *not* to have been if it was *not* allowed.

Hence the propriety shown by Albucius (who generally used to put his declamation into the form of some figure or other) in pleading first for wrongful divorce, then for ingratitude: "Who would think you had received any benefit from a woman whom you have so inequitably divorced?"[1] As a result he could deal freely with all questions relating to barrenness and the reckoning of the five years, then pass on to the accusation for ingratitude.

Cestius, for the husband, introduced the following 18 *colour*: "When my wife was tortured, I had as yet no thought of killing the tyrant. Afterwards, I did

---

[1] The reading is very doubtful. I have emended the text in such a way that Albucius is enabled to start on the *repudium* and proceed to the ingratitude.

fuit uxoris ultio. Utrumque secutus est, ut ⟨et⟩ [1] illa
marito silentium imputare non posset et maritus imputare illi tyrannicidium posset.   Latro dixit se iam
tunc de tyrannicidio cogitasse, sed uxori non indicasse.   Fabianus philosophus colorem ⟨non⟩ [2] magis
bono viro convenientem introduxit quam oratori cal-
lido.   Dixit enim et cogitasse ⟨se⟩ [3] tyrannicidium et
uxori indicasse et illam tum quidem fecisse quod probam feminam facere oportuit, nunc peccare quod putet
beneficium esse recte facere.   Hic color illi et in illa
parte profuit: si beneficium putas te dedisse quod
tyrannicidium non prodidisti, ego prior dedi, qui tibi
tyrannicidium credidi.   †Repudium ex tuo quo ius
liberorum cupiditatem, quo [4] semper uti tamquam
civis [5] debuisset, postea magis tamquam tyrannicida.†

19   L. Vinicius, †vinci fater†, [6] Fabiani colorem valde
probabat, et aiebat onerari uxorem uno modo posse,
si nihil umquam secretum ab illa maritus habuisset.
Si dixerit, inquit, post tormenta se de tyrannicidio
cogitasse, tum tyrannicidium uxori debemus.   Melius
de viro meruit si torta tyrannicidam fecit quam si
tacuit.   Sed [7] apparet ei aliquid de tyrannicidio
cogitatum, de quo tyrannus usque eo suspicatus est

[1] *Supplied by Müller.*
[2] *Supplied by Müller.*
[3] *Supplied by Bursian.*
[4] *I have translated my own dubious emendation of this passage:*
⟨In⟩ repudii excusationem usus ⟨est⟩ liberorum cupiditate,
qua.
[5] civis *Kiessling:* eius.

think of it, and the avenging of my wife was the real motive for my idea." He had two aims: *she* would not be able to make a virtue of her silence in the eyes of her husband, and *he* would be able to make a virtue of his tyrannicide in the eyes of his wife. Latro said he had already thought of killing the tyrant at that stage, but hadn't told his wife. Fabianus the philosopher brought in a *colour* that is worthy both of a good man and a cunning orator. He said that he had both thought of killing the tyrant and told his wife of it: and that she had *then* done what a good woman ought to have done—but *now* she is in the wrong in thinking it a good deed to do what is right. This *colour* came to his aid in the following part too: " If you think it a good deed that you did in not betraying the plan to murder the tyrant, *I* did you a good deed first in letting you know about the plot." He excused his divorcing his wife by his desire for children: he ought always to have used that excuse qua citizen—but more so later qua tyrannicide.

Lucius Vinicius, father of Lucius Vinicius, strongly 19 supported Fabianus' *colour*, and said the wife could only be made odious in one way—if the husband had kept nothing from her at any time. " If he says he considered tyrannicide after the torture, then we owe the killing to the wife. She deserved better of her husband if she made him into a tyrannicide by being tortured than if she merely kept quiet. But it is obvious that he *had* had some thoughts of tyrannicide —for the tyrant had formed such suspicions about the

---

⁶ *I translate Nipperdey's* L. Vinici pater: *the manuscripts differ.*
⁷ tacuit. Sed *Haase:* tacuisset.

ut torqueret. ⟨Si⟩ [1] dixerit cogitasse quidem se de tyrannicidio ante tormenta, sed uxori non indicasse, augebit uxoris beneficium: liberius enim potuit tyrannicidium indicare quod illi commissum non erat; potuit enim uxor etiam non indicante marito tam magni consili molitionem deprehendere. At si hunc colorem Fabiani sequor, multa efficiam. Si olim de tyrannicidio cogitavi, honestior sum vetus tyrannicida et non privatis sed publicis malis ad ultionem inpulsus. Si cum cogitarem non celavi uxorem, facilius persuadebo malum me hodie maritum non esse, qui [2] semper tam deditus fui. Ad ultimum hoc consequar, quod, *si quod audierat tacuit, non beneficium est sed fides.*

20 Hic est *L. Vinicius quo nemo civis Romanus in agendis causis praesentius habuit ingenium: quidquid longa cogitatio alii praestatura erat, prima intentio animi dabat; ex tempore causas agebat, sed non desiderabat hanc commendationem, ut ex tempore agere videretur. De hoc eleganter dixit divus Augustus: L. Vinicius ingenium in numerato habet.*

Hispo Romanius maligne et accusatorie "Nihil" inquit "ego isti narraveram; ista, ut erat necesse, 1 aliquid ex vultu, aliquid ex nocturnis vigiliis suspicata est. Unde emanaverit sermo scietis—videtis quo

---

[1] *Supplied by Schultingh.*
[2] qui *ed.:* cum.

plot that he put her to the torture. If he says that he had had thoughts of tyrannicide before the torture, but had not told his wife, he will increase the benefit conferred by his wife. For she could more freely have betrayed the killing if details of it had not been entrusted to her;[1] she could have detected the preparations for so vast a plot even if her husband didn't tell her of it. But if I follow this line of Fabianus', I achieve many results. If I thought about the killing some time ago, that makes me more honourable, a long-term tyrannicide impelled to revenge by public, not private wrongs. If, when I was plotting, I did not keep it from my wife, I shall be able the more easily to prove today that I am no bad husband, seeing that I was always so close to her. Finally, I shall ensure that her silence on anything she had heard is no benefit but a mere act of loyalty."

This is the Lucius Vinicius whom no compatriot 20 rivalled for presence of mind in the pleading of a case. What anyone else might have got from long preparation, he derived from the first impulse of his mind. He pleaded extempore, without being in need of the credit accruing to one seen to be pleading extempore. The blessed Augustus had a nice saying about him: "Lucius Vinicius has his genius in ready money."[2]

Romanius Hispo said in his malicious and accuser-like manner: "I had told her nothing; she, inevitably, had her suspicions from my look, from my sleepless nights. You can tell who let the story out

---

[1] i.e. she might have betrayed the plot without realising her husband's association in it.

[2] Cf. Quintilian 6.3.111; J. de Decker, *Rev. instr. publ. Belg.* 53 (1910), 371–4.

veniat tyrannus: non ad amicum meum, non ad servum, sed ad istam, quae nihil negoti habuisset si tacuisset. Tua etiam causa tacuisti: sciebas te perituram si confessa esses tyrannicidium."

Hybreas dixit: †ἀνάξαις οὖν ἐπὶ τὴν ἄκραν ἐπιών, καὶ εἰ εὐτολμεῖς, νῦν λαβὲ τὸ ξίφος.† [1]

VI

PATER ET FILIUS LUXURIOSI

Quidam luxuriante filio luxuriari coepit. Filius accusat patrem dementiae.

1 PORCI LATRONIS. Utriusque tamen conparetur luxuria. Tu consumis patrimonium patris tui, ego accusatoris mei. Naviga, milita, peregrinare, quaere adulescens, senex utere. *Accusator meus diversos et inter se contrarios adfectus habet: cupit reum damnari, crimen absolvi.*

CESTI PII. Potest nobis convenire; similes sumus. Puta te patrem: dic quid me velis facere. Si tu [2] bona fide frugi es, et hoc imitor. Te ego imitor an tu me? Rogo vos: uter prior coepit? "Luxuriaris"

---

[1] *I print, and roughly translate, Müller's version of this doubtful sentence.*
[2] tu *ed.:* tam.

---

[1] i.e. under torture. Her "letting the story out" was an indiscretion that led up to the torture.
[2] For the *actio dementiae*, see *C.* 2.3 n. The theme is alluded to in Quintilian 11.1.79. Some of the epigrams

by observing whom the tyrant came to for information: no friend of mine, no slave, but this woman,
who wouldn't have got into trouble if she'd kept her
mouth shut. She kept quiet [1] for her own sake too:
she knew she'd be killed if she confessed to tyrannicide."

Hybreas said: "†Go up to the castle, and if you
have the nerve take your sword now.†"

6

THE FATHER AND SON WHO BECAME DEBAUCHEES

A man began to be a debauchee, his son already
being one; the son accuses his father of madness.[2]

For the father

PORCIUS LATRO. But let us compare the extrava- 1
gance of the pair. You spend your father's money—
I my accuser's.[3]—Sail the seas, campaign, travel;
acquire money as a young man and spend it as an old
one.[4]—My accuser has different and inconsistent feelings—he wants the defendant condemned but the
crime acquitted.

CESTIUS PIUS. We can agree: we are similar.—
Suppose you are the father: tell me what you want
me to do.—If *you* are really of good character, I imitate that too.—Am I imitating you or you me? I ask
you all: who began it?—"You are extravagant."

suggest that it originally contained mention of the son ceasing
to be debauched.

[3] i.e. money that will go to my son (and if he accuses me,
I am not sorry to deprive him of it).

[4] Cf. Sen. *Ep.* 36.4.

345

inquit. Patrimonium conputemus. " *Sed tu senex es* " *inquit.* *Hoc dicis: luxuria tua serius coepit, citius desinet.*

2   ARELLI FUSCI patris. " Sed tu "inquit" senex es." 17[1]
Unde scis te non futurum luxuriosum senem? Omnia
a te vitia: quod unguento coma madet, tuum est;
quod laxior usque in pedes demittitur toga, tuum est.
Quid est aliud quod non a te senes discant? Quid
porro? domus nostra luxuriosos duos non capit? In-
dulgentius te abdicare non potui. Ecquid mihi licet
seniles annos meliore vita reficere? Hoc novissimum
meum meritum est et quod tibi pro maximo imputo:
pro te etiam luxuriosus factus sum.

FABIANI. Noli pecuniam concupiscere. Quid tibi
dicam? Haec est quae auget discordiam urbis et
terrarum orbem in bellum agitat, humanum genus
cognatum natura in fraudes et scelera et mutuum
odium instigat, haec est quae senes corrumpit.
Quidam summum bonum dixerunt voluptatem et omnia ad
corpus rettulerunt. *Nihil est mihi opus praecipienti-
bus: habeo exemplum,* proposui quidquid tu feceris
facere; navigabo si navigaris, militabo si militaris:
dic hodie, quid putes melius. Sed illud excipio: non
obicies quod elegeris.

BLANDI. Obicit luxuriam; poteram ei hoc dicere:

---

[1] You will find that it is *I* who have the money—and
therefore I am justified in spending it (cf. §5).

Let us reckon up our bank balances.[1] "But *you* are old." What you mean is: your extravagance began later, and will finish sooner.

ARELLIUS FUSCUS SENIOR. "But *you* are an old 2 man." How do you know *you* won't be extravagant in old age?—All my faults arise from you; that my hair is soaked in perfume is your doing. That my toga droops too loosely right to my feet is your doing. What else is there that old men could not go to you for lessons in?—Well: is there no room in our house for two debauchees?—I could not have found a kinder way to disinherit you.[2]—Why can't I give my old age the refreshment of a little comfort?—This is my last service—the one I claim the most credit with you for: it was for you that I even became a debauchee.[3]

FABIANUS. Do not covet money.[4] What am I to say to you? It is this that feeds the discord of a city and drives the world into war, spurring on the human race, that is by nature akin, to fraud, crime and mutual hatred, this that corrupts old men.— Some[5] have called pleasure the highest good, and measured everything by the body. I need no teachers; I have a model—I have decided to do everything *you* do. I shall sail the seas if you sail, campaign if you campaign. Say now what you think best. But I make one condition: you are not to reproach me with a course that is *your* choice.

BLANDUS. He reproaches me with extravagance.

---

[2] Than by spending all the money before you get it.

[3] With an allusion to the "plot" of which we shall hear much later on.

[4] For this *locus*, see *C*. 2.1.10, 21 nn.

[5] The Epicureans, Fabianus' natural enemies.

347

adulescens, frugaliter vixi quamdiu patrem habui. 177
Ante me desisti, ante me coeperas.

3 †BLANDI.† " Senex luxuriaris." Respondeo tibi:
adulescens enim navigavi. " Ego " inquit " iam
desii, tu nondum." Non miror si prior desisti; prior
coeperas.

MENTONIS. Quid? gaudiorum taedium cepisti?[1]
Vere luxurior.

POMPEI SILONIS. Si modo emendatus est filius
meus—solet enim etiam luxuria dissimulari—, suo
quisque ordine reus sit. Vis me ducere uxorem? Si
novercam haberes, iam abdicatus esses.

VIBI GALLI. Convivae certe tui dicunt: vivamus,
moriendum est. Si intellego, hoc nulli magis in domo
dicitur quam mihi. *Ostendi tibi luxuriam quam* [2] *in te
non videbas.* Adliga me, dum te custodias.

P. ASPRENATIS. Quia nihil proficiebam obiur-
gando, volui illi vitam suam ostendere.

IUNI OTHONIS. Malam causam haberem si alium
accusatorem haberem; malam causam haberem si te
filium non haberem.

4 Pars altera. IUNI GALLIONIS. A laudibus patris
incipiam. Fuit hic adulescens temperatissimus, et
lubricum tempus sine infamia transit; duxit uxorem,

[1] gaudiorum taedium cepisti *Thomas:* gaudium accepisti.
[2] luxuriam quam *E:* lumina qu(a)e *ABV.*

348

I could reply: " Young man, I lived frugally as long
as *I* had a father. You stopped before me—but you
began before me."

** " You are an old man wasting money." I 3
reply: " Yes—when I was young I sailed the seas." [1]
—"*I* have stopped: you haven't, yet." There is no
wonder you stopped first: you started first.

MENTO. What? You have grown tired of
pleasure? I really am in luxury now!

POMPEIUS SILO. If my son *has* reformed now (even
extravagance is often kept hidden), let each be accused in turn.—You want me to marry? If you had
a step-mother, you would already have been disinherited.

VIBIUS GALLUS. Doubtless your supper-com-
panions say: Let us live—we must die. If I understand aright, this is addressed to no-one in this house
more than me.[2]—I have shown you the extravagance
you did not see in yourself.—Tie me up—but put a
guard on yourself.

PUBLIUS ASPRENAS. Because I made no headway
criticising him, I decided to *show* him his way of life.

JUNIUS OTHO. I should have a weak case if I had a
different accuser; I should have a weak case if I
didn't have you for son.

The other side

JUNIUS GALLIO. I shall begin with praise of my 4
father. He was moderate in his youth, and passed
through that slippery time without blemish. He

---

[1] To make money, unlike you.
[2] Being old, I can best appreciate the wisdom of " Eat,
drink and be merry . . ."

filium sustulit, ad aetatem perduxit. Iam senex
factus est, nisi quod sibi nondum videtur; ⟨in⟩ [1]
luxuriam usque eo se proiecit ut accusem. Senex
amans, senex ebrius, circumdatus sertis et delibutus
unguentis et in praeteritos annos se retro agens ct   178
validius in voluptatibus quam iuvenis exultans,
nonne portentum est? *Luxuriosus adulescens peccat;*
at *senex luxuriosus insanit;* aetas exhaurit ⟨virtutes⟩: [2]
vitia lasciviunt.

PAPIRI FABIANI. Navem in portu mergis. Alter
solito tempore labitur, alter insolito; alter alieno,
alter suo; alter annos sequitur, alter senectuti re-
pugnat. Non est luxuria tua qualem videri velis:
non simulas ista sed facis, nec amantem agis sed
amas, nec potantem adumbras sed bibis, nec te dicis
bona dissipare sed dissipas. *Nemo*, puto, *vitia quia
odit imitatur. Quis imperator ob hoc ipse de proelio
fugit, ut bene pugnaret exercitus?* quis, ut ambitum
comprimeret, ipse honores mercatus est? quis, ut
seditionem leniret, turbavit rem publicam? *Non
coercet vitia qui provocat.*

5   Latro sic divisit: an ob hoc accusari pater possit,
⟨quod luxuriatus sit⟩. [3] Hic illam volgarem quaes-

----

[1] *Added by Thomas.*
[2] *Supplied by the editor.*
[3] *Supplied by Müller.*

----

[1] You are slipping just when you are safe. Otto, *Sprichwörter*, 284–5.

married, reared a son, brought him through to maturity. Now he is old, except that he doesn't yet think he is. He has flung himself so deep in debauchery that I am prosecuting him. An old man in love, an old man drunk, decked in garlands, steeped in perfumes, driving himself backwards into past years, revelling in pleasure more vigorously than a youth—is this not a prodigy! An extravagant youth is misbehaving; an extravagant old man is mad. Age exhausts the stock of virtues—but vice goes wantoning on.

PAPIRIUS FABIANUS. You are sinking the boat in the harbour.[1] One totters at the usual time, the other at an unusual time, one in his own time, the other in another's; one follows the lead of his years, the other kicks against his old age. Your debauchery is not what you would have us think it;[2] you are not pretending to do these things—you are doing them. You are not acting the lover but loving, not feigning the role of the toper but drinking. You are not saying you are dissipating your wealth—you are dissipating it. No-one, I think, imitates vices because he hates them.[3] What general ever fled from the battle himself to make his army fight well? Who traded in honours to suppress bribery? Who disturbed the state to calm rebellion? The provoker of vice is not restraining vice.

Latro's division was as follows: Can a father be 5 accused for extravagance? Here he put the well-

---

[2] i.e. it's not designed to reform your son.
[3] Cf. Sen. *Ir.* 2.6.2: "nec umquam committet virtus ut vitia dum compescit imitetur."

tionem posuit quam solebat fastidire: †se leviter†
minime patri obici solere luxuriam, non magis quam   17
avaritiam, quam iracundiam; non vitia patris accusari solere, sed morbum.   Ut possit aliquid praeter
dementiam obici patri, ⟨an⟩ [1] luxuria non possit.
" Alioqui filiis " inquit " abdicare permittitis ⟨patres;
sed lex patri filium quia de alieno consumit abdicare
permittit⟩,[2] hic de suo consumit."   Etiamsi ob hoc
accusari pater a filio ⟨potest, an a tali filio⟩ [3] possit?
Hic vitiorum exprobratio.   " Sic *ebrietatem patri obicis
ebrius,* sic petulantiam iniuriarum [4] damnatus? "
Etiamsi ob hoc accusari potest, etiamsi a tali filio, an,
si ad castigandum filium hoc consilio usus est, dam-
nandus sit.   Ait enim adulescens: Quolibet alio
genere debuisti me obiurgare.   Quid si adulterium
velles vindicare committendo?   Turpe est sic casti-
gare vitia ut imiteris.   Deinde, an consilio luxurietur.
Non enim concedit hoc filius: " alioqui " inquit
" quare, si coepisti sic emendare filium, cum emen-
daveras non desinis? "

6   Cestius ⟨a⟩ parte [5] patris aiebat simulationem
luxuriae significandam magis quam profitendam.
Ita, inquit, apparebit illum simulasse si etiamnunc
simulat; si desinit simulare, ostendit iam sibi nihil
opus esse eo consilio, quasi filius emendatus sit;

[1] *Supplied by Müller.*
[2] *Supplied by Gertz.*
[3] *Supplied by Müller after Gertz.*
[4] iniuriarum *Kiessling:* iniuria(m).
[5] a parte *Bursian:* pater.

known question that he usually scorned:[1] Extravagance is not generally made a reproach to a father, any more than avarice or choler; it is not a father's faults that are normally accused but his sickness. Even if something apart from madness can be made a reproach to a father, can luxury? "No. Otherwise," he said, "you are allowing sons to disinherit their fathers; but the law allows a *father* to disinherit his son for spending money out of another's pocket—*this* man is spending out of his own." Even if a father can be accused by a son for this, can he be by such a son as this? Here came a castigation of his faults. "Do you, then, a drunkard, reproach your father with drunkenness? Do you—once condemned for injury[2]—reproach him with his vicious temper?" Even if he can be accused of this and by such a son, is he to be condemned for using this means of reproving his son? For the son says: "You should have used any method but this of reproving me. What if you wanted to punish adultery by committing it? It is shameful to reprove faults by imitating them." Then Latro asked whether he *is* being debauched as part of a plan. For the son does not admit this: "Otherwise why, if you began to use this method of reforming your son, do you not stop now that you have reformed him?"

Cestius, for the father, said that the pretence of 6 debauchery should be hinted at rather than professed. "If he goes on pretending, it will be obvious that he was pretending before. If he stops pretending, he shows that he no longer needs that stratagem, his son

---

[1] Cf. *C.* 2.3.12, 10.3.7.
[2] An invented addition to the son's misdemeanours.

emendatum autem esse non concessit, et adsidue dixit 180
nihil magis se quam intervallum hoc luxuriae timere;
intermissa vitia vehementius surgere.

Latro aperte putabat simulationem confitendam.
Incipio, inquit, non tantum honestum senem sed
prudentem defendere si, quod vitium videri poterat,
efficio consilium. Quare potius significet quam dicat
frugi ⟨se⟩ [1] esse?

Blandus hac figura declamavit filium: ut pro abdicato respondit.

7 Cestius aiebat adulescentis partem diligentius
colorandam: facere illum rem non ita probam: patri
non remittere quod a patre ipsi remissum sit. Itaque
sic narravit ut *suam quoque luxuriam imputaret
patri. Non severam fuisse disciplinam, non bene in-
stitutam domus legem, quae posset adulescentis mores
formare et a vitiis aetatis abducere.* " *Quodammodo* "
inquit " *ad luxuriam a patre praemissus sum.*[2]
... *unguento canos madentis et comissatorem senem:* utique
nulli nimis luxuriosus sed parum sanus videbatur.
Merito in adulescentibus ⟨non⟩ omnem luxuriam
vindicant: cito desinunt. Desii, cum haberem
luxuriae istius exemplum. Quaeritis quae res mihi 181

---

[1] *Supplied by Schultingh.*
[2] praemissus sum *supplied by the editor from E. To fill the
remaining gap, I have translated* Mirabantur omnes (*Gertz*).

now apparently being reformed." But he did not admit that the son had reformed, and constantly said that he feared nothing so much as this interval in his debauchery: vices that have been halted for a while start up again with all the more strength.[1]

Latro said the pretence should be openly acknowledged. "I am beginning," he said, "the defence of an aged man who is both honourable and sensible, if I can show to be a plan what might have been thought a vice.[2] Why should he hint at his own honesty rather than declare it?"

Blandus used the following figure to declaim the part of the son: he made his reply as if on behalf of a son who had been disinherited.

Cestius said the role of the son should be given a 7 more elaborate *colour*: he was doing something not altogether honest in refusing to allow to his father what his father had allowed to him. And so Cestius slanted his narration in such a way as to blame even the son's own debauchery on to the father, saying there had been no rigorous discipline, no rules imposed by a well-conducted home to form a youth's character and lead him away from the vices normal to his age. "In a way I was sent ahead into debauchery by my father. People were astonished when they saw his white hair soaked in perfumes, an old man constantly at orgies; in fact, he was thought unanimously to be not excessively extravagant but rather mad. It is right that not every youthful extravagance is penalised: they soon stop. *I*

[1] Cf. Sen. *Ep.* 25.3, 29.8.
[2] Latro means: "If I can show an apparent vice to be a plan, it follows I am defending an honest man."

remedio fuerit? aetas: illa quae faciebam iam puta-
bam me non decere."

8 Hunc sensum ipse Cestius sano genere dixit;
Flavum Alfium, auditorem suum, qui eandem rem
lascivius dixerat, obiurgavit. Flavus hoc modo dixit:
cum desidiae se eripuisset,[1] paulatim se ad frugali-
tatem redisse et odio se vitiorum captum.[2] " Hoc
fuit " inquit " quare desinerem: sentiebam " inquit
" me senem fieri." Cestius hoc aiebat dulcius
quidem ⟨esse⟩,[3] sed corrumpi ultimam[4] sententiam.
" Incredibile est," inquit " cum iuvenis sit, sensisse
illum se senem fieri, et nolim videri tam diu luxuri-
atum donec sentiret senem se fieri."

9 Fuscus Arellius dixit: Non accusaturus patrem sed
me defensurus sum, ne aliena luxuria male audiam.
Hoc consilium luxuriante filio honestum emendato
⟨est⟩[5] supervacuum. In narratione hunc colorem
habuit: subito furore conlapsam patri mentem.
Meretricem vidi pendentem collo senis et parasitorum circumfusum patri gregem, turpes cum rivali-   18
bus rixas et ebrietati nocturnae additum diem.
Putavi initio et ego consilium esse, non morbum:
desii luxuriari; desinet, inquam, si propter me coepit.
Permanet in iuvenalibus vitiis et turpius luxuriosus et

---

[1] desidiae se eripuisset *Kiessling:* desiderio scripsisse.
[2] se vitiorum captum *Müller:* sibi uitiosum factum.
[3] *Supplied by C. F. W. Müller.*
[4] corrumpi ultimam *Madvig, C. F. W. Müller:* corrupit et
unam.
[5] *Supplied by Kiessling.*

stopped, even though I had a model in my debauchery. You ask what cured me? My age: I
began to think that what I did was unsuitable
for me." [1]

This idea was put over in a reasonable manner by 8
Cestius himself; but he told off his pupil Alfius
Flavus, who had said the same thing in less good
taste, thus: " When I had snatched myself out of
sloth, I gradually returned to good ways and began to
hate vice. This was why I stopped: I began to feel
that I was getting to be an old man." Cestius said
this was not unattractive, but that there was a flaw at
the end. " It is incredible that though a youth he
should have felt he was becoming an old man; and I
shouldn't want it thought that he had been debauched
for so long that he really was beginning to feel old."

Arellius Fuscus said: " I don't propose to accuse 9
my father, but to defend myself, in case I get a bad
reputation because of another's debauchery. This
' plan,' which was honourable during the son's debauchery, is superfluous now that he is reformed."
In his narration his *colour* was that his father's mind
had given way to sudden madness. " I saw a whore
hanging on my old father's neck, a flock of parasites
around him, shameful quarrels with rivals in love, day
merged with night in drunken revel. I myself
thought at first that this was a plot rather than a
disease. I stopped being debauched. He will stop,
I said to myself, if it was because of me that he began.
Yet he goes on indulging vices that suit youth; *his*
debauchery has been longer and more shameful than

---

[1] Contrast the father, who had not learned this lesson.

diutius. Quid faciam? ex suo more emendare patrem volo: luxuriandum est.

10 Silo Pompeius patronum adulescenti dedit; quod non putabat in accusatoris persona Latro faciendum: ⟨numquam certe esse factum⟩ [1] ut aliquis per patronum accusaret patrem.

Rufus Vibius ⟨a parte⟩ [2] adulescentis: festivum senem! in honorem filii sui ebrius fit. In narratione hoc usus est colore: solutum patrem iam mente eius labente laudare coepisse luxuriam; dicere enim eos felicius ⟨vivere⟩ [3] qui sibi amare permitterent nec cessarent tantum habere quantum cuperent; obiurgare interim ⟨se⟩ [4] quasi non commodaret. "Rusticum" inquit "iuvenem! Praematura" inquit "severitas non est frugalitas sed tristitia: quid tu senex facies?" Non creditis haec illum dixisse qui vitia dum obiurgare vult luxuriatur?

11 Argentarius hoc colore declamavit: Duo luxuriantur una in domo: alter iuvenis, alter senex; alter filius, alter pater; uterque aeque licenti cultu per publicum incedit. Alter vobis hoc ait: "Concessis aetati iocis utor et iuvenali lege defungor; id facio quod pater meus fecit cum iuvenis esset. Negabit? Bona ego aetate coepi; simul primum hoc tirocinium adulescentiae quasi debitum ac sollemne persolvero, revertar ad bonos mores." Qui qualem causam habeat videritis; facit etiamsi non quod oportet fieri,

---

[1] *Supplied by Gertz.*

[2] *Supplied by Kiessling.*

[3] *Supplied by Müller. The exact form of the whole passage is uncertain.*

[4] *Supplied by Gertz.*

mine. What am I to do? I want to reform my father in his own manner: I must be extravagant.''

Pompeius Silo gave the youth an advocate. Latro 10 thought this wrong for the role of an accuser: at least it had never happened that someone had accused his *father* by means of an advocate.

Vibius Rufus on the youth's side: " Splendid old man! He gets drunk for the sake of his son." In his narration this was the *colour* he used: " The old man, enfeebled, his mind already tottering, began to praise debauchery, saying that the happy men are those who allow themselves to love and don't hesitate to satisfy all their desires, and sometimes reproaching his son for not obliging. ' Unsophisticated youth!' said he. ' Austerity in the young is not uprightness but melancholia. What will you be like when you're an old man?' You can easily believe these were the words of one who has got debauched in an attempt to reprove vice." [1]

Argentarius' declamation had this *colour*: " Two 11 are debauched in one house, one young, one old; one son, one father. Both stalk the streets in equally outré costumes. One says to you: ' I am having the fun allowable at my age: [2] I am taking advantage of the law for young men. I am doing what my father did when he was young. Will he deny it? *I* began at the right age; as soon as I have got through this normal and indeed almost obligatory apprenticeship, I shall return to good ways.' You may decide how good his case is: he acts as is usual, even if not as is

---

[1] Ironical (like Vibius' first remark): the son refutes the *colour* of the father that it was all a plot.

[2] For the *locus indulgentiae*, see *C.* 2.4.10 n.

at quod solet. Alter ait: " scio me novum civitatis miraculum incedere, luxuriosum senem, sed hoc castigandi genus commoventius visum; ut emendarem filium, ipse peccare coepi." Ita, si avos viveret, ut nemo in domo luxuriosus esset, tres luxuriosi fuissetis.

12 A parte patris Glycon Spyridion dixit: ἐγὼ μὲν ἄρχομαι δαπανῶν, σὺ δ᾽ οὐ παύῃ.

Agroitas Massiliensis longe vividiorem sententiam dixit quam ceteri Graeci declamatores, qui in hac controversia tamquam rivales rixati sunt. Dicebat 184 autem Agroitas arte inculta, ut scires illum inter Graecos non fuisse, sententiis fortibus, ut scires illum inter Romanos fuisse. Sententia quae laudabatur haec fuit: ἐπὶ τῆς ἀσωτίας τοῦτο διαπεφωνήκαμεν · σὺ μὲν δαπανᾷς ἡδόμενος, ἐγὼ δὲ λυπούμενος.

Damas Scombrus: ἐστυγημένην[1] ἀσωτίαν ἀσωτεύῃ.

13 Diocles Carystius: εἶθ᾽ εὐχαριστοίης · ἄρτι ἐκ τῆς ἀσωτίας μεταβάλλομαι.

Hermagoras raras sententias dicebat, sed argutas et quae auditorem diligentem penitus adficerent, securum et neglegentem transcurrerent. In hac controversia dixit: ὦ τύχης δεινῆς · ταῦτα ἐπιτάττοντες ἀλλήλοις ἐποιοῦμεν.[2]

Barbarus dixit vulgarem sensum satis vulgariter: γνώσῃ, τέκνον, ὅτι νοῦς γήρᾳ συνανθεῖ.

Elegantius hoc conposuit Hispo Romanius: Placet

---

[1] ἐστυγημένην *Thomas:* CTHTHMENNN (*or similar*).
[2] ἐποιοῦμεν *vulg.:* ΕΠΙΟΟΜΕΝ.

---

[1] This is spoken by the father to the son, the next two by the son to the father (the text of both is dubious).
[2] The connection is in the stress on old age bringing a peak of wisdom and uprightness.

right. The other says: ' I know they think me, as I strut along, a prodigy new to our city, a debauched old man—but this seemed a more effective method of reproof. I began to do wrong myself so as to put my son on the right road.' So if *your* father were alive, you would all three of you have been debauchees to make sure no-one in the family was debauched."

For the father Glycon Spyridion said: " *I* am begin- 12 ning to be extravagant: *you* are not stopping."

Agroitas of Marseille produced a much more forceful epigram than the other Greek declaimers, who brawled in this *controversia* as though they were rivals in love. Now Agroitas had an unpolished technique (which showed he had not frequented the Greeks) and employed vigorous epigrams (which showed he had frequented the Romans). This was the epigram which won applause: " This is where we are at discord in our debauchery: you are debauched and enjoy it; I am debauched and do not." [1]

Damas Scombrus: " You are living a life of debauchery—which you hate."

Diocles of Carystos: " Be grateful! *I* am just 13 changing from being debauched."

Hermagoras spoke few epigrams, but they were sharp and liable to make a deep impression on the careful listener, while being missed by the careless and inattentive. In this *controversia* he said: " O unlucky fate! To think we have been acting thus to give each other precepts! "

Barbarus uttered a common idea—in a pretty common manner: " You will find, my child, that the mind blossoms in old age."

Romanius Hispo put this [2] more elegantly: " You

vobis frugalitas mea, quod patrimonium servavi, quod 185¹
adquisivi, quod uxorem mature duxi, semper dilexi,
quod ab omni me tutum fabula praestiti. Illud ad-
firmo, nihil tota vita frugalius feci.

Rem ab omnibus dictam celerrime Syriacus Vallius
dixit: fili, quando vis desinamus?

VII

PEREGRINUS NEGOTIATOR

Quidam, cum haberet formonsam uxorem,
peregre profectus est. In viciniam mulieris
peregrinus mercator commigravit; ter illam
appellavit de stupro adiectis pretiis; negavit
illa. Decessit mercator, testamento heredem
omnibus bonis reliquit formonsam et adiecit
elogium: "pudicam repperi." Adit hereditatem. Redit maritus, accusat adulteri ex sus-
picione.

1   PORCI LATRONIS. Quamquam eo prolapsi iam
mores civitatis sunt ut nemo ad suspicanda adulteria
nimium credulus possit videri, tamen ego adeo longe

---

¹ Than trying to reform you thus.
² He appears also in *Decl.* 363.
³ "Appellare est blanda oratione alterius pudicitiam
attentare" (*Dig.* 47.10.15.20).
⁴ The *Lex Iulia de adulteriis* of c. 16 B.C. set up a *quaestio
perpetua* to deal with adultery. The declaimers, however,
seem to have no real legal situation clearly in mind, because
"divorce must precede any accusation . . . by a husband"

are glad of my uprightness, the way I preserved my heritage, made money, married at the right age, cherished my wife, kept free of all gossip. This is my claim: I have done nothing more uprightly [1] during the whole of my life."

A thing that everybody said was put most concisely by Vallius Syriacus: " Son, when would you like us to stop? "

7

THE FOREIGN MERCHANT [2]

A man with a beautiful wife went off abroad. A foreign trader moved into the woman's neighbourhood. He three times made her propositions [3] of a sexual nature, offering sums of money. She said no. The trader died, leaving her all his wealth in his will, to which he added the clause: " I found her chaste." She took the bequest. The husband returned and accuses her of adultery [4] on suspicion.

For the husband

PORCIUS LATRO. [5] Although the morals of the state 1 have already declined so far that no-one can be thought too credulous in suspecting adulteries,[6] yet

(P. E. Corbett, *The Roman Law of Marriage* [Oxford, 1930], 143), and there is no mention of this.

[5] It is tiresome that this, the most complete of the declamations, is cut short in the manuscripts and can only be supplemented by the excerpts.

[6] Adultery was a favourite topic in the *locus de saeculo*: see, e.g., Sen. *Ben.* 1.9.4, 3.16.3; Juvenal (particularly *Sat.* 6) and Martial *passim*.

ab eo vitio afui ut magis timeam ne quis in me aut nimiam patientiam aut nimium stuporem arguat quod tam *seram querellam detuli.* *Non accuso adulteram nisi divitem factam;* ex ea domo ream protraho in qua iam nihil meum est. Cum ego tamdiu peregrinatus sim, nullum periculum terra marique fugerim, plus ⟨ista⟩ 186M intra unam viciniam quam ego toto mari quaesit. *Post tantos inpudicitiae quaestus si tacere possum, confitendum habeo hac me causa afuisse,* ut in accessionem patrimoni peregrinando cum uxore certarem. Illud, iudices, mihi tormentum est, quod notata iudicio vestro, ut multiplicatam dotem perdat, plus tamen ex quaestu habitura est quam quantum damnatae perdendum est; tantum in istam dives amator effudit ut post poenam quoque expediat fuisse adulteram.

2 Quae praeceperim uxori proficiscens, scio; cetera, quemadmodum adulescens formonsus, dives, ignotus in viciniam formonsae et in absentia viri nimium liberae mulieris commigraverit, quemadmodum adsidua satietate cotidianae per diem noctemque libidinis exhaustis viribus perierit, interrogate rumorem. Vos interrogo, iudices, quid offici mei fuerit: poteram ego salvo pudore meo nihil de hereditate suspicari in qua etiam nomen auctoris ab uxore doctus [1] sum?

---

[1] doctus *Bornecque:* ductus *A:* dictus *BV.*

---

[1] That is, I should be agreeing that I had connived (for connivance, see Juvenal 1.55–6 and the commentators *ad loc.*).

[2] Strictly, the loss of her dowry would have been a result of the divorce preceding the accusation for adultery (above,

I was so far from fault in this respect that I am afraid
rather that I may be accused of being too tolerant or
too dull for bringing my complaint so late in the day.
I am accusing her of adultery only now that she has
become rich; I hale her to the courts from a house
where nothing any longer belongs to me. Though I
was abroad for so long a time, though I have shirked
no danger by land or sea, *she* has acquired more in a
single neighbourhood than *I* did on all the seas there
are. If I were capable of keeping silent after such
great profits have rewarded shamelessness, I should
be avowing that I absented myself in order to compete on my travels with my wife in the increasing of
our property.[1] What tortures me, judges, is that if
she is condemned by your judgement, even if she
loses her dowry and the interest on it,[2] she will still
have more as a result of her profiteering than she must
forfeit on condemnation; so much has this millionaire
lavished on his mistress that even after she has been
punished adultery will still have been profitable.

I know what instructions I gave my wife on my de- 2
parture; you must apply to rumour for the rest, for
the story of how a handsome, rich and unknown
young man moved into the neighbourhood of a
beautiful woman, one who was all too free in the
absence of her husband, how by continually satisfying
his lusts night and day he exhausted his strength and
died. I ask *you*, judges, what my duty was: could I,
without hurting my pride, have no suspicions about a
bequest when I had to learn from my wife even the
name of the person who made it? I come here for no

p. 362 n. 4): the husband, if he could prove misconduct, would
be able to keep a sixth of the dowry (Corbett, 193).

Veni nihil aliud quam ut fortunam meam querar; nam causam melius vos nostis.

3 *Tempus est*, iudices, *de uxore marito credi* mulierem tam formonsam amari potuisse pudice; certe sic 187M amari, ne sollicitaretur, potuit; neque est quod dicat: non in meo istud arbitrio positum ⟨erat⟩.[1] Erratis vos, iudices, si non maius ad sollicitandam matronam putatis inritamentum spem corrumpendi quam faciem quamvis amabilem venustam.[2] Si tantum in formonsa sperari posset quantum placere potest, omnes formonsae in se universos oculos converterent. *Matrona,* quae ⟨tuta⟩[3] esse adversus sollicitatoris lasciviam volet, prodeat in tantum ornata quantum ne inmunda sit; habeat comites eius aetatis quae inpudicum, si nihil aliud, in verecundiam annorum movere possit; *ferat iacentis in terram oculos; adversus officiosum salutatorem inhumana potius quam inverecunda sit;* etiam in necessaria resalutandi vice multo rubore confusa ⟨sit⟩.[4] Sic se in verecundiam pigneret ⟨ut⟩[5] *longe ante inpudicitiam suam ore quam verbo neget.* In has servandae integritatis custodias nulla libido in- 188M rumpet.

4 Prodite mihi fronte in omne lenocinium composita, paulo obscurius quam posita veste nudae, exquisito in omnes facetias sermone, tantum non ultro blandientes ut quisquis viderit non metuat accedere:

---

[1] *Supplied by Kiessling.*
[2] venustam *Kiessling:* sensum.
[3] *Supplied by Bursian.*
[4] *Supplied by Kiessling.*
[5] pigneret ut *Bursian:* pignori.

other purpose than to complain of my fortune: *you* know my case better than I.

It is time, judges, that credence is given to the 3 husband on the topic of his wife, when he says that it was possible for so beautiful a woman to be loved chastely—and certainly without being pestered. There is no reason for her to say: " I couldn't help it." You are mistaken, judges, if you think that the prospect of being able to seduce her is not a greater incentive to make proposals to a married woman than a face however pretty and attractive. If a beautiful woman offered as much hope as pleasure to the beholder, all beauties would turn the eyes of the world upon them. A married woman who wants to be safe from the lust of the seducer must go out dressed up only so far as to avoid unkemptness. Let her have companions old enough, at the very least, to make the shameless respect their years. Let her go about with her eyes on the ground. In the face of the over-attentive greeting, let her be impolite rather than immodest. Even where she *has* to return a greeting, let her show confusion, with many a blush. Let her guarantee her modesty by denying her unchastity with her look well in advance of her words. No lust will be able to force its way past these guardians and preservers of her honour.

Very well, go out with your face made up to look 4 utterly seductive, naked hardly less obviously than if you had taken off your clothes,[1] your conversation carefully set to find room for every jest, all but making eyes invitingly to ensure that no-one who sees you is afraid to approach: *then* be surprised if, having

[1] See *C.* 2.5.7 n.

deinde miramini si, cum tot argumentis inpudicitiam praescripseritis, cultu, incessu, sermone, facie, aliquis repertus est qui incurrenti adulterae se non subduceret. Internuntium, puto, illa sollicitatoris arripi et denudari iussit, flagella et verbera et omne genus cruciatus poposcit, in plagas deterrimi mancipi vix inbecillitatem muliebris manus continuit. *Nemo sic negantem iterum rogat.*[1]

5 Quotiens absentis viri nomen inploravit? quotiens quod non una peregrinaretur questa est? cum quo questa es? apud quem indignata es? Abunde te in argumentum pudicitiae profecturam putas si stuprum tantum negaveris, quod plerumque etiam inpudicissima, spe uberioris praemi, de industria simulat? Quando de iniuria tua viro scripsisti et, ne in occasionem similis iniuriae solitudo tua pateret, maturiorem reditum rogasti? Et quanto decentius contumeliam penetralium meorum uxoris epistula quam 189M testamento sollicitatoris cognoscerem! Miserrimus omnis saeculi maritus sic contempta absentia mea etiamnunc iniuriam meam nescirem si qui fecerat tacere voluisset.

6 Totiens sollicitata non istam faciem qua placere poteras convestisti? non omne ornamentum veluti causam talis iniuriae exsecrata es? Quod proximum est a promittente, rogata stuprum tacet. Inspicite adulterae censum; ex eo inpune sit quod adulter isti

---

[1] *This sentence was transferred by Wachsmuth from before* cum quo (§5).

given advance warning of your shamelessness by so
many signs—dress, walk, talk, appearance—, you find
someone turning up who didn't get out of the way of
the adulteress looming up on him. No doubt she
ordered the seducer's go-between to be seized and
stripped, called for whips and lashes and every variety
of torture, scarcely restrained her feeble woman's
hands from flogging the worthless slave. No-one
asks again when he receives a refusal like that.

How often did she invoke the name of her absent 5
husband? How often complain that she hadn't
accompanied him abroad? To whom did you complain, to whom express your indignation? You think
you'll prove your chastity quite sufficiently if you
merely say no to sex—a refusal that often even the
most shameless woman purposely feigns in the hope
of a fatter price? When did you write to tell your
husband of the wrong done you, ask him to return
sooner so that in your solitary state you should not
remain open to the possibility of a similar outrage?
How much more proper it would have been for me to
learn of the insult offered to the inner sanctity of my
household from a letter of my wife than from the will
of her seducer! I am the most unhappy husband
there ever was—I was so despised while I was away
that even now I should be ignorant of the wrong done
me if the author of it had preferred to keep quiet.

If you were so often pestered, did you not veil the 6
beauty which could give the beholder such pleasure?
Did you not loathe every ornament as the motive for
such an outrage? Asked for sex, she keeps silent—
the next thing to promising it. Look at the adulteress' wealth. Let her go unpunished for the

dedit si est aliquid quod non dederit. Quid singil-
latim omnia percenseo? quid ego non emi in mundo
tibi? ⟨Me⟩[1] miserum: maritus cum omni censu
meo inter munera adulteri lateo. "Sola heres esto."
Quid ita? Habes, inquit; scripsit causas: "quia,
cum semel appellassem, ⟨cum iterum appellassem⟩,[2]
7 cum tertio appellassem, non corrupi." O nos nimium
felici et aureo, quod aiunt, saeculo natos! Sic etiam
qui inpudicas quaerunt pudicas honorant? "*Omnium
bonorum* meorum, omnis pecuniae meae *sola heres esto*
quia corrumpi non potuit, quia tot sollicitationibus
expugnari non potuit, *quia tam fideliter pudicitiam
custodivit.*" *Tace paulisper nomen auctoris: numquid
non testamentum viri creditis?* Ecce nullam in uxore
suspicatus infamiam, inter mutuum eius amorem aut
certe ita creditum iam moriturus tabellas occupare si
volo et[3] muneribus meis inponere elogium, ex testamento adulteri petendum est.

"Sola heres esto, quamvis aliena, quamvis ignota;
8 tantum quia pudica, quia incorrupta est." Quid? isti
tam censorio adultero non mater est? non soror? non
propinqua? an nulla earum pudica est? Idcirco
scilicet cum tantis divitiis peregrinas urbes in
honorem pudicitiae ignotae perambulat. Illic ubi
natus est nulla pudica erat, atque illic ubi negotiatus
est nulla non prostituta erat; vacuo testamento
pudica heres per errorem quaesita est.

---

[1] *Supplied by Gertz.*
[2] *Supplied by Kiessling.*
[3] volo et *ed.:* uoleti (-tis *V*) cum.

presents he gave her—if there is anything at all that he did *not* give her. Why go through it in detail? I bought everything for you all over the world: but, alas, I the husband, with all my wealth, am swamped beneath the presents of a seducer. " Let her be sole heir." Why so? " You know," she says. " He has written down the reason: Because I could not corrupt her, though I asked once, twice, a third time." We are indeed born in a fortunate and as 7 they say a golden age! Can it be that even men who go in search of unchaste women pay tribute to the chaste ones? " Let her be sole heir of all my property, all my money, because she could not be seduced, because she could not be won over despite so many attempts, because she guarded her chastity so faithfully." Suppress for a moment the name of the writer; would you not suppose this was the will of a *husband*? Look! Suppose that, suspecting no infamy on the part of my wife, loving and loved (or so I believe), I want to get my will made just before my death and write a codicil to go with my bequests to her: I must borrow the language of her lover's will.

" Let her be sole heir; she may not be my own, she may not be known to me: but she is chaste, and uncorrupted—just that." What, has this censor of an 8 adulterer no mother, no sister, no relative? Is none of *them* chaste? That, I suppose, is why he wanders round foreign cities with such riches, ready to pay tribute to unknown chastity. Where he was born there were no chaste women, and where he did his business everyone was a prostitute; there was a gap in his will—in his wanderings he was looking for a chaste heir.

Ego adulteram arguo, qui in matrimonium recepi,
qui communis ex ista liberos precatus sum, qui pudicam libentissime crederem. *Adeone iam ad omnem
patientiam saeculi mos abiit ut adversus querimoniam viri* 1
uxor alieno teste defendatur? At hercules adversus
externorum quondam opiniones speciosissimum
patrocinium erat: ego viro placeo.

9 Atque ego, si hunc morem scribendi recipitis, in
conspectu vestro ita scribam: " uxor mea heres ⟨ne⟩ [1]
esto, quod peregrinante me adamata est, quod heres
ab adulescente alieno ac libidinoso relicta est, quod
tam infamem hereditatem adit." A duobus vos
testamentis in consilium mitto: utrum secuturi estis?
quo ab adultero absolvitur, an quo damnatur a viro?
Unus pudicitiae fructus est pudicam credi, et adversus omnes inlecebras atque omnia delenimenta
muliebribus ingeniis est veluti solum ⟨ac⟩ firma-
mentum in nullam incidisse fabulam. †novos fortasse
non in omnium existimationem ocure et horrendum
multa deinde ab variae daturis experimenta.† [2]
Feminae quidem unum pudicitia decus est; itaque
ei curandum est esse ac videri pudicam. . . . [3]

Muliebrium vitiorum fundamentum avaritia est. 2
Quae potest non timere opinionem adulterii, potest
non timere adulterium. Ex omni rupe conchylium

[1] *Supplied by Schultingh.*
[2] *These words are quite uncertain: I translate Müller's version* Non est fortasse ⟨facile⟩ non in hominum e. incurrere et h. m. decentiae ac varia d. e.
[3] *The declamation is from this point preserved only in the excerpta.*

I accuse her of adultery; yet I received her in marriage, prayed for children from her that we could share, would be very ready to believe her chaste. Has our age become so permissive that a wife has to be defended against the complaints of her husband by means of the testimony of a stranger? Once, by heaven, the most plausible defence against the views of outsiders used to be: " *I* please my husband."

If you approve of this style of writing, I will write 9 thus in your presence: " Let my wife not be my heir, because while I was away she had a passionate affair, because she was left money by an unrelated and lustful youth, because she accepted so shameful a bequest."[1] You have heard these two wills: I direct you to deliberate on them. Which will you follow? The one where her lover acquits her, or the one where her husband convicts her? The one fruit of chastity is to be believed chaste, and woman's nature is such that the ground and bulwark against all snares and all lures is never to have caused gossip. It is perhaps difficult not to come under the judgement of men, even frightening when one has to give so many varied proofs of propriety. For a woman, in fact, the one glory is chastity; so she must take care to be chaste— and to be seen to be chaste. . . .

FROM THE EXCERPTA

The root of the vices of woman is avarice.—The woman capable of not fearing a reputation for adultery is capable of not fearing adultery.—From every

---

[1] Cf. the parody will in Quintilian 9.2.34.

contrahitur quo vestis cruentetur. Infelices ancillarum greges laborant ut adultera tenui veste perspicua sit et nihil in corpore uxoris suae plus maritus quam quilibet alienus peregrinusque cognoverit. Futuram eius aestimabo pudicitiam;[1] interim, quod negat, conperi[2] inpudicam. Omnes te inpudicam locuntur, pudicam tantum et unus et peregrinus, qui plus laudator quam accusator nocet. Uxorem meam nusquam pudicam audivi nisi in adulteri elogio. Deice in terram oculos et aures externorum vocibus claude: sibi quisque pro te neget. Pudicam ille dixit, ego inpudicam: puto, plus credetis civi quam peregrino, marito quam adultero. Ipsum elogium scripsit corruptoris animo. Quia pudicam, inquit, conperi: quod nulli praeter me contigit.

Pars altera. Formosa est: hoc natura peccavit. Sine viro fuit: hoc maritus peccavit. Appellata est: hoc alius peccavit. Negavit: hoc pudice. Heres relicta est: hoc feliciter. Hereditatem adiit: hoc consulte fecit.

---

[1] futuram eius—pudicitiam *Kiessling:* futura etus—iuditia.
[2] negat conperi *Müller, after Gertz:* rogat conperit.

rock the shellfish[1] is collected to stain your dress blood-red. Wretched flocks of maids labour so that the adulteress may be visible through her thin dress, so that her husband has no more acquaintance than any outsider or foreigner with his wife's body.—I will assess her future chastity; meanwhile, despite her denials, *I* have found her unchaste.—Everyone talks of you as unchaste. You are called chaste by only one man, a foreigner; on his lips praise is more harmful than accusation.—I have never heard my wife called chaste except in her lover's codicil.—Cast your eyes on the ground, and close your ears to the voices of foreigners: leave others, each for himself, to do the denying for you.—*He* said she is chaste, *I* say she is unchaste; doubtless you will prefer to believe a citizen rather than a foreigner, a husband rather than an adulterer.—He wrote even the codicil with the intent of a seducer.—"Because I found her to be chaste—something that has happened only to me."

The other side

She is beautiful: that was nature's fault. She was alone: that was her husband's fault. She was tempted: that was the fault of another. She said no: that was done chastely. She was left money: that was a stroke of good fortune. She took the bequest: that was only prudent.

---

[1] A great luxury, attacked by Sen. *Helv.* 11.2; Quintilian 1.2.6. Generally on shellfish, see Pliny *N.H.* 9.125 *seq.*

CONTROVERSIARUM

LIBER TERTIUS

SENECA NOVATO, SENECAE, MELAE FILIIS SALUTEM.

1   Quosdam disertissimos cognovi viros non respondentes famae suae cum declamarent, in foro maxima omnium admiratione dicentes, simul ad has domesticas exercitationes secesserant desertos ab ingenio suo. Quod accidere plerisque aeque mihi mirum quam certum est. Memini itaque me a Severo Cassio quaerere quid esset cur in declamationibus eloquentia illi sua non responderet.

2   In nullo enim hoc fiebat notabilius. Oratio eius erat valens, culta, vigentibus plena sententiis; nemo minus passus est aliquid in actione sua otiosi esse; 205 nulla pars erat quae non sua virtute staret, nihil in quo auditor sine damno aliud ageret, omnia intenta, aliquid petentia; nemo magis in sua potestate habuit

---

[1] The main witnesses to this apart from Seneca are Tac. *Dial.* 26.4-5 and Quintilian 10.1.116-17. Both stress Cassius' vigour and bitter tongue. Seneca's account is of the greatest

BOOK 3

PREFACE

SENECA TO HIS SONS NOVATUS, SENECA AND MELA
GREETINGS

I know several cases of gifted speakers who did not 1
match up to their reputation when they declaimed.
In the forum they spoke to the admiration of all who
heard them, but as soon as they retreated to our
private exercises they were deserted by their talents.
This frequent occurrence I find as surprising as it is
undeniable. And I remember that I once asked
Cassius Severus why it was that *his* eloquence failed
him in declamation.

Now in no-one could the contrast have been more 2
striking. His oratory [1] was strong, polished, full of
striking ideas; no-one was less tolerant of the superfluous in his pleading; [2] there was no part that did
not stand on its own feet, no place where the listener
could afford to let his attention wander. Everything

interest, for it was to Cassius that Tacitus (*Dial.* 19.1) attributed the change in oratorical style that marked what we call
the Silver Age.

[2] Cf. the story of someone who spoke in court of " Iberian
grasses ": " he means esparto," said Cassius (Quintilian 8.2.2).

audientium affectus. Verum est quod de illo dixit
Gallio noster: " Cum dicebat, rerum potiebatur:
adeo omnes imperata faciebant; cum ille voluerat,
irascebantur. Nemo non illo dicente timebat ne
desineret."

3   Non est quod illum ex his quae edidit aestimetis;
sunt quidem et hic [1] quibus eloquentia eius ⟨agnos-
catur; tamen auditus⟩ [2] longe maior erat quam
lectus. Non hoc ea portione illi accidit qua omnibus
fere, quibus maiori commendationi est audiri quam
legi, sed in illo longe maius discrimen est.

    Primum tantundem erat in homine quantum in
ingenio: corporis magnitudo conspicua, suavitas
valentissimae vocis—quamvis haec inter se raro
coeant, ut eadem vox et dulcis sit et solida—, pro-
nuntiatio quae histrionem posset producere, ⟨nec⟩ [3]
4 tamen quae histrionis posset videri. Nec enim quicquam magis in illo mirareris quam quod gravitas, 206
quae deerat vitae, actioni supererat: quamdiu citra
iocos se continebat, censoria oratio erat. Deinde
ipsa quae dicebat meliora erant quam quae scribebat.
Vir enim praesentis animi et maioris ingenii quam

---

[1] hic *Gertz:* haec.
[2] *Supplied by Bursian.*
[3] *Supplied by Bursian.*

---

[1] The manuscripts have probably omitted by accident other
instances of his control over emotions.
[2] Even more impossible for us: they are lost.

was vigorous and pointful. No-one was in more complete control of the emotions of his audience. My friend Gallio truly said of him: " When he spoke, he was a king on his throne, so religiously did everyone do what they were told. When he required it, they were angry.[1] Everyone was afraid, while he was speaking, in case he should stop."

It is impossible to judge him from his publica- 3 tions,[2] though even there one may sense his eloquence; he was far greater heard than read. It happens to almost all people that they gain from being heard rather than read, but to a smaller degree: in him there was a vastly greater gulf.

First of all, the man was as impressive as the talent. His body was remarkably large,[3] his voice both sweet and strong (an infrequent combination, this, in a voice), while his delivery would have made any actor's reputation, without being at all reminiscent of an actor's.[4] For—and this is perhaps the most 4 remarkable thing about him—the dignity which he lacked in his life he possessed in plenty in his speech. So long as he steered clear of jokes,[5] his oratory was worthy of a censor. Again, what he actually said was better than what he wrote. A man of resource,

---

[3] Indeed, he was twitted with looking like a gladiator (Plin. *N.H.* 7.55).

[4] For the orator " plurimum aberit a scaenico ": Quintilian 1.11.3, where the contribution of actors to an orator's education is discussed. See also Quintilian 1.12.14, 11.3.181. The orator Trachalus had " a delivery that would have been worthy of the stage " (10.1.119: cf. 12.5.5, where Quintilian quotes Cicero *de Orat.* 1.128).

[5] Some of these Seneca relates in this preface; Quintilian adds others.

studii magis placebat in his quae inveniebat quam in
his quae attulerat. Iam vero iratus commodius dicebat, et ideo diligentissime cavebant homines ne
5 dicentem interpellarent. Uni illi proderat excuti;
melius semper fortuna quam cura de illo merebatur.
Numquam tamen haec felicitas illi persuasit negle-
gentiam. Uno die privatas plures ⟨quam duas⟩ [1]
non agebat, et ita ut alteram ante meridiem ageret,
alteram post meridiem; publicam vero numquam
amplius quam unam uno die. Nec tamen scio quem
reum illi defendere nisi se contigerit: adeo nusquam
rerum ullam materiam dicendi nisi in periculis suis
6 habuit. Sine commentario numquam dixit, nec hoc
commentario contentus erat in quo nudae res
ponuntur, sed ex maxima parte perscribebatur actio;
illa quoque quae salse dici poterant adnotabantur;
sed cum procedere nollet nisi instructus, libenter ab
instrumentis recedebat. Ex tempore coactus dicere 207M
infinito se antecedebat. Numquam non utilius erat
illi deprehendi quam praeparari; sed magis illum
suspiceres quod diligentiam non relinquebat cum illi
tam bene temeritas cederet.
7   Omnia ergo habebat quae illum ut bene declamaret
instruerent: phrasin non vulgarem nec sordidam sed

[1] *Supplied by Müller.*

---

[1] For this "naturalism" in oratory, and for Cassius in
general, see my article in *J.R.S.* 54 (1964), 90–7.
[2] Quintilian is witness to his enthusiasm for accusation
(11.1.57); contrast Maternus in Tac. *Dial.* 11.4: " And I have

talented rather than studious,[1] he gave more pleasure
by his improvisations than by his prepared version.
He spoke better when in a temper, and hence men
took great care not to interrupt him—he was the only 5
one to benefit by any attempt to put him out;
chance always served him better than preparation.
All the same, this gift never enticed him into negligence. In one day he would not give more than two
private speeches, one before, one after mid-day. In
public cases, his limit was one a day. I don't know
that he ever defended anyone except himself:[2] so true
is it that the only dangers that gave him any scope for
oratory were his own.[3] He never spoke without 6
notes, and he was not content merely with the sort
that contain the bare bones of the speech, but to a
large extent the whole would be written out. In this
text, he used to note even possibilities for wit.
However, though he was not ready to set off without
equipment, he was glad to lay it aside. When he
had to speak extempore, he far excelled himself, and
it always paid him to find himself in a tight corner
rather than to be prepared; all the more admirable
that he did not abandon his care, considering that his
daring was so successful.

So he had everything that could equip him to be a 7
good declaimer: choice diction, neither common nor

no fear that I shall ever have to make a speech in the senate—
except where another is in danger." All the same, Cassius'
accusations tended to be unsuccessful (Macrob. *Sat.* 2.4.9).
His defence of himself was on a charge of *maiestas* as a result
of his libels on great personages under Augustus (Tac. *Ann.*
1.72.4, 4.21.5).

[3] i.e. other people's dangers (as defendants) did not inspire
him to come to their aid.

electam, genus dicendi non remissum aut languidum
sed ardens et concitatum, non lentas nec vacuas
explicationes, sed plus sensuum quam verborum
habentes, diligentiam, maximum etiam mediocris ingenii subsidium. Tamen non tantum infra se cum
declamaret sed infra multos erat; itaque raro declamabat et non nisi ab amicis coactus.

8   Sed quaerenti mihi quare in declamationibus impar
sibi esset, haec aiebat: Quod in me miraris, paene
omnibus evenit. Magna quoque ingenia—a quibus
multum abesse me scio—quando plus quam in uno
eminuerunt opere? Ciceronem eloquentia sua in
carminibus destituit; Vergilium illa felicitas ingenii
in oratione soluta reliquit; orationes Sallustii in
honorem historiarum leguntur; eloquentissimi viri
Platonis oratio, quae pro Socrate scripta est, nec   208M
9 patrono nec reo digna est.   Hoc non ingeniis tantum
sed corporibus videtis accidere, quorum vires non ad
omnia quae viribus efficiuntur aptae sunt: illi nemo
luctando par est; ille ad tollendam magni ponderis
sarcinam praevalet; ille quidquid adprehendit non
remittit, sed in proclive nitentibus vehiculis mora-
turas manus inicit. Ad animalia venio: alii ad
aprum, alii ad cervum canes faciunt; equorum non
omnium, quamvis celerrimi sint, idonea curriculis
velocitas est; quidam melius equitem patiuntur,

---

[1] Cf. below, §18, and Hor. *Sat.* 1.4.73–4: "nec recito cuiquam nisi amicis, idque coactus, / non ubivis coramve
quibuslibet."

low; a style of oratory that was not relaxed or languid but burning and spirited; developments neither slow nor empty, but richer in content than words; and finally the painstaking approach which is so great a stand-by even for the mediocre talent. But when he declaimed he fell below his own level—and that of many others: so he rarely did declaim—and only when his friends insisted.[1]

Now when I asked him why he was below his own 8 standard in declamation, he replied: " What surprises you in me happens to almost everybody. When has even great genius (not my category at all, I know) ever shown itself in more than one field? Cicero lost his eloquence when he wrote poetry;[2] the felicity of Virgil's touch deserted him in prose; Sallust's speeches are read only as a compliment to the author of the *Histories*; the speech[3] of the eloquent Plato written on behalf of Socrates is worthy neither of defender nor defendant. As with minds, 9 so you see with bodies —their strength is not suited to everything that strength can accomplish. One man is unequalled in wrestling; one excels at raising a heavy load; one will not let go of what he has taken a grip on, and when he puts his hands to a carriage careering downhill they will keep their hold. Animals also: some dogs are good for hunting the boar, others the stag. Not all horses, however swift, have speed suitable for the racecourse; some bear a

---

[2] Cicero's poems are sneered at in, e.g., Tac. *Dial.* 21.6 (where see Gudeman).

[3] Meaning his *Apology*—but that was no law-court speech: it never " saw even the door of the law-court " (Dion. Hal. *Dem.* 23).

10 quidam iugum. Ut ad meum te morbum vocem,
Pylades in comoedia, Bathyllus in tragoedia multum
a se aberrant; nomini meo cum velocitas pedum non
concedatur tantum sed obiciatur, lentiores manus
sunt; quidam cum hoplomachis, quidam cum Thrae-
cibus optime pugnant, quidam sic cum scaeva conponi
cupiunt quomodo alii timent. In ipsa oratione
quamvis una materia sit, tamen ille qui optime argu-
mentatur neglegentius narrat, ille non tam bene
implet quam praeparat. Passienus noster cum coepit
dicere, secundum principium statim fuga fit, ad
epilogum omnes revertimur, media tantum quibus 209
11 necesse est audiunt. Miraris eundem non aeque
bene declamare quam causas agere, aut eundem non
tam bene suasorias quam iudiciales controversias
dicere? Silo Pompeius sedens et facundus et lit-
teratus est, et haberetur disertus si a praelocutione
dimitteret; declamat tam male ut videar belle optasse cum dixi: numquam surgas. Magna et varia
res est eloquentia, neque adhuc ulli sic indulsit ut tota
contingeret; satis felix est qui in aliquam eius
partem receptus est.
12 Ego tamen et propriam causam videor posse reddere: adsuevi non auditorem spectare sed iudicem;
adsuevi non mihi respondere sed adversario; non
minus devito supervacua dicere quam contraria. In

---

[1] i.e. theatre mania.
[2] The text is dubious, and a name should perhaps replace
nomini meo. But presumably a boxer or the like is in question.

rider better, some a yoke.   To call your attention to 10
my own pet failing:[1] Pylades in comedy, Bathyllus
in tragedy are quite unlike their normal selves.   My
namesake's[2] feet are swift—everyone concedes that,
he is even criticised for it—but his hands are slower.
Some fight better with fully-armed gladiators, others
with the lighter-equipped; some desire, others fear
to be matched against a left-hander.   As to oratory,
the material may be the same, but the good arguer
narrates carelessly, in another the development is
inferior to the preliminaries.   When my friend
Passienus begins to speak, there is a general flight
after his proem—but we return in force for his epilogue: what comes between is heard only by those
who cannot avoid it.   Is there anything odd in a man 11
not declaiming as well as he pleads ?   Or in another
not treating *suasoriae* so well as legal *controversiae*?
Pompeius Silo, when he is seated,[3] displays eloquence
and education, and would be regarded as an orator if
he got rid of his audience after his preamble.   But he
declaims so badly that I fancy I made a neat point in
begging him never to get up.   Eloquence is something great and varied, and it has never yet been so
indulgent as to attend one man without flaw; you are
lucky if you are received into some part of it.

"However, *I* may be able to give you a reason 12
peculiar to me.   I am used to keeping my eye on the
judge, not the audience.   I am used to replying to
my opponents, not to myself.[4]   I avoid the super-

[3] Cf. Latro (*C.* 1 pr. 21), who remained seated while sketch-
ing the *quaestiones* involved in the declamation.
[4] Declaimers constantly raised and answered imaginary
objections.

scholastica quid non supervacuum est, cum ipsa
supervacua sit? Indicabo tibi affectum meum: cum
in foro dico, aliquid ago; cum declamo, id quod bel-
lissime Censorinus aiebat de his qui honores in muni-
cipiis ambitiose peterent, videor mihi in somniis
13 laborare. Deinde res ipsa diversa est: totum aliud
est pugnare, aliud ventilare. Hoc ita semper habitum
est, scholam quasi ludum esse, forum arenam; et ideo
ille primum in foro verba facturus tiro dictus est.
Agedum istos declamatores produc in senatum, in 210
forum: cum loco mutabuntur; velut adsueta clauso
et delicatae umbrae corpora sub divo stare non possunt, non imbrem ferre, non solem sciunt, vix se
inveniunt; adsuerunt enim suo arbitrio diserti esse.
14 Non est quod oratorem in hac puerili exercitatione
spectes. Quid si velis gubernatorem in piscina aestimare? Diligentius me tibi [1] excusarem, tamquam
huic rei non essem natus, nisi scirem et Pollionem
Asinium et Messalam Corvinum et Passienum, qui
nunc primo loco stat, minus bene videri ⟨dicere⟩ [2]
15 quam Cestium aut Latronem. Utrum ergo putas

[1] diligentius me tibi *Kiessling:* diligentissime sibi.
[2] *Supplied by Müller.*

---

[1] For the following criticisms of declamation, cf. *C.* 9 pr.:
the start of the extant part of Petronius' *Satyricon:* Tac. *Dial.*
35: and in general Bonner, c. 4.
[2] Normally used of new recruits to the army, then of
inexperienced gladiators (e.g. Suet. *Caes.* 26).
[3] This is literal as well as metaphorical. Declamation was

fluous as well as what tells against myself. Everything is superfluous in a declamation: declamation is superfluous.[1] I will tell you what I feel. When I speak in the forum, I am *doing* something. When I declaim I feel, to use Censorinus' excellent phrase of zealous candidates for local office, that I am struggling in a dream. Again, the two things are quite different: 13 it is one thing to fight, quite another to shadow-box. The school has always been taken to be a sort of school for gladiators, the forum as an arena—hence the word tiro [2] for the man who is going to make his first speech in the courts. Come on, bring your declaimers into senate and forum! With their surroundings they will change their character. They are like bodies used to the closet and the luxury of the shade, unable to stand in the open and put up with rain and sun.[3] They scarcely know where they are: [4] they are used to being clever at their own rating. There is no point in trying to test an orator amid these 14 childish pursuits. You might as well judge a helmsman on a fish-pond. I should take more pains in my defence (pleading that I was not born for such things) if I didn't know that Asinius Pollio, Messala Corvinus and Passienus (now our leading orator) are rated as declaimers below Cestius or Latro. Do you think this the fault of the speakers—or their hearers? *They* are 15

carried on indoors, law-courts might be open to the weather: cf. Quintilian 11.3.27 (" If we have to speak in the sun or on a windy, wet or hot day, shall we throw up the case? ") and the story about Latro in *C.* 9 pr. 3–4. There is constant reference to the difficulty found by declaimers in adapting to the courts: see Mayor on Juvenal 7.173.
   [4] Cf. Petr. 1.2: " When they get into the forum, they think they've been deposited in another world."

hoc dicentium vitium esse an audientium? Non illi
peius dicunt, sed hi corruptius iudicant: pueri fere
aut iuvenes scholas frequentant; hi non tantum
disertissimis viris, quos paulo ante rettuli, Cestium
suum praeferunt sed etiam Ciceroni praeferrent, nisi
lapides timerent. Quo tamen uno modo possunt
praeferunt; huius enim declamationes ediscunt, illius
orationes non legunt nisi eas quibus Cestius rescripsit.

16 Memini me intrare scholam eius cum recitaturus 21¹
esset in Milonem; Cestius ex consuetudine sua
miratus dicebat: si Thraex essem, Fusius essem; si
pantomimus essem, Bathyllus essem, si equus, Melissio. Non continui bilem et exclamavi: si cloaca esses,
maxima esses. Risus omnium ingens; scholastici intueri me, quis essem qui tam crassas cervices haberem.
Cestius Ciceroni responsurus mihi quod responderet
non invenit, sed negavit se executurum nisi exissem
de domo. Ego negavi me de balneo publico exiturum
nisi lotus essem.

17 Deinde libuit Ciceroni de Cestio in foro satis facere.
Subinde nanctus eum in ius ad praetorem voco et,
cum quantum volebam iocorum conviciorumque
effudissem, postulavi ut praetor nomen eius reciperet
lege inscripti maleficii. Tanta illius perturbatio fuit

---

¹ Cf. Tac. *Dial.* 26.9: "Almost every schoolman likes to
think that he can reckon himself above Cicero—though, of
course, far behind Gabinianus."

² In reply to Cicero's defence: cf. Quintilian 10.5.20.

³ i.e. a type of gladiator; in each case Cestius names a
notable example of the class.

⁴ The canal that drained Rome's sewage into the Tiber.

not worse speakers; the audience is judging by worse standards. It is boys, usually, or youths who throng the schools: and they prefer their Cestius to the eloquent men I have just mentioned—and they'd prefer him to Cicero if they didn't fear a stoning.[1] They do prefer him to Cicero, in fact, in the one way open to them: they learn off Cestius' declamations while not reading Cicero's speeches—except the ones to which Cestius has written replies.

" I recall going into his school when he was going 16 to recite a speech against Milo.[2] Cestius, with his usual admiration for his own works, said: ' If I were a Thracian,[3] I should be Fusius. If I were a mime, I should be Bathyllus. If I were a horse, I should be Melissio.' I couldn't contain my rage. I shouted: ' If you were a drain, you'd be the Great Drain.'[4] Universal roars of laughter. The schoolmen looked at me to discover who this bull-necked lout was. Cestius, who had taken on himself to reply to Cicero, could find nothing to reply to *me*, and he said he wouldn't go on if I didn't leave. *I* said I wouldn't leave the public bath until I'd had my wash.

" After that, I resolved to revenge Cicero on 17 Cestius, in the courts. Soon, I met him and summoned him before the praetor, and when I'd had enough of deriding and abusing him, I requested the praetor to admit a charge against him under the law on unspecified offences.[5] Cestius was so worried that

[5] See below, *C.* 5.1 n., and for the charge of ingratitude, *C.* 2.5 n. It is probable that neither charge would have stood up in a Roman court, and Cassius clearly chose them for their declamatory connections. But one could request a *curator* from the praetor (the real-life parallel to the *actio dementiae*: see *C.* 2.3 n.) in cases of insanity (Bonner, p. 93).

ut advocationem peteret. Deinde ad alterum praetorem eduxi et ingrati postulavi. Iam apud praetorem urbanum curatorem ei petebam; intervenienti- 212
bus amicis, qui ad hoc spectaculum concurrerant, et
rogantibus dixi molestum me amplius non futurum si
iurasset disertiorem esse Ciceronem quam se. Nec
hoc ut faceret vel ioco vel serio effici potuit.

18   Hanc, inquit, tibi fabellam rettuli ut scires in declamationibus tantum non aliud genus hominum esse.
Si comparari illis volo, non ingenio mihi maiore opus
est sed sensu minore. Itaque vix iam obtineri solet
ut declamem; illud obtineri non potest, ut velim aliis
quam familiarissimis audientibus. Et ita faciebat.

Declamationes eius inaequales erant, sed ea quae
eminebant, in quacumque declamatione posuisses,
inaequalem eam fecissent. Conpositio aspera et
quae vitaret conclusionem, sententiae vivae. Ini-
quom tamen erit ex his eum aestimari quae statim
subtexam; non enim haec ille optime dixit, sed haec
ego optime teneo.

he asked for an adjournment. Next, I haled him off to a second praetor and accused him of ingratitude. Finally, before the Urban Praetor, I requested a guardian for him. His friends, who had thronged to the spectacle, put in a word for him, and in response to them I said I should give no further trouble if he swore he was less eloquent than Cicero. But neither joke nor serious argument would induce him to do that.

" I've told you this little tale to show that declama- 18 tions breed a virtually separate race of men. To be comparable with them, I need not more genius but less sense. So now I can scarcely be persuaded to declaim: and when I am, it is only before my best friends." And so he did.

His declamations were uneven, but what stood out in them were things that would have made any declamation you put them in look unequal. His word-arrangement was harsh, and avoided periodic structure. His epigrams were lively. But it would be unfair to judge him from the extracts that immediately follow.[1] They don't show him at his best; but they are what I best remember.

---

[1] It is tiresome that we cannot, because of the excerpting of Book 3, know which of the epigrams were actually Cassius': not, anyway, all of them, though Seneca's practice would suggest that the first epigrams in each declamation have a good chance of being Cassius'.

EXCERPTA

CONTROVERSIARUM

LIBRI TERTII

I

Luxuriosus a Sodalibus Excaecatus

Caecus de publico mille denarios accipiat.

Decem adulescentes, cum bona comedissent, sortiti sunt ut cuius nomen exisset ex pacto excaecaretur et ita acciperet mille denarios. Exiit sors cuiusdam; excaecatus est. Petit mille denarios. Negantur.

Hi sunt oculi quos timuistis, mariti. O legem, si excaecat homines, abrogandam! Mille denarios nulli res publica dat nisi qui invitus accipit. Dic nunc: miserere; hoc, cum excaecareris, non dixisti. Res publica debilitatem consolatur, non emit. Con-

---

[1] Bonner, p. 96. No Roman parallel is available. At Athens the disabled received a small daily pension (Aristotle *Ath. Pol.* 49.4).

EXCERPTS FROM BOOK 3

1

The Debauchee who was Blinded by his Friends

A blind man shall receive a thousand denarii
from the state.[1]

Ten youths, having eaten up their estates, drew
lots on the understanding that the one whose
name came out should be blinded and so receive
a thousand denarii. The lot for one of them
came out, and he was blinded. He asks for a
thousand denarii; they are refused.

Against the youth: These are the eyes you feared,
husbands.[2]—What a law! It deserves to be annulled
if it causes men to be blind!—The state gives a
thousand denarii to no-one who is not sorry to receive
them.[3]—Say now: " pity me "—you did not say that
when you were being blinded.—The state consoles a
man for disability—it doesn't purchase it.—Having

[2] The youth is represented as a womaniser as well as a
debauchee.
[3] i.e. involuntary blindness is the pre-requisite.

sumptis patrimoniis membra conferunt. Utilius est rei publicae unum caecum repelli quam novem fieri. Non solus a vobis petit alimenta, sed primus. Alam qui propter debilitatem alitur, non alam qui propter alimenta debilitatur. Sic fit, ubi homines maiorem vitae partem in tenebris agunt, ut novissime solem 214 quasi supervacuum fastidiant.

Pars altera. Illis novem nihil daturus est: nulli non favorabilis erit si eos a quibus excaecatus est decipit. "Circumventus adulescens ab illis novem veteranis consumptoribus solus" inquit "novem consentientibus non potui resistere." Omnia ex composito facta sunt: unus mentionem intulit, omnes adprobaverunt; electus est qui sortiretur; sors huius quae exiret prima subiecta est. Cum repugnaret, excaecatus est. Si circumventus, inquit, est, persequatur iniuriam, de vi agat, talionem petat. Videbimus; primum est ut habeat unde vivat.

---

[1] With a probable allusion to the Greek habit of meals where the expenses were shared between the guests (ἔρανος).

[2] Athenaeus 273C tells of a luxurious Sybarite who said he had not seen the sun rise or set for twenty years (cf. Cic. *Fin.* 2.23). See Mayor on Juvenal 8.11, and especially Sen. *Ep.* 122.

eaten up their estates, they pay contributions [1] in limbs.—It is more expedient for the state that one blind man should be rebuffed than that nine men should be blinded. He is not the only one who seeks support from you—merely the first.—I will feed the man who is being fed because of his disability, not the man who gets disabled to be given food.—So it is that, when men spend the greater part of their lives in darkness,[2] they end up despising the daylight as unnecessary.

The other side: He [3] doesn't propose to give the other nine anything; he will be popular with everybody if he deceives those who blinded him.—" A youth outwitted by those nine experienced debauchees," he says, " I could not on my own resist nine in full accord." Everything was prearranged; one of them brought the idea up, all the rest approved of it. They chose who was to win the draw; his lot was put in in such a way that it would come out first. He struggled, but he was blinded.—" If he was tricked," it is said, " let him go to law about the injury done him, sue for violence, seek retribution in kind." [4] We shall see; meanwhile, let him have something to live on.

[3] The youth is given an advocate (perhaps as being blind, perhaps as being too young to plead).

[4] Retribution in kind was provided for in the Twelve Tables (8.2), and is discussed by Gellius 20.1.14 *seq.*

THE ELDER SENECA

II

Parricida Aequis Sententiis Absolutus

Quidam filium accusavit parricidii. Aequis
sententiis absolutum abdicat.

Minus est iam quod rogo; non peto ut me a parricida vindicetis, sed ut separetis. Parricidam non
accuso, sed fugio. Quomodo iste accusatori parcet
qui patri non pepercit? Ergo nihil medium est inter
testamentum et culleum? Non absolutus parricida
sed dubius: ut absolvaris, multis tibi sententiis opus
est, ut damneris, una. Non absolverunt reum, sed
saeculo pepercerunt. Miraris in hac civitate misericordiam, in qua lex absolutionem et paribus tabulis 215¹
dat? Quaeris quam multis non placeas? si unum
adiecero, parricida es. Absolutionem legi, non innocentiae debes. Absolutus, inquit, sum. Non abdico

---

¹ Murder of parents or near relations: though the concept
could be extended (see *C.* 1.1.23 n.). Here, clearly, of
attempted murder of the father.

² See *C.* 2.3.3 n.

³ That is, must I make him my heir if I cannot get him convicted of parricide? The traditional punishment for a
parricide was to be tied in a sack (*culleus*) and drowned: cf.

2

The Parricide who was Acquitted on a Tied Vote

A man accused his son of parricide.[1]   He was acquitted on an equal vote.[2]   He is disinherited.

For the father: What I ask on this occasion is less; I do not ask you to avenge me on this parricide, but to separate me from him.   I do not accuse the parricide—I am trying to escape from him.—How will he keep his hands off his accuser?—he didn't keep them off his father.—Is there then no half-way house between the will and the sack?[3]—You are not an acquitted parricide, but a " not proven " one: you need many votes to be acquitted, to be condemned, one.[4]—They did not acquit the defendant, they spared the age.[5]—Are you surprised to see this pity [6] displayed in a state where the law grants acquittal even on equal votes?—You ask how many are against you?   If I add one more, you are a parricide.—You owe your acquittal to the law, not to your innocence. —" I was acquitted."   I do not disinherit you for

e.g. *Dig.* 48.9.9: " parricida . . . culleo insuatur cum cane, gallo gallinaceo, vipera et simia, deinde in mare profundum iactetur "; Cic. *Rosc. Am.* 70 (with Landgraf's note).

[4] i.e. many more favourable votes to be properly acquitted, only one more to be condemned.

[5] Spared it the spectacle of a condemned parricide and the trouble of so unpleasantly punishing him.

[6] Shown by the jury in the murder trial.   The speaker says this pity is only to be expected (and deplored) in a state where laws are so lenient.   This and the previous epigram should perhaps be run together.

te propter parricidium, sed propter alia vitia, quae te fecerunt tam credibilem parricidam.

Pars altera. Manifestus adulescentis color est ut se dicat patris auctoritate oppressum.

III

ABDICANDUS QUI ABDICATUM FRATREM ADOPTAVIT

Cum tricenario filio pater patrimonium dividat.

Quidam habuit filios, frugi et luxuriosum. Abdicavit luxuriosum. Frugi peregre profectus est; captus est a piratis; de redemptione scripsit patri. Patre cessante luxuriosus praevenit et redemit. Redit frugi; adoptavit fratrem suum. Abdicatur.

Nec est quod quisquam me laudet: prior frater inter nos fecit pietatis exemplum; una navigavit, una periclitatus est, una omnes emensus est terras, reliquit me tantum ad paternam domum. Non est quod excusatione aetatis utaris: potes navigare. Utrique gratias agere deberet: frater me isti reduxit, ego isti fratrem. Si tamquam inertem abdicasti, navigavit,

---

[1] Probably fictitious: Bonner, 106.
[2] That is, after redeeming him from the pirates.
[3] From which, of course, he was excluded.
[4] The father, who is addressed in the previous epigram.
[5] By adopting him and so bringing him back into the family.

parricide, but for the other vices that made you so plausible in the role of parricide.

The other side: The obvious *colour* for the youth is that he should say he was a victim of his father's prestige.

3

THE MAN WHO ADOPTED HIS DISINHERITED BROTHER AND WAS HIMSELF TO BE DISINHERITED

When a son reaches the age of thirty, his father must divide his property with him.[1]

A father had two sons, a good one and a debauched one. He disinherited the debauchee. The good one set off abroad. He was captured by pirates, and wrote to his father to get a ransom. The father was dilatory; the debauchee got in first and redeemed him. The good son returned home, and adopted his brother. He is being disinherited.

For the good son: There is no call for anyone to praise me. Of the two of us, it was my brother who first provided an example of affection: he sailed with me,[2] shared my dangers, travelled over the whole world with me, and abandoned me only when I returned to my father's house.[3]—Don't make your age an excuse: you are quite capable of going to sea.— He [4] ought to be grateful to both of us: my brother brought me back to him, *I* brought my brother back to him.[5]—If you disinherited him for being lazy, well,

si tamquam impium, suos redemit. Non potest eripi 216
filio quod accepit a lege. Quomodo enim potest
pater eripere quod non potest non dare?

Pars altera. Per alterum mihi necesse est abdicare
quem nolo. Hoc uno alter alteri placet, quod uterque
patri displicet. Utamur medicina qua cogimur:
quod in vulneribus fieri periculosis solet, ut malum
cum ipso corpore exsecetur. Adoptare permittitis
adulescenti, quem lex in patrimonio dividendo
experitur? Lex te ad ministerium patrimonii ad-
misit, non in dominium. Est aliqua aetas a qua
aliquis filius esse desinat? Ne tricenario quidem
adoptare filio licet; neque enim quisquam alium
potest in manum suam recipere qui ipse in aliena
manu est. Quomodo fieri potest ut tibi potestas vitae
necisque [aut] in fratrem sit, mihi¹ in filium non sit?
Si bene de te meruerat, patrem pro illo rogasses.

¹ in fratrem sit, mihi *Gronovius:* aut in fratrem sit aut.

---

¹ It is clear from this and other epigrams that the theme
should mention that the good son was over thirty, and had in
accordance with the law received a share of the estate.

² i.e. get rid of the bad son from the family even at the
expense of the good. Cf. *C.* 9.5.6: " medici alligant et corporibus nostris ut medeantur vim adferunt "; Curt. 5.9.3: " sed
medici quoque graviores morbos asperis remediis curant."

³ This was certainly the position in strict Roman law. For
" the civil law rule was that a *filiusfamilias* could own nothing . . . It became customary for the *paterfamilias* to allow

he went to sea; if for lacking affection, he ransomed a relation.—A son cannot be deprived of what he has received under the law. How can a father snatch away what he cannot withhold? [1]

The other side: Thanks to one of my sons, I have to disinherit the other—against my will.—What makes my sons get on with each other is merely that their father fails to get on with both.—Let us use the inescapable medicine: [2] as is the way with dangerous wounds, the evil must be cut away with a part of the body.—Will you allow adoption to be exercised by a young man who is only being tried out by the law in the division of the estate? The law brought you in to help with the estate, not to own it.[3]—Is there an age at which one stops being a son? Not even at thirty can a son adopt: you cannot take control of another when you yourself are in the control of a third.[4] How can *you* have power of life and death over a brother when *I* don't have it over my son.[5]—If he deserved well of you, you could have begged your

his son the free use of some property (his *peculium*) . . . In law this *peculium* remained the property of the *paterfamilias* " (B. Nicholas, *An Introduction to Roman Law* [Oxford, 1962], 68).

[4] This again would be true under Roman law. But the declamation—whose validity turns on the possibility of such an adoption—may have been framed with Greek conditions in view. There a son presumably could adopt, for his coming of age gave him almost complete release from his father's control (see A. R. W. Harrison, *The Law of Athens* [Oxford, 1968], 75, 82 *seq.*).

[5] The text is uncertain. As here printed, it seems to mean that the good son cannot acquire what the father had renounced, *patria potestas* over the bad son.

Nam quod ego non redemi, paupertatis fuit: nihil in medio conparebat; quidquid tricenarius reliquerat, abdicatus abstulerat. Quid facerem solus, senex, inops, cuius patrimonium alter diviserat, alter absumpserat?

IV

SERVATUS A FILIO

Servatus contra servatorem ne quam habeat actionem.

Servatus a filio abdicat. Ille praescribit.

⟨O si⟩ [1] licuisset perire, si loqui non licet! Servatum me putatis? captus sum. Redde me hosti; 217 captivis loqui licet. Quoniam tantopere vitae beneficia iactat, audite quis prior dederit. Si quis me hosti reddiderit, servatorem vocabo. An vos abdicationem actionem putatis? Etiamsi actio est, lex quae de servato loquitur ad personas tantum extraneas pertinet, ad filium et ad patrem non magis quam ad servum et ad dominum, libertum et patronum. Ut a patris potestate discedas et ad aestimationem

[1] *Supplied by C. F. W. Müller.*

---

[1] There is no evidence for the existence of such a law (Bonner, 106).

[2] On the grounds of the conflicting law (cf. *RLM* p. 382.7 *seq.* for the type of *praescriptio* that involved " persona, ut . . . magistratus sum, accusari me non licet*, et talia "). This is the Greek παραγραφή, and is not properly a Roman practice (see Adamietz on Quintilian 3.6.72).

father on his behalf.—That I did not ransom him was due to my poverty; there was no money available: what the thirty-year-old son had left, the disinherited son had removed. What was I to do, a poor solitary old man, whose estate had been shared with one son and squandered by the other?

4

THE FATHER SAVED BY HIS SON

One who has been saved shall have no right of action against his saver.[1]

A man who has been saved by his son disinherits him. The son brings an objection.[2]

For the father: Would that I had been allowed to die, if I am not allowed to speak.—Do you think I was saved? I was taken captive.—Send me back to the enemy—prisoners are allowed to speak.—Since he boasts so loudly of the value of life, hear who was the first of us to bestow it.[3]—Anyone who gives me back to the enemy I shall call my saviour.—Do you regard disinheriting as an " action "?[4] Even if it is, the law when it speaks of people saved refers only to non-relations; it applies to father and son no more than to master and slave, freedman and patron.—Leave the power exercised by a father and come to a

---

[3] The father, that is, on him.

[4] The question is posed, though not answered, by Quintilian 3.6.77 (where see Adamietz). It is not one that makes sense in terms of Roman law, because *abdicatio* was not a legal act (see note on *C.* 1.1).

beneficii venias, qui vitam dat, si prior accepit, non obligat sed reddit. Processi in aciem exemplum filio meo; vicit me non hostis sed aetas. Servavit quem saepe servaveram. Redivivum me senem meretrix vocat, parasitorum iocantium materia sum; omnibus istis tamquam servatoribus tacere iubeor. Fili, si vivere mihi non licet, cur perire non licuit? Ego te, inquit, protexi. Ita tu adulescens in acie non ante patrem stetisti? Audite filii mei gloriam: parricidium non fecit; cum posset servare, servavit.

Pars altera. Hic me genuit; hic mihi spiritum, hic has manus quibus servaretur dedit.

V

Pater Raptam Continens

Rapta raptoris aut mortem aut indotatas nuptias
optet.

Raptor postulat ut rapta educatur. Pater non vult.

Iste raptor est, ego in ius educor. Non est tam facile homini probo occidere quam perdito mori. 218

---

[1] She and the parasites (boon companions) are hangers on of the son, and had provoked his disinheritance (cf. *Decl.* 296: " obicimus adulescenti ante omnia quod parasitum habuerit ").

[2] That is, I shouldn't have got into such danger in the first place if you had been in your rightful position.

reckoning of the service rendered. One who gives life after first receiving it puts the other under no obligation—he is merely making a return.—I went into battle as an example to my son. I was conquered not by the enemy but by my age.—I was saved by one whom I had often saved.—The whore [1] calls me an old man resurrected. I am a joke to parasites. They all tell me to keep quiet, as though *they* are my saviours.—Son, if I am not allowed to live why was I not allowed to die?—" I protected you." So you, a youth, did not stand before your father in the battle line? [2]—Hear my son's boast: he did not commit parricide; when he was in a position to save my life, he did so.

The other side: This man begot me; he gave me breath—and these hands to save him.

5

THE FATHER WHO DETAINED HIS DAUGHTER AFTER SHE WAS RAPED

A girl who has been raped may choose either marriage to her ravisher without a dowry or his death.[3]

A ravisher demands that the girl he raped be brought before the magistrate. The father refuses.[4]

For the father: He is the ravisher—yet *I* am brought to court.—It is not so easy for an upright

---

[3] See note on *C.* 1.5.
[4] The theme is briefly dealt with by Calp. Flacc. 34.

Communis, inquit, lex est. Dii faciant ne me experiri cogas an tota ista mea sit. Quando ergo, inquit, optabis? Hoc tempore non possum; curo vulnera, familiam reficio, expugnatam domum lugeo, ereptam virginitatem consolor, minantem sibi ipsi custodio. Quando optabis? Cum rapta voluerit, non cum raptor. Quando optabis? Cum tu noles. Quando, inquit, optabis? Paro me optioni, confirmo animum; non est facile hominem occidere; premo interim gemitus meos et introrsus erumpentes lacrimas ago. Scio quid futurum sit: vultus te meus decepit. Stulte, quemquam putas morari filiae suae nuptias? In securem incurris et carnificem ultro vocas. Cum rogare debeas, convicium facis. Nemo vindicare se cogitur.

Pars altera. Nihil est miserius quam incertum inter vitam mortemque destitui. Iam beneficium erit, etiamsi mortem optaverit. In amorem filiae istius incidi. Appellare debui de nuptiis patrem: feci; sed videtis quam etiam in lege lentus sit. Raptor vitam alieni arbitrii habet, libertatem sui. Lex ista communis est: habet hic raptor quod timeat,

---

[1] The father would in effect make the choice; cf. *C*. 8.6: "mortem optaturus est." But this could be disputed (see Quintilian 4.2.68).

[2] i.e. we both have rights under it. The father in reply hints that he will choose death (cf. below: "I know . . .").

[3] Into supposing that I shall choose marriage.

[4] Therefore my delay means that I am contemplating the other choice.

[5] A hint at suicide (cf. *C*. 2.3.23).

man to kill [1] as for a depraved one to die.—" The law is common to all." [2]   God forbid that you should force me to test out whether it is all on my side.—" When will you make your choice?" I cannot at this moment; I am salving wounds, rebuilding my household, lamenting the despoilment of my house, consoling my daughter for the loss of her virginity, guarding her when she threatens to take her own life. " When will you choose?" When the girl who was raped wishes, not her ravisher. "When will you choose?" When *you* do not wish it. "When will you choose?" I am preparing myself for the choice, strengthening my resolve. It is not easy to kill a man; meanwhile I suppress my groans, and drive within the tears that burst forth.—I know what will happen. You have been deceived by my countenance.[3] Fool, do you suppose that anyone would be prepared to delay his daughter's marriage? [4] You are running on to the axe, summoning the executioner of your own accord.—You should be imploring —yet you insult.—No-one can be forced to avenge himself.

The other side: Nothing is more wretched than to be left uncertain whether one will live or die. By now, it will be a boon even if he chooses death.—I fell in love with the girl. You say I should have asked her father for her hand. I *did*, but you see how slow he is even where the law insists that he should choose.— A ravisher's life is in another's power, but his freedom is in his own.[5]—That law has something for both of us. In it a rapist has something to fear, but he has some-

habet et quod sperare possit. In lege, inquit, non est
scriptum quando. Immo statim; quotiens tempus
non adicitur, praesens intellegitur. Tam longum tibi
ius in caput civis permittitur? Crudelius est quam
mori semper mortem timere.

VI

DOMUS CUM TYRANNO INCENSA

Damni inlati actio sit.

Quidam tyrannum ex arce fugientem cum
persequeretur, in privatam domum conpulit.
Incendit domum: tyrannus cum domo con-
flagravit. Praemium accepit. Agit cum illo
dominus damni.

219

Quem exclusisti et quem recepisti? Quare nullam
aliam domum tyrannus petit? nemo non venienti
domum clusit. Aditum in domum non habui qui in
arcem habui. Non gaudes impendisse te aliquid
publicae libertati? " Hic est in cuius domo tyrannus
occisus est": tamquam tyrannicida monstraris.
Redde, inquit, domum. Ita vivo tyranno non perdi-

---

[1] A fixed declamatory (if not legal) principle; cf. *Decl.* 280:
" quoniam omnium vel poenarum vel praemiorum tempus aut
constitutum est aut praesens."

[2] There was naturally provision for this in Roman as in
Greek law (by the *Lex Aquilia de damno*; cf. c. 3: " si quis
alteri damnum faxit, quod *usserit* fregerit ruperit iniuria . . .").
But the theme is Greek in setting, even if the declaimers
naturally used Roman terminology (for *damnum sarcire*, see
Bonner, 117).

thing to hope for too.—" The law does not specify when the choice is to be made." Then it means at once; for where the time is not mentioned, the present is understood.[1]—Is so prolonged a power over a citizen's life permitted you ? Constant fear of death is crueller than death itself.

6

THE HOUSE THAT WAS BURNT DOWN WITH A TYRANT IN IT

An action may lie for damage to property.[2]

A man pursuing a tyrant in flight from his castle cornered him in a private house, and set fire to it. The tyrant went up in flames along with the house. The other man got the reward;[3] the house-owner sues him for the damage caused.

For the " tyrannicide ": Whom did you shut out, whom did you let in ? [4]—Why didn't the tyrant make for some other house ? Everyone shut their doors as he approached.—I couldn't get into your house— though I had got into the castle.—Aren't you glad to have made some sacrifice for the people's liberty ? —People say: " This is the man who owned the house where the tyrant was killed." You are pointed out as if you were the killer of the tyrant.— " Give me back my house." That means you hadn't

---

[3] i.e. as killer of the tyrant.

[4] Answer: tyrannicide and tyrant. The implication here and in many of the other epigrams is that the house-owner was a friend of the tyrant and admitted him voluntarily.

deras? Tyranni amicus, tyranni satelles, certe, quod negare non potes, hospes. Diu expectavi an eiceretur tyrannus. Facilius potes accusare aut te, qui tam familiaris tyranno fuisti ut illi tua maxime placeret domus, qui illum recepisti, aut tyrannum, qui tibi damnum dedit, quod in domum tuam confugit, aut, ut culpa te liberem, facilius potes accusare fortunam, quae tyrannum potissimum ad te detulit.

Pars altera. Eius debet esse damnum cuius praemium est. Non est iniquum eius rei tibi iniuriam inputari cuius fructum percepisti. Non elegit domum tyrannus—nec enim hoc illi vacabat—, sed in eam quam potuit inrupit, cum ego in ea non essem. Nactus hic occasionem nocendi intrare noluit, sed tyrannicidium elegit dubium, lentum, periculosum urbi. Accepit praemium maius sine dubio quasi damnum sarcire deberet.

lost it while the tyrant was alive.[1] You were his
friend, his hireling, at least (and this you cannot
deny) his host.—I waited for a long time to see if the
tyrant would get thrown out.—Better either blame
yourself—*you* were so friendly to the tyrant that he
chose your house particularly, *you* took him in—or
blame the tyrant, who caused you damage by resort-
ing to your house, or (to free you from guilt) blame
Chance, which sent the tyrant to your house in particular.

The other side: The loss ought to be borne by the
recipient of the reward. You may fairly be blamed
for damage involved in something from which you
drew the profit.—The tyrant didn't *choose* my house—
he hadn't time. He burst in where he could, at a
time when *I* wasn't there.—This man took the opportunity of doing me harm. He chose not to enter,
but instead selected a method of killing the tyrant
that was uncertain, slow and dangerous for the city.
—He surely got a bigger reward on the understanding that he must repair the damage.

[1] As you would have done had you not been friendly with
him.

THE ELDER SENECA

VII

220

Venenum Furenti Filio Datum

Filio furenti et membra sua lanianti pater venenum dedit. Accusatur ab uxore malae tractationis.

Non mirum est quare vivat quae filium perdidit: vivit qui occidit.

Pars altera. Quem cotidie perdebam aliquando extuli. Falleris, misera mulier, in orbitatis tuae tempore: non tunc perdidisti filium, sed tunc extulisti.

Extra. Alfius Flavus hanc sententiam dixit: ipse sui et alimentum erat et damnum. Hunc Cestius quasi corrupte dixisset obiurgans: Apparet, inquit, te poetas studiose legere: iste sensus eius est qui hoc saeculum amatoriis non artibus tantum sed sententiis implevit. Ovidius enim in libris metamorphoseon dicit:

ipse suos artus lacero divellere morsu
coepit et infelix minuendo corpus alebat.

---

[1] The exercise is alluded to by Quintilian 8.2.20, 8.5.23.

[2] Bonner, 94–5. Quintilian 7.4.11 remarks that this declamatory law is parallel to the *actio rei uxoriae,* when a divorced wife reclaimed her dowry and "quaeritur utrius culpa divortium factum sit"; but this need not imply any special connection between the *actio malae tractationis* and divorce. In Seneca (cf. *C.* 4.6, 5.3) the cases generally concern wives distressed by the ill-treatment of their children; but contrast *C.* 1.2.22.

7

A MAD SON GIVEN POISON

A father gave his son poison when he was mad and tearing his flesh.[1] His wife accuses him of ill-treatment.[2]

For the mother: It is not surprising that a mother is alive after losing her son. His murderer is alive.

The other side: I finally saw to his grave one whom I had been losing each day. You are mistaken, poor woman, in the date of your bereavement; it was not then that you lost your son—merely then that you buried him.

By the way: Alfius Flavus spoke this epigram: " He was his own nourishment—and his own damage." [3] Cestius reproved him for something in such bad taste, and said: " It is obvious you are a careful reader of poetry. That idea came from a man who filled this generation with erotic handbooks—and erotic epigrams." For it is Ovid who says in the *Metamorphoses*: [4]

" He began to tear his own limbs, biting and rending; Wretched man, he nourished his body—by taking from it."

[3] Cf. Quintilian 8.2.20: ". . . qui suos artus morsu lacerasse fingitur in scholis *supra se cubasse* " (explained by W. Heraeus, *Rh. M.* 79 [1930], 256).

[4] 8.877–8 (of the hungry Erysichthon). The erotic handbooks were the three books of the *Ars Amatoria*.

VIII

Olynthius Pater Reus Concursus

Qui coetum et concursum fecerit, capital sit.

Victa Olyntho cum filio adulescente Olynthius
senex Athenas venit.   Athenienses omnibus civi-
tatem Olynthiis decreverunt.   Invitatus ad
cenam ab adulescente luxurioso cum filio venit.   22
Ibi cum de stupro filii mentio esset, pater pro-
fugit, adulescens retentus est.   Pater flere ante
domum coepit; incensa est domus; decem
adulescentes perierunt et filius Olynthii.   Accusatur pater quod coetum concursumque fecerit.

Misero si flere non licet, magis flendum est.   Im-
perari dolori silentium non potest.   Fuerunt ex
populo qui dicerent: " hic meum filium, hic meam
corrupit uxorem "; suum quisque illo et ignem attulit
et dolorem.   Timeo, fili, ne, dum te quaero, in ossa
raptoris alicuius incidam.   Ubi Athenarum fides ? ubi

---

[1] This law (also mentioned in *RLM* p. 344.21) has Roman
parallels (Bonner, 113), but the setting is so thoroughly Greek
that this is hardly relevant.   However, the law certainly
sounds a little drastic for Athens, even in a crisis.

[2] Olynthus, on the Chalcidic peninsula in northern Greece,
was destroyed by Philip of Macedon in 348 B.C. (see also *C.*
10.5).   The remnants of the population were scattered, and
many certainly took refuge in Athens; but it is unlikely that
(despite Suidas s.v. κάρανος) they were granted citizen rights,

8

THE FATHER FROM OLYNTHUS ACCUSED OF PROVOKING AN ASSEMBLY

Whoever causes a gathering and assembly shall die.[1]

After the defeat of Olynthus, an old man of that city came with his youthful son to Athens. The Athenians decreed that all Olynthians should receive Athenian citizenship.[2] The father was invited to supper by a debauched youth, and went, along with his son. There was talk at the party of raping the boy; the father fled, but his son was kept behind. The father started to weep in front of the house, which got burned down.[3] Ten youths died, and so did the son of the Olynthian. The father is accused of causing a gathering and assembly.

For the father: If a wretched man is not allowed to weep, he must weep the more.[4]—Silence cannot be imposed on grief.—There were people in the crowd who said: " This man seduced my son, that my wife." Everyone brought there his own brand, and his own grievance.—I am afraid, son, that while I search for your body I may stumble on the bones of someone who ravished you.—Where is the good faith of Athens? Where the hands that gave and received

though they probably received some privileges (*RE* s.v. Olynthos col. 329).

[3] i.e. by an angry crowd.

[4] Cf. *C.* 4.1: " nulla flendi maior est causa quam flere non posse."

415

hospitales invicem dexterae? Capti, inquam, fili, sumus; dum licet, fugiamus, sed tamquam a Philippo, pariter. Apud Philippum certe viri fuimus. Lacrimae meae vocantur in crimen, quasi ex quo Olynthos capta est flere desierim. Tantus scilicet sum ut in ea civitate populum concitare potuerim in qua filium servare non potui. Non quotiens convenerunt in aliquem locum plures coetus et concursus est, sed quotiens convocati, quotiens parati quasi ad ducem suum concurrerunt; non si una vicinia coit aut transeuntium paucorum numerus adfluxit, sed ubi totus aut ex magna parte populus, ubi divisa in partes civitas. Coetus multitudinis magnae nomen est coeuntis ex consensu quodam: at illic initio pauci fuerunt, deinde reliqui non ad me convenerunt, sed ad incendium, quod tamen populus spectare maluit 22 quam extinguere. Lex non eum punit propter quem coetus factus est sed eum a quo factus est. Non mihi tanti ultio fuit ut amittere filium vellem; et temptavi populum rogare nec potui.

Pars altera. Quid coetu opus est? Sunt scriptae ad vindictam iniuriarum omnium leges. Mota semel multitudo modum non servat. Ardere illo incendio civitas potuit.

---

[1] Or perhaps: "We have been tricked."

pledges of hospitality?—" We're trapped,[1] son," I said. " Let us get out while we can, but together, as though we were escaping from Philip."—At least we were *men* when Philip was our enemy.[2]—My tears are brought up against me—as though I have ever stopped crying since Olynthus fell.—Apparently [3] I am so important that I had the power to arouse the people in a city where I hadn't the power to save my son.—It is not a gathering and assembly whenever a number of people have come together to a certain place, but only when they have been called together, when they have assembled, as if ready to follow their leader: not if one district has gathered, or a few passers-by have drifted up, but where a whole people or a good part of it, a state divided into factions, has assembled. An assembly is the name for a large crowd gathering in pursuance of some common plan. But on that occasion there were few people at first; the rest came later not because I summoned them, but because of the fire. And the populace preferred gaping at that to putting it out.—The law doesn't punish the man who was the occasion of an assembly, but the man who was the instigator of it.—Revenge wasn't worth the loss of my son; I tried to beg the people off, but I failed.

The other side: What need is there of a crowd? There are laws prescribed to avenge any injury.— Once a crowd is aroused it cannot control itself.— Thanks to that fire the city might have gone up in flames.

[2] But not now, if you should be seduced.

[3] Of course sarcastic.

THE ELDER SENECA

IX

Crux Servi Venenum Domino Negantis

Aeger dominus petit a servo ut sibi venenum daret; non dedit. Cavit testamento ut ab heredibus crucifigeretur. Appellat servus tribunos.

Lex Cornelia, te appello; ecce erus iubet quod tu vetas. Ne quis illum displicuisse domino putet, tunc huic parari iussit crucem cum sibi venenum. Plura servi crimina confitemur: intempestivas potiones, inutiles cibos desideranti negavit. Quid enim ille non voluit qui venenum petivit? Malui crucem pati quam mereri. Si vincitur, periturus est, si non vincitur, serviturus ei a quo in crucem petitur. Ex altera parte lex est, ex altera testamentum, crux utrimque. Furiosus servum sine causa voluit occidere. Quaeritis insaniae argumentum? Et se voluit occidere. Servo, inquit, tribuni non possunt

---

[1] There is a brief treatment of this theme in *Decl.* 380, where what is only implicit in Seneca is made more clear, that the master is now dead.

[2] For a similar appeal by a slave, see *RLM* p. 96.21. The *tribuni plebis* had during the republic had the right to aid the oppressed (*latio auxilii*), which passed to the emperors as part of their *tribunicia potestas*. Slaves would not have been able to appeal thus, but in a declamation this could be disregarded (or disputed: see below, " The tribunes cannot . . .").

[3] The *Lex Cornelia de sicariis et veneficis* (81 B.C.), which

9

The Crucifixion of a Slave who Refused to Give his Master Poison [1]

A sick master asked his slave to give him poison; he refused. The master put a provision in his will that the slave should be crucified by his heirs. The slave appeals to the tribunes.[2]

For the slave: I appeal to you, law of Sulla: [3] take notice, a master is ordering what *you* forbid.—Do not suppose that he [4] displeased his master: his master ordered a cross for him at the same time as poison for himself.[5]—We have many crimes on the part of the slave to confess: [6] he refused when he was asked to serve unseasonable drinks, harmful food. For his master wanted everything—after all he asked for poison.—" I preferred enduring the cross to deserving it."—If he loses the case he will die; if he wins, he will be the slave of the man who now seeks to crucify him.—On one side is the law, on the other the will: on both sides the cross.[7]—He was mad, and wanted to kill his slave for no reason. You require proof of his insanity? He wanted to kill himself too.—" The

established a standing court to deal with poisoners and murderers (Bonner, 111–12).

[4] An advocate, here and elsewhere, speaks for the slave.

[5] That is, the owner always intended to kill the slave, and the episode over the poison was irrelevant to his intention.

[6] Of course ironical.

[7] The dilemma of the slave when the master made his request (not, as Bornecque implies, when his master was dead): so too below: " Then it makes . . ."

THE ELDER SENECA

succurrere. Serva natum regem habuimus; servo indice patefacta est Bruti liberorum cum Tarquiniis coniuratio. Ergo nihil interest venenum domino dederit aliquis an negaverit? Etiam ubi remedium est mori, scelus est occidere. Tam cito vos de vita domini servum desperare vultis quam heredem? Mortem si supplicium putas, quid rogas, si beneficium, quid minaris? Venenum quisquam obicit nisi datum? Ullum tu finem facies tribuniciae potestati, quam populus Romanus, ut ipse plurimum posset, plus valere quam se voluit? Venenum habere scelus est tam magnum quam dominum occidere.

Pars altera. Mori volens elegit huic ministerio nequissimum servum, audacem, infestum sibi. Ille non saluti consuluit domini, quem videbat insanabili morbo tabescere, sed tormenta eius extendit. Servus erilis imperii non censor est sed minister. Agitur de iure testamentorum, quorum interiit omnis potestas si vivorum imperia neglexerint ⟨servi⟩,[1] mortuorum tribuni. Itane, furcifer, tu non morieris domini arbitrio, morietur dominus tuo?

[1] *Supplied here by the editor (before* vivorum *by C. F. W. Müller).*

---

[1] Servius Tullius, a common rhetorical example (see Index of Names).
[2] Livy 2.4.5 *seq.* For Brutus' punishment of his children, see *C.* 10.3.8.
[3] The dead owner is addressed.
[4] The tribunate grew up as a plebeian counterweight to the power of the aristocratic magistrates.
[5] The *Lex Cornelia* punished anyone who " fecerit vendi-

tribunes cannot go to the help of a slave." We had a king born of a slave woman;[1] a slave was the informer who revealed the conspiracy of Brutus' children with the Tarquins.[2]—Then it makes no difference whether someone gave his master poison or refused it?—Even where the remedy is to die, it is a crime to kill.—Do you want a slave to despair of his master's life as readily as an heir does?—If you[3] regard death as a punishment, why ask it for yourself? If you regard it as a boon, why do you use it as a threat?—Is poison being made a charge without its having been administered?—Will *you* put any limits to the power of the tribunes, whom the Roman people, in order to ensure its own supreme power, wanted to be more powerful than itself?[4]—To possess poison[5] is as great a crime as to kill one's master.

The other side: Wishing to die, he chose for this service a good-for-nothing slave, a bold man who hated him.—He wasn't interested in saving his master's life (he saw he was wasting away under an incurable disease) but in prolonging his agonies.—A slave is not the judge of his master's orders but their agent.—What is at stake is the law relating to wills, which have lost all their validity if slaves neglect the orders of the living, tribunes those of the dead.—Jailbird, do you refuse to die at the will of your master?—though your master has to die when *you* want him to.[6]

derit emerit *habuerit* dederit " poison (Cic. *Cluent.* 148). The point here is that the master was himself guilty of possessing poison, and the slave was justified in not aiding him.

[6] i.e. the slave, by refusing to administer poison, prevented his master from dying at the time he had chosen.

LIBER QUARTUS

Seneca Novato, Senecae, Melae filiis salutem.

1   Quod munerarii solent facere, qui ad expectationem populi detinendam nova paria per omnes dies
dispensant, ut sit quod populum et delectet et revo-
cet, hoc ego facio: non semel omnes produco; aliquid
novi semper habeat libellus, ut non tantum sententiarum vos sed etiam auctorum novitate sollicitet.
Acrior est cupiditas ignota cognoscendi quam nota
repetendi. Hoc in histrionibus, in gladiatoribus, in
oratoribus, de quibus modo aliquid fama promisit, in
omnibus denique rebus videmus accidere: ad nova 22
2 homines concurrunt, ad nota non veniunt.[1] Non
tamen expectationem vestram macerabo singulos
producendo: liberaliter hodie et plena manu faciam.
    Pollio Asinius numquam admissa multitudine de-

[1] nota non veniunt *Kiessling:* noua conueniunt.

BOOK 4

PREFACE

SENECA TO HIS SONS NOVATUS, SENECA AND MELA
GREETINGS

I am doing what gladiator-producers often do 1
when, in order to maintain the suspense of the
populace, they distribute new pairs over each day of
the games, so that there is always something to please
the spectators and bring them back—I am not bringing all my declaimers on at once; let a book always
have something new, to keep you on your toes by
means of the novelty of the speakers as well as of the
epigrams.[1] The desire to get to know the unknown
is keener than the desire to go back to the known.
We see this everywhere—in connection with actors,
gladiators and orators, at least where reputation has
promised something beforehand: men flock to the
new, avoid the old. But I won't keep you on tenter- 2
hooks by bringing them on only one at a time; today
I shall be liberal and open-handed.

Asinius Pollio never let a crowd in when he de-

[1] Seneca's children were particularly keen on epigrams (C.
1 pr. 22).

423

clamavit, nec illi ambitio in studiis defuit; primus enim omnium Romanorum advocatis hominibus scripta sua recitavit.[1] Et inde est quod Labienus, homo mentis quam linguae amarioris, dixit: " ille triumphalis senex ἀκροάσεις [tuas id est declamationes] suas numquam populo commisit ": sive quia parum in illis habuit fiduciam, sive—quod magis crediderim—tantus orator inferius id opus ingenio suo duxit, et exerceri quidem illo volebat, gloriari

3 fastidiebat. Audivi autem illum et viridem et postea iam senem, cum Marcello Aesernino nepoti suo quasi praeciperet. Audiebat illum dicentem, et primum disputabat de illa parte quam Marcellus dixerat: praetermissa ostendebat, tacta leviter implebat, vitiosa coarguebat. Deinde dicebat partem contrariam. Floridior erat aliquanto in declamando quam in agendo: illud strictum eius et asperum et nimis iratum ingenio suo iudicium adeo cessabat ut in multis illi venia opus esset quae ab ipso vix inpetra- 226²

4 batur. Marcellus, quamvis puer, iam tantae indolis erat ut Pollio ad illum pertinere successionem eloquentiae suae crederet, cum filium Asinium Gallum relinqueret, magnum oratorem, nisi illum, quod semper evenit, magnitudo patris non produceret sed obrueret.

---

[1] Recitation was well-known in Rome before this. See A. Dalzell, *Hermathena* 86 (1955), 20–28 for a discussion of this passage.

[2] Labienus behaved in precisely the same way himself (*C.* 10 pr. 4): but he was no friend of Pollio's (see Quintilian 4.1.11).

claimed; but he was not without scholarly ambition —indeed he was the first of all the Romans to recite what he had written before an invited audience.[1] Hence the remark of Labienus [2] (who had a sharper mind than tongue): "That old man, hero of triumphs,[3] never put his declamations in the firing-line against the people." Perhaps it was that he lacked confidence in them; or perhaps (as I prefer to suppose) so distinguished an orator regarded this occupation as unworthy of his talents, and, while prepared to get exercise from it, scorned to make a parade of it. However, I heard him both in his prime 3 and afterwards when he was an old man and as it were instructing his grandson, Marcellus Aeserninus. He would listen to him speaking; then first of all he would argue on the side Marcellus had taken, showing him what he had left out, filling out what he had skimmed over, and criticising faulty passages: next he would speak on the other side. He was rather more flowery in declamation than in making speeches: that stern and harsh judgement, that he turned too angrily on his own genius, was so much in abeyance that in many respects he needed allowances made for him that *he* hardly granted to others. Marcellus, 4 though only a boy, was already so clever that Pollio held him heir-apparent to his own eloquence, though he left in his son, Asinius Gallus, a fine orator; the trouble was that, as always happens, the son was swamped rather than helped by the father's greatness.

[3] Pollio celebrated a triumph over the Parthini behind Durazzo in 39 B.C.

Memini intra quartum diem quam Herium filium amiserat declamare eum nobis, sed tanto vehementius quam umquam ut appareret hominem natura contumacem cum fortuna sua rixari; nec quicquam ex
5 ordine vitae solito remisit. Itaque cum mortuo in Syria C. Caesare per codicillos questus esset divus Augustus, ut erat mos illi clementissimo viro, non civiliter tantum sed etiam familiariter, quod in tam magno et recenti luctu suo homo carissimus sibi pleno convivio cenasset, rescripsit Pollio: " eo die cenavi quo Herium filium amisi." Quis exigeret maiorem ab amico dolorem quam a patre?

6 O magnos viros, qui fortunae succumbere nesciunt et adversas res suae virtutis experimenta faciunt! Declamavit Pollio Asinius intra quartum diem quam filium amiserat: praeconium illud ingentis animi fuit malis suis insultantis. At contra Q. Haterium scio 2? tam inbecillo animo mortem Sexti fili [1] tulisse ut non tantum recenti dolori cederet, sed veteris quoque et oblitterati memoriam sustinere non posset. Memini, cum diceret controversiam de illo qui a sepulchris trium filiorum abstractus iniuriarum agit, mediam dictionem fletu eius interrumpi; deinde tanto maiore

---

[1] mortem Sexti fili *Kiessling:* mortis sex filiorum.

I recall that Asinius spoke a declamation to us within three days of losing his son Herius, but so much more forcefully than usual that you could tell that this naturally defiant man was quarrelling with his fate. Nor did he make any relaxation in his ordinary routine. Thus when Gaius Caesar had died 5 in Syria, and the blessed Augustus had complained in a letter (using the polite and even familiar tone customary in that most forbearing of men) that despite this great recent bereavement of his one of his dearest friends had had a full-dress supper-party, Pollio wrote back: " *I* dined the day I lost my son Herius." And who would ask for greater grief from a friend than from a father?

How great these men are, who do not know what it 6 means to yield to fortune and who make adversity the touchstone of their virtue![1] Asinius Pollio declaimed within three days of losing his son; that was the manifesto of a great mind triumphing over its misfortunes. On the other hand, I know that Quintus Haterius took the death of his son so hard that he not only succumbed to grief when it was recent, but could not bear the memory of it when it was old and faded. I remember that when he was declaiming the *controversia*[2] about the man who was torn away from the graves of his three sons and sues for damages, Haterius' tears interrupted him in mid-speech; after that he spoke with so much greater force, so much more pathos, that it became clear how

---

[1] Seneca dwells on this fortitude in a way characteristic of the rhetoricians: cf. *S.* 2.15; Sen. *Ep.* 99.6, *Marc.* 14 *seq.*; Val. Max. 5.10.

[2] *C.* 4.1.

impetu dixit, tanto miserabilius, ut appareret quam magna interim pars esset ingenii dolor.

7 Declamabat autem Haterius admisso populo ex tempore: solus omnium Romanorum, quos modo ipse cognovi, in Latinam linguam transtulit Graecam facultatem. Tanta erat illi velocitas orationis ut vitium fieret. Itaque divus Augustus optime dixit: "Haterius noster sufflaminandus est": adeo non currere sed decurrere videbatur. Nec verborum illi tantum copia sed etiam rerum erat: quotiens velles eandem rem et quamdiu velles diceret, aliis totiens figuris, aliis tractationibus, ita ut regi posset nec consumi.

8 Regi autem ab ipso non poterat; †alioqui† libertum habebat cui pareret; sic ibat quomodo ille aut concitaverat eum aut refrenaverat. Iubebat eum ille transire, cum aliquem locum diu dixerat: transibat; insistere iubebat eidem loco: permanebat; iubebat epilogum dicere: dicebat. In sua potestate habebat ingenium, in aliena modum.

9 Dividere controversiam putabat ad rem pertinere si illum interrogares, non putabat si audires. Is illi erat ordo quem impetus dederat; non dirigebat se ad

228M

---

[1] Repeated by St. Jerome (*PL* 23.365): Seneca the younger discusses speed in oratory in *Ep.* 40, and mentions Haterius (his "rush" Seneca thought to be far from the mark of a sane man).

great a part grief can sometimes play in a man's talents.

Haterius used to let the public in to hear him de- 7 claim extempore. Alone of all the Romans *I* have known he brought to Latin the skill of the Greeks. His speed of delivery was such as to become a fault. Hence that was a good remark of Augustus': "Haterius needs a brake "[1]—he seemed to charge downhill rather than run. He was full of ideas as well as words. He would say the same thing as often as you liked and for as long as you liked, with different figures and development on every occasion. He could be controlled—but not exhausted.

But he couldn't do his own controlling. He had a 8 freedman to look to, and used to proceed according as *he* excited or restrained him.[2] The freedman would tell him to make a transition when he had been on some topic for a long time—and Haterius would make the transition. He would tell him to concentrate on the same subject—and he would stay on it. He would tell him to speak the epilogue—and he would speak it. He had his talents under his own control—but the degree of their application he left to another's.

He thought it relevant to divide up a *controversia*— 9 if you questioned him; if you listened to his declamation, he didn't think so.[3] His order was the one his flow of language [4] dictated; he did not regulate him-

---

[2] Rather as Gaius Gracchus was said to have relied on a pipe-player (Cic. *de Orat.* 3.225).

[3] i.e. in theory he believed in a logical *divisio*; in practice he didn't seem to.

[4] Tacitus (*Ann.* 4.61) says Haterius " impetu magis quam cura vigebat."

declamatoriam legem. Nec verba custodiebat. Quaedam enim scholae iam quasi obscena refugiunt, nec, si qua sordidiora sunt aut ex cotidiano usu repetita, possunt pati. Ille in hoc scholasticis morem gerebat, ne verbis calcatis et obsoletis uteretur; sed quaedam antiqua et a Cicerone dicta, a ceteris deinde deserta dicebat, quae ne ille quidem orationis citatissimae cursus poterat abscondere: adeo quidquid insolitum est etiam in turba notabile est.

10   Hoc exempto nemo erat scholasticis nec aptior nec similior, sed dum nihil vult nisi culte, nisi splendide dicere, saepe incidebat in ea quae derisum effugere non possent. Memini illum, cum libertinum reum defenderet, cui obiciebatur quod patroni concubinus fuisset, dixisse: inpudicitia in ingenuo crimen est, in servo necessitas, in liberto officium. Res in iocos 229¹ abiit: "non facis mihi officium" et "multum ille huic in officiis versatur." Ex eo inpudici et obsceni aliquamdiu officiosi vocitati sunt.

11   Memini et illam contradictionem sic ab illo positam magnam materiam Pollionis Asinii et tunc Cassi Severi iocis praebuisse: "at, inquit, inter pueriles condiscipulorum sinus lasciva manu obscena iussisti." Et pleraque huius generis illi obiciebantur. Multa erant quae reprehenderes, multa quae suspiceres,

---

¹ Quintilian (2.10.9, 8.3.23) protested against the avoidance of ordinary words in declamation. Cf. also *C.* 7. pr. 3–4.
² Bornecque compares Trimalchio in Petr. 75.11: " tamen

self by the rules of declamation. Nor did he keep a
guard over his words. Some the schools avoid nowadays as if they were obscene, regarding as intolerable
anything rather low or in everyday use.[1] Haterius
bowed to the schoolmen so far as to avoid cliché and
banality. But he would employ old words that
Cicero had used but that had later fallen into general
disuse, and these caught the attention even in that
break-neck rush of language. How true it is that the
unusual stands out even in a crowd!

With this exception, no-one was better adapted to 10
the schoolmen or more like them; but in his anxiety
to say nothing that was not elegant and brilliant, he
often fell into expressions that could not escape
derision. I recall that he said, while defending a
freedman who was charged with being his patron's
lover: " Losing one's virtue is a crime in the free-
born, a necessity in a slave,[2] a duty [3] for the freedman." The idea became a handle for jokes, like
" you aren't doing your duty by me " and " he gets
in a lot of duty for him." As a result the unchaste
and obscene got called " dutiful " for some while
afterwards.

I recall that much scope for jest was supplied to 11
Asinius Pollio and then to Cassius Severus by an
objection raised by him in these terms: " Yet, he
says, in the childish laps of your fellow-pupils, you
used a lascivious hand to give obscene instructions."
And many things of this sort were brought up against
him. There was much you could reprove—but much

ad delicias ipsimi annos quattuordecim fui: nec turpe est quod
dominus iubet."
[3] For the *operae officiales* of freedmen, see on *C.* 4.8.

cum torrentis modo magnus quidem sed turbidus flueret. Redimebat tamen vitia virtutibus et plus habebat quod laudares quam cui ignosceres, sicuti in ea in qua flevit declamatione.

to admire; he was like a torrent that is impressive, but muddy in its flow.[1]   But he made up for his faults by his virtues, and provided more to praise than to forgive: as in the declamation in which he burst into tears.

[1] Reminiscent of Horace on Lucilius (*Sat.* 1.4.11: cf. Quint. 10.1.94).

EXCERPTA

CONTROVERSIARUM

LIBRI QUARTI

I

Pater a Sepulchris a Luxurioso Raptus

Amissis quidam tribus liberis cum adsideret sepulchro, a luxurioso adulescente in vicinos hortos abductus est et detonsus coactus convivio veste mutata interesse. Dimissus iniuriarum agit.

Numquam lacrimae supprimuntur imperio, immo etiam inritantur. Nulla flendi maior est causa quam flere non posse. Rapuit me qualem in convivium puderet venire, dimisit qualem redire ad sepulchrum puderet. Credo mirari aliquem quod in forum amissis modo liberis veniam: at ego iam in convivio fui. Quousque, inquit, flebis? Est quaedam in ipsis malis miserorum voluptas et omnis adversa fortuna habet in querellis levamentum. Ibi me flere pro-

---

[1] Bereavement manifested itself in long hair and dark clothes (Cic. *Sest.* 32: "erat . . . in luctu senatus, *squalebat civitas . . . veste mutata*"). Hence the hair-cut and the change.
[2] For the width of the *actio iniuriarum*, see Bonner, 115–16.

EXCERPTS FROM BOOK 4

1

The Father who was Dragged from a Graveyard by a Debauchee

A man who had lost three sons was sitting by their grave, when he was carried off by a debauched youth into a nearby garden, given a haircut, and forced to attend a party in different clothes.[1] When they let him go, he sues for injury.[2]

For the father: An order never stifles tears—in fact it provokes them. There is no better cause for tears than to be unable to shed them.—I was in such a state when he hauled me off that I was ashamed to go to a party; I was in such a state when he let me go that I was ashamed to go back to the tomb.—I believe some people are surprised to see me in court when I have just lost my sons; but after all I *have* already been to a party.—" How much longer will you weep? " The wretched find a certain pleasure even in their miseries,[3] and all adversity discovers a relief

[3] Cf. Sen. *Ep.* 99.25: " ait Metrodorus esse aliquam cognatam tristitiae voluptatem." Seneca proceeds to dispute it.

hibes ubi crudeliter ipse non fleres. Cum miser-
rimum sit flere, quam infelix sum cui ne hoc quidem
licet! Vidi ebriorum sitim et vomentium famem. 23
Quis est iste qui supra flentem patrem censuram
lugendi postulat? Proiectus in omnia gulae libidi-
nisque flagitia, omnibus notandus censoribus, saeculo
praecepta conponit; scit quantum super amissos tres
liberos patri flendum sit, quem si viveret pater fleret.
Senex, orbus, infelix, hoc tantum inter miserias
solacium capio, quod miserior esse non possum.
Cineres meorum in sepulchro video. Magnum solacium est saepius appellare liberorum non responsura
nomina. Hic mihi vivendum est, ne cui de nuptiis,
ne cui de liberis cogitanti dirum omen occurram.
Cogit flere qui non sinit. In illo convivio morari
etiam felicis patris esset iniuria.

Pars altera. Questus prius sum de inhumanitate
eorum qui illum propinquitate contingerent: nemo
amicus, nemo, inquam, propinquus est? Sed melius
illi eius rabiem, ut video, noverant. ⟨Erant⟩ [1] festo
die sodales amicique mecum, quorum unus: " Quid

---

[1] *Supplied by Thomas.*

---

[1] For debauchees " vomit so as to eat, eat so as to vomit "
(Sen. *Helv.* 10.3).

in complaint.—You stop me weeping in a place where you would be cruel to refrain from weeping yourself. —It is wretched to weep: how unhappy am *I*, who am not even allowed to do that.—I saw the thirst of the drunk, the hunger of the vomiting.[1]—Who is this man who claims to be censor of grief over a weeping father? Flung among all the disgraceful actions provoked by greed and lust, worthy of branding by every censor, he makes up rules for the age; he claims to know how much a father should weep for three lost sons: his father would weep for *him*, if he were alive.—Old, bereaved, unhappy, I have only one solace amid my wretchedness: I cannot be more wretched than I am.—I look on the ashes of my sons in their grave. It is a great comfort to keep calling the names of sons who will answer nothing.—" *This* is where I must live, to avoid bringing ill luck if I meet someone with thoughts of marriage and children." [2]— He who forbids you to weep compels you to weep.—It would be an injury even to a happy father to have to stay at a party like that.

The other side: First of all, I complained of the cruelty of his nearest and dearest. " Have you no friend? " I asked, " no relation? " But they—I see it now—knew his madness better than I.[3]—It was a feast-day; I had with me friends and acquaintances. One of them said: " Why let this poor man perish?

[2] This epigram (perhaps also the previous one) is an extract from the words of the father addressing the youth in the graveyard.

[3] Knew, that is, that he was not to be diverted from his insensate grief.

hunc miserum perire patimur? Nemo sibi ipse finem flendi facit; pudet illos desinere, cogi volunt." Consolarer te diutius, nisi iam et accusare posses.

II

METELLUS CAECATUS

Sacerdos integer sit.

Metellus pontifex, cum arderet Vestae templum, dum Palladium rapit oculos perdidit. Sacerdotium illi negatur.

Vesta mater, fortasse nullum sacerdotem haberes 232 nisi Metellum habuisses. Sacrorum causam ago, non Metelli: plus illorum interest ne Metellum sacerdotem quam Metelli ne sacerdotium perdat. Non erat tantus Metellus cum illi sacerdotium dedimus.

---

[1] i.e. for consoling him. The youth's *colour* is that that is what he was trying to do on the day of the party.

[2] That L. Caecilius Metellus rescued the Palladium from the temple of Vesta in 241 B.C. seems certain (Livy *Per.* 19). That he was blinded for setting eyes on the image is an invention of the declamation schools: and our passage is the first appearance of it. Fact and fiction are disentangled by O. Leuze, *Philologus* 64 (1905), 95–115. That dubious author the pseudo-Plutarch (*Parall.* 17) tells much the same story of Ilus; but this may be a late story, based on the Roman one. Tiresias, blinded for seeing what he should not have seen, comes to mind.

[3] Bonner, 104. Compare the provision for priestesses in *C.* 1.2. The " wholeness " of the priest was demanded both

No-one can put a stop to his own tears. People are ashamed to stop—they want to be *made to*."—I should go on comforting you, but there!—you might accuse me.[1]

2

METELLUS BLINDED [2]

A priest must be without defect.[3]

When the temple of Vesta was on fire, the high priest Metellus lost his sight grabbing the image of Pallas.[4] His rights as priest are refused him.

For Metellus: Mother Vesta, you would perhaps have no priest now [5] if you had not had Metellus then. —It is the cause of the religious rites [6] that I am pleading, not Metellus'. It is more important to them not to lose Metellus as their priest than to Metellus not to lose his priesthood.—Metellus was not so great when we gave him his priesthood.[7]—The

in Greece and Rome: cf. Dion. Hal. 2.21.3; Plut. *Quaest. Rom.* 73 (sores disqualified from taking the auguries). See G. Wissowa, *Religion und Kultus der Römer* [2] (Munich, 1912), 491 n. 3.

[4] For the different legends about the Palladium, see R. G. Austin on Virg. *Aen.* 2.163. Its presence in the temple of Vesta in Rome was a guarantee of the safety of the city (e.g. Cic. *Scaur.* 48).

[5] i.e. your temple, and indeed the whole city, would have been destroyed.

[6] Or, perhaps, as elsewhere, "the holy objects" (the Palladium not being the only relic in the shrine).

[7] i.e. far from becoming less "whole" as a result of this episode, he has become greater.

THE ELDER SENECA

Civitas sollicita pendebat; duo periclitabantur quibus nihil habebat populus pretiosius, sacra et Metellus. O faciendum sacerdotem nisi esset! Lex integrum ad animum refert, non ad corpus. Lex hoc aestimari tunc voluit cum quis peteret, non cum haberet sacerdotium. Habes, Vesta, duplex pontificis tui meritum: servavit sacra nec vidit.

Extra. Pollio: ante hoc si caecus factus esset, non sustulisset; si postea caecus factus est, vidit.

Pars altera. Sacerdos non integri corporis quasi mali ominis res vitanda est. Hoc etiam in victimis notatur, quanto magis in sacerdotibus? Post sacerdotium magis est observanda debilitas; non enim sine ira deorum debilitatur sacerdos. Apparet non esse propitios deos sacerdoti quem ne servati quidem servant.

Extra. Hunc colorem Gallio non probavit, summo cum honore Metelli adserens contra Metellum agendum, ita ut cogatur cum iudicibus officio pontificum et ipse consulere.

---

[1] Cf. Ovid's account of the incident, *Fast.* 6.437 *seq.*: "heu quantum timuere patres . . . attonitae flebant demisso crine ministrae."

[2] The law, that is, posited in this declamation; in fact, the body would be specifically mentioned.

[3] Pollio's characteristically tart comment on the bad logic of the preceding epigram.

city was anxious and in suspense:[1] danger threatened the two most precious possessions of the people
—the holy objects and Metellus.—How worthy he
would be of being made priest—were he not priest
already!—The law alludes to a whole mind, not a
whole body.[2]—The law intended this assessment to
be made when someone sought the priesthood, not
when he already held it.—Vesta, your priest has done
you a double service; he preserved the holy objects—
and did not see them.

By the way: Pollio: "If he had been blinded
beforehand, he would not have taken them. If he
was blinded later, he saw them."[3]

The other side: A priest whose body has a blemish
is to be avoided like something of ill omen.—This is
an object of censure even in sacrificial victims:[4]
how much more in priests!—Once a man becomes
priest, more careful watch must be paid for any disability; if a priest is maimed, the gods must be
angry.—The gods obviously do not favour a priest
whom they don't preserve even after he has preserved
them.[5]

By the way: Gallio did not approve of this *colour*;
he asserted that the case against Metellus must be
put with all due honour paid him, so that *he*, like the
judges, is forced to have regard to the duty of priests.

[4] Victims had to be without blemish (*purae*): for details,
see Wissowa, *op. cit.*, 416.
[5] So Augustine on the incident, *Civ. Dei* 3.18: " homo igitur
potius sacris Vestae quam illa homini prodesse potuerunt."

THE ELDER SENECA

III

Exul Raptae Pater

Inprudentis caedis damnatus quinquennio exulet.
Rapta raptoris mortem aut indotatas nuptias
optet.

⟨Quidam⟩,[1] cum haberet filiam et filium, in- 23:
prudentis caedis damnatus in exilium abiit. Filia
eius rapta est; raptor ad patrem puellae se contulit, impetravit ab illo ut iuberet filiam nuptias
optare et epistulam daret ad filium. Fratre
auctore mortem optavit puella. Pater rediit;
abdicat filium.

Quomodo me excusabo rei publicae, cui duos
abstuli, neutrum mea culpa? In altero me fortuna
decepit, in altero filius. Filia etiam fratri paruit,
filius nec patri. Per humanos, inquit, errores:
agnovi preces meas. Potes omnibus, inquit, ostendere hominem quam non possis occidere. Scis me
civem debere rei publicae: hoc intererit tamen, quod

---

[1] *Supplied by Gertz.*

---

[1] Bonner, 98–100. The law agrees with Greek custom
(though the term may not always have been five years), and
is not inconsistent with Roman practice.

3

The Exile whose Daughter was Raped

One convicted of unintentional homicide shall go
into exile for five years.[1]
A girl who has been raped
may choose between her ravisher's death
and marriage to him without dowry.[2]

A man who had a son and a daughter was convicted of unintentional homicide and went off to
exile. His daughter got raped; the ravisher
sought out the girl's father, and got him to order
the girl to choose marriage and give him a letter
to his son. On her brother's advice the girl
chose death. The father returned, and disinherits the son.

For the father: How shall I make my excuses to the
state, which I have deprived of two men—neither by
my own fault: in the one case, I was let down by
fortune, in the other by my son.—My daughter
obeyed even her brother, my son disobeyed even his
father.—" In the name," he said, " of the errors men
are liable to commit ": I recognised the terms of my
own entreaties.—" You can show all men how incapable you are of killing a man." [3]—" You know
that I owe a citizen to the state; the difference will

---

[2] Cf. note on *C.* 1.5.
[3] Rapist to father; the next words were written by father
to son.

inprudentes occidimus, prudentes servavimus. Aliquem in exilio infra fortunam meam vidi.

Pars altera. Inrupit contumeliose tamquam in exulis domum. Pervenit ad patrem, non pepercit eius pudori. At ego querebar quod absenti fecit iniuriam. Non possum ob hoc abdicari quod lege factum est. Non potuisti, pater, de iniuria iudicare quam non noveras. Multa nobis extorquentur quae nolumus scribere. Et tu in ea fortuna eras in qua posses iniuriam accipere, et ille is erat qui etiam in patria facere iniuriam posset. Quia sciebat malam causam suam, egit apud eum qui illam non noverat. Redit superbus, iubebat nos optare nuptias, cogebat: videbatur sic et illic coegisse. Aliquid tamen epistulis consecutus est: nemo umquam tardius perit. 234M Collegit ingentem numerum perditorum, expugnavit domum, vexavit puellam: haec tibi raptor non narraverat.

Extra. Latro aiebat semper invisum esse qui reum alium pro se subiceret. Non oportere hic derivari factum in sororis voluntatem. Qui defendit, inquit, crimen, auditur tamquam reus, qui transfert

---

[1] i.e. the ravisher.

[2] i.e. the rapist returning to the son with the letter (cf. below " all high and mighty ").

[3] The son draws a parallel between the rapist's behaviour to the daughter and to the father.

[4] This will be a modified excerpt from a division: cf. *C*. 10.2.8.

[5] Cf. below: " Because he knew . . ." The father only heard one side of the story (cf. " *This* is what . . .").

still be that I killed unwittingly, saved wittingly."—
While I was in exile I saw someone more miserable
than myself.[1]

The other side: He [2] burst insultingly into the house
—as though it belonged to an exile.—He went to my
father: he did not spare his shame.[3]—But my complaint was that he did him an injury while he was
away.—I cannot be disinherited for doing something
legal.[4]—You could not, father, be the judge of an
injury that you did not know about.[5]—We can be
made to write much that we do not want to.—Fortune
had made *you* vulnerable to injury; *he* was a man
capable of doing an injury—even in his own country.
—Because he knew his case was weak, he pleaded it
before someone who was ignorant of the facts.—He
returned all high and mighty, told us to choose
marriage, tried to force us to. It looked as if he had
used similar force over there,[6] too.—However, he got
one thing out of the letter: no-one ever took longer
to die.[7]—He collected a gang of desperadoes,
stormed the house, violated the girl. *This* is what
the ravisher had *not* told you.

By the way: Latro said that unpopularity always
attends someone who shifts guilt to another; in this
case the deed [8] should not be shrugged off on to the
sister. "If you defend a crime, you are heard as
defendant; if you seek to transfer guilt, you are

---

[6] i.e. to the exiled father.
[7] i.e. the choice was held up by the letter.
[8] i.e. the decision to choose death.

tamquam accusator. Malo autem loco est qui habet rei fortunam, accusatoris invidiam. Asinius Pollio dicebat colorem in narratione ostendendum, in argumentis exsequendum: non prudenter facere eos qui in narratione omnia instrumenta coloris consumerent; nam et plus illos ponere quam narratio desiderasset et minus quam probatio.

IV

Armis Sepulchri Victor

Sepulchri violati sit actio.

Bellum cum esset in quadam civitate, vir fortis in acie armis amissis de sepulchro viri fortis arma sustulit. Fortiter pugnavit et reposuit. Praemio accepto accusatur sepulchri violati.

Arma vix contigeram: secuta sunt. Haec si sumo, arma sunt, si relinquo, spolia. Vidisses vere violari sepulchrum si illo venisset hostis. Uterque quod alteri deerat commodavimus: ille viro arma, ego armis virum. Res publica multum consecuta est, vir fortis nihil perdidit. Necessitas est quae navigia iactu exonerat, necessitas quae ruinis incendia op- 235

---

[1] Bonner, 119: "Violation of sepulchre could give rise at Rome to a private action before the praetor."

[2] The same subject is dealt with in *Decl.* 369, and discussed summarily in *RLM* p. 599.21 *seq.* At Quintilian 5.10.36 we find mention of a similar theme: is it sacrilege to remove arms from a temple to repel the enemy?

446

heard as accuser. You are in a bad way if you're as unfortunate as a defendant *and* as unpopular as an accuser." Asinius Pollio said that the *colour* should be *shown* in the narration and followed through in the proofs. He said it was unwise to use up all one's resources for a *colour* during the narration; it meant putting more than was required in the narration and less than was required in the proofs.

4

The Victor who Used Weapons Taken from a Tomb

Violation of a tomb is to be actionable.[1]

While a certain city was at war, a hero lost his weapons in battle, and removed the arms from the tomb of a dead hero. He fought heroically, then put the weapons back. He got his reward, and is accused of violating the tomb.[2]

For the hero: I had scarcely touched the weapons: they followed me.[3]—If I take them, they are weapons for me; if I leave them, they are spoil for the enemy. —You would have seen the tomb really violated if the enemy had reached it.—We both lent what the other lacked: he gave a man arms, I gave the arms a man.—The state gained much, the hero lost nothing. —It is necessity that lightens a ship by casting out cargo, necessity that stops fires by pulling down

---

[3] A hint of supernatural intervention, proving the beneficence of the dead hero. Rather similarly in *Decl.* 369: " visus est mihi emergere tumulo vir fortis."

primit: necessitas est lex temporis. Quicquam non
fit legitime pro legibus? Melius cum ipso sepulchro
actum est, in quo notiora sunt iterum arma victricia.
Pro re publica plerumque templa nudantur et in
usum stipendii dona conflamus.

Pars altera. Reum habemus in proelio inertem, in
fuga audacem, turpem non minus patrocinio quam
crimine. Arma sua perdidit: hoc excusare non
poterat nisi aliena rapuisset. Aliena rapuit: hoc
excusare non poterat nisi sua perdidisset. Arma
victricia, arma consecrata dis Manibus, arma quae te
quoque fecerunt virum fortem. Reposui, inquit,
arma. Gloriatur quod non et illa perdiderit. " Non
teneor lege, quia reposui." Tam teneris hercule
quam qui vulneravit aliquem licet vulnus sanaverit,
quam qui subripuit aliquid licet reddiderit deprehensus. Non est hoc illi crimen propter virtutem
donandum: iam gratiam virtuti rettulimus, praemium
consecuta est. Aequos esse nos convenit: unum
virum fortem honoravimus, alterum vindicemus.

houses. Necessity is the law of the moment.—Is anything illegal which is done on the law's behalf?— Even the tomb has benefited: the weapons, victorious a second time, are all the more celebrated.— For the state's sake we often denude temples,[1] melting down offerings to use as pay.

The other side: Our defendant is lazy in battle, bold in flight: both his defence and the charge against him are disgraceful. He lost his own weapons. He could not have found an excuse for this if he had not stolen another's. He stole another's. He could not have found an excuse for this if he had not lost his own.[2]—Weapons that were victorious, weapons dedicated to the shades of the dead, weapons which could make even you a hero.—" I put the arms back." He is boasting that he didn't lose *them* too. " I am not liable under the law, because I put them back." You are just as liable surely as someone who has wounded a man, even though he then heals the wound, as someone who has stolen something, even though he then gets detected and makes restitution.—We must not let him get away with his crime because of his bravery; we have already recognised his courage— it gave him his reward. We must be fair; we have honoured one hero—let us avenge the other.

[1] Cf. *Decl.* 369: " sic Romani gloriose spoliarunt Iovem," where Burman compares Florus 1.22.23 " arma non erant: detracta sunt templis " (after Cannae).
[2] i.e. in each case the excuse is no less shameful than the charge.

V

Privignus Medicus

Abdicavit quidam filium. Abdicatus medici-
nae studuit. Cum pater aegrotaret et medici
negarent posse sanari, sanavit. Reductus est.
Postea aegrotare noverca coepit; desperaverunt   236
medici. Rogat pater filium ut curet novercam.
Nolentem abdicat. Contradicit.

Quo pacto istud evenit, ut abdicatione mea pater
aegrotaret, reditu noverca? Pietati cessere morbi.
Medicinam relinquo, multum laboris, multum vigili-
arum; adice huc et quod qui sanantur ingrati sunt.
Et medicus possum decipi et non possum privignus
excusari. Eundem, inquit, medici morbum esse
dicunt; nempe illi qui negaverunt te posse sanari.
Ego vero cedo domo si fateris illam sic posse sanari.
Timeo fortunam. Imputabitur mihi si quid acciderit.
Ecce tu me non posse non credis. Omnes medici

---

[1] Doctor sons appear in Quintilian 7.2.17, *RLM* pp. 90.13
seq., **333.33** *seq.* But the closest parallel is Lucian's *The
disinherited son* ('Αποκηρυττόμενος), where this theme is treated
at length, the only difference being that in Lucian the disease
is madness. Some detailed parallels are noted below. The
Greek declamation goes carefully into the legality of second
disinheritance, which is not mentioned in Seneca.

[2] Because the father loved his son and pined for him, the
step-mother hated him. The implication is that the son's
treatment would fail with the step-mother, for, as the next

5

THE DOCTOR STEP-SON

A father disinherited his son. The disinherited
son studied medicine. His father fell ill, and the
doctors said he could not be cured; his son cured
him, and was reinstated. Later, his step-
mother fell ill; the doctors gave up hope. The
father asks the son to treat his step-mother.
He refuses and is disinherited: he replies.[1]

For the son: How did it happen that my father fell
ill at my disinheritance, my step-mother at my
return? [2]—Diseases have been overcome by affection.
—I am giving up medicine, and with it much hard
work, much loss of sleep: quite apart from the fact
that people one cures show no gratitude.[3]—As a
doctor I may be wrong; as step-son I can find no
excuses.[4]—"The doctors say it's the same disease."
You mean the doctors who said *you* were incurable.—
I leave home if you claim that she can be cured thus.[5]
—I am afraid of my luck. If anything goes wrong, I
shall get the blame.[6]—Here you are refusing to be-

(closely related) epigram says, diseases may be cured by
affection (cf. below: " It was not as a doctor . . .").

[3] A point rubbed in by Lucian §§1, 13, 19.

[4] i.e. the case against me should anything go wrong would
be unanswerable; cf. below: " I am afraid . . ."

[5] i.e. the same way you were cured. The son is not prepared
to take the risk, and would leave home voluntarily rather than
try.

[6] So exactly Lucian 31: δεδιὼς τὴν τύχην καὶ τὴν παρὰ τῶν
πολλῶν δυσφημίαν.

negant, et nunc diligentiores fuerunt quia in te decepti sunt. Non sum tantae scientiae quantae videor: magnis praeceptoribus opus est; ego abdicatus studui. Quaeris quomodo te sanaverim? Non tibi medicus sed filius profui; desiderio laborabas; gratum tibi erat quidquid meis manibus acceperas. Ut primum intravi, recreatus es: quid in te curandum esset adverti. Haec non eodem morbo laborat. Multa sunt dissimilia: sexus, aetas, animus. Nihil magis aegris prodest quam ab eo curari a quo volunt. Temerariis remediis graves morbi curantur, quibus uti non audeo in noverca.

Extra. Non oportet adulescentem quicquam novercae suscensere; alioqui odit et gaudet. Ferendus est adulescens si se excusat, non est si ulciscitur.

Pars altera. Lugendum est, flendum est; in hoc me servasti? Hostis aliquando vulnus sanavit quod fecerat, ob hoc maxime, quia alius sanare non poterat.

---

[1] Lucian 24: οὐχ υἱὸς ὢν σὸς ἐξέμαθον—and he proceeds to elaborate on his poverty as a student: though in 4 he had said that he had attended the most eminent foreign teachers.

[2] Lucian enlarges on these differences (§§6, 26 *seq.*).

lieve I can do nothing. All the doctors say she can't be saved, and after being mistaken about you they have been all the more careful this time. I'm not so knowledgeable as I seem; one needs eminent teachers—but when I was a student I had been disinherited.[1] You may ask how then I cured *you*. It was not as a doctor that I did you good, but as your son. You were suffering from missing me; you liked everything you received from my hands. As soon as I entered the house, you were a new man—I saw from that what your treatment should be. *She* has a different disease. There are many differences—sex, age, attitude.[2]—Nothing is better for the sick than to be treated by those they *want* to have treating them.—Grave illness requires bold remedies—which I dare not use, on a step-mother.

By the way: The youth ought not to show any annoyance with the step-mother.[3] Otherwise they will say he hates her, and is glad she is ill. The youth can get away with excusing himself—not with taking his revenge.[4]

The other side: I cannot but grieve, cannot but weep: is it for this you saved my life?—There was once a case of an enemy curing a wound he had inflicted, just because no-one else could cure it.[5]—

---

[3] Observe Lucian's care to be agreeable to the step-mother: she is χρηστή (2, cf. 31).

[4] i.e. by refusing out of ill-will.

[5] Telephus was wounded by Achilles, then healed by the rust from Achilles' spear. In gratitude, he guided the Greeks to Troy.

Negant posse sanari; nemo suscipit. Nemo enim vult curationem filio praeripere.

Extra. Pollio dicebat: inter patres et filios id 2³ solum iudex putat licere quod oportet.

VI

INDISCRETI FILIUS ET PRIVIGNUS

Quidam mortua uxore, quae in partu perierat, alteram duxit; puerum rus misit. Ex illa subinde filium sustulit. Utrumque puerum ruri educavit; post longum tempus redierunt similes. Quaerenti matri uter eius sit, non indicat. Accusatur ab ea malae tractationis.

Quid fletis, pueri? Securi estote; non memini. Iam lites sunt, et nondum indicavi. Qualis eris noverca quae sic fieri cupis? Alter tuus est, alter tui frater est, et si per te licuerit neuter privignus est. Dum alterius vis esse mater, utriusque es noverca. Si coegeris, mentiar: non mater sed noverca deci-

---

[1] i.e. (one supposes) there was no legal compulsion on the son to obey, but a strong moral one.

[2] See note on *C*. 3.7.

[3] Many of the epigrams in this declamation depend for their point on the step-mother's reputation, with the Romans especially, as a prodigy of cruelty: " saeviores tragicis novercas " (Quintilian 2.10.5, with an allusion to mythological prototypes such as Ino). They were particularly liable to poison their step-sons: see *C*. 9.5 and Virg. *Georg.* 2.128: " poc-

"They say she is incurable. No-one will take the case." That is because no-one wants to deprive my son of the chance of curing her.

By the way: Pollio said: "Between fathers and sons, the only law in the eyes of a judge is an ought."[1]

6

THE SON AND THE STEP-SON WHO COULD NOT BE TOLD APART

A man, on the death of his wife in childbirth, married another, and sent the child off into the country. Soon he acknowledged a son by his new wife. He brought both boys up in the country. After a long while they returned, looking alike. When the mother asks which hers is, he refuses to tell her. She accuses him of ill-treatment.[2]

For the father: Why weep, children? Don't worry: I don't remember. Here we are at law—and I haven't told her yet.—What sort of a step-mother will you be if this is the way you desire to become one?—One is yours, the other is the brother of yours: and if you will allow it, neither is a step-son.—In wanting to be mother of one, you are a step-mother[3] to both.—If you use force, I shall lie; you will be deceived, not as a mother but as a step-

ula si quando saevae infecere novercae." They appear *passim* in declamation (see esp. *Decl.* 1), for (Jerome *Ep.* 54.15) "omnes . . . communes rhetorum loci in novercam saevissi-mam declamabunt."

pieris. Hos ipsa noluit natura distingui. Indicarem
nisi tam pertinaciter quaereres. " Hic tuus est ":
quid alterum novercalibus oculis intueris? " Ille
tuus est." ... [1] Uni tibi contigit ut habeas privignum
et non sis noverca.

Pars altera. Malae tractationis agit; filius enim
rus ablegatus a patre et educatus est sic ut ignotus
esse posset et matri. Tibi rediit uterque filius, huic
uterque privignus. Eo crudelius filio caret quo propius accessit. Times huius iniquitatem, cum iniquus
ipse magis ames eum cui alterius donare vis matrem [2]
quam cui non vis suam reddere.

Extra. Quod ad colorem pertinet viri, Hispo
Romanius et Silo Pompeius hoc usi sunt: nescio et
ideo non indico. Quidam miscuerunt et utroque usi
dixerunt: nescio, sed etiamsi scirem non indicarem,
quod Latro et Cestius. Sed Asinius Pollio neutrum
colorem probabat. Si dicit, inquit, " nescio," nulli
fidem facit: uxor ipsa non quaereret ab illo nisi ille
scire posset. Dici enim contra virum potest: quaere
a nutrice, a paedagogo. Verisimile non est neminem

---

[1] *Lacuna observed by Thomas.*

---

[1] i.e. I shall say that the step-son is the true son, thus
ensuring that the wife maltreats her own son.
[2] Thus revealing a bad motive in asking.
[3] The parallel retort has slipped out of the text.
[4] A woman could not act in person, and an advocate
presents her case.

mother.[1]—Nature herself wanted these two not to be distinguished from each other.—I should tell you—if you didn't ask so persistently.[2]—" This one is yours "; why do you look at the other with a step-mother's eyes? " That one is yours "; . . .[3]—You are the only woman lucky enough to have a step-son without being a step-mother.

The other side: She [4] sues for ill-treatment; for her son was exiled to the country by his father, and brought up in such a way that even his mother could not get to know him.—Both returned to you as sons, both to her as step-sons.—It is the crueller that she lacks a son, having got so near to it.—You fear her unfairness; but you are unfair yourself—you love the one you wish to provide with the other's mother more than the one to whom you refuse to give his own back.

By the way: As to the husband's *colour*, Romanius Hispo and Pompeius Silo used this one: " I do not know, and so I do not say." Some mixed these up,[5] and used both for their speeches: " I do not know, but even if I did know, I should not say." So Latro and Cestius. But Asinius Pollio disliked both these colours. " If he says, I do not know, he wins no-one's belief; his very wife would not ask him unless he was in a position to know. For one can reply to the husband: Ask the nurse, ask the boy's slave. It

---

[5] This is loosely worded. Bornecque supposed that another *colour* has dropped out of the text before this sentence. But Asinius Pollio's criticisms concern only two *colours*, and the ones we are given.

domi esse qui sciat. Ille autem mixtus color utrumque corrumpit, et ignorantis fidem et non indicantis
fiduciam. Nam cum dicit " etiamsi scirem non indicarem," efficit ut illum scire iudex putet; cum dicit
" nescio," efficit ut videatur indicare debere si scit.
Ipse autem hoc colore usus est, quem aiebat sim-
plicissimum: scio, sed non indico, quia pueris hoc
utile est; et tuo filio: magis amaturus sum eum qui
matrem videbitur non habere.

VII

Tyrannicida Adulter Tyranni

Tyrannicidae praemium.

In adulterio deprehensus a tyranno gladium
extorsit tyranno et occidit eum. Petit praemium. Contradicitur.

Non fecisset tyrannicidium nisi illum tyrannus
armasset. Cuius adulter non fuit qui etiam tyranni
fuit? Inputat nobis quod deprehensus in adulterio 2
mori noluit. Tyrannicida vester iure occidi potuit a

---

[1] The sense is (though the Latin can hardly mean): " that
it is obvious that he recognises he ought . . ."
[2] i.e. I shall favour the step-son, if he is identified. So it is
in the interests of the mother and her true son that the boys
should *not* be identified.

is improbable there is *no-one* in the house who knows. But the mixed *colour* spoils both his credit as not knowing and his self-confidence in not saying. For when he says, Even if I knew, I should not say, he makes the judge think he does know. When he says, I don't know, he ensures that it looks as if he ought to say if he knows." [1] Asinius himself used this *colour*, which he said was the most straightforward: " I know, but I do not say, because this is in the children's interests—even your own son's: I am liable to love more the one who obviously has no mother." [2]

7

THE TYRANNICIDE WHO CUCKOLDED THE TYRANT [3]

A tyrannicide shall have a reward.[4]

A man who was caught in bed with a tyrant's wife snatched the sword from the tyrant's hand and killed him. He asks for the reward. There is an objection.

Against the killer: He would not have killed the tyrant if the tyrant had not armed him.—Whom did he not cuckold if he cuckolded even the tyrant?—He tries to gain credit with us for being caught in adultery—and not wanting to die.—Your precious tyrant-

---

[3] The theme is mentioned by Quintilian 5.10.36. For tyrants, see note on *C.* 1.7.

[4] The reward normally given to Olympic victors, plus " whatever he likes " (Cic. *Inv.* 2.144); cf. *Decl.* 288: " tyrannicida optet quod volet." The custom would be Greek, but Bonner (p. 104) points out that the senate considered rewarding the murderers of Julius Caesar (Appian *Bell. Civ.* 2.127).

tyranno. Certamen in pari condicione contractum
publica fortuna distraxit. Non innocentior vicit, sed
fortior. Tulit secum tyrannus gladium; sic enim
occisuri veniunt. Cur solus ad praemium venis?
Tyrannum certe occidisti cum adultera. Non lori-
cam clipeumve sumpsit, sed tenuem ac perlucidam
vestem; perfusus unguento intravit cubiculum, in
quo tyrannum non esse diligenter agnoverat. Tyrannicida noster ne tyrannum inveniret optavit. Ducat
tyrannicidam in arcem tyrannus, non uxor, odium,
non amor; ascensurus ferat animum, ferat ferrum;
eat illo ubi inveniat tyrannum. Omnia honesta opera
voluntas inchoat, occasio perficit. Saepe honorata
virtus est et ubi eam fefellit exitus; scelera quoque,
quamvis citra exitum subsederint, puniuntur; nec
infelix virtus amittit gloriae titulum, nec gloriam
virtutis intercipit fortuita felicitas. Numquam
maiorum nostrorum prudentia tantis muneribus
tyrannicidium emeret si illud etiam libido promit-
teret. Novo inauditoque more pugnabant, tyrannicida pro adulterio, tyrannus pro pudicitia. Occidisti

---

[1] For "adulterum cum adultera qui deprehenderit dum
utrumque corpus interficiat sine fraude sit" (*C*. 1.4). This
is why the contest was on equal terms—both had a legal right
to kill the other; what made the killer win was his superior
strength, which was lucky for the state but not a sign of his
innocence.

[2] Not, that is, to a room where he had "made quite sure
there was no tyrant."

[3] It is the intention, not the result, that is to be taken into

killer could, legally, have been killed by the tyrant.[1]
A contest that was joined on equal terms was parted
by the fortune of the state. It was not the more
innocent party that won, it was the stronger.—The
tyrant brought a sword with *him*: *that* is how men
come when they *mean* to kill.—Why do you alone ask
for the prize? Surely you had your mistress to help
you when you killed the tyrant.—He took no breast-
plate, no shield—but a thin, transparent robe;
bathed in perfume, he entered the bedroom—where
he had made quite sure there was no tyrant.—Our
tyrant-killer prayed not to meet the tyrant.—A
tyrant-killer should be led to the castle by the
thought of the tyrant, not his wife, by hate, not love.
When he is to climb up there, let him bring a purpose
with him, and a sword: let him go where he can
expect to find the tyrant.[2]—All good deeds are begun
by will, only *completed* by opportunity. Often
bravery has been honoured even when the outcome
has let it down; crimes, too, get punished even if
they collapse short of their aim. Unlucky virtue
does not lose its title to glory, but fortuitous success
does not appropriate the glory that virtue deserves.[3]—
Our ancestors were sensible: they would not have
paid such rewards for tyrannicide if even lust gave an
opportunity to win them.—It was a novel and un-
precedented fight they fought, the tyrant-killer
defending adultery, the tyrant chastity.—You killed

account in judging a deed. Cf. Sen. *Ben.* 7.15.2: " semper
contra fortunam luctata virtus etiam citra effectum propositi
operis enituit. Plus praestitit qui fugientes occasiones secutus
est . . . quam quem sine ullo sudore gratum prima fecit
occasio."

tu maritum, fortuna tyrannum. Tyrannum cadere
rei publicae volo: occidat illum civis iratus, misceat
maledicta vulneribus, qualia in adulterum maritus
⟨iacere solet, non qualia in maritum⟩ [1] adulter. Ab [2]
adulterae osculis ad praemium curris: nolo tyrannicida imitetur antequam occidat tyrannum. Populus
Romanus veneno vinci hostem noluit, proditione 240
noluit. Honorabo subitum tyrannicidium, non
honorabo fortuitum, non coactum.

Pars altera. Non habebas, inquit, ferrum. Quid
enim tyranno profuit quod habuit? In eo qui inermis
ad tyrannum venit non virtus minor est sed periculum maius. Non quaeras quid in arcem tulerim;
tyrannicidium detuli. Non est gladius meus; sed
manus mea est, sed animus meus est, sed consilium,
sed periculum, sed tyrannicidium meum est. Adulterium vocas quo effectum est ne quis timeat adulterium? Diligenter arce munita occasionem
requirens temptavi servos, temptavi amicos; per
uxorem solam refulsit occasio. Non putavi adulterium uxorem tyranni polluere, sicut nec homicidium
tyrannum occidere. Ferrum in arcem ferre periculosum erat, invenire facile. Si tyrannum, inquam,

---

[1] *Supplied by Gertz.*
[2] adulter. Ab *ed. after Gertz:* adulterat ab.

the husband, chance killed the tyrant.—I want the
tyrant to fall a victim to the state; let him be killed
by an angry citizen, who mixes curses with his blows
—the kind a husband usually hurls at an adulterer,
not an adulterer at a husband.—You run from your
mistress's kisses to ask for the reward; I don't want
the tyrant-killer to behave like the tyrant [1] before he
kills him.—The Roman people did not want their
enemy defeated by poison or treachery.[2]—I will
reward the impulsive killing of a tyrant—but not an
accidental killing, not an enforced killing.

The other side: " You had no sword." What good
did having one do the tyrant? The man who goes
unarmed to meet the tyrant is not the less brave—he
runs the more danger.—Don't enquire what I took
up to the castle: what I brought down was my deed.
—The sword is not mine—but the hand is mine, mine
the intention, the plan, the danger, the killing.—Do
you call adultery something that resulted in no-one
having to fear adultery?—The castle was well forti-
fied; I sought out an opportunity, tampering with
slaves and friends; the wife was the only opportunity
that shone out.—I didn't regard it as adultery to
seduce a tyrant's wife, just as it is no murder to kill a
tyrant. It was dangerous to take a sword into the
castle—but easy to find one there. " If I find the

[1] i.e. by womanising, a characteristic of declamatory
tyrants. Cf. below " Do you call . . .," and also *C.* 5.8
" nulla rapietur."
[2] With particular allusion to the refusal of the senate to
have Pyrrhus poisoned and to defeat the Faliscans by treachery: two stories linked by Frontinus *Strat.* 4.4. and Val. Max.
6.5.1.

invenero, obvia quaelibet res telum erit. Certe
semper secum solet habere ferrum tyrannus. Gladius
inter duos fortioris est. Quam sollicitus adulter fui,
ne non deprehenderer!

VIII

Patronus Operas Remissas Repetens

Per vim metumque gesta irrita sint.

Bello civili patronus victus et proscriptus ad
libertum confugit. Receptus est ab eo et rogatus ut operas remitteret. Remisit consignatione
facta. Restitutus indicit operas. Contradicit.

Patronus a liberto restitutionem peto. Si pacisci 241
tunc a me voluisses operas, spopondissem. Bona
bello perdidi, ad restitutionem nudus veni; nunc
libertorum operas desidero. Profer tabellas illa pro-
scriptionis tabula crudeliores: persequebatur illa
quos vicerat, hae persecutae sunt quos receperant; in

---

[1] " Generally agreed to be a clause (put into statute-form)
of a genuine praetorian edict " (Bonner, 114). Much turns
(as in *C*. 9.3) on what exactly counts as *vis*.

[2] That is, outlawed and stripped of his property. Doubtless
the triumviral proscription of 43–2 B.C. (of which the principal
victim was Cicero: see *S*. 6 and 7) is in question, though Sulla
also employed this method of purging his enemies in 82 B.C.

[3] Sen. *Ben*. 3.25 tells the story of a slave who concealed and
impersonated her mistress. See also Val. Max. 6.8.

[4] The former owner (*patronus*, here for convenience translated " patron ") could, beside automatic rights over a man
he had freed, contract on manumission that the freedman

tyrant," I said to myself, " anything to hand will serve
as a weapon. Anyway, a tyrant generally has a
sword about him. Where two men fight, the sword
goes to the stronger."—How anxious a seducer I was
—anxious I might not get caught!

8

THE PATRON WHO TRIED TO GET BACK SERVICES
HE HAD RENOUNCED

Things done through force or fear are not
to stand.[1]

A patron who was on the losing side in the civil
war and proscribed [2] took refuge with a freedman
of his.[3] The freedman took him in, and asked
him to waive the services [4] he owed him. He did
waive them, in writing. Restored to his estate,
he demands the services. The freedman makes
objection.

For the patron: I am patron, and I seek restitution
from my freedman.[5]—If, on that occasion, *you* had
wanted to bargain for services from *me*, I should have
promised them.[6]—I lost my property in the war, and
it is naked that I have come to seek restitution. *Now*
I need the services of my freedman.—Produce the
document—it is more cruel than the notorious proscription list. *That* harried the defeated, *this* has

should perform services (*operae*), domestic (*officiales*) or skilled
(*fabriles*). See A. M. Duff, *Freedmen in the Early Roman
Empire* (Oxford, 1928), 44 *seq*.
  [5] Paradox!
  [6] So great, that is, was my fear.

illa ultio fuit, in his perfidia; denique illa iam desiit,
hae perseverant. Non mea, inquit, sed aliena vis
fuit. Aeque dignus est poena qui ipse vim adhibet et
qui ab alio admota ad lucrum suum utitur. In hunc
primum incidi et, dum timeo ne offenderem, secutus
sum hoc exigentem. Non recepit me, sed inclusit.
Nihil est venali misericordia turpius.

Pars altera. Nihil tibi opus est potestas: scis tibi
illum parere, etiam cum cogi non potest. Quaslibet
indicas operas, numquam tamen indices tam pericu-
losas quam indixisti. Habeo iudicia tua; bene de
servo iudicasti: manu misisti; bene de liberto:
proscriptus mihi potissimum te commisisti. Si
noluissem patronum habere, potui. Unus ex pro-
scriptis fuisti qui tunc posses etiam rogari. Resti-
tutio tibi proscriptionem remisit, non quidquid in
proscriptione gessisti rescidit.

Extra. Omnes invecti sunt in libertum. Varius
Geminus et Otho Iunius egerunt lenius, ut patronus
remissurus videretur operas si obtinuisset. Nam 242M
Otho dixit: Sine me iudicio meo videri remi-
sisse; faciam, remittam. Quid me sic times, tam-

---

[1] i.e. the man responsible for the proscription.

[2] Cf. Sen. *Ben.* 4.25.3: " pudeat ullum venale esse beneficium."

[3] From the episode during the proscription.

[4] i.e. that of sheltering him during the proscription. That
would hardly be an *opera*, though it might be represented to
be part of the freedman's *officium* (for which see Duff, 40).

[5] The rest being dead. The freedman emphasises his own
services.

harried a guest. That was an act of revenge, this is an act of treachery. That is no longer in effect, this still continues.—"*I* did not use force—someone else [1] did." The man who applies force himself and the man who makes use to his own profit of force applied by another are equally deserving of punishment.— This man was the first I came across. I was afraid of offending him, and I went along with him even when he demanded this.—He didn't let me in: he shut me in.—Nothing is more disgusting than pity that demands a price.[2]

The other side: You do not need power. You know [3] that he obeys you even when he cannot be coerced.—You may impose whatever services you like—you will never impose such dangerous ones as those you have already insisted on.[4]—I have your judgements. You judged well of your slave: you freed him. You judged well of your freedman: when you were proscribed, it was to me that you chose to entrust yourself.—If I had wished to have no patron, I could have rid myself of him.—You were the only one of the proscribed who at that period was capable even of being begged.[5]—Your restitution has invalidated your proscription, but it has not annulled anything you did while you were proscribed.

By the way: Everyone went for the freedman. Varius Geminus and Junius Otho pleaded more calmly, intending it to seem as if the patron would waive the services if he won the case. Indeed, Otho said: " Let it look as if I waived them on my own decision. I will do it—I will waive them. Why fear

quam invitus promiserim? Contra Cestius ait:
Tunc eiusmodi utendum coloribus ubi verendum est
ne videamur rem duram postulare, ubi contra
honestam personam promissione iudex molliore fal-
lendus est. Quid in hac persona veremur et causa
nisi hoc unum, quod ex hoc colore metuendum est,
ne, si volumus hoc remittere, et voluisse videamur?

me—as if I have promised against my will?"[1]
Cestius, on the other hand, said that one should use
colours of this kind where there is a danger that we
may be thought to be making a harsh demand, where
to get the better of an honourable character the judge
has to be misled by a promise of gentler things to
come. "But what is there to be afraid of with this
character and this case?—except only the danger
arising from this *colour*, that it may look as though we
were willing[2] to waive before if we are willing to
waive now."

[1] As I did last time.
[2] i.e. and were not coerced into it.

EXCERPTA

CONTROVERSIARUM

LIBRI QUINTI

I

LAQUEUS INCISUS

Inscripti maleficii sit actio.

Quidam naufragio facto, amissis tribus liberis et uxore incendio domus, suspendit se. Praecidit illi quidam ex praetereuntibus laqueum. A liberato reus fit maleficii.

Tres, inquit, liberos perdidi. Utinam et illos servare potuissem! Vive; mutantur vices felicitatis humanae: proscriptus aliquando proscripsit. Victi fugiunt, proscripti latent, naufragi natant. Amisi, inquit, uxorem, liberos, patrimonium. Tu putabas te ea condicione accepisse, ne perderes? Ludit de suis Fortuna muneribus et quae dedit aufert, quae abstulit reddit, nec umquam tutius est illam experiri

470

EXCERPTS FROM BOOK 5

1

The Cut Noose

An action may lie for an offence not specified
in the law.[1]

A man who had been shipwrecked, and had
lost three children and his wife in a fire at his
house, hung himself.   A passer-by cut the noose.
He is accused of an offence by the man he saved.

For the passer-by: " I have lost three children."
Would that I could have saved *them* too!—Live:
human happiness has its vicissitudes: the proscribed
have sometimes themselves proscribed.[2]—The defeated fly, the proscribed lie hidden, the shipwrecked
swim to shore.—" I have lost my wife, children,
estate."   Do you think that you received them on
terms that precluded your losing them?   Fortune
plays with its gifts, taking away what it gave, returning what it took away: it is never more safe to make

[1] Cf. *C.* 3 pr. 17, with note: Bonner, 86–7, is perhaps too
insistent that Quintilian 7.4.36 does not prove the fictitiousness
of this law.
[2] With a probable allusion to Marius (cf. *C.* 1.1.5).

quam cum locum iniuriae non habet. Cn. Pompeius in Pharsalia victus acie vixit: maius tu tuum putas esse naufragium? Crassus vixit: et non privatas perdiderat, sed publicas opes. Omnia tibi fortuna abstulit, sed spem reliquit. Tolle spem 244M hominibus, nemo victus retemptabit arma, nemo infeliciter experta negotiatione alios appetet quaestus, nemo naufragus vivet. Spes est ultimum adversarum rerum solacium. Ut viveres, natasti. Miseritus sum nec in te amplius quam periculum cogitavi; non attendi incendium, non orbitatem, aut, si attendi, memineram te post illa vixisse. Non visus est mihi moriendi animum habere: elegerat locum in quo interpellari posset.

Pars altera. Tot ille fundorum dominus aliena arbore suspendo laqueum. De fortuna nihil queror: mori permittit. " Nunc " inquit " morere." Iniuria est ut qui meo arbitrio debui tuo moriar. Amisi uxorem, liberos, patrimonium; fortuna mihi nihil praeter laqueum reliquit, iste nec laqueum. Sumpsi instrumenta mortis solitudinem et laqueum, alterum aptum morituro, alterum misero. Quisquis intervenis, si amicus es, defle, si inimicus es, specta. Cum

---

[1] Neither was a compelling instance. Pompey died soon after Pharsalus, Crassus even sooner after Carrhae. But doubtless the point is that neither committed suicide.

[2] An idea often recurring in the younger Seneca; e.g. *Ep.*

trial of it than when it has no more scope for harm.—
Pompey was defeated in battle at Pharsalus, yet
lived. Do you think your shipwreck worse than
that? Crassus lived, though he had lost not his
private fortune but the state's.[1]—Fortune has taken
everything from you—but it has left hope. Remove
men's hopes—and no-one who has been defeated will
resort to arms again, no-one who has failed in business
will have the heart to pursue further gain, no-one
who has been shipwrecked will survive. Hope is the
last solace of adversity.—It was in order to live that
you swam.—I pitied you, and had thought only for
your danger; I did not bother about the fire or your
bereavement—or if I did I remembered you had gone
on living after those events.—I didn't think he intended to die: he had chosen a place where he could
be interrupted.

The other side: Once the owner of so many estates,
I hang my noose from a tree that belongs to another.
—I make no complaints about fortune—it allows me
to die.[2]—" Die *now*." It is a wrong done me if I have
to die at your will when I should have died at mine.—
I have lost wife, children, estate; my luck left me
nothing but the noose—and this man left me not even
the noose.—I took as the means of my death solitude
and a noose, the one suitable for a man proposing to
die, the other for a man encompassed by misery.—
Whoever you may be who come on the scene, weep
if you are a friend, look on if you are an enemy.[3]—*I*

24.11: " adeo mors timenda non est ut beneficio eius nihil
timendum sit."

[3] But in neither case interfere.

a me iste accusetur, graviorem de me quam de reo
ferte sententiam: ego ut moriar, iste ne prohibeat.
Ne haec narrarem mori volui. Praecidit remedium
meum. Si qua est fides, non enatavi, sed eiectus
sum. Nihil iam timebam nisi vivere. Domus meae
fata claudo, nullo miserior quam quod ultimus
morior. Cui me vitae reservas? Ut aedificem?
aspice incendium. Ut navigem? aspice naufragium.
Ut educem? aspice sepulchrum. In tam calamitosa
domo feliciores fuistis, uxor et liberi: vobis mori
contigit.

II

Gener Inimici Divitis

Pauper, cum haberet filium et divitem inimicum filiam habentem, peregre profectus est.
Rumor fuit de morte eius. Filius cum divite in
gratiam rediit et eius filiam duxit. Reversus
pater cogit illum uxorem repudiare; nolentem
abdicat.

Nemo quicquam facile credit quo credito dolendum
sit. Ego diu non credidi de nuptiis tuis. Desertor
patris, inimici cliens, uxoris mancipium, non flevisti
patrem, non quaesisti; sic inimico placuisti. Rumor,

am accusing *him*; but you must pass a harsher verdict on me than on the accused—that *I* should die, that *he* should not prevent me.—It was so as not to have to tell this story that I wanted to die.—He cut through my solace.—If you will believe me, I did not swim to safety: I was cast up.—I had no further fear—except of life.—I bring the story of my house to a close, in nothing more wretched than that I am the last to die. —What life is it you preserve me to live? To build? Look at the fire. To go to sea? Look at the wreck. To rear children? Look at the tomb. In so disaster-ridden a house, my wife and children were more fortunate—*they* succeeded in dying.

2

THE SON-IN-LAW OF A RICH ENEMY

A poor man had a son, and an enemy [1] who was a rich man with a daughter. He set out overseas. There was a rumour that he had died. The son came to be on good terms again with the rich man, and married his daughter. The father returned and is trying to force his son to divorce his wife. He refuses, and is disinherited.

For the father: No-one is quick to believe where belief must bring pain. *I* did not believe for a long time that you had married.—Traitor to your father, client of an enemy, slave to your wife, you did not weep for your father or look for him; that is how you

---

[1] Such enmities frequently occur in declamation: cf. *C.* 10.1; Petr. 48.5; and the similar theme in *Decl.* p. 48.25 Ritter.

inquit, fuerat te decessisse. Mirabar si talem uxorem vivo patre habere potuisses. Non quaeris ubi perierim? Mors mea tibi debet esse suspecta: inimicum habeo. Quis alius hanc famam potuit inmittere nisi qui me vivo filiam conlocare non poterat? Non times ne inter ipsas nuptias tuas patris ossa referantur? Tot servi secuntur, tot liberti, tot clientes, ut quidquid dixerit rumor sit. Fabricius aurum a Pyrrho accipere noluit; beatior fuit ille animo quam ille regno. Plures insidias in itinere fugi, et factum dives quod faciendum mandaverat credidit.

Pars altera. Vanum gloriae genus odium divitiarum. Mortales esse inimicitiae debent. Scipio Gracchi inimicus et tamen postea socer. Cuius vitio 246M inimicitiae contractae sint apparet: ille amat filium tuum, tu nec tuum.

Extra. Saenianus rem stultissimam dixit: dives me semper contempsit, numquam nisi pro mortuo habuit. Ut aliquid et ipse simile Saeniano dicam, post hanc sententiam semper Saenianum pro mortuo habui.

found favour with my enemy.—" There was a rumour you had died." I would be surprised if you could have taken such a wife while your father lived.—No enquiries about the place of my death? My death ought to arouse suspicions in you—I have an enemy. —Who else could have put the story about unless it was one who could not marry off his daughter while I was alive?—Aren't you afraid your father's bones may be brought back on your wedding-day?—He has so many slaves, freedmen and clients in his retinue that whatever he says becomes a rumour.[1]—Fabricius did not want to take gold from Pyrrhus; he was more fortunate in his character than Pyrrhus in his empire.[2] —I had many ambushes to escape on my way: and the rich man believed that what he had ordered to be done had been done.

The other side: Hatred of wealth is an empty kind of fame.—Enmities ought to be mortal.—Scipio [3] was Gracchus' enemy—but later on his father-in-law.— It's obvious whose fault it was that the enmity grew up—*he* loves your son, *you* don't love even your own.

By the way: Saenianus said a very stupid thing: " The rich man always despised me, always counted me as dead." To rival Saenianus' saying, after this epigram *I* always counted Saenianus as dead.

---

[1] A rumour being " the agreement of the state and, as it were, the testimony of the people " (Quintilian 5.3); the retinue was so large that it was equivalent to a whole people.
[2] Cf. *C.* 2.1.29.
[3] See Index of Names s. vv. P. Cornelius Scipio Africanus major and Ti. Sempronius Gracchus. For the marriage, see Liv. 38.57.

III

FRATRES PANCRATIASTAE

Malae tractationis sit actio.

Quidam duos filios pancratiastas instituit;
eduxit ad Olympia. Cum conpositi essent ut
simul pugnarent, accessit ad pugnantes pater et
ait abdicaturum se si quis perdiderit. Con-
mortui sunt iuvenes et decreti his divini honores.
Reus fit pater malae tractationis ab uxore.

Tertius sine sorte pugnasti et utrumque vicisti.
Stetit cruentus pater; iam perierant et adhuc mina-
batur. Moriuntur non alter ab altero sed uterque a
patre. Misera mater odisse non potest qui filium
suum occidit. Iuvenes invicti, nisi habuissent
patrem. Pii iuvenes nec parricidium patri negare
potuistis. Vincere propter parricidium nolunt, vinci
propter abdicationem. "Abdico eum qui victus 247
erit." Demens, meliorem abdicaturus es. Invoco
Iovem, cuius Olympia parricidiis polluta[1] sunt.

---

[1] polluta *Bursian:* absoluta.

---

[1] The *pankration* was an event combining boxing and
wrestling.
[2] Cf. *C.* 3.7 with note.
[3] i.e. the father.
[4] Which would normally be a safety-valve for her emotions;

478

3

THE BROTHERS WHO WERE PANCRATIASTS [1]

An action may lie for maltreatment.[2]

A man trained his two sons as pancratiasts, and presented them to compete at the Olympic games. They were paired off to fight each other. The father went to the combatants and said he would disinherit the one who lost. The youths were both killed together, and had divine honours decreed them. The father is accused of maltreatment by his wife.

For the wife: You[3] were the third combatant, though you drew no lot: and you defeated the other two.—The father stood there, covered with blood; they had already perished—and still his threats continued.—They died, not at each other's hands, but both at their father's.—Poor mother—she cannot hate the killer of her son.[4]—Youths whom no-one would have defeated—if they had had no father.—These dutiful youths could refuse nothing to their father—even parricide.—They do not want to win—it means parricide, or to lose—it means disinheritance.—" I disinherit the one who loses." Madman, your intention is to disinherit the better of the two.[5]—I invoke Jupiter, whose Olympic festival has been profaned by parricide.

in this case the killer of each son is the other, and neither is guilty.

[5] The better one would be the one whose *pietas* (and fear of killing) restrained him from the effort necessary for victory.

Pars altera. Non facturus dixi et, si facturus, pro gloria dixi. Non debeo in invidia solus esse, cum luctus communis sit. Omnes aiebant fratres conlusuros. Minatus sum non ut filiis metum inponerem sed ut populo satis facerem.

IV

Damnatus Parricidii Alligans Fratrem

Qui falsum testimonium dixerit vinciatur apud eum in quem dixerit.

Ex duobus filiis profectus est cum uno pater; adulescens solus rediit. Accusatus est a fratre parricidii et damnatus. Diebus festis intercedentibus poena ex lege dilata est; rediit pater. Accusavit damnatus fratrem falsi testimonii et obtinuit et vinxit. Cogit pater ut vinctum solvat; nolentem abdicat.

Falsum, inquit, in fratrem testimonium dixit. Si vis grave illius crimen facere, te exorabilem praesta. Crudelis in fratrem miraris si in te parricidium creditum est? Ergo ego duos filios habere non possum?

---

[1] i.e. a real fight.

[2] The law is certainly not Greek, and probably not Roman either (Bonner, 92).

[3] Bornecque compares Suet. *Tib.* 61: under Tiberius' reign of terror " no day was free from punishments, not even holy

The other side: I did not say it with the intention of acting—and, if I did intend, it was for their glory that I spoke.—I ought not get all the odium: our grief is common to us both.—They all said the brothers would collude. I threatened not in order to intimidate my sons but in order to give the populace what it wanted.[1]

4

THE CONVICTED PARRICIDE WHO KEPT HIS BROTHER A PRISONER

The false witness shall be the prisoner of the man he slandered.[2]

Of two sons, one set off with his father. Only the youth returned. He was accused by his brother of parricide and convicted. A festival intervening, the punishment was delayed, according to the law's requirements.[3] The father came back. The convicted son accused his brother of false witness, won the case and imprisoned him. His father tries to force him to release his prisoner. On his refusal, he disinherits him.

For the father: " He gave false witness against his brother." If you want to add weight to the charge against him, show that you can be won over. If you are cruel to your brother, can you wonder if people thought you a parricide?—Can I not then have *two*

and sacred days." See also G. Wissowa, *Religion und Kultus der Römer*[2], 432.

Adulescens, iam potes et parricidium facere. Alli- 248.
gatus est alter filius quia non revertebar, alter quia
redii. Numquam solves fratrem? Si talis es, nihil
testis mentitus est: parricida es. Non impio in te
sed in patrem pio animo dixit: suspectum habuit
quod reliqueras patrem. Inter catenas filii mei
iaceo, eodem clausus ergastulo. Ingrate, testem
tuum simul alligasti.

Pars altera. Meo periculo solutus, meo alligatus.
Vix solvi poterat si testimonium falsum pro fratre
dixisset. Parricidium de patre finxit, de fratre commisit. Venisse patrem mihi carnifex nuntiavit.
Parricida sum, sicut obicitur, ⟨si⟩ [1] huic leviter irascor.
Miraris si eum fratrem alligare possum qui me potuit
occidere? Ingrata erat ipsa poenae meae dilatio:
expectare gravius videbatur quam pati; imaginabar
mihi culleum, serpentis, profundum.

[1] *Supplied by Bursian.*

sons?—Young man, now we can see you are capable
of parricide too.—One son went to prison because I
hadn't returned, the other because I did.—Will you
never release your brother? If you are this sort of
man, the witness told no lies: you *are* a parricide.—
When he spoke it was not out of cruelty to you but
out of kindness to his father; he regarded it as
suspicious that you had left your father behind.—I
wear my son's chains, I lie shut in the same slaves'
prison: ungrateful boy, you have bound *your* witness
as well.[1]

The other side: He was free to my peril—and to my
peril he was imprisoned.[2]—He could hardly be
released if he had given false witness on his brother's
behalf.[3]—He fabricated a parricide about his father—
and committed one on his brother.—It was the executioner who announced my father's return to me.—I
am a parricide as they charge me if my anger with
this man is only mild.—Do you wonder that I am
capable of making a prisoner of a brother who was
capable of killing me?—The delay in my punishment
was itself unwelcome; it seemed worse to wait than
to suffer; I pictured to myself the sack, the serpents,
the deep.[4]

[1] The father (" your witness ": his return has disproved the
parricide) so much sympathises with his captive son that he
represents himself as captive too.
[2] He gave false witness when free; his captivity resulted in
the father's accusation.
[3] Let alone against him.
[4] For the punishment of parricide, see *C*. 3.2 n.

V

Domus Cum Arbore Exusta

Qui sciens damnum dederit, quadruplum solvat,
qui inscius, simplum.

Dives pauperem vicinum rogavit ut sibi
arborem venderet quam sibi dicebat obstare.
Pauper negavit; dives incendit platanum, cum
qua et domus arsit. Pro arbore pollicetur quadruplum, pro domo simplum.

Excitatus flammarum sono, vicinorum primo fidem
imploravi. Arbor ramis excurrentibus totam domum
texerat. "Non potest exorari; incendatur." Est 249
hoc inpotentiae, sine fine concupiscere, sine modo
irasci. "Non potest expugnari precibus; expellatur
ignibus." Nihil inter te et pauperem interest, si iure
agamus. Liceat et pauperem gaudere prospectu.
Vos possidetis agros, urbium fines, urbesque domibus impletis; intra aedificia vestra undas ac nemora
conprehenditis. Nihil lautius occurrit oculis tuis
quam ruinae meae. Domum perdidi, qui carere ne
arbuscula quidem poteram. Deliciis tuis, dives,
ardebimus? Oculis voluptas incendio quaeritur et

---

[1] The law is discussed by Bonner, 117–19, who feels able to
relate it to true Roman legislation before 287 B.C.

[2] Of whom the rich man was of course one.

[3] And he, it seemed, enjoyed the view of the tree.

5

The Burning of the House and the Tree

The penalty for malicious damage is to pay four
times the amount of the loss, for unintentional
damage only the amount of the loss.[1]

A rich man asked his poor neighbour to sell him
a tree which he said blocked his view. The poor
man refused. The rich man burned down the
plane-tree, and the house went up in flames at
the same time. For the tree he is ready to pay
four times the amount, for the house only the
amount.

For the poor man: Awaked by the sound of the
flames, I first begged help from my neighbours.[2]—
The tree had covered the whole house with its spread-
ing branches.—" He cannot be won over; let it be
burned." This is a sign of immoderation, to covet
without end, to be angry without limit. " He cannot
be stormed by entreaties; let him be driven out by
flames." There is no difference at law between you
and a poor man. May a poor man, too, be allowed to
enjoy the view.[3]—You rich possess for fields the
territory of cities, and cities you fill with your houses.
Within your buildings you confine waters and groves.[4]
Yet nothing in your eyes gives the impression of
luxury more than the ruins that were my home.—I
have lost my house, though I wasn't ready to do

[4] Cf. below: " fictive groves and fishponds like straits,"
with my note on *C.* 2.1.13 and Sen. *Thy.* 464–5.

prospectus ignibus relaxatur. " Prospectui ob-
stabat." Quid? inambulantibus nobis non obstant
servorum catervae? excitati in immensam altitudinem
parietes lucem non impediunt? infinitis porrectae
spatiis ambulationes et urbium solo aedificatae
domus non nos prope a publico excludunt? Sub hac
arbuscula imaginabar divitum silvas. Quantum
perdidi quem fatetur iratus inimicus plus perdidisse
quam voluit! Non iniquum postulo: eius damno
desinat incendium cuius consilio coepit. Scilicet ut
domus ad caelum omne conversae brumales aestus
habeant, aestiva frigora, et non suis vicibus intra
istorum penates agatur annus, ⟨ut sint⟩ [1] in summis 250
culminibus mentita nemora et navigabilium pisci-
narum freta, arata quondam populis rura singulorum
nunc ergastulorum sunt latiusque vilici quam reges
imperant. Maria proiectis molibus submoventur.
Nesciebas quanta sit potentia ignium, quam inrevo-
cabilis, quemadmodum totas absumat urbes, quam
levibus initiis oriantur incendia? Etiamsi partem
damni dare noluisti, si tamen voluisti partem, in
totum, quasi prudens dederis, tenendus es; ex toto
enim noluisse debet qui inprudentia defenditur. Si

[1] ut sint *Gertz: omitted by M (some manuscripts give* agunt).

---

[1] Cf. the lampoon quoted in Suet. *Ner.* 39.2: " Roma
domus fiet; Veios migrate, Quirites, / si non et Veios occupat
ista domus."
[2] A feature stressed in later descriptions of rich men's villas,

without even a little tree.—Rich man, are we to burn
for your whim? Here is fire being used to give the
eye pleasure, to clear a view.—" It blocked the view."
Well, don't hordes of slaves block *our* way when we
walk the streets? Do not walls, raised immensely
high, impede the light? Promenades stretching
over vast distances, houses on the ground of whole
cities [1]—do not these virtually keep us out of public
places?—Beneath this little tree I used to picture to
myself the forests owned by the rich.—How great my
loss!—an angry enemy agrees that I have lost more
than he intended.—What I ask is only fair: let the
fire's end bring loss to the man who planned its start.
—Yes, it is so that houses facing every quarter of the
heavens [2] should have heat in winter and cold in
summer, so that in these men's homes the passage of
the year should not bring its normal changes, so that
on the highest roofs there should be fictive groves and
fishponds like straits on which boats can sail, it is for
all this that country once ploughed by whole peoples
belongs to single slave-farms and bailiffs have wider
sway than kings.—Masonry is thrown in—and seas
are cleared out of the way.[3]—Didn't you know the
strength of fire, how irreversible it is, how it con-
sumes whole cities, from what trivial beginnings
blazes can start?—You did not intend one part of the
loss: but if you intended the other part, you are
liable for the whole as if you had caused it purposely;
a man who defends himself by a plea of non-intention
must not have intended the act even in part.—If you

e.g. Stat. *Silv.* 2.2.45–7, and many remarks in Plin. *Ep.* 2.17
and 5.6.
[3] See *C.* 2.1.13 n.

fatereris te scientem ianuam incendisse, si unum
tignum,[1] puto, tota domus intellegeretur ex parte;
nec enim quisquam omnia incendit, sed unam aliquam rem, ex qua surgat in omnia se sparsurus ignis.
Atqui pars domus est arbor quae in domo est.

Pars altera. Pestilentem mihi faciebat domum
arbor: caelum omne per quod salubris spiritus venire
posset obduxerat. Rogavi pauperem et dixi: nihil
tibi nocet arbor recisa, mihi plurimum non recisa.
Quid ad te illi rami pertinent qui extra domum sunt?
Quasdam partes domus meae radices [2] premebant;
iam etiam quosdam parietes moverant. Scitis quanta
vis sit arborum; muros discutiunt.

VI

Raptus in Veste Muliebri

Inpudicus contione prohibeatur.

Adulescens speciosus sponsionem fecit muliebri veste se exiturum in publicum. Processit;   25
raptus est ab adulescentibus decem. Accusavit
illos de vi et damnavit. Contione prohibitus a
magistratu reum facit magistratum iniuriarum.

[1] si unum tignum *appears in M after* parte *below.*
[2] radices *Warmington:* rami.

---

[1] That is, if you set fire to a house purposely, you start the
fire by burning a single part. If then the rich man intended
to burn the tree, he must be supposed to have intended the
burning of the whole house. Objections might be found to
this argument.

acknowledged that you set fire intentionally to a door, or a single timber, I suppose the whole house would be understood in the part; for one doesn't set fire to everything, only some one thing from which a fire can arise—a fire which will spread to the whole. But a tree in a house is part of a house.[1]

The other side: The tree was making my house un-healthy. It had shut off all the sky [2] that could give passage to sound air. I asked the poor man, saying: "The tree does you no harm if it is cut down, it does me a lot of harm if it is not."—What have you to do with those branches that are outside the house?— The roots were endangering parts of my house; they had already caused some of the walls to shift. You know what trees can do; they shatter walls.

6

THE MAN WHO WAS RAPED IN WOMEN'S CLOTHES

An unchaste man shall be barred from speaking in public.[3]

A handsome youth betted he would go out in public in women's clothes. He did so, and got raped by ten youths. He accused them of violence,[4] and had them convicted. Forbidden by a magistrate to speak to the people, he accuses the magistrate of injuring him.[5]

[2] For trees as an obstruction to the view, see *Dig.* 8.2.17 and 43.27.1.
[3] There are both Greek and Roman parallels to this law (Bonner, 105).
[4] See *C.* 9.5 n.
[5] See *C.* 4.1 n.

Muliebrem vestem sumpsit, capillos in feminae habitum conposuit, oculos puellari lenocinio circumdedit, coloravit genas. Non creditis? at qui non crediderant, victi sunt sponsione. Et hoc de sponsione forsitan venerit, ut auderet inpudicus contionari. Date illi vestem puellarem, date noctem: rapietur. Sic illum vestis sumpta decuit ut videretur non tunc primum sumpsisse. Facta totius adulescentiae remitto, una nocte contentus sum: sic imitatus est puellam ut raptorem inveniret. Numquid cecidi? numquid carmen famosum conposui, aut, ut proprium genus iniuriae tuae dicam, numquid te rapui? Apud patres nostros, qui forensia stipendia auspicabantur nefas putabatur brachium toga exserere. Quam longe ab his moribus aberant qui tam verecunde etiam virtute utebantur! Constat hunc stupratum, cum damnati sint qui rapuerunt.

Pars altera. Constat semper gravem, semper serium fuisse; sed hoc iocis adulescentium factum est. Ceterum tam nota erat verecundia eius ut nemo iam sine sponsione crediderit.

---

[1] i.e. in court.

[2] Cf. Gaius 3.220: "*Iniuria* is committed not only when someone is struck . . . but also . . . if one writes . . . in

For the magistrate: He put on women's clothes,
made his hair look like a woman's, put on the alluring
eye-shadow girls use, coloured his cheeks. Don't
you believe it? Yet it was those who had disbelieved
him who lost the bet.—Perhaps this too is the result
of a bet, that he should dare to speak in public,[1]
though unchaste.—Give him girls' clothes, give him
darkness—he will get raped.—He was so suited by
the dress he put on that it looked as though it wasn't
the first time he had put it on.—I pass over everything
he did as a youth—I am satisfied to talk only of a
single night; he imitated a girl to such effect that he
found someone to rape him.—Have I struck a blow?
Have I written a slanderous lampoon, or, to mention
your particular type of injury, have I raped you?[2]—
In our fathers' time, those who were starting off their
career in the courts were thought to be acting out-
rageously if they poked an arm out of their toga.[3]
How far from such a character[4] were those who were
so modest even in the use they made of something
good!—It is agreed that this man was violated—those
who raped him have been convicted.[5]

The other side: It is agreed that he was always
grave, always serious; but *this* was the outcome of a
youthful prank.—Yet his modesty was so well-known
that no-one would believe his challenge without a bet.

defamation of another or follows a matron or youth, and in
many other ways."

[3] See Austin's note on Quintilian 12.10.21, citing Aeschin.
Tim. 25.

[4] As this youth's. Or maybe " from the morals of today."

[5] Presumably an extract from the *divisio*.

VII

Non Recepti ab Imperatore

Nocte in bello portas aperire ne liceat.
Imperator in bello summam habeat potestatem.

Trecenti ab hoste captivi ad portas nocte
venerunt, imperator non aperuit; ante portas
occisi sunt. Imperator post victoriam reus est
laesae rei publicae.

Non putavi meos: noverant legem. Cur, inquit,
trecenti perierunt? Immo cur ne perirent capti
sunt? Hos ego interdiu non recepissem nisi victores,
noctu ne victores quidem. Procedens postridie in
proelium pugnaturis ostendi trecentos, in quibus nihil
laudari potest praeter fugam, nihil desiderari praeter
numerum. Fugiunt ut leges relinquant, revertuntur
ut tollant. Populus Romanus Cannensi proelio in
summas redactus angustias, cum servorum desideraret auxilia, captivorum contempsit, et credidit
eos libertatem magis tueri posse qui numquam
habuissent quam qui perdidissent. Nocte quomodo

---

[1] These " laws " are clearly statements of Roman (or any
other) military practice: for the second cf. *Decl.* 348, for the
first Cic. *Inv.* 2.123, where a very similar theme is touched on
(so too in the Greek rhetors, e.g. *Rhet. Gr.* 2.196, 198 Spengel).
[2] See *C.* 10.4 n.

7

THE MEN THE GENERAL WOULD NOT LET IN

In time of war it shall be illegal to open the gates
at night.
In wartime a general shall have
supreme power.[1]

Three hundred prisoners, escaped from the
enemy, came to the gates at night. The general
would not open up, and they were killed before
the gates. After the victory the general is
accused of harming the state.[2]

For the general: I did not think they were my men.
They knew the law.—"Why did three hundred
die?" Rather, why did they let themselves be
captured to avoid death?—I should not have let them
in by day unless they had conquered; at night not
even if they *had* conquered.—Going into battle next
day, I pointed out the three hundred to the men
about to fight—the three hundred who cannot be
praised except for their flight or missed except for
their number.—They flee to escape the laws, return
to destroy them.—The Roman people was reduced to
extreme straits by the battle of Cannae: needing re-
inforcement from slaves, they yet despised reinforce-
ment from prisoners, believing that those who had
never had freedom could defend it more ably than
those who had lost it.[3]—By night, how am I to tell

[3] The senate refused to redeem the prisoners (Liv. 22.58
seq.; Cic. *Off.* 3.114), after having enrolled slaves (Liv.
22.57.11: cf. *C.* 9.4.5).

hostem civemque distinguam? quam mihi das notam
ut arma cognoscam? Credo in insidiis hostes fuisse,
ut exclusos occiderent, sequerentur admissos.

Pars altera. Infestus trecentis fuit; iniquo conlo-
cavit loco; hoc ne argui posset non recepit. Capti
sunt fortissimi duces, Regulus, Crassus. Haec pos- 253ᴺ
trema rogantium vox erat: mitte arma; certe lex non
vetat.

VIII

TYRANNUS POST ABOLITIONEM CANDIDATUS

Conpetitori liceat in conpetitorem dicere.

Tyrannus dominationem sub abolitione deposuit ut si quis obiecisset tyrannidem capite
puniretur. Petit magistratum; conpetitor contradicit.

Candidatus anno meo spondeo: nulla rapietur,
nullus occidetur, nullum spoliabitur templum. Cur

---

[1] Crassus surrendered to the Parthian Surenas after Carrhae
(Plut. *Crass.* 31). As in *C.* 5.1, the length of Crassus' captivity
seems to be exaggerated.

[2] The law "may be taken from an enactment on the
conduct of elections . . . or may merely reflect custom"
(Bonner, 106). Cf. *C.* 7.7.4 for a case where the freedom to
criticise is not made use of.

enemy and citizen apart? What mark do you give me by which I can recognise their weapons?—I think there were enemy in ambush, to kill them if they were shut out—but follow them in if they were admitted.

The other side: He had a down on the three hundred; he put them in an unfavourable position. He refused to let them in so that this could not be proved against him.—The most brave of leaders, Regulus, Crassus, were made prisoner.[1]—These were the last words of the pleading men: " Send us down weapons. At least the law does not forbid *that*! "

8

The Tyrant who Stood for Office After an Amnesty

Candidate may speak against candidate.[2]

A tyrant laid down his power under an amnesty [3] which provided that anyone charging him with tyranny should be executed. He is standing for a magistracy; his rival speaks against him.[4]

For the rival: As candidate, I promise that in *my* year no-one will be raped,[5] no-one killed, no temple despoiled.—Let him tell us why he has not held

---

[3] This situation recurs in Quintilian 9.2.97, *RLM* pp. 59.6, 85.31, and *Decl.* 267.

[4] At an election meeting rather than in court.

[5] As under a tyranny (cf. *C.* 4.7 n.). The competitor throughout has to avoid direct attack on the ex-tyrant (as in the Quintilian passage and the quotation in *RLM* p. 59.7 *seq.*).

honores tamdiu non gesserit narret. Per communem deprecor libertatem, moriar: obicietur tibi quod occideris civem. Vult aliquo imperio, aliqua potestate distingui, homo magnae nobilitatis, magnae gratiae, ingentis pecuniae. Siciliae fuisse dicitur dominus qui inclusos aeneis tauris homines subiectis urebat ignibus, ut mugitum ederent, verba non possent. O hominem in sua crudelitate fastidiosum, qui, cum vellet torquere, tamen nolebat audire!

Pars altera. Quidquid egi, quidquid gessi, rei publicae causa feci. Peto ne mihi lex pro me lata noceat, neu quid noceat quia non obicitur quod non noceret obiectum.

---

[1] Answer: because he was sole tyrant—which does not count as a magistracy.

[2] Phalaris, listed as a rhetorical *exemplum* in Val. Max. 9.2 ext. 9.

[3] Thus acting like the tyrant in the present *controversia*.

magistracies over so long a period.[1]—I beg, by the freedom of the state, let me die: it will be made a reproach to *you* that you caused a citizen's death.—This man, very well-born, very influential and extremely rich, wants to have some power, some office to mark him off.—There was once (we are told) a ruler[2] of Sicily who shut men in brazen bulls and roasted them over fires, so that they could bellow without uttering intelligible words. What a man, choosy yet cruel, who wanted to torture—without having to hear.[3]

The other side: Whatever I did, whatever I performed was for the state.—What I seek is that a law carried on my behalf should not harm me[4]—and that something[5] which would not harm me if it were made the subject of a charge should not harm me because it is not made the subject of a charge.

[4] Because the execution, or forcible silence, of his competitor would work against the ex-tyrant (cf. above: "It will be made a reproach to *you* . . .").

[5] His having been a tyrant. The ex-tyrant is afraid that the indirect hints of his competitor may harm his chances.

EXCERPTA

CONTROVERSIARUM

LIBRI SEXTI

I

Chirographum Cum Abdicato

Abdicato frater chirographum dedit dimidiam se partem daturum hereditatis si non respondisset. Ille tacuit. Abdicatur alter a patre.

Tantum aeris alieni habet quantum vivo patre non possit solvere.[1] Vis scire cuius fidei sis? ne frater quidem tibi sine chirographo credidit. Alterius spem moror, alterius fidem. Vivo, et iam patrimonium meum divisum est. Nisi succurritis,[2] vincet me et ille[3] qui tacuit. Non dissimulo me hodie duos abdicare. Chirographum prode,[4] parricidarum foedus et nefariae spei pactum, chirographum danti impium, accipienti turpe, patri periculosum.

---

[1] i.e. by staying alive.
[2] The judges.
[3] By receiving half the bequest (cf. "defeat my father" below).
[4] Contrast the son's secretiveness.

EXCERPTS FROM BOOK 6

1

The Arrangement with a Disinherited Brother

A brother gave a written undertaking to a son who had been disinherited that he would give him half the bequest if he did not protest at disinheritance. He kept quiet. The other son is disinherited by his father.

For the father: He is so far in debt that he cannot discharge it while his father is alive.—Do you want to know what your credit is like? Not even your brother believed you without a written undertaking. —I am delaying [1] the hopes of one son, and the test of the other's loyalty.—I still live—and already my estate has been divided.—Unless you [2] come to my aid, even the one who kept quiet will defeat me.[3]—*I* am not trying to conceal [4] the fact that today I am disinheriting two sons.—Bring out the undertaking, a parricides' treaty, an agreement based on wicked hopes, an undertaking that is nefarious on the part of the giver, shameful to the recipient and dangerous to the father.

Pars altera. In omnem me fortunam, frater, comitem tibi iungam: si militandum, una militabimus, si peregrinandum, una urbes peragrabimus, si cotidianam rogavero stipem, et illam tecum dividam. Nolui recentem iram exagitari patris; malui ut tacendo patrem vinceret. Meae partis heres ero, tuae custos. Et quia de re maxima melius sibi quisque credit, do chirographum; tu da operam ut istud magis a patre accipere quam a fratre videaris. Hoc, quod honeste, quod pie gerebamus, tam palam egimus ut pater sciret. Quid enim timebam? ne, si rescisset pater, moleste ferret filium suum hominem avarum non esse, fratrem pium esse? Ita mihi contingat patrem utrique nostrum placare.

255ℕ

II

Exul Pater Fundo Prohibitus

Exulem tecto et cibo iuvare ne liceat.
Inprudentis caedis damnatus quinquennio exulet.

Quidam, cum filium et filiam haberet, inprudentis caedis damnatus in exilium profectus solebat venire in possessionem vicinam finibus.

---

[1] By affectionate behaviour towards your father.

[2] Bonner argues (pp. 110–11) that this is a genuine law, part of the " aquae et ignis interdictio " (he observes there is mention of " shelter " in this context in Cic. *Dom.* 78).

[3] See *C.* 4.3 n.

The other side: Brother, I will be at your side as companion in the face of every turn of events. If we must be soldiers, we will campaign together. If we must travel, we will travel through the cities of the world together. If I have to beg my daily bread, I will divide it too with you.—I did not want my father's recent rage to be aroused anew; I preferred that he should defeat my father by keeping quiet.—" I shall be heir to my part, guardian of yours. And because, in an important matter, everyone trusts himself best, I give a written undertaking; *you* must ensure [1] that you appear to be receiving it more from your father than from your brother."—We did this honourably and with affection—and we did it so openly that my father got to know of it. What had I to fear ? That, if my father got to know, he would be annoyed that his son was not avaricious, but an affectionate brother ?—May I succeed in reconciling our father to us both!

2

The Exiled Father who was Barred from his Estate

It shall be illegal to help an exile with shelter and food.[2]
One convicted of unintentional homicide shall go into exile for five years.[3]

A man with a son and a daughter was convicted of involuntary homicide, and went off into exile; he made a practice of coming to an estate of his near the border. The son got to know of this, and

Resciit hoc filius, cecidit vilicum; vilicus exclusit patrem. Coepit ire ad filiam. Accusata illa quod exulem recepisset advocato fratre absoluta est. Post quinquennium pater abdicat filium.

Accusator civium me fecit exulem, filius etiam 256 meorum. Filiam honestiorem inveni, quod accusata est, servum frugaliorem, quod caesus est. Male meruisti de patre, quem exclusisti, de sorore, cui praeiudicio nocuisti, de iudicibus, quos in tam bona timuisti causa. Aut tu peccasti aut soror. Filius me meus docuit quod illum non recipio. Absoluta est, inquit, me advocato soror. Ita tu patrem non recipiebas, cum tam bene istam causam agere posses? Cum absoluta est quae receperat, damnatus est qui expulerat. Filia me patrem iudicavit, servi dominum; uni filio exul fui. Ignosce, fidelissime servulorum, et tibi inprudens nocui. Quam bonam eius causam putas fuisse, quae ne te quidem advocato damnata est? Si te herede possum mori, dignus sum qui tibi etiam hunc servum relinquam. Alii exul est, tibi pater est. Nulla lex scelus imperat: certe quae fecit absoluta est. Lex eum tenet qui iuvat exulem, non qui patitur iuvari. Ignora, dissimula: lex te in-

---

[1] By being her advocate when she needed none.

[2] Any more than the man he accidentally killed.

[3] In my will. The father means he will not do either, but will manumit the slave.

[4] Your father's presence in the country.

beat the bailiff, who henceforth excluded the
father. He then began to visit his daughter.
She was accused for taking in the exile, but
acquitted with the help of her brother. After
the five years, the father disinherits the son.

For the father: My accuser made me an exile from
my fellow-citizens, my son from my relations also.—I
found my daughter more honourable—she was
accused: the slave more virtuous—he got beaten.—
You have deserved ill of your father, whom you kept
out, of your sister, whom you harmed by the example
you gave, of the judges, of whom you showed fear [1] in
so good a cause.—Either you have done wrong, or
your sister has.—That I do not take my son in is
something that I learned from *him.*—" My sister was
acquitted with my aid." Yet you refused to take in
your father, despite being so good at pleading this
case?—When the girl who had received him got
acquitted, that meant the condemnation of the man
who had turned him out.—My daughter judged me
her father, the slaves their master; I was an exile
only in the eyes of my son.—Forgive me, most faith-
ful of my dear slaves, I didn't mean to harm you
either.[2]—Her case *must* have been a good one if she
wasn't convicted even with you as her advocate.—If
I am capable of dying with you as my heir, I am bad
enough to leave you [3] even so good a slave as this.—
To another he is an exile, to you a father.—No law
orders a crime; anyway, the girl who committed one
was acquitted.—The law applies to someone who
helps an exile, not someone who allows him to be
helped.—Take no notice, pretend you do not know; [4]

nocentem esse, non curiosum iubet. Si mea causa faciebas, me admonuisses, servum prohibuisses, non cecidisses.

Pars altera. Facere lege prohibente non potui. Accusata et absoluta est quia muliercula videbatur non nosse leges. Non pro me timui sed pro te: res in notitiam hominum pervenerat; captabaris; timui ne occidereris. Vis scire notum fuisse? soror est accusata. Malui servum frugalissimum caedere quam patrem optimum amittere. 257

III

Mater Nothi Lecta Pro Parte

Maior frater dividat patrimonium, minor eligat.
Liceat filium ex ancilla tollere.

Quidam, cum haberet legitimum filium, alium ex ancilla sustulit et decessit. Maior frater sic divisit ut patrimonium totum ex una parte poneret, ex altera matrem nothi. Minor elegit matrem et accusat fratrem circumscriptionis.

Unus omnium exheredatus sum dividendo. Legisset, inquit, alteram partem. Tu solus talis potuisti

---

[1] See Bonner, 128–31, where it is argued that this law goes back to the Twelve Tables.

[2] The meaning is that such a child may be legitimised. Bonner (pp. 127–8) suggests that this may be a fragment of Augustan legislation, codifying something that had always been possible.

[3] Doubtless under the *Lex Plaetoria* (c. 200 B.C.).—The subject is found elsewhere, e.g. *RLM* p. 336.8.

the law orders you to be innocent, not to spy on others.—If you had been acting in my interests, you would have warned me off, prevented the slave taking me in—not beaten him.

The other side: I could not do what the law forbade. —She was accused—and acquitted because a mere woman was thought to be ignorant of the law.—I was not afraid for myself, but for you; the affair had come to public notice; they were looking for you; I feared you might get killed. Do you want evidence that the story had got around?—my sister was accused.—I preferred beating the most decent of slaves to losing the best of fathers.

3

THE BASTARD'S MOTHER WHO WAS CHOSEN AS PART OF AN ESTATE

The elder brother shall divide an estate,
the younger make the choice.[1]
It shall be legal to acknowledge a child born
of a slave-girl.[2]

A man with a legitimate son acknowledged another by a slave-girl, and died. The elder brother made a division by which he put the whole estate in one part and the mother of the bastard in the other. The younger son chose his mother and accuses the brother of fraud.[3]

For the younger brother: I am the only son who has ever been deprived of his patrimony by means of a division.—" He should have chosen the other part."

esse filius qualis frater es. Lex te dividere, me eligere iussit: aperte ne minor circumscribatur timet. Sic divisit ut, si vellem non esse mendicus, relinquerem fratrem in egestate, matrem in servitute. Non est dividere ex altera parte patrimonium ponere, ex altera onus. Talis fuit ut illi coheredem pater ex ancilla tolleret. Elige ut aut patrimonio careas aut scelere. Circumscriptores dici solent qui aliquid abstulerunt: iste nihil reliquit. Tu, inquit, voluisti pauper esse. Cur ergo queror, si egestate delector? Obici, inquit, non potest quod lege factum est. Immo nihil nisi quod lege factum est; nam si quid aliter gestum est, per se inritum est. Circumscriptio semper crimen sub specie legis involvit: quod apparet in illa legitimum est, quod latet insidiosum. Semper circumscriptio per ius ad iniuriam pervenit. Lex iubet maiorem dividere, minorem eligere: nec tu divisisti nec hic elegit; sic a te alligatus est ut necesse haberet quod non expediebat malle. Nota fuit in matrem mea pietas; non timuit ne eligere possem alteram partem.

Pars altera. Ego nihil aliud quam divisi. Circumscriptio non in divisione est, sed in electione. Habes matrem, quam totis quidam bonis redemerunt;

258

You alone were capable of being as cruel a son as you
are a brother.—The law ordered that you should
make the division, I the choice; clearly it is afraid
that the younger son may get tricked.—He made the
division in such a way that if I wanted to avoid
beggary I had to leave my brother poor and my
mother a slave.—It is no division to put the estate in
one part and a burden in the other.—Such was his
character that his father provided him with a legitimised co-heir—by a slave-girl.—Choose between
beggary and crime.[1]—The fraudulent, by normal
reckoning, are those who have removed something;
he has *left* nothing.—" You chose to be poor."
Why then am I complaining if I enjoy poverty?—
" There can be no charge where something is done
legally." On the contrary, there can only be a
charge where an act *is* legal; where it is illegal, it is
automatically invalid. Fraudulence always wraps
crime in a show of legality; the obvious part is legal,
the hidden is the trap. Fraudulence always proceeds to illegal ends by legal means.—The law orders
the elder to make the division, the younger to choose;
you did not divide, and *he* did not choose: he was so
trammelled by you that he had to choose what went
against his interests.—My affection towards my
mother was well-known; he did not need to fear I
was capable of choosing the other part.

The other side: I did nothing but make the division.
Fraudulence lies not in division but in choice.—You
have your mother—some men have ransomed theirs

[1] This must be the sense, though the Latin means: " Choose
to be either without an estate or without a crime."

habes gloriam, quam per ignes quidam, per arma quaesierunt. Multa de patrimonio rapuit, cum haberet ius dominae ancillae inpudentia. Timebas ne in illam saevirem? Non expediebat mihi, cum in illa totum patrimonium habiturus essem. Nunc tantundem habes; habes enim partem quam voluisti. Ut tantundem haberes, nec pater voluerat; ideo matrem tuam ancillam reliquit.

IV

Potio Ex Parte Mortifera

Veneficii sit actio.

Proscriptum uxor secuta est. Quodam tempore secreto poculum tenentem ⟨deprehendit⟩,[1] interrogavit quid esset; ille dixit venenum et mori se velle. Rogavit illa ut partem sibi daret, et dixit se nolle sine illo vivere. Partem bibit ipse, partem uxori dedit. Perit illa sola. Testamento inventus est maritus heres. Restitutus arguitur veneficii.

Sic egit ut deprehenderetur, sic deprehensus est ut exoraretur, sic bibit ut viveret. Quod est istud

259

[1] *Supplied by Müller.*

---

[1] Compare the argument in *RLM loc. cit.*: " He has no cause for complaint—he has his liberty, he is a citizen, and he has achieved the freeing of his mother." The " through fire, through weapons " has a Virgilian ring: cf. *Aen.* 2.664 " per tela per ignis " in another notable instance of *pietas*.

[2] i.e. by spending money before the father's death.

at the cost of all their wealth; you have fame, which men have sought through fire and through weapons.[1] —She stole much of the estate from me,[2] for this impudent maid had a mistress' rights.—Were you afraid I might be cruel to her?[3] It was not in my interests, for she would have formed the whole of my inheritance. As it is you have as much as I; for you have the part you wanted.—Not even our father wanted you to have as much as me; that was why he left your mother a slave.[4]

4

THE DRINK THAT WAS PARTLY FATAL

An action may lie for poisoning.[5]

His wife followed into exile a man who had been proscribed.[6] On one occasion she found him in private, a cup in his hand. She asked what it was; he said that it was poison, and that he wanted to die. She asked him to give her part of it, and said she didn't want to live without him. He drank a part, and gave part to his wife. Only she died. In her will her husband proved to be her heir. After restitution, he is accused of poisoning.

Against the husband: He acted in such a way as to be caught, was caught in such a way as to be talked

---

[3] If I got the share consisting of the woman.

[4] Thus emphasising the inequality of his two sons.

[5] Not an *actio* in real life: cases of poisoning would be brought before Sulla's standing court on assassination and poisoning (see on *C.* 3.9).

[6] For the civil war setting, see *C.* 4.8, with notes.

venenum quod tantum heredi non nocet? Nemo
umquam tam palam uxori venenum dedit. Fugit ne
occideretur qui dicit se mori cupere. Unus proscriptione locupletior factus est. Ut vivere vellet
uxor illi persuadere non potuit; persuasit res blan-
dior, uxoris hereditas. Sciit quam partem potionis
hauriret. Contrarias partes gladio persecutus est,
suas veneno. Occidendi finem prius victores fecere
quam victi. Quid iam putabatis futurum cum in
exilium uxor testamentum tulisset, maritus venenum?
Ubi est uxor? ecquid te pudet? Iam etiam proscripti
redeunt. Statim sumpta potione conlapsa est.
Nolite mirari si tam efficax venenum est: heres est
qui dedit. Summis fere partibus levis et innoxius
umor suspenditur, gravis illa et pestifera pars pondere
suo subsidit. Apparet te diu praeparatum venenum
habuisse: scisti dividere. Etiamsi potest defendi qui
volenti dedit, tu potes qui fecisti ut vellet? Id genus
veneni fuit quod pondere subsideret in imam po-
tionem. Bibit iste usque ad venenum, uxor venenum.

Pars altera. Virum in pace dilexit, in bello secuta
est, in consilio ultimo non reliquit. O dignam quam
innocens sequar! Bellum civile egi, proscriptus sum, 260

---

[1] This explains itself through comparison with what is said
below, e.g. " The light harmless liquid . . ."

[2] By dying now.

[3] That is, even granted I had no ulterior motive.

over, drank in such a way as to live.—What sort of a poison is it that spares only the heir?—No-one has ever given his wife poison so openly.—This man who says he wants to die fled so as to avoid being killed.—He alone has got richer by being proscribed.—His wife could not persuade him to want to live; what persuaded him was something more alluring—his wife's bequest.—He knew which part of the drink to drain.[1]—He attacked the other side with his sword, his own with poison.—The victors made an end of killing sooner than the vanquished.—What do you think was likely to happen when the wife carried her will into exile, the husband poison?—Where is your wife? Are you not ashamed? Now even the proscribed are returning.—Having drunk the draught, she fell dead at once. Don't be surprised the poison is so effective—it was an heir who administered it.—The light harmless liquid generally hangs about the top part, while the heavy noxious part is carried down by its own weight.—It's obvious you had had the poison ready for a long time; you knew how to divide it.—It may be defensible to give poison to a willing victim—but what of you, who arranged that she *should* be willing?—It was the sort of poison that was carried by its weight to the bottom of the drink; he drank as far as the poison—his wife drank the poison.

The other side: She loved her husband in peace, followed him in war, did not abandon him in his last resolution. How well she deserves that I should follow *her*[2]—even though I am innocent![3]—I fought in the civil war, I was proscribed, I went into exile;

exulavi; quid his malis adici potest nisi ut venenum
bibam et vivam? Venenum, inquam, est. Hoc qui
daturi sunt dissimulant. Venenum Cato vendidit.
Quaerite an proscripto licuerit emere quod licuit
Catoni vendere.

V

IPHICRATES REUS

Qui vim iudicio fecerit capite puniatur.

Missus Iphicrates adversus Thracum regem
bis acie victus foedus cum eo percussit et filiam
eius uxorem duxit. Cum Athenas redisset et
causam diceret, visi sunt circa iudicium quidam
Thracum cultris armati, et ipse reus gladium
strinxit. Cum iudices citarentur ad iudicandum,
palam absolutorias tulerunt sententias. Accusatur quod vim iudicio fecerit.

Nemo iudicum tuorum non sic timuit tamquam tu
de illis iudicaturus esses. Cum toto tibi regno suo

---

[1] During the sale of the property of the King of Cyprus
(58 B.C.). See Plin. *N.H.* 29.96; *RE* s.v. Porcius 16) col. 182.

[2] The setting is Greek, but the law was of course applicable
in Rome too, though not necessarily with so stern a sanction
(Bonner, 113–14).

[3] The theme is treated briefly in *Decl.* 386, to which parallels
will be noted.—Iphicrates did fight in Thrace, successfully, in
386 B.C. (e.g. Nep. *Iph.* 2.1), and did marry the daughter of the
Thracian king, Cotys (*ibid.* 3.4). He *was* accused of high

what can be added to these misfortunes except that I should take poison—and survive!—" It is poison," I said. Those who intend to give poison pretend that it is something else.—Cato sold poison.[1] Ask whether a proscribed man was allowed to buy what Cato was allowed to sell.

<h1 style="text-align:center">5</h1>

<h2 style="text-align:center">IPHICRATES ON TRIAL</h2>

The man who brings violence to bear on a trial shall die.[2]

Iphicrates, sent to fight the king of Thrace, was twice defeated in battle, signed a treaty with him and married his daughter. Back in Athens, when he stood trial, there were seen about the court-room men armed with Thracian knives, and the defendant himself drew his sword. When the judges were summoned to give judgement, they openly voted for acquittal. Iphicrates is accused of bringing violence to bear on the trial.[3]

Against Iphicrates: All of your judges were afraid, as if it was you who were going to judge *them*.[4]—Your advocate [5] came with his whole kingdom to aid you;

treason, much later (355 B.C.), and is said to have intimidated the jurors on that occasion (Polyaen. 3.9.29: cf. 15?). The theme is fiction woven round these facts.

[4] Cf. *Decl.* 386: " It was not the judges who acquitted the accused, but the accused who acquitted the judges."

[5] The Thracian king, whose presence at the trial is specifically mentioned in *Decl.* 386.

venit advocatus; non maioribus copiis bellum in-
struxit quam iudicium. Iphicrate, conde gladium;
iudicium est. Quid tibi cum gladio? certe bis victis
arma ponenda sunt. Quae est ista contra rerum
naturam permutatio, in bello nuptiae, in iudicio
bellum?

Pars altera. Ego vim non feci; omnia enim legi- 261M
tima peracta sunt: accusator suo loco dixit, reus suo
respondit; perfectum per omnes numeros suos iudicium est. Cum iudices sententias ferrent, strinxi
gladium ut occiderem me si damnatus essem.
Iudices tulerunt palam absolutorias ut gratiam duci
suo referrent. Nuptiarum causa utilitas rei publicae
fuit. Miles pulsus saepius erat infelici proelio.
Barbaros circa iudicium fuisse non propter officium
armatos, sed propter morem suum. Quid potestis,
inquit, queri? quod vobis obsidem adduxi?

VI

ADULTERA VENEFICA

Veneficii sit actio.

Quidam, cum haberet uxorem et ex ea filiam
nubilem, indicavit uxori cui eam conlocaturus
esset. Illa dixit: celerius morietur quam illi

he brought up as many troops for the trial as for the battle.—Iphicrates, sheathe your sword—this is a trial.—What have you to do with swords?[1] Surely the twice defeated should lay down their arms.— What is this unnatural exchange?—marriage in war and war in the court-room.

The other side: I did nothing by force. Everything the law prescribed was carried out. The accuser spoke in his turn, the defendant replied in his; the trial was completed in all its details. When the judges were passing sentence, I drew my sword—to kill myself if I should be convicted.[2]—The judges openly voted for acquittal, to show their gratitude to their general.—The marriage was motivated by the interests of the state. The soldiers had been defeated in unsuccessful combat too often.—The barbarians surrounded the court in arms not to do their duty by me, but because that is their custom.—" What can you complain about?" says Iphicrates. " That I have brought you a hostage?"[3]

6

THE ADULTERESS WHO WAS A POISONER

An action may lie for poisoning.[4]

A man with a wife and, by her, a marriageable daughter, told his wife whom he proposed to marry their daughter to. She said: " She will

[1] Cf. Ov. *Fast.* 2.101.
[2] So too in *Decl.* 386 *sermo.*
[3] The father-in-law. " You " = the judges.
[4] See note on *C.* 6.4.

nubat. Decessit puella ante diem nuptiarum, dubiis signis cruditatis [1] et veneni. Torsit ancillam pater; dixit illa nihil se scire de veneno, sed de adulterio dominae et eius cui conlocaturus filiam erat. Accusat uxorem veneficii et adulterii.

"Morietur": teneo veneficam; "celerius quam nubat": teneo adulteram. "Morietur": factum est; "celerius quam nubat": factum est. Adulterium deprehendi serius quam factum est, veneficium antequam fieret. Duo crimina ad vos detuli et duas indices: altera dicit quod factum est, altera 262M etiam quid futurum sit. Generi adultera, filiae paelex. Quam infelix domus est in qua adulterium argumentum est ⟨veneficii⟩! [2] Dixi: honestus est; dixi; pulcher est; dum laudo generum, commendavi adulterum. O me tardissimum in malis meis! veneficium ne denuntiatum quidem credidi, adulterium in veneficio demum deprehendi. Versae sunt in exsequias nuptiae mutatusque genialis lectus in funebrem, subiectae rogo felices faces. Profertur putre

---

[1] cruditatis *early editors:* crudelitatis.
[2] *Added here by the editor (after* adulterium *by Kiessling).*

---

[1] Specified as "livores et tumores" in *Decl.* 354; the idea recurs often elsewhere, e.g. *C.* 9.5; *Decl.* p. 252.11 Ritter; Calp. Flacc. 35; Quintilian 5.9.11, 7.2.8 and 13.
[2] Themes exploiting the ambiguity of "die sooner than" (a phrase used in the "daily language of the people": *Decl.* p. 385.22 Ritter) recur elsewhere, e.g. *Decl.* 354 and esp. Calp. Flacc. 40, *RLM* pp. 331.12 *seq.*, 376.34, and *Rhet. Gr.* 2.143.27 *seq.* Spengel.

die sooner than marry him." The girl died
before the wedding-day, with doubtful symptoms
that might have suggested either indigestion or
poisoning.[1] The father tortured a slave-girl,
who said she knew nothing of poison but was
aware of an affair between her mistress and the
man to whom he had proposed to marry his
daughter. He accuses his wife of poisoning and
adultery.[2]

For the husband: "She will die." I have got the
poisoner. "Sooner than marry." I have got the
adulteress. "She will die." It has happened.
"Sooner than marry." It has happened.—I detected
the adultery after it took place, the poisoning before.
—I have brought before you two charges, and two
witnesses: one woman says what happened, the
other what is going to happen as well.—Mistress of
her son-in-law, rival of her daughter.[3]—How unhappy
the house where adultery is the proof of poisoning![4]
—I said: "He is honourable." I said: "He is
handsome." I was praising a son-in-law—and
recommending a rival to myself.—How slow I was
amidst my troubles! I did not believe the poisoning
even when it was denounced, and I only found out
about the adultery in the middle of the poisoning.—
The marriage turned into a funeral, the wedding-bed
was changed to a funeral couch, the torches of joy
were used to light the pyre.—The body is brought

[3] Cf. Cic. *Cluent.* 199: "uxor generi, noverca fili, filiae
paelex."
[4] The two were thought to be closely connected: cf. *C.*
7.3.6; Cato *ap.* Quintilian 5.11.39.

corpus et venenis tumens. Quid ultra quaeritis?
verbis signa, signis tormenta conveniunt. Ad vocem
tuam facta conveniunt. "Morietur antequam
nubat": factum est. Vidimus fluens corpus, et in
cadavere illius materna verba credidimus. Generum
adulterio perdidi, uxorem parricidio, filiam veneficio.

Pars altera. Duo gravissima crimina obiecit, adulterium et veneficium: adulterium ancilla teste, veneficium ne ancilla quidem. Cum indignaretur se non
rogatam, exciderunt illi verba quae non minus quam
filiam luget. At quare dixisti: "celerius morietur
quam illi nubat"? Verba dolori parum considerata
exciderunt. Et est saepissime fortuita divinatio.

VII

DEMENS QUI FILIO CESSIT UXOREM

Dementiae sit actio.

Qui habebat duos filios duxit uxorem. Alter
ex adulescentibus cum aegrotaret et in ultimis
esset, medici dixerunt animi vitium esse. Intravit ad filium stricto gladio pater; rogavit ut
indicaret sibi causam. Ait amari a se novercam.

2631

---

[1] Because she had poisoned the daughter.
[2] *Rhet. Gr.* 2.144.2 *seq.* recommends throwing doubt on the
evidence of the slave.
[3] Cf. *Decl.* p. 385.24 Ritter: "But she, as well as the
accuser, will lament the fate of the girl."

out, rotten and swollen with poisons.—Need I say more? The words agree with the symptoms, the symptoms with the evidence of the torture.—What took place agrees with your words: " She will die sooner than marry." So it turned out. We have seen the putrescent body; and when we saw her corpse we believed her mother's words.—I have lost my son-in-law by adultery, my wife by parricide,[1] my daughter by poisoning.

The other side: He has brought two very serious charges, adultery and poisoning: the adultery on the evidence of a slave-girl,[2] the poisoning not even on that.—Angry that she had not been consulted, she let fall words which she regrets as much as she regrets her daughter.[3]—" But why did you say: ' She will die sooner than marry him'? " The words slipped out without sufficient thought amid her grief. And often divination is successful by chance.

7

THE MADMAN WHO LET HIS SON HAVE HIS WIFE

An action may lie for madness.[4]

A man with two sons married a wife. One of the youths fell ill and was breathing his last; the doctors said that it was his state of mind that was the trouble. The father went into his son's room with a drawn sword;[5] he asked him to

---

[4] See *C*. 2.3 n.
[5] With which, as we are told explicitly in *Decl.* 291, he proposed to kill himself if he did not learn the truth.

Cessit illi uxore sua pater. Ab altero accusatur dementiae.

Audite rem novam: fratrem crudelem, novercam misericordem. Insanus sum quia aliquis meo beneficio sanus est. Tradidi illi uxorem; sed eripueram. "Testor" inquit "praesides pietatis deos, amare antequam duceres coepi." Ita tu iniuriam vocas quod fratrem habes, non habes novercam? Transii praeter istius oculos cum ferro; gladium mihi nemo nisi aeger extorsit. Patri qui periculum filii morientis sustinere non potuit ignoscendum in qualicumque facto est.

Pars altera. Alter lenocinio curavit, alter parricidio convaluit. Quid? hoc adulterium esse non putas quod marito conciliante committitur? Nescio furiosius uxorem duxerit an habuerit an dimiserit an conlocarit. Quam demens est cui adulterium pro beneficio imputatum est! Strinxit gladium maritus non ut vindicaret adulterium sed ut faceret. Mori potius debuit frater quam sanari turpiter. Quid enim si matrem, si sororem concupisset? Quaedam remedia graviora ipsis periculis sunt. Omnia inter pri-

---

[1] The illness and the cession of the wife come from the story of Antiochus and Stratonice, told in Val. Max. 5.7 ext. 1 and Lucian *Syr. Dea* 17–18. Variants on the theme appear in *Decl.* 291 and Calp. Flacc. 48.

[2] That is, they call me mad. The epigram depends on the ambiguity of *sanus* = "sound," "well" and also "sane."

tell him the reason. The son said he loved his step-mother. The father let him have his wife.[1] His other son accuses him of madness.

For the father: Hear a novel thing: a cruel brother, a step-mother who feels pity!—I am mad [2] because someone else is better, thanks to me.—I handed my wife over to him; but I had stolen her from him. " I call," he says, " on the gods who look after family affection to witness that I fell in love with her before you married her."—Do you call it a wrong done you that you keep a brother—and have lost a step-mother?—I passed before his eyes with a sword; no-one could get it away from me except a sick man.[3] —A father who could not tolerate the danger run by his dying son must be forgiven whatever he does.

The other side: The one used pandering to treat the patient, the other got better by means of a parricide.[4] —Don't you count it adultery where the husband plays the middle-man?—I don't know whether he was the more mad to marry his wife, or to keep her, or to let her go, or to marry her off.—How mad a man must be if adultery is marked up to him as a good deed!—The husband drew his sword not to punish adultery but to cause it.—My brother should have died rather than be cured by shameful means.[5]— What if he had lusted after his mother, or his sister? —Some cures are worse than the dangers they

---

[3] That is, by telling him what he wished to know.

[4] Stealing his father's wife.

[5] Cf. Sen. *Oed.* 517: " ubi turpis est medicina, sanari piget."

vignum et novercam conposita: simulatum morbum
et derisum animo turpissimo patrem.

VIII

Versus Virginis Vestalis

Virgo Vestalis scripsit hunc versum: felices nuptae!
moriar nisi nubere dulce est.   Rea est incesti.

" Felices nuptae " cupientis est; " peream nisi "
adfirmantis est; " nubere dulce est ": aut experta
iuras aut inexperta peieras; neutrum sacerdotis est.
Tibi magistratus suos fasces submittunt, tibi consules
praetoresque via cedunt; numquid exigua mercede
virgo es? Sacerdos raro iuret nec umquam nisi per
suam Vestam. " Moriar ": numquid perpetuus
ignis extinctus est? " Moriar ": numquid de
nuptiis appellata es? ⟨Te⟩ [1] ad ultimum, Vesta,
invoco, ut tam infesta sis sacerdoti quam invisa es.
Recita carmen, dum quaero quale sit. Tu carmen
scribas, tu verba pedibus tuis emollias et severitatem
templo debitam modulatione frangas? Quodsi

---

[1] *Supplied by Bursian.*

---

[1] Cf. Sen. *Med.* 433–4: " remedia . . . invenit nobis
deus / periculis peiora "; *Decl.* p. 420.5 Ritter.

[2] Or perhaps: " the illness was feigned, the father shame-
fully gulled." The indirect speech shows that this is not an
epigram, but Seneca's report of a *colour*.

[3] Bornecque compares the case of a Vestal who was accused
because of her " over-gay dress and a wit freer than befits a
virgin " (Liv. 4.44.11).—The verse is a hexameter.

combat.[1]—It was all worked out between the step-son and the step-mother—the pretended illness and the shameful deception of the father.[2]

8

THE VESTAL'S VERSE

A Vestal virgin wrote the following verse: "How happy married women are! O, may I die if marriage is not sweet." She is accused of unchastity.[3]

Against the virgin: "How happy married women are!" are the words of one who wants something; "may I perish if . . .!" those of one who asserts something. "It is sweet to marry": you either swear from experience, or, if you have no experience, you are foresworn. Neither befits a priestess.—The magistrates lower their *fasces* to you, consuls and praetors make way for you: [4] isn't that a good wage for your virginity?—A priestess should rarely swear—and then only by her own goddess, Vesta.—"May I die." Has the eternal fire been extinguished? "May I die." Have you been asked in marriage?—I invoke you, finally, Vesta: be as harsh towards your priestess as she is hostile to you.—Recite the verse, while I investigate what it is like.[5]—Are *you* to write a verse, soften your words with the metre you give them, enervate with its rhythm the austerity that properly belongs to a temple?—If you really want to

---

[4] For the privileges of Vestals, cf. *C.* 1.2.3 n.

[5] This perhaps prefaced an analysis such as appears in the first epigram.

utique laudare vis nuptias, narra Lucretiam, de illius
morte scribe antequam iurabis de tua. O te omni
supplicio dignam cui quicquam sacerdotio felicius est!
" Dulce est ": quam expressa vox, quam ex imis
visceribus emissa non expertae tantum sed delec-
tatae! Incesta est etiam sine stupro quae cupit
stuprum.

Pars altera. Unus illi versus obicitur, ne hic 265M
quidem totus. Non oportet, inquit, scribere carmen.
Multum interest obiurges an punias. Incesti damnari nulla potest nisi cuius violatum corpus est.
Quid, tu putas poetas quae sentiunt scribere? Vixit
modeste, castigate; non cultus in illa luxuriosior, non
conversatio cum viris licentiosior; unum crimen eius
vobis confiteor: ingenium habet. Quidni invideat
Corneliae, quidni illi quae Catonem peperit, quidni
sacerdotes parientibus?

Extra. Varius Geminus apud Caesarem dixit:
Caesar, qui apud te audent dicere magnitudinem
tuam ignorant, qui non audent humanitatem.

praise marriage, tell the story of Lucretia, write about *her* death before swearing by your own.—You indeed deserve every punishment if you find anything more agreeable than your office.—" It is sweet ": the phrase is clear-cut, despatched from the very heart of a woman who has had experience—and, what is more, enjoyed it.—A woman is unchaste if she wants sex, even if she has not had it.

The other side: One verse is made subject of a charge against her—and not even the whole verse.—" She should not write poetry." There is a lot of difference between reproaching and punishing.—No-one can be convicted of unchastity unless her body has been violated.[1]—Do you imagine that poets write what they really mean?[2] She lived modestly and strictly; she wore no finery that was over-luxurious, had with men no dealings that were over-free. I have only one crime to confess for her—she has talent.—Why should she not envy Cornelia,[3] or Cato's mother, or those who give birth to priestesses?

By the way: Varius Geminus said in the presence of Caesar:[4] " Caesar, those who venture to speak in your presence are unaware of your greatness; those who do not venture are unaware of your kindness."

[1] Cf. the discussion of Latro, *C.* 1.2.13.
[2] Compare the protestations of Catullus 16.5 (with Kroll's note): cf. Plin. *Ep.* 4.14 (with Sherwin-White's note).
[3] As mother of the Gracchi.
[4] Doubtless Augustus.

525

Printed in Great Britain by
Richard Clay (The Chaucer Press), Ltd.,
Bungay, Suffolk

THE LOEB CLASSICAL LIBRARY

VOLUMES ALREADY PUBLISHED

Latin Authors

AMMIANUS MARCELLINUS. Translated by J. C. Rolfe. 3 Vols.

APULEIUS: THE GOLDEN ASS (METAMORPHOSES). W. Adlington (1566). Revised by S. Gaselee.

ST. AUGUSTINE: CITY OF GOD. 7 Vols. Vol. I. G. E. McCracken. Vol. II. and VII. W. M. Green. Vol. III. D. Wiesen. Vol. IV. P. Levine. Vol. V. E. M. Sanford and W. M. Green. Vol. VI. W. C. Greene.

ST. AUGUSTINE, CONFESSIONS OF. W. Watts (1631). 2 Vols.

ST. AUGUSTINE, SELECT LETTERS. J. H. Baxter.

AUSONIUS. H. G. Evelyn White. 2 Vols.

BEDE. J. E. King. 2 Vols.

BOETHIUS: TRACTS and DE CONSOLATIONE PHILOSOPHIAE. Rev. H. F. Stewart and E. K. Rand. Revised by S. J. Tester.

CAESAR: ALEXANDRIAN, AFRICAN and SPANISH WARS. A. G. Way.

CAESAR: CIVIL WARS. A. G. Peskett.

CAESAR: GALLIC WAR. H. J. Edwards.

CATO: DE RE RUSTICA; VARRO: DE RE RUSTICA. H. B. Ash and W. D. Hooper.

CATULLUS. F. W. Cornish; TIBULLUS. J. B. Postgate; PERVIGILIUM VENERIS. J. W. Mackail.

CELSUS: DE MEDICINA. W. G. Spencer. 3 Vols.

CICERO: BRUTUS, and ORATOR. G. L. Hendrickson and H. M. Hubbell.

[CICERO]: AD HERENNIUM. H. Caplan.

CICERO: DE ORATORE, etc. 2 Vols. Vol. I. DE ORATORE, Books I. and II. E. W. Sutton and H. Rackham. Vol. II. DE ORATORE, Book III. De Fato; Paradoxa Stoicorum; De Partitione Oratoria. H. Rackham.

CICERO: DE FINIBUS. H. Rackham.

CICERO: DE INVENTIONE, etc. H. M. Hubbell.

CICERO: DE NATURA DEORUM and ACADEMICA. H. Rackham.

CICERO: DE OFFICIIS. Walter Miller.

CICERO: DE REPUBLICA and DE LEGIBUS: SOMNIUM SCIPIONIS. Clinton W. Keyes.

CICERO: DE SENECTUTE, DE AMICITIA, DE DIVINATIONE. W. A. Falconer.

CICERO: IN CATILINAM, PRO FLACCO, PRO MURENA, PRO SULLA. Louis E. Lord

CICERO: LETTERS to ATTICUS. E. O. Winstedt. 3 Vols.

CICERO: LETTERS TO HIS FRIENDS. W. Glynn Williams, M. Cary, M. Henderson. 4 Vols.

CICERO: PHILIPPICS. W. C. A. Ker.

CICERO: PRO ARCHIA POST REDITUM, DE DOMO, DE HARUS-PICUM RESPONSIS, PRO PLANCIO. N. H. Watts.

CICERO: PRO CAECINA, PRO LEGE MANILIA, PRO CLUENTIO, PRO RABIRIO. H. Grose Hodge.

CICERO: PRO CAELIO, DE PROVINCIIS CONSULARIBUS, PRO BALBO. R. Gardner.

CICERO: PRO MILONE, IN PISONEM, PRO SCAURO, PRO FONTEIO, PRO RABIRIO POSTUMO, PRO MARCELLO, PRO LIGARIO, PRO REGE DEIOTARO. N. H. Watts.

CICERO: PRO QUINCTIO, PRO ROSCIO AMERINO, PRO ROSCIO COMOEDO, CONTRA RULLUM. J. H. Freese.

CICERO: PRO SESTIO, IN VATINIUM. R. Gardner.

CICERO: TUSCULAN DISPUTATIONS. J. E. King.

CICERO: VERRINE ORATIONS. L. H. G. Greenwood. 2 Vols.

CLAUDIAN. M. Platnauer. 2 Vols.

COLUMELLA: DE RE RUSTICA. DE ARBORIBUS. H. B. Ash, E. S. Forster and E. Heffner. 3 Vols.

CURTIUS, Q.: HISTORY OF ALEXANDER. J. C. Rolfe. 2 Vols.

FLORUS. E. S. Forster; and CORNELIUS NEPOS. J. C. Rolfe.

FRONTINUS: STRATAGEMS and AQUEDUCTS. C. E. Bennett and M. B. McElwain.

FRONTO: CORRESPONDENCE. C. R. Haines. 2 Vols.

GELLIUS, J. C. Rolfe. 3 Vols.

HORACE: ODES AND EPODES. C. E. Bennett.

HORACE: SATIRES, EPISTLES, ARS POETICA. H. R. Fairclough.

JEROME: SELECTED LETTERS. F. A. Wright.

JUVENAL and PERSIUS. G. G. Ramsay.

LIVY. B. O. Foster, F. G. Moore, Evan T. Sage, and A. C. Schlesinger and R. M. Geer (General Index). 14 Vols.

LUCAN. J. D. Duff.

LUCRETIUS. W. H. D. Rouse. Revised by M. F. Smith

MARTIAL. W. C. A. Ker. 2 Vols.

MINOR LATIN POETS: from PUBLILIUS SYRUS to RUTILIUS NAMATIANUS, including GRATTIUS, CALPURNIUS SICULUS, NEMESIANUS, AVIANUS, and others with "Aetna" and the "Phoenix." J. Wight Duff and Arnold M. Duff.

OVID: THE ART OF LOVE and OTHER POEMS. J. H. Mozley.

OVID: FASTI. Sir James G. Frazer.

2

OVID: HEROIDES and AMORES. Grant Showerman.
OVID: METAMORPHOSES. F. J. Miller. 2 Vols.
OVID: TRISTIA and EX PONTO. A. L. Wheeler.
PERSIUS. Cf. JUVENAL.
PETRONIUS. M. Heseltine; SENECA; APOCOLOCYNTOSIS. W. H. D. Rouse.
PHAEDRUS AND BABRIUS (Greek). B. E. Perry.
PLAUTUS. Paul Nixon. 5 Vols.
PLINY: LETTERS, PANEGYRICUS. Betty Radice. 2 Vols.
PLINY: NATURAL HISTORY. Vols. I.–V. and IX. H. Rackham. VI.–VIII. W. H. S. Jones. X. D. E. Eichholz. 10 Vols.
PROPERTIUS. H. E. Butler.
PRUDENTIUS. H. J. Thomson. 2 Vols.
QUINTILIAN. H. E. Butler. 4 Vols.
REMAINS OF OLD LATIN. E. H. Warmington. 4 Vols. Vol. I. (ENNIUS AND CAECILIUS.) Vol. II. (LIVIUS, NAEVIUS, PACUVIUS, ACCIUS.) Vol. III. (LUCILIUS and LAWS OF XII TABLES.) Vol. IV. (ARCHAIC INSCRIPTIONS.)
SALLUST. J. C. Rolfe.
SCRIPTORES HISTORIAE AUGUSTAE. D. Magie. 3 Vols.
SENECA, THE ELDER: CONTROVERSIAE, SUASORIAE. M. Winterbottom. 2 Vols.
SENECA: APOCOLOCYNTOSIS. Cf. PETRONIUS.
SENECA: EPISTULAE MORALES. R. M. Gummere. 3 Vols.
SENECA: MORAL ESSAYS. J. W. Basore. 3 Vols.
SENECA: TRAGEDIES. F. J. Miller. 2 Vols.
SENECA: NATURALES QUAESTIONES. T. H. Corcoran. 2 Vols.
SIDONIUS: POEMS and LETTERS. W. B. Anderson. 2 Vols.
SILIUS ITALICUS. J. D. Duff. 2 Vols.
STATIUS. J. H. Mozley. 2 Vols.
SUETONIUS. J. C. Rolfe. 2 Vols.
TACITUS: DIALOGUS. Sir Wm. Peterson. AGRICOLA and GERMANIA. Maurice Hutton. Revised by M. Winterbottom, R. M. Ogilvie, E. H. Warmington.
TACITUS: HISTORIES AND ANNALS. C. H. Moore and J. Jackson. 4 Vols.
TERENCE. John Sargeaunt. 2 Vols.
TERTULLIAN: APOLOGIA and DE SPECTACULIS. T. R. Glover. MINUCIUS FELIX. G. H. Rendall.
VALERIUS FLACCUS. J. H. Mozley.
VARRO: DE LINGUA LATINA. R. G. Kent. 2 Vols.
VELLEIUS PATERCULUS and RES GESTAE DIVI AUGUSTI. F. W. Shipley.
VIRGIL. H. R. Fairclough. 2 Vols.
VITRUVIUS: DE ARCHITECTURA. F. Granger. 2 Vols.

3

Greek Authors

ACHILLES TATIUS. S. Gaselee.

AELIAN: ON THE NATURE OF ANIMALS. A. F. Scholfield. 3 Vols.

AENEAS TACTICUS, ASCLEPIODOTUS and ONASANDER. The Illinois Greek Club.

AESCHINES. C. D. Adams.

AESCHYLUS. H. Weir Smyth. 2 Vols.

ALCIPHRON, AELIAN, PHILOSTRATUS: LETTERS. A. R. Benner and F. H. Fobes.

ANDOCIDES, ANTIPHON, Cf. MINOR ATTIC ORATORS.

APOLLODORUS. Sir James G. Frazer. 2 Vols.

APOLLONIUS RHODIUS. R. C. Seaton.

THE APOSTOLIC FATHERS. Kirsopp Lake. 2 Vols.

APPIAN: ROMAN HISTORY. Horace White. 4 Vols.

ARATUS. Cf. CALLIMACHUS.

ARISTIDES: ORATIONS. C. A. Behr. Vol. I.

ARISTOPHANES. Benjamin Bickley Rogers. 3 Vols. Verse trans.

ARISTOTLE: ART OF RHETORIC. J. H. Freese.

ARISTOTLE: ATHENIAN CONSTITUTION, EUDEMIAN ETHICS, VICES AND VIRTUES. H. Rackham.

ARISTOTLE: GENERATION OF ANIMALS. A. L. Peck.

ARISTOTLE: HISTORIA ANIMALIUM. A. L. Peck. Vols. I.–II.

ARISTOTLE: METAPHYSICS. H. Tredennick. 2 Vols.

ARISTOTLE: METEOROLOGICA. H. D. P. Lee.

ARISTOTLE: MINOR WORKS. W. S. Hett. On Colours, On Things Heard, On Physiognomies, On Plants, On Marvellous Things Heard, Mechanical Problems, On Indivisible Lines, On Situations and Names of Winds, On Melissus, Xenophanes, and Gorgias.

ARISTOTLE: NICOMACHEAN ETHICS. H. Rackham.

ARISTOTLE: OECONOMICA and MAGNA MORALIA. G. C. Armstrong; (with METAPHYSICS, Vol. II.).

ARISTOTLE: ON THE HEAVENS. W. K. C. Guthrie.

ARISTOTLE: ON THE SOUL. PARVA NATURALIA. ON BREATH. W. S. Hett.

ARISTOTLE: CATEGORIES, ON INTERPRETATION, PRIOR ANALYTICS. H. P. Cooke and H. Tredennick.

ARISTOTLE: POSTERIOR ANALYTICS, TOPICS. H. Tredennick and E. S. Forster.

ARISTOTLE: ON SOPHISTICAL REFUTATIONS. On Coming to be and Passing Away, On the Cosmos. E. S. Forster and D. J. Furley.

ARISTOTLE: PARTS OF ANIMALS. A. L. Peck; MOTION AND PROGRESSION OF ANIMALS. E. S. Forster.

ARISTOTLE: PHYSICS. Rev. P. Wicksteed and F. M. Cornford. 2 Vols.

ARISTOTLE: POETICS and LONGINUS. W. Hamilton Fyfe; DEMETRIUS ON STYLE. W. Rhys Roberts.

ARISTOTLE: POLITICS. H. Rackham.

ARISTOTLE: PROBLEMS. W. S. Hett. 2 Vols.

ARISTOTLE: RHETORICA AD ALEXANDRUM (with PROBLEMS. Vol. II). H. Rackham.

ARRIAN: HISTORY OF ALEXANDER and INDICA. Rev. E. Iliffe Robson. 2 Vols.

ATHENAEUS: DEIPNOSOPHISTAE. C. B. Gulick. 7 Vols.

BABRIUS AND PHAEDRUS (Latin). B. E. Perry.

ST. BASIL: LETTERS. R. J. Deferrari. 4 Vols.

CALLIMACHUS: FRAGMENTS. C. A. Trypanis. MUSAEUS: HERO AND LEANDER. T. Gelzer and C. Whitman.

CALLIMACHUS, Hymns and Epigrams, and LYCOPHRON. A. W. Mair; ARATUS. G. R. Mair.

CLEMENT OF ALEXANDRIA. Rev. G. W. Butterworth.

COLLUTHUS. Cf. OPPIAN.

DAPHNIS AND CHLOE. Thornley's Translation revised by J. M. Edmonds: and PARTHENIUS. S. Gaselee.

DEMOSTHENES I.: OLYNTHIACS, PHILIPPICS and MINOR ORATIONS. I.–XVII. AND XX. J. H. Vince.

DEMOSTHENES II.: DE CORONA and DE FALSA LEGATIONE. C. A. Vince and J. H. Vince.

DEMOSTHENES III.: MEIDIAS, ANDROTION, ARISTOCRATES, TIMOCRATES and ARISTOGEITON, I. AND II. J. H. Vince.

DEMOSTHENES IV.–VI.: PRIVATE ORATIONS and IN NEAERAM. A. T. Murray.

DEMOSTHENES VII.: FUNERAL SPEECH, EROTIC ESSAY, EXORDIA and LETTERS. N. W. and N. J. DeWitt.

DIO CASSIUS: ROMAN HISTORY. E. Cary. 9 Vols.

DIO CHRYSOSTOM. J. W. Cohoon and H. Lamar Crosby. 5 Vols.

DIODORUS SICULUS. 12 Vols. Vols. I.–VI. C. H. Oldfather. Vol. VII. C. L. Sherman. Vol. VIII. C. B. Welles. Vols. IX. and X. R. M. Geer. Vol. XI. F. Walton. Vol. XII. F. Walton. General Index. R. M. Geer.

DIOGENES LAERTIUS. R. D. Hicks. 2 Vols. New Introduction by H. S. Long.

DIONYSIUS OF HALICARNASSUS: ROMAN ANTIQUITIES Spelman's translation revised by E. Cary. 7 Vols.

DIONYSIUS OF HALICARNASSUS: CRITICAL ESSAYS. S. Usher. 2 Vols.

EPICTETUS. W. A. Oldfather. 2 Vols.

EURIPIDES. A. S. Way. 4 Vols. Verse trans.

EUSEBIUS: ECCLESIASTICAL HISTORY. Kirsopp Lake and J. E. L. Oulton. 2 Vols.

GALEN: ON THE NATURAL FACULTIES. A. J. Brock.

THE GREEK ANTHOLOGY. W. R. Paton. 5 Vols.

GREEK ELEGY AND IAMBUS with the ANACREONTEA. J. M. Edmonds. 2 Vols.

THE GREEK BUCOLIC POETS (THEOCRITUS, BION, MOSCHUS). J. M. Edmonds.

GREEK MATHEMATICAL WORKS. Ivor Thomas. 2 Vols.

HERODES. Cf. THEOPHRASTUS: CHARACTERS.

HERODIAN. C. R. Whittaker. 2 Vols.

HERODOTUS. A. D. Godley. 4 Vols.

HESIOD AND THE HOMERIC HYMNS. H. G. Evelyn White.

HIPPOCRATES and the FRAGMENTS OF HERACLEITUS. W. H. S. Jones and E. T. Withington. 4 Vols.

HOMER: ILIAD. A. T. Murray. 2 Vols.

HOMER: ODYSSEY. A. T. Murray. 2 Vols.

ISAEUS. E. W. Forster.

ISOCRATES. George Norlin and LaRue Van Hook. 3 Vols.

[ST. JOHN DAMASCENE]: BARLAAM AND IOASAPH. Rev. G. R. Woodward, Harold Mattingly and D. M. Lang.

JOSEPHUS. 9 Vols. Vols. I.–IV. H. Thackeray. Vol. V. H. Thackeray and R. Marcus. Vols. VI.–VII. R. Marcus. Vol. VIII. R. Marcus and Allen Wikgren. Vol. IX. L. H. Feldman.

JULIAN. Wilmer Cave Wright. 3 Vols.

LIBANIUS. A. F. Norman. Vol. I.

LUCIAN. 8 Vols. Vols. I.–V. A. M. Harmon. Vol. VI. K. Kilburn. Vols. VII.–VIII. M. D. Macleod.

LYCOPHRON. Cf. CALLIMACHUS.

LYRA GRAECA. J. M. Edmonds. 3 Vols.

LYSIAS. W. R. M. Lamb.

MANETHO. W. G. Waddell: PTOLEMY: TETRABIBLOS. F. E. Robbins.

MARCUS AURELIUS. C. R. Haines.

MENANDER. F. G. Allison.

MINOR ATTIC ORATORS (ANTIPHON, ANDOCIDES, LYCURGUS, DEMADES, DINARCHUS, HYPERIDES). K. J. Maidment and J. O. Burtt. 2 Vols.

MUSAEUS: HERO AND LEANDER. Cf. CALLIMACHUS.

NONNOS: DIONYSIACA. W. H. D. Rouse. 3 Vols.

OPPIAN, COLLUTHUS, TRYPHIODORUS. A. W. Mair.

PAPYRI. NON-LITERARY SELECTIONS. A. S. Hunt and C. C. Edgar. 2 Vols. LITERARY SELECTIONS (Poetry). D. L. Page.

PARTHENIUS. Cf. DAPHNIS and CHLOE.

PAUSANIAS: DESCRIPTION OF GREECE. W. H. S. Jones. 4 Vols. and Companion Vol. arranged by R. E. Wycherley.

PHILO. 10 Vols. Vols. I.–V. F. H. Colson and Rev. G. H. Whitaker. Vols. VI.–IX. F. H. Colson. Vol. X. F. H. Colson and the Rev. J. W. Earp.

PHILO: two supplementary Vols. (*Translation only.*) Ralph Marcus.

PHILOSTRATUS: THE LIFE OF APOLLONIUS OF TYANA. F. C. Conybeare. 2 Vols.

PHILOSTRATUS: IMAGINES; CALLISTRATUS: DESCRIPTIONS. A. Fairbanks.

PHILOSTRATUS and EUNAPIUS: LIVES OF THE SOPHISTS. Wilmer Cave Wright.

PINDAR. Sir J. E. Sandys.

PLATO: CHARMIDES, ALCIBIADES, HIPPARCHUS, THE LOVERS, THEAGES, MINOS and EPINOMIS. W. R. M. Lamb.

PLATO: CRATYLUS, ZARMENIDES, GREATER HIPPIAS, LESSER HIPPIAS. H. N. Fowler.

PLATO: EUTHYPHRO, APOLOGY, CRITO, PHAEDO, PHAEDRUS. H. N. Fowler.

PLATO: LACHES, PROTAGORAS, MENO, EUTHYDEMUS. W. R. M. Lamb.

PLATO: LAWS. Rev. R. G. Bury. 2 Vols.

PLATO: LYSIS, SYMPOSIUM, GORGIAS. W. R. M. Lamb.

PLATO: REPUBLIC. Paul Shorey. 2 Vols.

PLATO: STATESMAN, PHILEBUS. H. N. Fowler; Ion. W. R. M. Lamb.

PLATO: THEAETETUS and SOPHIST. H. N. Fowler.

PLATO: TIMAEUS, CRITIAS, CLITOPHO, MENEXENUS, EPISTULAE. Rev. R. G. Bury.

PLOTINUS: A. H. Armstrong. Vols. I.–III.

PLUTARCH: MORALIA. 16 Vols. Vols. I.–V. F. C. Babbitt. Vol. VI. W. C. Helmbold. Vols. VII. and XIV. P. H. De Lacy and B. Einarson. Vol. VIII. P. A. Clement and H. B. Hoffleit. Vol. IX. E. L. Minar, Jr., F. H. Sandbach, W. C. Helmbold. Vol. X. H. N. Fowler. Vol. XI. L. Pearson and F. H. Sandbach. Vol. XII. H. Cherniss and W. C. Helmbold. Vol. XV. F. H. Sandbach.

PLUTARCH: THE PARALLEL LIVES. B. Perrin. 11 Vols.

POLYBIUS. W. R. Paton. 6 Vols.

PROCOPIUS: HISTORY OF THE WARS. H. B. Dewing. 7 Vols.

PTOLEMY: TETRABIBLOS. Cf. MANETHO.

QUINTUS SMYRNAEUS. A. S. Way. Verse trans.

SEXTUS EMPIRICUS. Rev. R. G. Bury. 4 Vols.

SOPHOCLES. F. Storr. 2 Vols. Verse trans.

STRABO: GEOGRAPHY. Horace L. Jones. 8 Vols.

THEOPHRASTUS: CHARACTERS. J. M. Edmonds. HERODES, etc. A. D. Knox

THEOPHRASTUS: ENQUIRY INTO PLANTS. Sir Arthur Hort, Bart. 2 Vols.

THUCYDIDES. C. F. Smith. 4 Vols.

TRYPHIODORUS. Cf. OPPIAN.

XENOPHON: CYROPAEDIA. Walter Miller. 2 Vols.

XENOPHON: HELLENICA. C. L. Brownson. 2 Vols.

XENOPHON: ANABASIS. C. L. Brownson.

XENOPHON: MEMORABILIA AND OECONOMICUS. E. C. Marchant. SYMPOSIUM AND APOLOGY. O. J. Todd.

XENOPHON: SCRIPTA MINORA. E. C. Marchant and G. W. Bowersock.

IN PREPARATION

Greek Authors

AELIAN: VARIA HISTORICA. C. Pritchet.

MUSAEUS: HERO AND LEANDER. T. Gelzer and C. H. Whitman.

Latin Authors

MANILIUS. G. P. Goold.

DESCRIPTIVE PROSPECTUS ON APPLICATION

CAMBRIDGE, MASS. HARVARD UNIVERSITY PRESS
LONDON WILLIAM HEINEMANN LTD

8